MARION MERRELL DOW INC.

9300 Ward Parkway
MAIL: P.O. Box 8480
Kansas City, Missouri 64114-0480
Telephone: 816/966-4000

Dear Health Professional:

Please accept this book, *The Living Heart Brand Name Shopper's Guide,* as part of the continuing dedication of Marion Merrell Dow Inc. to help your patients live a healthier life. It is our sincere wish that this material will help you obtain better patient compliance with your dietary recommendations.

At Marion Merrell Dow, our oommitmont to health goes far beyond the development of pharmaceutical products. It is our goal to help improve longevity and quality of life in a variety of ways. Providing health information is part of that effort.

Many consumers find it confusing to choose heart-healthy products from the thousands of products displayed in supermarkets. This user-friendly reference book cuts through that confusion by identifying more than 5,000 food products low enough in fat, saturated fat, and cholesterol to be good choices on a cholesterol-lowering diet. The calorie and sodium content of each food is also included. The result will be more healthful food selections and a healthier life-style.

When patients receive our medications like Cardizem® CD (diltiazem HCl), Cardizem® Injectable (diltiazem HCl), or Lorelco® (probucol), they get not only the highest quality medication, but also our full commitment to their health. It is for this reason that we are pleased to make this book available to you.

Sincerely,

MARION MERRELL DOW INC.

COMDJ066/6759

THE LIVING HEART
BRAND NAME SHOPPER'S GUIDE

MICHAEL E. DeBAKEY, M.D.
ANTONIO M. GOTTO, JR., M.D., D.PHIL.
LYNNE W. SCOTT, M.A., R.D./L.D.
JOHN P. FOREYT, PH.D.
Edited by Mary McMann, M.P.H., R.D./L.D.

THE LIVING HEART BRAND NAME SHOPPER'S GUIDE

MASTERMEDIA LIMITED
NEW YORK

MASTERMEDIA and colophon are registered trademarks of MasterMedia Limited.

Inclusion of a food in this Guide does not imply an endorsement and is not meant to classify any food as "good" or "bad." Although brand names have been used for your convenience, the authors have not included information on the status of brand names as registered trademarks.

Library of Congress Cataloging-in-Publication Data
The Living heart : brand name shopper's guide / Michael E. DeBakey
. . . [et al.].
     p. cm.
   Includes index.
   ISBN 0-942361-43-1 (paper)
   1. Food—Cholesterol content—Tables. 2. Low-cholesterol diet.
3. Low-fat diet. 4. Coronary heart disease—Prevention.
I. DeBakey, Michael E. (Michael Ellis), 1908–
TX553.C43L58   1992
641.1'4—dc20   91-42946
                                                              CIP

Designed by Jacqueline Schuman

Production services by Martin Cook Associates, Ltd.
Manufactured in the United States of America
10 9 8 7 6 5 4 3 2

CONTENTS

FOOD SECTIONS

FOOD SECTIONS

ACKNOWLEDGMENTS

We are extremely grateful to The Abercrombie Foundation for its assistance in the development of *The Living Heart Brand Name Shopper's Guide.*

Many devoted individuals worked on the preparation of this Guide, making its development a pleasurable and satisfying experience. We especially wish to thank Mary C. McMann and Myrthala Miranda-Guzman for their extraordinary efforts in preparing material for the book and the standard of excellence they maintained throughout the project. Mary worked tirelessly to evaluate information on over 10,000 foods and estimated missing values for foods qualifying for the Guide. We are also indebted to her for editing and proofreading the manuscript. Myrthala was involved with the project since its inception; we thank her for the hundreds of hours spent entering and organizing food information in the computer. We owe special thanks to Samantha, Myrthala's new daughter, for waiting to arrive until the day after data entry was completed.

Organizing data received from food manufacturers is a massive task. We especially thank Angi Stewart for managing the correspondence, typing the manuscript, and reformating computer data for the manuscript. A special thanks goes to D'Laine Westmoreland and Kay Zercher for reviewing and organizing data when they were first received from the food manufacturers.

We are very grateful to Suzanne Jaax and Danièle Brauchi for their excellent information, encouragement, and thoughtful review of the manuscript, and for continually testing parts of the Guide with their patients. We also thank Mary Beth Pigneri for her work on the Guide during the initial phase and for reviewing the completed manuscript.

Supermarkets in different parts of the country vary as to the brand-name products they carry. We are very grateful to our consultants—Ruth Johnson (California), Patricia Snyder (Minnesota), and Lynn Baughman (Colorado)—for their valuable input to this Guide.

We believe that for a book like this to be useful, it needs to be evaluated by the people who will actually be using it. We are very grateful to Jenny

Harding, Burniece and Winfred Harding, Dana Petri, John and Eleanor Egan, and Sandra Kimbrow for their excellent suggestions.

A special thanks goes to Jack Fox for his encouragement and insight and, most of all, for putting us in touch with Susan Stautberg, President of MasterMedia. Working with Susan, our enthusiastic, innovative, and creative publisher, has been an invigorating and rewarding experience.

We thank Mary Carroll, Allen Jones, and Andrew Ellner for their special assistance in reformating the food sections of this Guide.

We express our deepest appreciation to the numerous food manufacturers who provided information to us about their products and especially to the 280 manufacturers who have developed foods that are low enough in fat, saturated fatty acids, and dietary cholesterol to be included in this Guide.

PREFACE

In 1977 we published *The Living Heart,* which answered many of the questions about heart disease most frequently asked by patients and their families. In the following years, the importance of maintaining the health of the heart became increasingly apparent. It also became clear that diet is one of the most crucial aspects of preventive maintenance.

In 1984 we responded to this new interest in diet by publishing *The Living Heart Diet.* It appeared on the *New York Times* best-seller list and continues to be a popular book, both for patients and for those individuals interested in changing their eating habits to promote a living heart. The subject of heart disease is of immense interest to the public today, and the relationship between diet and a healthy heart continues to increase in significance. This growth is shown in the thousands of new food products developed specifically for people trying to follow a diet lower in fat, saturated fat, cholesterol, and calories. It is also illustrated in the massive overhaul of the nation's food labeling system mandated by the Nutrition Labeling and Education Act signed by President George Bush in 1990, which is presently in the process of being carried out by the Food and Drug Administration and the Food and Safety Inspection Service of the U.S. Department of Agriculture.

Since the authors started working together in 1971, teaching patients about selecting appropriate foods to help control blood cholesterol, body weight, and blood pressure has been a basic part of our nutrition program. Over the years, we have seen an increasing demand from patients for information on brand name foods. With the development of so many new foods containing less fat, saturated fat, and cholesterol, the task of keeping up with them has become a major challenge. *The Living Heart Brand Name Shopper's Guide* is intended to make it easier for consumers to select foods low in fat, saturated fat, and cholesterol. The Guide's practical format is designed to make it easy to use while making out a shopping list or in the supermarket.

The authors hope that this Guide will help you in your efforts to consume a diet providing no more than 30% of calories from fat, less than

10% of calories from saturated fat, and less than 300 milligrams of cholesterol as a way of promoting a living heart. Remember:

You are what you eat . . .
You eat what you buy . . .
Buy wisely . . .

The Living Heart Brand Name Shopper's Guide will help you.

The content of *The Living Heart Brand Name Shopper's Guide* is unique in several ways. The Guide is the first book to help consumers choose both brand-name and generic foods appropriate for a cholesterol-lowering eating pattern. Although consumers buy many products by brand name, most books on the market include only values for generic products (skim milk, bread, lean meat, etc.). Brand name and generic products listed in the Guide have been evaluated to see if they meet or are under the cutoff points for fat, saturated fatty acids, and cholesterol. Values for foods high in fat but low in saturated fatty acids (such as oil and margarine) that play a role in a well-balanced cholesterol-lowering eating pattern have also been included in the Guide. In addition, where values for saturated fatty acids and cholesterol were not available, these values are estimated (and appear in parentheses). In spite of increasing evidence indicating that reducing the intake of saturated fatty acids is a crucial factor in a cholesterol-lowering eating pattern, many food labels do not yet provide this information.

There have been many changes in the field of heart disease since *The Living Heart Diet* was published in 1984. These changes have occurred primarily in the areas of identifying factors that increase the risk of heart disease and developing techniques for reducing these risk factors. One of the greatest advances has been in the initial identification and treatment of people with high blood cholesterol levels. Due to efforts by the National Cholesterol Education Program (NCEP), the American Heart Association, the media, and food manufacturers, both the medical profession and the general public have experienced a dramatic increase in their awareness of the importance of elevated blood cholesterol as a major risk factor for heart disease.

In 1983 approximately 1,600 physicians who responded to the National Physician and Public Survey (sponsored by the National Heart, Lung, and Blood Institute) identified a total cholesterol of 260 to 279 mg/dL as the range at which they initiated diet therapy. In 1986 an equal number of physicians reported prescribing diet therapy for patients with blood cholesterol levels of 240 to 259 mg/dL. From 1987 to 1988 there was an organized campaign to circulate the NCEP guidelines for treatment of high blood cholesterol. The Report of the NCEP Expert Panel on Detection, Evaluation, and Treatment of High Blood Cholesterol in Adults classified patients based on total and low density lipoprotein cholesterol and made recommendations for treatment with diet and with diet and drugs. The success of this program is reflected in the lower median range of blood cholesterol—200 to 219 mg/dL—at which 1,600 physicians reported initiating diet therapy in 1990.

Changes have also been taking place in the public sector. One of the aims of the NCEP was to raise the awareness of the American public about risk associated with elevated blood cholesterol. In 1983 77% of approximately 4,000 people surveyed had heard of "high serum cholesterol," the amount of total cholesterol in the blood. This number had grown to 81% by 1986 and to an impressive 93% by 1990. Increasingly large numbers of individuals are taking more responsibility for their own health. A 1990 Gallup Survey of opinions concerning nutrition and health identified several areas of public concern and change. Of the people surveyed, 83% said that they were either "very concerned" or "fairly concerned" about the effect of what they ate on their future health. Part of this concern with the effect of nutrition on health took the form of eliminating certain types of food from the diet. Almost 75% of the adults surveyed said that they were eliminating fats and saturated fats from their diet. Of those making changes in fat intake, most reported that they had quit eating high-fat foods, butter, fried foods, tropical oils, and red meats.

There has been rapid growth in both the number of products being marketed to health-conscious consumers and the amount of information about health provided to the public. Currently, most supermarkets carry about 30,000 food and non-food items, and about 800 new brand name items appear on grocery-store shelves each month (some also disappear). In spite of the 400 to 500 cookbooks printed each year, many of which specialize in low-cholesterol cooking, consumers following a cholesterol-lowering eating pattern don't always have an easy time identifying the foods they need. The practical information provided in *The Living Heart Brand Name Shopper's Guide,* however, fills the gap between what you know about eating "healthy" and putting this knowledge to work in your daily life.

Michael E. DeBakey
Antonio M. Gotto, Jr.
Lynne W. Scott
John P. Foreyt

THE LIVING HEART
BRAND NAME SHOPPER'S GUIDE

Chapter 1

The Living Heart Diet— an Update on Diet and Heart Disease

Two of the more common questions asked about health care today are "Does high blood cholesterol increase the risk of having heart disease?" and "Will lowering blood cholesterol help prevent heart disease?" In 1984, when *The Living Heart Diet* was published, the authors researched these questions and gave the best possible answer to both "yes." Since that time, numerous research studies reported from around the world have provided additional information about the causes and treatment of heart disease. However, these new and convincing scientific data have strengthened the evidence supporting the "yes" answer to these two questions.

The evidence linking blood cholesterol level to heart disease is now overwhelming. It is based on many years of epidemiologic studies, clinical studies, genetic studies, and studies conducted with laboratory animals. All of these research studies indicate that high blood cholesterol is related to increased risk of heart disease. Important points of the new research are summarized in the answers to frequently asked questions about diet and heart disease.

- *Is heart disease still as big a problem as it was a few years ago?*

More than 25% of the adult American population—more than 68 million people—suffer from some form of cardiovascular disease (CVD), which includes all diseases of the heart and blood vessels. Although death rates from CVD have been declining in recent years, these diseases are still responsible for almost half of all deaths in the United States. Coronary heart disease (CHD), which is a disease of the arteries in the heart, remains the leading cause of death in the United States. More than 6 million Americans have a history of heart attack and/or symptoms of the disease. Each year, about 1,500,000 people suffer a heart attack, and more than 500,000 of these attacks are fatal. The second leading cause of death in the U.S. is cancer, followed by stroke (another type of CVD).

● *Is diet related to heart disease?*

There is substantial evidence from laboratory, epidemiologic, and clinical studies showing a powerful link between diet and coronary heart disease (CHD). High intakes of saturated fatty acids and cholesterol and excess calories (which lead to obesity) are related to heart disease. This relationship is based on the effect saturated fatty acids, cholesterol, and obesity have on blood cholesterol levels. Diet plays a significant role in determining a person's blood cholesterol level. A high blood cholesterol level is one of the major risk factors for CHD.

● *What is blood cholesterol?*

Cholesterol, an odorless, white, waxy substance present in every cell in the body, is carried by blood. Most of the cholesterol in your blood has been manufactured by your own body, especially your liver. Medical research has shown that high levels of cholesterol in the blood are a major risk factor for cardiovascular disease. The only way to know whether your cholesterol level is high is to have a laboratory analyze a sample of your blood. The results are given in milligrams of cholesterol in a deciliter (mg/dL) of blood.

● *What should my blood cholesterol level be?*

In 1987 the National Cholesterol Education Program classified levels of blood cholesterol for adults.

Although a blood cholesterol level of less than 200 mg/dL puts you at lower risk for heart disease, it does not mean no risk. A level between 200 and 239 mg/dL increases your risk of developing heart disease. If your blood cholesterol is 240 mg/dL or higher, you have more than twice the risk of heart disease of someone whose cholesterol is 200 mg/dL. If you are in this high-cholesterol category, you should seek the advice of a physician. The significance of your cholesterol value depends on your

TOTAL BLOOD CHOLESTEROL
CATEGORIES FOR ADULTS*

Category	Total Cholesterol
Desirable	Less than 200 mg/dL
Borderline-High	200 to 239 mg/dL
High	240 mg/dL or greater

*20 years of age and older.

levels of LDL-cholesterol and HDL-cholesterol. (LDL- and HDL-cholesterol are explained later in this section.)

- *What is an acceptable level of cholesterol for children?*

In the spring of 1991, the National Cholesterol Education Program recommended that children two years of age and above from families with high blood cholesterol or premature heart disease have their blood cholesterol measured. The categories for total cholesterol for children are shown below:

TOTAL BLOOD CHOLESTEROL
CATEGORIES FOR CHILDREN*

Category	Total Cholesterol
Acceptable	Less than 170 mg/dL
Borderline	170 to 199 mg/dL
High	200 mg/dL or greater

*2 through 19 years of age.

- *Is a high cholesterol level the only risk factor for coronary heart disease?*

No, there are a number of risk factors for coronary heart disease:

- High blood cholesterol
- Cigarette smoking
- High blood pressure
- Obesity
- Diabetes
- Being a male
- Family history of heart disease by age 55
- Low HDL-cholesterol (less than 35 mg/dL)
- Circulation disorders of blood vessels in the legs, arms, and brain (peripheral vascular disease and stroke)

If you have one risk factor, your likelihood of developing heart-related problems increases. If you have two risk factors, however, you are at much higher risk than you might think from "adding up" the risk. An individual with two risk factors actually has four times the risk of heart disease as someone without any risk factors. Someone with the top three controllable risk factors—high blood cholesterol, cigarette smoking, and high blood pressure—has eight times the risk of someone without any risk factors.

- *What is LDL-cholesterol?*

The letters LDL stand for low density lipoprotein. The body makes lipoproteins (combinations or packages of protein, cholesterol, and fat) to carry cholesterol and fat in blood. LDL is the major carrier of cholesterol in the blood. High levels of LDL are strongly correlated with premature coronary heart disease, and this is why LDL is called "bad cholesterol." LDL is found only in blood and does not occur in food. You can calculate your LDL value if you know your levels of cholesterol, triglyceride, and HDL. (The formula works if your triglyceride level is under 400 mg/dL; if it is higher, your physician can order a special blood test to determine your LDL.)

$$LDL = total\ cholesterol - HDL - (triglyceride/5)$$

The categories of LDL-cholesterol are shown below:

Children*		Adults**	
Category	LDL-cholesterol	Category	LDL-cholesterol
Acceptable	Less than 110 mg/dL	Desirable	Less than 130 mg/dL
Borderline	110–129 mg/dL	Borderline–	
		High-Risk	130–159 mg/dL
High	130 mg/dL or greater	High-Risk	160 mg/dL or greater

*2 through 19 years of age.
**20 years of age and older.

- *What is HDL-cholesterol?*

HDL, or high density lipoprotein, is called "good cholesterol" because this lipoprotein removes cholesterol from the blood and prevents the buildup of cholesterol in the walls of arteries. Evidence from research studies suggests that high levels of HDL protect against coronary heart disease and that low levels of HDL (below 35 mg/dL) increase the risk of coronary heart disease.

- *Is the level of triglyceride in my blood important?*

Yes, triglyceride level is important, even though it has not received as much publicity as cholesterol. Although triglyceride differs from cholesterol, it is also a normal component of blood. The triglyceride in your blood can come from the diet or be manufactured by the body. Triglyceride levels can usually be lowered by weight reduction (if overweight), decreased alcohol intake (or avoidance of alcoholic beverages), and a diet low in fat and saturated fatty acids.

The level of triglyceride in your blood gradually increases after a meal, reaches its highest point about four hours after eating, and then begins to fall. To get an accurate measurement of triglyceride level, you must fast (nothing to eat or drink except plain water) for 12 to 14 hours before your blood is drawn. If your triglyceride level is above 150 mg/dL, your level of risk is determined by the other risk factors you have. Your risk increases if you have a low HDL (below 35 mg/dL), high blood pressure, or diabetes, or if you smoke. The combination of high triglyceride and high LDL-cholesterol levels appears to carry a very high risk of coronary heart disease.

- *Does diet play a role in reducing risk factors?*

Yes, diet plays an important role in controlling four of the nine risk factors—high blood cholesterol, high blood pressure, obesity, and diabetes. High blood pressure can often be lowered by losing weight (if overweight) and by decreasing the intake of sodium and salt. Blood cholesterol can be lowered by decreasing the intake of saturated fatty acids, dietary cholesterol, and excess calories (leading to overweight). Decreasing the amount of food eaten helps control weight and reverse obesity. Both the amount and type of food eaten are important factors in the control of blood cholesterol and diabetes.

- *What are the latest facts about obesity?*

We continue to be a heavy population. Almost a quarter of the adult population of the U.S. is overweight. The states with the highest prevalence of overweight are Wisconsin (26%), Indiana (26%), and West Virginia (25%). States with the lowest prevalence are New Mexico (15%), Hawaii (16%), and Utah (17%). Overweight also differs by region, with the Midwest having the highest prevalence (23%), followed by the South (22%), the Northeast (20%), and the West (17%). A recent study reporting the results of a national sample of U.S. adults found that women are twice as likely as men to have a major weight gain over a ten-year period and that the gain is highest in women aged 25 to 34 years.

A report on weight fluctuation suggests that "yo-yo" dieting may be very bad for your health. In that report, researchers examined the associations between variability in body weight and a number of health measures in people who are participants in a long-term project called the Framingham Heart Study. They found that people who had the greatest weight fluctuation had both increased death rates overall and increased rates of illness and death from coronary heart disease. Dieting, which is frequently associated with weight fluctuation in many people who lose and regain weight a number of times, may be a contributor to the problem. The data suggest that people who need to lose weight should be very serious in their attempt and be determined to maintain any weight loss. The "yo-yo" cycle may be harmful to your health.

Finally, for people who are obese, new data suggest that the location of fat on the body may be a more important factor in the risk of cardiovascular disease than the total amount of fat. People carrying their fat in the abdomen (those with a beer belly or pot belly) appear to be at greater risk than those carrying fat elsewhere on their bodies (those with fat thighs, buttocks, or hips). In other words, upper-body obesity—the apple-shaped body—is more dangerous than lower-body obesity—the pear-shaped body. One of the easiest ways to determine your pattern of obesity is to obtain waist and hip measurements, and then calculate a waist-to-hip ratio (WHR) by dividing your waist measurement by your hip measurement. For example, if your waist and hips are the same size, your WHR is 1. The larger your abdomen is in comparison to your hips, the larger the WHR. The WHR appears to be a powerful predictor of cardiovascular disease and diabetes, independent of and in addition to the effects of the obesity itself. The risk is greatest when the WHR is equal to or greater than 1.0 in men and 0.8 in women.

- *What are the dietary guidelines?*

The dietary guidelines provide recommended intakes of several nutrients for all healthy Americans two years of age and older. They are designed to lower blood cholesterol levels in children, adolescents, and adults with the aims of reducing the incidence of coronary heart disease and generally improving health. The guidelines are consistent with recommendations made by the American Heart Association (1983), the National Cholesterol Education Program by the Expert Panel on Population Strategies for Blood Cholesterol Reduction (1990) and the Expert Panel on Blood Cholesterol Levels in Children and Adolescents (1991), the U.S. Surgeon General (1988), the U.S. Department of Agriculture and the Department of Health and Human Services (1990) in the "Dietary Guidelines for Americans," the National Research Council (1989), and the National Cancer Institute (1987). These recommendations are for a diet that provides the following:

DIETARY RECOMMENDATIONS

- Less than 10% of calories from saturated fatty acids
- No more than 30% of calories from fat
- Less than 300 milligrams of cholesterol per day
- Up to 10% of calories from polyunsaturated fatty acids
- About 10% to 15% of calories from monounsaturated fatty acids
- About 50% to 55% of calories from carbohydrates
- About 15% to 20% of calories from protein
- Total calories to reach and maintain a desirable body weight

● *Does reducing the amount of total fat eaten lower blood cholesterol?*

The total amount of fat you eat usually does not independently affect your level of blood cholesterol. However, preliminary data indicate that very-low-fat diets are associated with low cholesterol levels. The types of fatty acids making up the fat you get in food are more important than the total amount of fat. Fat in food is made up of saturated and unsaturated fatty acids; unsaturated fatty acids consist of monounsaturated and poly-unsaturated fatty acids. A high intake of saturated fatty acids contributes to an elevation of blood cholesterol. The dietary recommendation of limiting fat to no more than 30% of calories is a practical way of keeping the intake of saturated fatty acids to less than 10% of calories. This level allows enough fat: (1) to provide essential fatty acids, (2) for absorption of fat-soluble vitamins, and (3) to supply calories for normal growth and development (in children). Since the recommendation of no more than 30% of calories from fat is vague when it comes to guiding you in the selection of individual foods, steps for converting it into practical terms are presented in chapter 4.

● *Why is decreasing saturated fatty acids so important?*

The saturated fatty acids you get in food raise blood cholesterol levels. The major emphasis in a cholesterol-lowering eating plan is on reducing saturated fatty acid intake to less than 10% of calories. At present, adults and children get about 14% of their calories from saturated fatty acids (about 50% more than the recommended level). Meat, poultry, and dairy products are the primary sources of saturated fatty acids in the diet of adults and children. Saturated fatty acids are present in both animal and plant foods. Animal sources include meat fat, poultry skin, and the butter-fat in high-fat dairy products. Vegetable sources of saturated fatty acids include the tropical oils (coconut, palm kernel, palm oil), cocoa butter, and coconut. These vegetable sources make up only a small percent of the total saturated fatty acids in the typical American diet. The individual saturated fatty acids occurring most often in food are palmitic, stearic, myristic, and lauric acids.

- *What is the role of monounsaturated fatty acids in a cholesterol-lowering diet? Which foods are good sources?*

Data from the Mediterranean countries and the results of small re-search studies indicate that monounsaturated fatty acids neither increase the total blood cholesterol level nor decrease the level of HDL-cholesterol (good cholesterol). Replacing saturated fatty acids with either carbohy-drates or unsaturated fatty acids (polyunsaturated or monounsaturated) helps lower blood cholesterol levels. Monounsaturated fatty acids should make up 10% to 15% of total calories. In the typical American diet, monounsaturated fatty acids supply about 14% of calories.

The most concentrated sources of monounsaturated fatty acids are olive, canola, and peanut oil and partially hydrogenated soybean oil. Other sources of monounsaturated fatty acids in the American diet are nuts (especially hazelnuts, pecans, and macadamia nuts) and the fat on beef and pork. The fat found in beef steak, for example, has about equal amounts of monounsaturated and saturated fatty acids. Although trim-ming the fat off meat reduces both saturated and monounsaturated fatty acids, decreasing the amount of saturated fatty acids by this process is far more important than preserving the level of monounsaturated fatty acids.

- *What are polyunsaturated fatty acids? What are good sources?*

Replacing saturated fatty acids with either unsaturated fatty acids (monounsaturated or polyunsaturated) or carbohydrates helps lower blood cholesterol. Polyunsaturated fatty acids include omega-6 and omega-3 fatty acids. Linoleic acid, an omega-6 fatty acid containing 18 carbon atoms and 2 double bonds, is the major polyunsaturated fatty acid in the American diet. It is found primarily in vegetable oils such as safflower, sunflower, corn, and soybean oil. These oils are used in most commercial salad dressings and are used to make margarines.

The primary omega-3 fatty acids are eicosapentaenoic acid (EPA) with 20 carbon atoms and 5 double bonds and docosahexaenoic acid (DHA) with 22 carbon atoms and 6 double bonds. They are found primarily in fish oils.

Recent studies have shown that levels of HDL (the good cholesterol) may decrease in people consuming diets high in polyunsaturated fatty acids. Preliminary data raised the possibility that diets high in polyunsaturated fatty acids (greater than 10% of calories) may increase the risk of cancer. However, this finding was controversial and further analysis of the data did not confirm it. There are no population studies that document the overall health and safety of consuming diets containing greater than 10% of calories from polyunsaturated fatty acid. The recommended level of intake of polyunsaturated fatty acids is "up to 10% of calories."

- *Does it matter how much vegetable oil I use? Which oil is the best?*

All of the fat in the diet should be accounted for in calculating total fat intake. This includes fat naturally occurring in food (cheese, meat, cream), used in preparation (cake, cookies, candy, sauces), added to food in processing (luncheon meat, ground beef, salad dressing), and added at the table (spread on bread). All of this fat should provide no more than 30% of total calories for the day. The actual amount of fat recommended depends on calorie intake—at 1,200 calories, 3 teaspoons of oil and margarine are included, whereas at 2,000 calories, 6 teaspoons per day are allowed. More information on the amount of fat to use is given on pages 45 and 47–48.

All vegetable oils are a combination of polyunsaturated, monounsaturated, and saturated fatty acids. Even those oils highest in polyunsaturated and monounsaturated fatty acids provide some saturated fatty acids. Research with several oils is under way; until the data identify one or more particular oils as having superior cholesterol-lowering qualities, we recommend a variety of oils low in saturated fatty acids. The following table lists common vegetable oils (listed in ascending order of saturated fatty acid content).

Oil, 1 tablespoon*	Saturated (g)	Monounsaturated (g)	Polyunsaturated (g)
Canola	0.8	8.4	4.2
Safflower	1.2	1.6	10.1
Walnut	1.2	3.1	8.6
Sunflower	1.4	2.7	8.9
Corn	1.7	3.3	8.0
Olive	1.8	9.9	1.1
Soybean (hydrogenated)	2.0	5.9	5.1
Peanut	2.3	6.2	4.3
Soybean (hydrogenated) and cottonseed	2.4	4.0	6.5

*Adapted from "Composition of Foods: Fats and Oils," Agriculture Handbook No. 8-4, 1979.

- *What about fish in a cholesterol-lowering diet?*

Fish (finfish and shellfish) are a good choice on a cholesterol-lowering diet. Most fish are low in both total fat and saturated fatty acids, and any fat that is present is high in polyunsaturated fatty acids (omega-3). Including fish on a regular basis has several benefits. A study reported from the Netherlands showed that the group of men consuming as little as 1 ounce of fish per day had less than half the deaths from coronary heart disease as the group that did not eat fish. This effect may be due to the omega-3 fatty acids in fish fat or to something else in fish. The fat level in fish ranges from less than 1 gram to about 15 grams in a 3-ounce cooked portion. Warm water varieties are usually lower in fat, and cold water varieties are usually higher in omega-3 fatty acids. The following table lists some common fish and their level of fat, omega-3 fatty acid, and cholesterol.

Fish, 3 Oz Cooked*	Total Fat (g)	Omega-3 Fatty Acid** (g)	Cholesterol (mg)
Finfish: Cooked by Dry Heat			
Mackerel, Atlantic	15.1	1.0	64
Salmon, Sockeye	9.3	1.0	74
Swordfish	4.4	0.7	43
Trout, Rainbow	3.7	0.6	62
Halibut	2.5	0.4	35
Tuna, White (canned in water)	2.1	0.6	35
Flounder	1.3	0.4	58
Haddock	0.8	0.2	63
Cod, Atlantic	0.7	0.1	47
Shellfish: Cooked by Moist Heat			
Clam	1.7	0.2	57
Crab, Blue	1.5	0.4	85
Crayfish	1.2	0.2	151
Shrimp	0.9	0.3	166
Lobster, Northern	0.5	0.1	61

*Adapted from "Composition of Foods: Finfish and Shellfish Products," Agriculture Handbook 8-15, 1987.
**Includes eicosapentaenoic acid (EPA) and docosahexaenoic acid (DHA).

- *Does taking fish oil capsules lower cholesterol?*

Large doses of fish oil may have a slight cholesterol-lowering effect. However, fish oil has more of an effect in lowering triglyceride. Health experts do not recommend taking fish oil capsules. A diet low in saturated fatty acids and dietary cholesterol is much more effective in lowering blood cholesterol. Large doses (12 to 18 capsules of 1,000 mg each) of fish oil have been reported to help lower triglyceride levels but should not be used except under a doctor's supervision. Long-term use of fish oil capsules may lead to the development of side effects, such as diarrhea and an increased tendency to bleed.

- *Should I avoid all foods containing cholesterol?*

No, the dietary guidelines recommend that the amount of cholesterol consumed be limited to less than 300 mg per day. A recent study estimated that for someone eating a 2,500-calorie diet, every 100 milligram decrease in dietary cholesterol will decrease blood cholesterol by about 4 mg/dL. This response appears to hold true even when a low level of cholesterol is consumed. Therefore, lowering your intake of dietary cholesterol will result in some decrease in blood cholesterol.

- *What are fat replacers? Are they safe?*

Fat replacers are designed to replace all or only part of the fat in a product. Replacements for dietary fat are intended to lower fat content in food while satisfying the desire for that "high fat" taste and "mouthfeel." Fat replacers are usually based on carbohydrate, protein, or fatty acids. However, the fat content of a product can also be reduced by adding ingredients such as water, juice, fruit, or vegetables. Reducing fat content decreases calories in a product, since fat is the most concentrated source of calories.

Carbohydrate-based fat replacers include modified cornstarch, cellulose gel, and natural gums like carrageenan and locust bean. They are fully digestible and provide 4 calories per gram. Maltodextrins, for example, which result from hydrolyzing cornstarch, can partially or totally replace fats in a variety of products, such as salad dressings, dips, margarines, and frozen desserts. Baked products will probably contain them in the future. Carrageenan, which has been used in food for centuries, is extracted from one of eight species of red algae. Its viscosity and gel-forming properties add body to frozen desserts, pie fillings, whipped products, yogurt, and sauces. It is also being used in the new lower-fat ground beef being served in some quick-service restaurants. When the fat content of regular ground beef is reduced to less than 10% (by weight), the meat loses texture and juiciness. Carrageenan helps retain moisture and natural juices, making very-low-fat ground beef acceptable.

Protein-based fat replacers are made from protein sources such as egg white and whey and casein from milk. Microparticulated protein is made by combining protein from egg white and milk with other substances and milling it into very tiny round particles, which feel creamy on the tongue.

These fat replacers can be used in foods needing a creamy texture, such as fat-free frozen desserts, cheeses, sour cream, salad dressings, and sauces. Protein-based fat replacers supply some calories. Since protein provides 4 calories per gram and fat 9 calories per gram, it is obvious that replacing the fat with protein in foods that have a high fat content will decrease overall calories. Simplesse, an example of microparticulated protein, has 1 to 2 calories per gram.

Olestra is the best-known example of fatty acid–based fat replacers that are made by combining fatty acids with some other substance, such as sucrose (sugar). Since the fat-like substance formed in this process is not broken down or absorbed in the body, it does not provide calories. These fat replacers are heat-stable and can be used for food preparation techniques requiring high temperatures, such as frying and baking. At this time, the FDA has not approved the use of fatty acid–based fat replacers.

The important thing to remember about fat replacers is that, with few exceptions, the reduced fat or fat-free products in which they are used are not calorie free. Fat replacers may replace all or only part of the fat in a product. In many products, when the fat is reduced or removed, other ingredients, such as sugar, may be increased to achieve an acceptable flavor. Always check the total calories listed on the label.

Although there have been no adverse effects reported from short-term metabolic studies, studies showing the long-term effects of introducing appreciable amounts of fat replacers in the diet have not been reported. We do not know how individuals will use products containing fat replacers over an extended period of time. People may compensate for the lower fat content of these foods either by consuming more fat from other sources or by consuming more calories from carbohydrates and protein.

- *What is stearic acid? How does it affect blood cholesterol?*
  Stearic acid is one of the saturated fatty acids found in certain foods. In the pure form, stearic acid does not raise blood cholesterol. In a study reported by Bonanome and Grundy (1988), the effect of stearic acid on blood cholesterol was compared with the effect of palmitic (saturated) and oleic (monounsaturated) fatty acids. The researchers found that when stearic acid replaced palmitic acid in the diet, it was as effective as oleic acid in lowering blood cholesterol. The problem is that foods containing stearic acid also contain other saturated fatty acids, such as palmitic, which do tend to cause an increase in blood cholesterol levels.

Examples of foods considered good sources of stearic acid are shown below along with their content of several other fatty acids. In the future, researchers will likely learn more about the effect of other individual fatty acids on blood cholesterol.

Fat, 100g*	Stearic (%)	Palmitic (%)	Oleic** (%)	Linoleic† (%)
Cocoa butter	33.2	25.4	32.6	2.8
Beef tallow	18.9	24.9	36.0	3.1
Lard (pork fat)	13.5	23.8	41.2	10.2
Chicken fat	6.0	21.6	37.3	19.5
Sunflower oil	4.5	5.9	19.5	65.7
Soybean oil (hydrogenated)	5.0	9.8	42.5	34.9

*Adapted from "Composition of Foods: Fats and Oil," USDA Handbook 8-4, 1979.
**Oleic is the major monounsaturated fatty acid in the American diet.
†Linoleic is the major polyunsaturated fatty acid in the American diet.

- *What is meant by hydrogenation?*

Hydrogenation is the process of adding hydrogen molecules to oils (usually those containing primarily monounsaturated or polyunsaturated fatty acids). Partially hydrogenating liquid oils changes them to a semi-solid form to produce margarines and shortenings. Hydrogenation makes oils more stable and able to withstand higher temperatures (as in deep-fat frying) without breaking down. Many oils used in commercial foods and institutional cooking, as well as shortening used at home, are partially hydrogenated. Total hydrogenation of an oil is not suitable for use in most foods. Fat that has been hydrogenated totally makes up a very small portion of the total fat blend in a food.

- *What are trans fatty acids and how do they affect blood cholesterol?*

Trans fatty acids are formed during the process of hydrogenating oils to make margarine and shortening. Although some trans fatty acids occur in milk fat, hydrogenated fats are the primary source in the American diet. From a practical standpoint, trans fatty acids have nothing to do with your blood cholesterol level. In 1990 Mensink and Katan reported a research study indicating that trans fatty acids decrease I IDL (good cholesterol) and increase LDL (bad cholesterol). However, subjects in this study, which was conducted in the Netherlands, consumed approximately four times the amount of trans fatty acids normally eaten in the United States. Since food manufacturers have been removing tropical oils (coconut, palm kernel, and palm) from their products, the use of hydrogenated fat has increased. However, both national and international organizations have concluded that the amount of trans fatty acids consumed in a balanced diet is safe. The authors do not recommend dietary changes based on this study.

- *What are antioxidants? Do they protect against heart disease?*

One of the new theories is that antioxidants protect body cells from the damage caused by free radicals. A free radical is an unstable molecule that is able to change another molecule, such as a polyunsaturated fatty acid or a protein, into a form that can damage body tissues. Our bodies can get free radicals from outside or form them internally. The free radicals cause serious damage when they interact with certain substances in the body, which may contribute to heart disease, cancer, immune diseases, cataracts, and even aging itself. One theory is that cholesterol causes the most injury to arteries when it is oxidized or damaged by free radicals.

Antioxidants are substances that stop chain reactions caused by free radicals. It has been suggested that antioxidant nutrients, such as beta carotene and vitamins E and C as well as certain medications, may help protect the body from harmful actions of free radicals. For example, if beta carotene can prevent the oxidation of cholesterol, it might minimize the damage to arteries.

Beta carotene is a precursor of vitamin A. However, unlike vitamin A, it is not toxic in excessive amounts and appears to have no dangerous side effects, even at high doses. The most visible side effect of too much beta carotene is the development of an orange color in the skin. This color change is harmless and fades once the level of beta carotene is decreased. The average American takes in from 1.5 to 1.9 mg of beta carotene per day. It would be impractical for most people to eat the large portions of foods rich in beta carotene necessary to get 25 mg (equivalent to the amount used in the study) each day. Some of the best food sources of beta carotene are shown below. Although the jury is still out on the antioxidant and beta carotene theory, the incorporation of some of these foods into a well-balanced diet may have some beneficial effect.

Studies are being conducted to shed more light on the antioxidant theory. The Physicians' Health Study, a ten-year study currently under way, is looking at the effect of beta carotene supplementation on cancer and heart disease. The physicians are assigned to one of four groups receiving beta carotene, aspirin, a placebo, or a combination of the three. Preliminary data on 333 of the 22,000 male doctors with cardiovascular problems show that those assigned 50 mg of beta carotene on alternate

Food, ½ Cup*	Beta Carotene (mg)	Food, ½ Cup*	Beta Carotene (mg)
Carrot juice	18.9	Beet greens, cooked	2.4
Yams, boiled	16.7	Squash, butternut, cooked	2.2
Pumpkin, canned	16.2	Mango, fresh	1.9
Carrots, cooked	11.5	Collards, cooked	1.4
Carrots, raw, grated	5.1	Cantaloupe, fresh	1.3
Spinach, cooked	4.4	Kale, cooked	1.1
Apricot, dried, uncooked	2.8	Broccoli, cooked	1.0
Squash, acorn, cooked	2.6		

*Adapted from Nutrition Coordinating Center database, University of Minnesota, Minneapolis, Minn.

days (the equivalent of about two cups of carrots) had a 44% reduction in all major coronary events, such as heart attack. This group also had a 49% reduction in all major vascular events, such as stroke.

Another ongoing study, known as PQRST (Probucol Quantitative Regression Swedish Trial), is under way in Sweden. It is designed to assess whether a cholesterol-lowering drug with antioxidant properties can inhibit or reverse atherosclerosis in humans. Recent research studies have shown that an antioxidant drug retards the development of atherosclerosis in animals.

Positive results from these studies would give additional support to the antioxidant hypothesis.

● *Will increasing the fiber content of the diet lower blood cholesterol?*
    The addition of 2 ounces of an oat cereal (oatmeal or oat bran) to a diet low in fat and saturated fatty acids lowers blood cholesterol by 2% to 3% in addition to the cholesterol-lowering effect of the diet. There are two types of fiber—soluble and insoluble—and they play different roles in the body. The fiber content of food is a combination of both types of fiber. The table below shows the amount of total fiber, soluble fiber, and insoluble fiber in several foods (listed in descending order of total fiber content).

Soluble fiber helps to lower blood cholesterol. Examples of soluble fiber are oat cereals, dried beans, legumes, guar gums, barley, pectins from fruit, and psyllium. A study by Davidson reported that 2 ounces (56 grams dry weight) of oat bran lowered LDL-cholesterol significantly more than the same amount of oatmeal. The main difference between oatmeal and oat bran is their content of beta-glucan, a particular type of soluble fiber

Food, ¾ Cup*	Total Fiber (g)	Soluble Fiber (g)	Insoluble Fiber (g)	Calories
100% Bran	14.0	1.2	12.8	106
Pinto Beans, cooked	9.0	2.8	6.2	177
Corn, cooked	2.3	0.3	2.0	100
Oat Bran Muffin** (1 medium)	1.0	0.5	0.5	142
Apple w/Skin (1 medium)	2.8	1.0	1.8	81
Oat Bran, cooked	4.0	2.0	2.0	68
Oatmeal, cooked	2.7	1.4	1.3	109

*Adapted from Nutrition Coordinating Center database, University of Minnesota, Minneapolis, Minn.
**Fat content is less than 2 g except in muffin, which contains 6 g of fat.

that is twice as high in the oat bran. The study data suggest that it takes 3 ounces of oatmeal to achieve the same reduction in blood cholesterol as that attributed to 2 ounces of oat bran.

Insoluble fiber is not soluble in the intestinal tract. It does not appear to help lower blood cholesterol, but does aid in normal bowel function. Insoluble fibers are found in the skin, peels, and husks of fruits, vegetables, and whole-grain products.

The recommended level of total fiber for adults is 20 to 35 grams per day. It is further recommended that good sources of both soluble and insoluble fiber be included. Most authorities feel that increasing fiber intake improves general health in most people by promoting normal gastrointestinal function. Fiber may also help decrease the risk of developing certain diseases, such as colorectal cancer.

Foods containing fiber can either be high or low in fat. High-fiber muffins and cookies, for example, can be high in fat because of the fat added in preparation. Read the label and list of ingredients on commercial products to identify those high-fiber products that may also be high in fat and saturated fatty acids.

● *Is a vegetarian diet the best way to eat?*
According to current research, the best way to eat is a balanced diet: (1) that includes a variety of foods, (2) that is low in saturated fatty acids and cholesterol, and (3) that provides sufficient calories to maintain a desirable body weight. A vegetarian diet is one but not the only way to meet these requirements. Vegetarian diets do not always fit the guidelines for a cholesterol-lowering diet. For example, a vegetarian diet that includes large amounts of eggs, whole milk, cheese, butter, and cream on a regular basis will be high in saturated fatty acids and cholesterol. Re-

search studies indicate that complete vegetarians (no meat, eggs, or dairy products) and lacto-ovo vegetarians (no meat but eggs and dairy products) have lower blood levels of total and LDL-cholesterol and triglycerides than nonvegetarians. It is not clear if these lower levels are due to vegetarians' consuming less fat and saturated fatty acids, more soluble fiber, or other factors. In preliminary studies, a very-low-fat vegetarian diet has been associated with low blood cholesterol levels.

Vegetarian diets are healthful and are nutritionally adequate when carefully planned. Some surveys of nutrient intake indicate that vegetarians average higher intakes of calcium, vitamins A and C, and magnesium than nonvegetarians. In addition, iron deficiency appears to be no more common among vegetarian women than among nonvegetarian women.

- *Does red meat cause a high blood cholesterol level?*

No, a research study conducted at Baylor College of Medicine showed that eating either lean beef or a combination of chicken and fish had the same effect on blood cholesterol when consumed as part of a diet with less than 30% of calories from fat and less than 10% of calories from saturated fatty acids. The beef used in the study was USDA Select grade (very lean), which had any external fat trimmed off before cooking. Chicken breasts without skin and red snapper were used in the study. The beef, chicken, and fish were cooked without additional fat. This study demonstrates that including very lean beef in a diet low in saturated fatty acids and cholesterol does not have a bad effect on blood cholesterol.

- *What effect does using alcohol have on heart disease?*

Based on current research, there is no general agreement on the role of alcohol in heart disease. The Seven Countries Study (Keys) showed that populations consuming 3% to 5% of calories from alcohol may have either very high or very low rates of coronary heart disease (CHD). The studies that have increased public interest in alcohol use and heart disease are those suggesting that male teetotalers have a somewhat higher risk of CHD than men who regularly consume less than 100 grams of alcohol per week. The following are examples of beverages providing about 100 grams of alcohol:

- 7 mixed drinks, each containing 1½ fluid ounces of 80 proof liquor, have approximately 98 grams of alcohol (however, 7 mixed drinks, each containing 1½ fluid ounces of *100 proof* spirits, provide about 124 grams of alcohol)

- 9 glasses (4 fluid ounces each) of table wine have about 96 grams of alcohol
- 8 cans (12 fluid ounces each) of regular beer have about 102 grams of alcohol

Other studies suggest that moderate alcohol consumption is associated with higher levels of HDL (good cholesterol). One difficulty in applying this information to your individual intake is that not all research studies define "moderate alcohol consumption" the same way.

Studies conducted with religious groups (Seventh-Day Adventists) indicate that abstaining from alcohol is associated with a low risk of CHD. Triglyceride is usually very sensitive to alcohol. In individuals with elevated triglyceride, eliminating alcohol usually causes a rapid decrease in triglyceride levels. An elevated triglyceride level increases the risk of heart disease.

A number of studies suggest that people consuming 2 alcoholic drinks a day (on average) or more have higher blood pressure than people drinking less than this amount. High blood pressure is one of the major risk factors for cardiovascular disease. Other studies have suggested that the use of alcohol increases the risk of hemorrhagic stroke, especially in women. Of course, these studies do not reflect the other terrible consequences to life and health of alcohol abuse. Health professionals do not recommend alcohol use as a way of lowering cardiovascular risk. Our dietary recommendation is that if you do use alcohol, do so in moderation, that is, no more than two drinks per day. One drink is defined as:

- 1½ fluid ounces (a jigger) of distilled spirits, such as bourbon, rum, gin, etc.
- 4 fluid ounces of table wine
- 12 fluid ounces of regular beer

The accompanying table shows the percent of alcohol and the grams of alcohol in one drink of various alcoholic beverages (in ascending order of percent alcohol).

AMOUNT OF ALCOHOL (ETHANOL)
IN ONE SERVING OF SELECTED ALCOHOLIC DRINKS

Drink	Calories*	Percent Alcohol	Weight of Alcohol (g)
Lite Beer (12 fl oz)	78–131	2.2–4.4	7.8–15.6
Regular Beer (12 fl oz)	146	4.5	12.8
Table Wine, all types (4 fl oz)	84	11.5	11.0
Dessert Wine, sweet type (2 fl oz)	90	18.8	9.0

Drink	Calories*	Percent Alcohol	Weight of Alcohol (g)
Liqueur, Coffee, 53 proof (1.5 fl oz)	160	26.5	11.3
Liqueur, Crème de Menthe, 72 proof (1.5 fl oz)	186	36.0	14.9
Distilled Spirits, 80 proof** (1.5 fl oz)	97	40.0	14.0
Distilled Spirits, 86 proof† (1.5 fl oz)	105	43.0	15.1
Distilled Spirits, 90 proof‡ (1.5 fl oz)	110	45.0	15.9
Distilled Spirits, 94 proof (1.5 fl oz)	116	47.0	16.7
Distilled Spirits, 100 proof (1.5 fl oz)	124	50.0	17.9

*Alcohol contributes 7 calories per gram.
**Examples of 80 proof spirits include rum and vodka.
†An example of 86 proof spirits is whiskey.
‡An example of 90 proof spirits is gin.
Adapted from "Composition of Foods: Beverages," Agriculture Handbook No. 8-14, 1986.

● *What role does exercise play in reducing the risk of heart disease?*

It is estimated that approximately 30% of the adults in the U.S. are sedentary. The large number of individuals with very low levels of physical activity is important, since exercise has both indirect and direct effects on the risk of heart disease. Indirectly, physical activity helps reduce other risk factors for heart disease, such as high blood pressure and overweight. Although exercise does not appear to have a great deal of effect on the level of total blood cholesterol, it helps to decrease triglyceride and to increase HDL (good cholesterol) levels. In a more direct way, physical activity helps increase the interior size of arteries in the heart and improves the function of the left ventricle of the heart.

Some people believe that in order to gain a health benefit from physical activity you must be extremely active. However, recent research indicates that moderate exercise may have great health benefits. A large research study looked at death rates (from all causes) for people at five levels of physical fitness, as measured by exercise testing. Death rates from cardiovascular disease and cancer were considerably lower in the most-fit group when compared to those with a lower level of physical fitness. The largest drop in these death rates, however, occurred between the least-fit and the next-least-fit group. In practical terms, this means that moderate levels of physical fitness—such as might be obtained by a brisk daily walk of from 30 minutes to one hour—may help protect you from early death from all causes and, more specifically, from early death due to cardiovascular disease.

Chapter 2

Feeding Children and Adolescents

CHOLESTEROL LEVELS IN CHILDREN AND ADOLESCENTS

Concerns about nutrition and preventing heart disease affect children and adolescents as well as adults in the United States. The "Report of the Expert Panel on Blood Cholesterol Levels in Children and Adolescents" was released by the National Cholesterol Education Program (NCEP) in April 1991. The NCEP report sent a message to a number of groups—parents, teachers, school-lunch providers, and physicians and other health professionals—that influence both the diet and health status of children and adolescents. That message is that it is much better to begin taking appropriate steps in childhood to prevent heart disease than to wait and treat the disease after it has developed.

In its report on children and adolescents, the NCEP made dietary recommendations for children (two years of age and above) that are similar to those for adults.

- The diet should consist of a wide variety of foods to achieve nutritional adequacy
- Calorie intake should be adequate to support growth and development and to reach and/or maintain a desirable body weight
- The diet should provide:
  1. an average of no more than 30% of calories from fat.
  2. less than 10% of total calories from saturated fatty acids.
  3. less than 300 milligrams of cholesterol per day

Much of the message about diet, cholesterol levels, and heart disease has already reached children in the U.S. In July 1991, 407 children in the fourth to eighth grades responded to a Gallup Survey about children's nutrition knowledge. The survey, which was commissioned by the International Food Information Council and the National Center for Nutrition and

Dietetics of The American Dietetic Association, is similar to one conducted with adults in 1990 (page xxii).

CHILDREN MAKE FOOD DECISIONS

In America today, young people are making more of their own decisions about what they eat. Sixty-five percent of the more than 400 children in the Gallup Survey said they usually decide what to eat for breakfast, 46% usually select their own lunch, and 74% usually select their own snacks.

The Gallup Survey indicated that more than half (57%) of the children interviewed are involved in the process of buying food for meals and snacks. Children and adolescents can be taught to use *The Living Heart Brand Name Shopper's Guide*. They should be encouraged to read labels and select foods that are either listed in the Guide or contain similar levels of fat.

WHEN CHILDREN AND ADOLESCENTS EAT

Although most young children eat breakfast, skipping this meal becomes more common during the teenage years. Statistics show that teenage girls are the group most likely to skip breakfast. Quick-and-easy breakfast suggestions that are low in fat and/or saturated fat include:

- Fruit and fruit juice
- Most breads, bagels (except the egg type), and English muffins with unsaturated margarine and jelly, low-fat cheese, low-fat cream cheese spread (see page 171), or peanut butter
- Cereals (except those containing nuts, coconut, or oil) with skim, ½%, or 1% low-fat milk
- Waffles or pancakes that are low in fat (see page 115) with unsaturated margarine and syrup or jelly

When there is no time at all to fix breakfast, fill in with instant breakfast mix made with skim milk.

Snacks are an important source of nutrition for children and adolescents. Young children have small stomachs and need to supplement meals with nutritious snacks. It is estimated that snacks provide 18% of the calories consumed by children age 6 to 11 and 21% of the calories consumed by teenagers. Since 83% of the children polled in the Gallup Survey said that they sometimes prepare their own snacks, it is increasingly important that appropriate snack foods be available. Encourage children to use foods that are low in fat and saturated fat for snacking instead of chips, candy, "regular" desserts, and other foods that are high in fat. Examples of snack foods low in fat and saturated fat include:

- Fruits and juices
- Vegetables
- Dairy products, such as skim, ½%, or 1% low-fat milk, low-fat cheese, and low-fat or nonfat flavored yogurt (see page 177)
- Ready-to-eat cereals (see page 125)
- Breads (see page 101)
- Crackers and rice cakes (see pages 149 and 163)
- Low-fat and nonfat frozen desserts (page 217), such as ice milk, frozen yogurt, fruit bars
- Angel food and other cakes (page 188), cookies (page 192), and muffins (page 197) that contain little or no fat or are prepared with unsaturated oil or margarine
- Fig bars, gingersnap cookies, graham crackers, and other commercial cookies that are fat-free or are low in fat (see page 192)
- Snack foods, such as fruit leathers (page 342), pretzels (page 346), popcorn (page 344), and baked tortilla chips (see page 341)

For a high-energy snack that is easy to carry, try mixing dried fruit, cereal, fat-free candy, and nuts or seeds that are low in saturated fat or use a commercial trail mix that does not contain chocolate chips or coconut.

WHERE CHILDREN AND ADOLESCENTS EAT

Today children and adolescents eat more of their food away from home than ever before. The school-lunch program accounts for many of the meals children eat away from home. Statistics indicate that about 60% of the children attending public schools in the U.S. buy the school lunch. This percent is higher for grades 1 through 6. The United States Department of Agriculture (USDA) requires that school lunches provide one-third of a child's daily calorie needs. The school lunch must offer the student 2 ounces of meat or meat alternate, two or more servings of fruit or vegetable (totaling ¾ cup), and one-half pint of milk per day and eight servings of bread per week. Surveys show that 15% to 17% of the calories provided in the school lunch come from saturated fat. With leadership from the USDA, the American Food Service Association, universities, and health professions, an increasing number of school-lunch programs are working to reduce the fat and saturated fat in the total school lunch.

Food-service directors and their cook-managers are modifying recipes and seeking out commercial products that are lower in fat. Many school-lunch programs offer skim chocolate milk, which helps provide the calories students often need without supplying fat. Parents should be aware of the foods being served in their child's school-lunch program and support the food service in its efforts to reduce fat in school lunches.

Many children and adolescents eat meals and snacks "on the go." Although most of the food eaten by school-age children comes from home, the number of children buying and consuming takeout food is growing. An estimated 83% of the restaurant visits made by children and adolescents (under age 18) are to fast-food establishments. However, the growing trend toward lower-fat eating has led to some changes in the choices offered at many fast-food restaurants. Since not all of the items served in restaurants are equally appropriate for a cholesterol-lowering eating plan, it is a good idea to help your child identify those choices that are lower in fat. At a fast-food restaurant or snack bar, choices that are lower in fat include:

- Grilled chicken breast (skinless) sandwich with mustard or catsup or a small amount of mayonnaise (ask that it be served on the side)
- Hamburger with lettuce, tomato, pickles, and onions; spread the bun with mustard or catsup or a small amount of mayonnaise (ask that it be served on the side). Request that hamburgers made with the lower-fat ground beef being offered at some fast-food restaurants be served without cheese
- Sandwiches made with sliced turkey, lean ham, or lean roast beef with mustard or catsup or a small amount of mayonnaise (ask that it be served on the side)
- Thin-crust pizza with single cheese and lots of vegetables
- Fat-free muffins
- Low-fat or nonfat frozen yogurt
- Skim or low-fat milk
- Fresh fruit

Some vending machines now offer choices that are lower in fat and/or saturated fat, such as:

- Fresh fruit
- Raisins and mixed dried fruit
- Fruit juice and vegetable juice

- Soft drinks containing carbonated water and fruit juice
- Cereal and dried fruit snack mixes containing a small amount of nuts and seeds
- Low-fat flavored yogurt
- Fat-free candy (see page 368)

When an adolescent or child eats foods that are high in fat away from home, serving foods low in fat at home helps compensate and brings fat and saturated fat for the day to a level within the dietary guidelines.

WHAT DO CHILDREN KNOW ABOUT FOOD?

The majority (94%) of the children interviewed in the Gallup Survey agreed that what they eat can affect their future health. It is interesting to note that 84% of the children agreed that it is best to eat small amounts of many different foods and not too much of any one thing. This attitude is similar to the dietary recommendation to eat a wide variety of foods. An even higher proportion (98%) of the group recognized the importance of eating plenty of fruits, vegetables, and high-fiber foods, such as whole-grain breads and cereals. Only 18% of the children surveyed said they believe it's okay to "eat anything you want, whenever you want to."

Some adults who are on cholesterol-lowering diets tend to restrict their food choices more than is necessary. This tendency, which is usually temporary, can lead to labeling some foods as "very good" and others as "very bad." The Gallup Survey indicates that this trend toward extremes may be carrying over to children. For example, 85% said that "to eat healthy you should avoid *all* high-fat foods." However, a well-balanced cholesterol-lowering diet includes limited amounts of high-fat foods, such as oil, margarine, regular salad dressing, nuts, and seeds. Children and adolescents need some fat in their diet to supply fat-soluble vitamins and essential fatty acids and to provide the calories necessary to support growth and development and physical activity. Seventy-seven percent of the children surveyed had this same all-or-nothing attitude about sweets. They agreed that "you should *never* eat foods with large amounts of sugar." Actually, a child or adolescent who is consuming a well-balanced diet can include a moderate amount of sweet foods. It is important to look at the type and amount of fat provided by some sweet foods. Sweets such as cookies, candy, and pastries may be very high in fat. *The Living Heart Brand Name Shopper's Guide* lists sweets that are low in fat or fat-free.

Perhaps the most disturbing survey answer was from 73% of the children who said that they *worry* about fat and cholesterol. The 1990 Gallup

Survey of adults showed that only 56% of them worry about these aspects of their diet. There is concern that this type of worry may lead to dietary extremes in children and adolescents, who have a very real need for appropriate amounts of fat. It is understandable that almost two-thirds (65%) of the children surveyed said that they are tired of hearing about what foods are good or bad for them.

Health experts favor an eating pattern that is flexible enough to cover the many different aspects of daily life. A food high in fat, saturated fat, and/or cholesterol can be part of an eating pattern that follows the dietary guidelines. It may be necessary to compensate for the food that is high in fat by serving other foods low in fat so that the average intake does not exceed the recommended amounts of fat, saturated fat, and cholesterol. This is often the best way to achieve a diet plan that fits into your child's lifestyle.

WHERE DO CHILDREN GET INFORMATION ABOUT FOOD?

The responsibility for educating children and adolescents about food and nutrition lies with several groups. Ninety-five percent of the children in the Gallup Survey relied on the school for information on food and nutrition. Parents were the second (86%) source and health professionals were listed third (73%). However, when the children were asked to rank sources of information on food and nutrition by how useful this information was to them, the highest rating (80%) went to health professionals, such as doctors, nurses, and dietitians.

Some of the most effective teaching is by example. What is eaten at home influences the overall dietary intake of children and adolescents. Of the children polled in the Gallup Survey, 54% eat with their families every day while 89% reported eating with their families at least three to five times a week. It is of interest that 60% of the children who rated their eating habits as "excellent" or "good" said they eat with their families every day. Of the children rating their own diets as "fair" or "poor," 44% ate with their families each day and 38% ate with families three to five times per week.

WHY CHANGE A CHILD'S EATING PATTERN?

Several accepted facts about the development of heart disease form the basis for the NCEP recommendations concerning children and adolescents. Atherosclerosis—the thickening of artery walls due to a buildup of fat, cholesterol, and other substances—is the process underlying most heart disease. Research clearly shows that atherosclerosis does not suddenly appear in older people but actually begins in childhood. Atherosclerosis usually progresses very slowly throughout childhood and usually leads to coronary heart disease (CHD) only after the individual reaches adulthood.

A high blood cholesterol level contributes to the process of atherosclerosis. Research studies suggest that a child or adolescent with an elevated blood cholesterol level is more likely than the general population to have high blood cholesterol as an adult. More specifically, research has shown that high levels of total cholesterol, LDL-cholesterol, and VLDL-cholesterol (very low density lipoprotein) and low levels of HDL-cholesterol in the blood are associated with the degree to which early signs of atherosclerosis are found in adolescents and young adults. Therefore, experts feel that steps taken to prevent or slow the progress of atherosclerosis in childhood and/or adolescence could very well increase the years of good health for many adults.

Studies of many countries from all over the world show that adults in the U.S. have higher blood cholesterol levels and higher rates of CHD and heart attack death than their counterparts in other countries. It is also true that children and adolescents in the U.S. have higher levels of blood cholesterol and consume a diet higher in saturated fat and cholesterol than children of other countries. Research has identified high intakes of saturated fat, cholesterol, and calories (when leading to obesity) as major dietary factors contributing to an elevated blood cholesterol.

Chapter 3

Saving Time and Money While Eating ''Healthy''

The basic facts are clear—you eat what you buy. Healthy eating begins with the food you purchase. If you buy foods low in fat, you will eat foods low in fat. If you fill your cabinets and refrigerator with foods high in fat, you are going to have trouble eating sensibly. Don't fall for the old excuses that eating ''healthy'' takes too much time or is too expensive. This chapter provides some basic, common-sense techniques to help you save time and money while eating well and staying on a healthy eating plan.

SAVING TIME

There are usually five steps involved in preparing a meal from first idea to completion. They all take time. You must: (1) plan the meal, (2) purchase the food, (3) store the food, (4) prepare the food, (5) serve the meal and clean up when it is over. Since time is often limited for today's busy people, here are a few suggestions for cutting the time required for each of these steps.

PLANNING AHEAD

- Prepare menus

    Although writing menus may take a little extra time when you first begin, it will save you much more time in the long run. As you organize the recipes needed for the week's menus, use the conversion tables on page 404 in the Appendix as a shortcut to help you total the amount of each food you will need. One of the primary advantages of writing menus is that a complete grocery shopping list can easily be developed from them.
- Shop from a list

    Having a complete grocery shopping list means making fewer trips to the supermarket—a tremendous saving of time. How often have you started preparing a meal only to find that you were missing one or more ingredients? Those "quick" trips to the supermarket to pick up one or two items waste a lot of time. Try comparing the time it takes to write a week of menus to the time spent making several extra trips to the store each week. Shopping lists are a key factor in an efficiently run kitchen. In addition to writing down those foods and ingredients you need for the week's menus, write down other foods when you notice they are running low. If you are in a hurry, place the empty container on the counter so that it will act as a reminder until you have time to add it to your shopping list. If you do happen to forget an ingredient you need, you may be able to substitute for it in your recipe. Check out the simple substitutions on page 401 in the Appendix before making an extra trip to the supermarket. Another way to save time is to organize the items on your shopping list according to the layout of your supermarket. This advance planning will help you move through the store more efficiently, avoiding backtracking. Use products listed in *The Living Heart Brand Name Shopper's Guide* to make up your shopping list. For example, if a recipe calls for cheese, use the information in the Guide to help you decide which of the cheeses are lower in fat before you go to the store. You may find it helpful to use a "standard" shopping list, such as the one on page 39, that can be photocopied for your convenience.

- Plan for holiday meals

    Have you ever wondered how some people seem so calm and organized while preparing a large holiday dinner? One trick is to keep a standard menu and shopping list for these special occasions, which can be used from one year to the next. Most people serve the same traditional meal each Thanksgiving, Christmas, New Year's Day, and 4th of July. Planning can help you avoid missing items and last-minute crises. Also, try preparing a standard shopping list for other special times, like hunting trips, picnics, and camp-outs.

- Organize your kitchen

    Another part of planning ahead is organizing your kitchen so that utensils and equipment used most often are within convenient reach. Ideally, your work area will be near the sink and the cooking surface. Utensils (can opener, cutting board, knives), spices, garbage disposal or trash container, and the equipment you use most frequently (food processor, blender, mixer) should be nearby. Several types of equipment are specially designed to reduce food-preparation time. These time-savers include a microwave oven, oven timer (to start and stop the cooking process when you aren't present), crockpot or slow cooker, countertop convection oven, food processor, toaster oven, blender, and pressure cooker or pressure saucepan.

PURCHASING FOODS

- Purchase large amounts of food

  Making fewer trips to the supermarket by purchasing large amounts of food on one shopping trip helps you save time, especially if you have been shopping two or three times a week. A recent survey reported that shoppers averaged 2.3 trips per week to the supermarket, with men usually making more shopping trips per week than women. Shoppers who have children average more trips to the store each week than shoppers without children. Another time-saving option is to have the supermarket deliver your food. When you use a shopping service, it is important to specify the exact brand of food you want, since different brands of the same food item may contain varying amounts of fat, saturated fat, and cholesterol.

- Purchase "quick" food

  The type of food you buy will determine the amount of time necessary for preparation. The items you buy may be in the form of raw food (fresh fruit, vegetables, meat), convenience food (foods partially prepared), or fully prepared takeout foods (ready to eat). Foods ready to pop into the microwave for a minute or two and then serve are now commonly available. Although convenience and microwaveable foods are often high in fat, *The Living Heart Brand Name Shopper's Guide* lists many convenience foods that are low in fat. Be sure to read the nutrition label before making your choice.

  Convenience foods, which are now available in most categories of the supermarket, can range from cleaned and sliced raw vegetables to frozen dinners. The usual meaning of "convenience food" is that someone else has done some (or all) of the preparation for you. This also usually means that the food will cost more than dishes you prepare from scratch. However, the amount of time busy people can save by using convenience foods may make the extra cost worthwhile. You are the best judge of how important saving time may be when it is weighed against the increased price of these food products. Many different types of convenience foods are listed in *The Living Heart Brand Name Shopper's Guide*. For example, prepared muffins, pie fillings, pre-seasoned vegetable mixtures, and single-serving entrées and dinners appear in the Guide. The single-serving entrées and dinners in the Guide are either shelf-stable (canned and retort-type packaging) or frozen. It is usually necessary to supplement these dinners and entrées with other foods to have a complete meal. Single-serving entrées and dinners may start out low in calories and fat, but the calorie and fat content of the finished meal will depend on the foods being added. Page 405 of the Appendix includes examples of quick-to-prepare foods which can be served with single-serving entrées and dinners that are low in calories and fat. You will also find menus at different calorie levels.

Takeout food is becoming increasingly popular in the United States. Fast-food restaurants are the most frequent source for takeout food, with restaurants taking second place. Supermarket deli shops are becoming a popular place to purchase prepared hot and cold food. Some supermarkets have salad bars where sliced fresh fruit and vegetables can be purchased and may even provide prepared gourmet and specialty foods. Some caterers are glad to prepare food to fit special requests, such as food low in calories and sodium. They may even agree to use your recipes. For an additional fee, they will often deliver the food to your home. Page 407 of the Appendix provides sample questions designed to help you find out whether prepared foods purchased outside the home are low in fat, saturated fat, and cholesterol.

STORING FOOD

- Preserve freshness

  Food should be stored in such a way that its freshness and nutrients are preserved. You can wash fruits and vegetables and partially prepare vegetables before they are ever put into the refrigerator. Try cleaning carrots and storing them in an air-tight container so that they are ready for slicing or grating. Storing foods in clear containers makes it easier to find them in the refrigerator.
- Divide foods into amounts most often used in recipes

  Before freezing meat, divide it into the amounts that will be needed in the recipes you have planned for the week. Packages of foods to be frozen should be clearly labeled with the name of the food and the date.

- Consider "active" and "passive" time

  The total time it takes to prepare a meal includes both active and passive time. Active time is the time you actually spend preparing food, such as trimming the fat off the meat and cubing it. Passive time is the time it takes the meat to cook while you are free to do something else.

- Combine simple and complicated dishes

  When an entrée takes a lot of active time to prepare, it is wise to choose salad and vegetables that require short active amounts of time for preparation. If the entrée takes very little active time to prepare and longer passive time, salad and vegetables can be prepared with short active-time requirements to yield a quick meal. Begin collecting quick-and-easy recipe and menu ideas. Recipes with just a few ingredients are often quicker to prepare than those with several ingredients and numerous steps.

- Cook extra food

  When you prepare a recipe, it takes very little added active time to double or triple the quantity. Part of the finished dish can be frozen and served later. Soups, stews, casseroles, chili, spaghetti sauce, cookies, and muffins lend themselves to freezing for future use.

- Use quick-to-fix foods and ingredients

  Keep a large number of quick-to-fix foods and ingredients on hand that can be prepared in several different ways. One popular example is chicken breasts (with bone and skin removed), which can be grilled, used as part of a salad plate, served with salsa, or topped with marinara sauce. Other examples of quick-to-fix foods are canned and frozen vegetables, rice, pasta, fish fillets, and lean ground beef.

- Prepare soup without meat

  Prepare your favorite soup recipe, omitting the meat. Freeze part of the soup and then add meat, fish, or poultry, allowing enough time to reheat the soup and cook the meat just before eating. This works especially well for tomato- and vegetable-based soups.

SERVING MEALS AND CLEANING UP

- Use fewer dishes

  You can save time by using the same dish for cooking, serving, and storing food. Use as few pieces of equipment as possible to shorten your clean-up time.

- Serve food directly onto the plate

    You can save time at informal meals by serving food directly from the cooking pan onto the plate instead of transferring it to a serving dish. In addition to saving clean-up time, this shortcut provides an easy way to pre-portion food, a helpful technique for people needing to lose weight.
- Store dishes near the dishwasher or sink

    You can save time by storing eating utensils (plates, glasses, and silverware) near the dishwasher or sink. Depending on the design of your kitchen, you may be able to remove dishes from the dishwasher or sink and put them away while standing in one place.
- Use disposable dishes

    Clean-up time after a meal can be cut to a minimum by using disposable plates, glasses, and plastic "silverware." You may want to invest in some sturdy plate liners, which can be used to strengthen less-expensive paper plates. Weigh the value to you of the time saved by using disposable dishes against their cost.

SAVING MONEY

Americans spend a lot of money on food. In 1990 Americans spent more than $546 billion for food and almost $80 billion on alcoholic beverages, according to data published by the United States Department of Agriculture. Individuals and families accounted for approximately 81% of this $546 billion spent on food—or in excess of $442 billion; most of the rest was spent by businesses and the government. Data indicate that average weekly food expenditures per person rose from $18.94 in 1980 to $25.68 in 1988. Increases in money spent for food were not evenly distributed between food consumed at home and that eaten away from home. Money spent for food eaten at home increased by 24% between 1980 and 1988, while money spent for food eaten away from home increased by 61%. According to a survey reported in "Trends—Consumer Attitudes & the Supermarket 1991," the average amount of money spent per person per week on groceries increased from $29 to $32 between January 1990 and January 1991.

The percent of a family's income spent on food decreased from 14% to 12% between 1970 and 1990 (USDA). This apparent reduction was primarily due to the fact that during this 20-year period money spent on food increased by only 24% while income increased by 42%. It is estimated that much of the 24% increase in food expenditures was due not to rising food prices but to increased eating away from home. Survey data show that meals eaten away from home and snacks accounted for 46% of the U.S. food dollar in 1990, almost double the amount in 1970.

In 1990 the amount of money families spent on groceries per person each week was at an all-time high. Households that don't include children usually spend more money per person on groceries than households with children. As a rule, larger households spend fewer food dollars per person than smaller households.

Most people like the idea of saving money on food as long as quality and convenience aren't sacrificed. Here are some tips to help you save money on the foods you purchase:

- Use price-off coupons

    According to "Trends—Consumer Attitudes & the Supermarket 1991," the use of coupons is one of the techniques shoppers most frequently employ to save money. Make it a habit to clip coupons for frequently used foods or new items you want to try that are low in fat, saturated fat, and cholesterol.

    To make using coupons more convenient, set up a filing system and arrange your coupons by type of product. Pull out your coupons at the same time you make out your shopping list. Then, make a note of those items on your shopping list for which you have coupons and place the coupons to one side for easy access at the check-out counter.

    Be sure to check your coupons each week before you go shopping and remove the outdated ones.
- Read the newspaper for grocery "specials"

    Spotting those special buys in weekly supermarket ads is another way careful shoppers stretch their food budget.
- Buy store brands or lower-priced products instead of national brands

    You can usually save money on a consistent basis and without compromising on quality by buying items with store labels instead of national brands.
- Compare prices and select the least expensive

    Many supermarkets provide a service called "unit pricing," which shows the price per ounce of a product. This information enables you to compare the price per ounce of several brands of the same product that may be available in different-size containers. Based on the price per ounce, it is often cheaper to buy larger-size containers of certain foods, even when they aren't on sale. Purchasing a large quantity of an item you use regularly when the price is marked down is an even better bargain. For example, fruits and vegetables are usually a good buy when they are in season. Try buying extra ears of fresh corn when the price is low and freezing them for use at a later time.

- Use a written shopping list

    Shoppers commonly find that purchasing only those foods on their shopping list is a good way to save money. This is especially true of compulsive shoppers, who may be swayed by the mouthwatering smells, attractive-looking foods, colorful displays, and tasty samples so popular in today's supermarkets. Many people are also influenced in the foods they purchase by their own degree of hunger. Using a list (and sticking to it) is one of the best ways to avoid expensive impulse buying.

- Buy commonly used products on "special" whenever you find them

    This is one exception to the "don't get anything not on your shopping list" suggestion. When you find a very good price on something commonly used that you have enough space to store, go ahead and buy it. If an item advertised at a special price is not available, be sure to request a "rain check" so that you can get the lower price when new stock arrives.

- Compare prices between supermarkets

    Don't be afraid to go to supermarkets other than your "old standby" to take advantage of advertised specials. Of course, if you spend an extra hour and burn a dollar's worth of gasoline to save 30 cents on cantaloupe, you haven't really found a bargain. Price is not always the only factor you will want to consider.

- Shop at a discount or warehouse food store for grocery items

    Buying large quantities of certain items at warehouse food stores can help stretch your food dollars. This type of food purchasing has many of the same pros and cons as shopping for specials at several supermarkets. If you waste a lot of time and gasoline to save a few pennies on items you don't actually use that often, you've bought a very expensive "bargain."

- Buy fewer luxury or gourmet items

    Luxury and gourmet foods tend to be expensive. Although we may enjoy eating these fancier foods, it may be easier on your pocketbook to buy them once in a while for a special occasion instead of on a routine basis.

- Buy fewer convenience foods

  The name says it all! Convenience foods carry a higher price tag because you are paying someone else to do all or part of the preparation and often the cooking. Weigh the extra cost of these food items against the value of the time you may save by using them.

- Purchase day-old bread products

  Most bakeries have some outlet for selling day-old bread, rolls, and sandwich buns at reduced prices. However, these products are truly bargains only if you can use them within a relatively short period of time.

You can also save money by employing the following techniques in your home.

- Do more meal planning

  Planning your meals ahead of time helps save both money and time. In writing your menus, pay close attention to advertised food "specials" and items for which you have coupons. Of course, price isn't the only consideration. It is also important that you include a variety of foods in your menus, and that they be low in fat, saturated fat, and cholesterol. Use your menus to make a shopping list of the foods and ingredients you will need. The information in "Some Interesting Food Facts to Make Cooking Easier" (page 402) can help you plan the amounts of certain basic foods that you will need to buy with more accuracy.

- Use more leftovers

  At times, you can plan "twice" for the foods you buy—once when the food is first prepared and served and a second time when it appears as leftovers. It makes good "money sense" to have a purpose in mind for food that remains after a meal. Don't just let bits of food get pushed to the back of the refrigerator until they have to be thrown out. Leftovers can be eaten alone or in combination with other foods to make a new dish. Serve leftovers as a tasty brown-bag lunch the next day or freeze them for later use. Instead of freezing the total amount of a leftover, try dividing it into servings on plates that can be stored in the freezer and heated in the microwave for quick meals at home or work.

- Use less meat, poultry, and fish

  Meat, poultry, and fish are more expensive per serving than most other foods you purchase. Decrease the cost of your entrée by mixing meat with beans, pasta, and/or vegetables. This technique can also help decrease the fat, saturated fat, and cholesterol in the entrée.

- Eat out less often

  Eating at home is normally less expensive than eating out. When you eat out, you are paying not only for the food but for someone to prepare it, serve it, and clean up afterward.

- Take your lunch to school or work

  Preparing food at home and taking it to school or work is usually less expensive than eating out. Food brought from home has the added advantage of being prepared in ways that keep it lower in fat, saturated fat, and cholesterol. This can also hold true if you need food low in calories and/or sodium. Use *The Living Heart Brand Name Shopper's Guide* to help you select those foods that are low in fat, sodium, etc.

GROCERY SHOPPING LIST

Fruit, Vegetables

_____

_____

_____

_____

Bakery: Bread, Rolls

_____

_____

_____

Canned: Fruit, Juice, Veggies,
Tuna, Soups, Entrées

_____

_____

_____

Ingredients: Oil, Flour, Sugar,
Spices, Dried Fruit

_____

_____

_____

Mixes: Bread, Cake, Pancake,
Muffin

_____

_____

_____

Rice, Pasta, Dried Beans

_____

_____

_____

Beef, Chicken, Fish, Pork, Lamb,
Luncheon Meat

_____

_____

_____

Condiments: Salad Dressing,
Mustard, Catsup

_____

_____

_____

Frozen: Juice, Fruit, Veggies,
Dinners, Desserts

_____

_____

_____

Dairy: Milk, Yogurt, Cheese,
Margarine

_____

_____

_____

Crackers, Chips, Cookies

_____

_____

_____

Beverages

_____

_____

_____

Cleaning Supplies & Paper Goods

_____

_____

_____

Other

_____

_____

_____

_____

Chapter 4

Planning a Cholesterol-Lowering Eating Pattern

Two methods that can be used to translate the dietary recommendations of "no more than 30% of calories from fat" and "less than 10% of calories from saturated fatty acids" into practical food choices are described in this chapter. Either method can help you control the amount of food containing fat and saturated fat you eat so that your intake does not exceed the levels in the dietary guidelines.

- Servings of Food Method
- Grams of Fat Method

Both the servings of food and the grams of fat (and saturated fat) methods are based on the number of calories you consume. Therefore, you will first need to determine about how many calories you need each day.

DETERMINING YOUR CALORIE NEEDS

In order to determine the approximate number of calories you need each day to maintain your present weight (or to lose weight), you need to know your height, frame size, and activity level. You will follow four steps to arrive at your calorie level.

1. *Height.* Measure your height without shoes.

2. *Frame size.* Use one of the following two simple tests to determine your frame size. The first method requires no equipment. Place the thumb and index finger of one hand around your other wrist. Be sure your thumb and index finger go around the radius and ulna bones at your wrist (the smallest part, closest to your hand).

- If thumb and index finger *overlap,* you have a *small* frame.
- If thumb and index finger *just touch,* you have a *medium* frame.
- If thumb and index finger *do not meet,* you have a *large* frame.

A second way to determine frame size is to use a flexible measuring tape to measure around your wrist at the smallest area, nearest your hand. Match your wrist measurement with your height in the table below to get your frame size.

Height	Small Frame	Medium Frame	Large Frame
Under 5′3″	Less than 5½″	5½″ to 5¾″	Greater than 5¾″
5′3″ to 5′4″	Less than 6″	6″ to 6¼″	Greater than 6¼″
Over 5′4″	Less than 6¼″	6¼″ to 6½″	Greater than 6½″

3. *Activity level.* Consider all of your activities for a typical day. This includes the amount of time you spend resting, walking around your house, sitting at a desk, watching television, and exercising. Then, use the list below to determine your level of activity.

ACTIVITY LEVEL*

- Very Light Activity

  Seated and standing activities, such as working as a house painter or in a laboratory, driving, typing, sewing, ironing, cooking, playing cards, playing a musical instrument.
- Light Activity

  Walking on a level surface at 2.5 to 3 mph, garage work, electrical work, restaurant work, carpentry, house-cleaning, child care, golf, sailing, table tennis.
- Moderate Activity

  Walking 3.5 to 4 mph, weeding, carrying a load, cycling, skiing, tennis, dancing.
- Heavy Activity

  Walking uphill with a load, heavy manual labor such as digging, climbing, basketball, football, soccer.

*Adapted from National Research Council. *Recommended Dietary Allowance,* 10th Edition. National Academy Press, Washington, D.C., 1989.

4. *Calorie level.* Use your height, frame size, and level of activity with the table for either males (page 42) or females (page 43) to determine the approximate number of calories you need each day. Remember, the

---

ADULT MALES

Height Without Shoes*	Frame Size	Desirable Weight**	Calorie Level Based on Physical Activity			
			Very Light (Calories)	Light (Calories)	Moderate (Calories)	Heavy (Calories)
5'5"	Small	129 (124–133)	1,700	1,950	2,200	2,600
	Medium	137 (130–143)	1,800	2,050	2,350	2,750
	Large	147 (138–156)	1,900	2,200	2,500	2,950
5'6"	Small	133 (128–137)	1,750	2,000	2,250	2,650
	Medium	141 (134–147)	1,850	2,100	2,400	2,800
	Large	152 (142–161)	2,000	2,300	2,600	3,050
5'7"	Small	137 (132–141)	1,800	2,050	2,350	2,750
	Medium	145 (138–152)	1,900	2,200	2,450	2,900
	Large	157 (147–166)	2,050	2,350	2,650	3,150
5'8"	Small	141 (136–145)	1,850	2,100	2,400	2,850
	Medium	149 (142–156)	1,950	2,250	2,550	3,000
	Large	161 (151–170)	2,100	2,400	2,750	3,200
5'9"	Small	145 (140–150)	1,900	2,200	2,450	2,900
	Medium	153 (146–160)	2,000	2,300	2,600	3,050
	Large	165 (155–174)	2,150	2,500	2,800	3,300
5'10"	Small	149 (144–154)	1,950	2,250	2,550	3,000
	Medium	158 (150–165)	2,050	2,350	2,700	3,150
	Large	169 (159–179)	2,200	2,550	2,850	3,400
5'11"	Small	153 (148–158)	2,000	2,300	2,600	3,050
	Medium	162 (154–170)	2,100	2,450	2,750	3,250
	Large	174 (164–184)	2,250	2,600	2,950	3,500
6'0"	Small	157 (152–162)	2,050	2,350	2,650	3,150
	Medium	167 (158–175)	2,150	2,500	2,850	3,350
	Large	179 (168–189)	2,350	2,700	3,050	3,600
6'1"	Small	162 (156–167)	2,100	2,450	2,750	3,250
	Medium	171 (162–180)	2,200	2,550	2,900	3,400
	Large	184 (173–194)	2,400	2,750	3,150	3,700
6'2"	Small	166 (160–171)	2,150	2,500	2,800	3,300
	Medium	176 (167–185)	2,300	2,650	3,000	3,500
	Large	189 (178–199)	2,450	2,850	3,200	3,800
6'3"	Small	170 (164–175)	2,200	2,550	2,900	3,400
	Medium	181 (172–190)	2,350	2,700	3,100	3,600
	Large	193 (182–204)	2,500	2,900	3,300	3,850

*Table adjusted for measurement of height without shoes.
**From 1959 Metropolitan Life Insurance Company, New York City. These tables are based on 1959 rather than 1983 Metropolitan Life Insurance Company height-weight tables because the earlier tables specify lower weights, more appropriate to health-related concerns.

ADULT FEMALES

Height Without Shoes*	Frame Size	Desirable Weight**	Calorie Level Based on Physical Activity			
			Very Light (Calories)	Light (Calories)	Moderate (Calories)	Heavy (Calories)
5'0"	Small	106 (102–110)	1,400	1,600	1,800	2,100
	Medium	113 (107–119)	1,450	1,700	1,900	2,250
	Large	123 (115–131)	1,600	1,850	2,100	2,450
5'1"	Small	109 (105–113)	1,400	1,650	1,850	2,200
	Medium	116 (110–122)	1,500	1,750	1,950	2,300
	Large	126 (118–134)	1,650	1,900	2,150	2,500
5'2"	Small	112 (108–116)	1,450	1,700	1,900	2,250
	Medium	119 (113–126)	1,550	1,800	2,000	2,400
	Large	129 (121–138)	1,700	1,950	2,200	2,600
5'3"	Small	115 (111–119)	1,500	1,750	1,950	2,300
	Medium	123 (116–130)	1,600	1,850	2,100	2,450
	Large	133 (125–142)	1,750	2,000	2,250	2,650
5'4"	Small	118 (114–123)	1,550	1,750	2,000	2,350
	Medium	127 (120–135)	1,650	1,900	2,150	2,550
	Large	137 (129–146)	1,800	2,050	2,350	2,750
5'5"	Small	122 (118–127)	1,600	1,850	2,050	2,450
	Medium	131 (124–139)	1,700	1,950	2,250	2,600
	Large	141 (133–150)	1,850	2,100	2,400	2,800
5'6"	Small	126 (122–131)	1,650	1,900	2,150	2,500
	Medium	135 (128–143)	1,750	2,050	2,300	2,700
	Large	145 (137–154)	1,900	2,200	2,450	2,900
5'7"	Small	130 (126–135)	1,700	1,950	2,200	2,600
	Medium	139 (132–147)	1,800	2,100	2,350	2,800
	Large	149 (141–158)	1,950	2,250	2,550	3,000
5'8"	Small	135 (130–140)	1,750	2,050	2,300	2,700
	Medium	143 (136–151)	1,850	2,150	2,450	2,850
	Large	154 (145–163)	2,000	2,300	2,600	3,100
5'9"	Small	139 (134–144)	1,800	2,100	2,350	2,800
	Medium	147 (140–155)	1,900	2,200	2,500	2,950
	Large	158 (149–168)	2,050	2,350	2,700	3,150
5'10"	Small	143 (138–148)	1,850	2,150	2,450	2,850
	Medium	151 (144–159)	1,950	2,250	2,550	3,000
	Large	163 (153–173)	2,100	2,450	2,750	3,250

*Table adjusted for measurement of height without shoes.
**From 1959 Metropolitan Life Insurance Company, New York City. These tables are based on 1959 rather than 1983 Metropolitan Life Insurance Company height-weight tables because the earlier tables specify lower weights, more appropriate to health-related concerns.

calorie levels in these tables are estimates. Each person is different, and this individual variation may mean that you actually need a higher or lower calorie level than shown in the table. Add calories, for example, if you wish to gain weight or during pregnancy or lactation. The calorie levels in this table are based on your ideal body weight. If you are overweight, the calorie levels in the tables are probably lower than what you typically are consuming each day. By using the lower calorie level, you will probably be able to lose weight. Overestimating your physical activity can cause the calorie level given in the table to be too high. For example, if you consider yourself moderately active, but you actually do mostly light physical activity, the calorie level indicated in the table will be too high for you. Very few people do heavy physical activity on a regular basis.

Combining a decrease in calories with an increase in physical activity makes the goal of lasting weight loss more attainable. Of course, losing excess weight is only the first battle of the war. It usually takes regular physical activity in addition to a controlled calorie intake to keep weight off after it initially has been lost.

METHODS FOR DEVELOPING EATING PLANS

The two methods for monitoring your cholesterol-lowering eating plan take different approaches. The Servings of Food Method is an excellent method for individuals who need to control their calorie intake. In addition, it helps control the level of fat and saturated fat from foods being eaten. The Grams of Fat Method allows you to be more precise in monitoring your intake of fat and saturated fat. With this method, you simply keep track of the grams of fat (and saturated fat) in foods eaten each day. Keeping the total grams of fat and saturated fat under the "goal" level keeps the level of fat at no more than 30% of calories and the saturated fat at less than 10% of calories.

SERVINGS OF FOOD METHOD

The Servings of Food Method for planning a cholesterol-lowering diet is especially useful for those people who want to eat about the same number of calories each day. It is based on average amounts of fat, saturated fat, cholesterol, and calories for each of eight food groups.

Use the preceding section to determine about how many calories you need. Then, compare your calorie needs to the eating patterns shown in the "Servings of Food Method—Sample Eating Patterns" table below. Choose the level nearest to your estimated calorie needs. Of course, the calorie levels in the tables are only approximate, since there is some variation in the calories provided by one serving of the different foods grouped together in a food group. The table lists the suggested number of servings from each of the eight food groups at each calorie level. Each of the food groups is described briefly. The amount considered to be a serving of each type of food in the "Servings of Food Method—Sample Eating Patterns" table is specified as part of the description of each food.

SERVINGS OF FOOD METHOD—SAMPLE EATING PATTERNS

	Number of Servings per Day*						
Food Groups	1,200 Cal.	1,400 Cal.	1,600 Cal.	1,800 Cal.	2,000 Cal.	2,200 Cal.	2,500 Cal.
Meat, Poultry, Fish	6 oz	6 oz	6 oz	6 oz	6 oz	6 oz	6 oz
Egg Yolk**	3/wk	3/wk	3/wk	3/wk	3/wk	3/wk	3/wk
Dairy Products	2	2	3	3	3	4	4
Fats and Oils	3	3	4	5	6	7	8
Bread, Cereal, Pasta, and Starchy Vegetables	3	4	4	6	7	7	10
Vegetables	4	4	4	4	4	4	4
Fruits	3	3	3	3	3	5	5
Optional Foods	0	1	2	2	2	2	2

*Each sample eating pattern has no more than 30% of calories from fat, less than 10% of calories from saturated fat, and averages less than 300 milligrams of cholesterol per day.
**The number of egg yolks per week is specified; everything else is specified as number of servings per day.

FOOD GROUPS AND SERVING SIZES

★ *Meat, Poultry, and Fish*
Meat, poultry, and fish provide large amounts of fat, saturated fat, and cholesterol in the diets of adults and children. However, these foods also supply high-quality protein and important vitamins and minerals (phosphorus and vitamins B_6 and B_{12}). All meat should be very lean, with any visible fat trimmed off before cooking. Choose cuts of red meat that have the least fat marbled throughout the muscle. The skin should be removed before poultry is cooked. Avoid self-basting poultry, since extra fat has been injected into these birds. Meat, poultry, and fish should be cooked with little or no added fat. It is recommended that your intake of lean meat, poultry without skin, and fish not exceed 6 ounces cooked per day. Three ounces is about the size of a deck of playing cards.

One ounce of cooked meat, fish, and poultry averages about:

> 60 calories
> 3 grams of fat
> 1 gram of saturated fat
> 27 milligrams of cholesterol

Food Sections in *The Living Heart Brand Name Shopper's Guide* where foods from this group are found include:

> Meat, Poultry, and Fish (page 273)
> Single-Serving Entrées and Dinners (page 323)

★ Eggs

Egg yolk is one of our most concentrated sources of dietary cholesterol. An average egg yolk provides 213 milligrams of cholesterol. Three egg yolks per week can be included in a cholesterol-lowering eating plan averaging less than 300 milligrams of cholesterol per day. It is important to account for all the eggs you eat. This includes not only eggs eaten alone but also whole eggs or yolks used in cooking. Egg whites have no cholesterol and can be used freely. Remember, meat, poultry, fish, and dairy products also provide cholesterol. (Notice that the egg group is the only one using a "weekly" instead of a "daily" amount.)

An average egg provides:

> 80 calories
> 6 grams of fat
> 2 grams of saturated fat
> 213 milligrams of cholesterol

The Living Heart Brand Name Shopper's Guide does not have a section on eggs.

> Egg Substitutes (page 209)

★ Dairy Products

Dairy products provide large amounts of saturated fat in the diets of children and adults. However, these foods not only provide high-quality protein and are the major source of calcium in the diet but also contribute vitamin A, riboflavin, and vitamins B_6 and B_{12}. Dairy products that are low in fat or nonfat contain the same nutrients as whole milk. Skim milk, ½%, and 1% low-fat milk actually have as much (or more) calcium and protein as whole milk.

One serving of dairy products provides about:

90 calories
3 grams of fat
2 grams of saturated fat
10 milligrams of cholesterol

Values listed in the Food Sections of *The Living Heart Brand Name Shopper's Guide* are for the manufacturer's serving size. You may need to adjust the amount you eat of these brand-name foods to provide about 90 calories. One serving of dairy products is:

Cheese—1 to 2 ounces of cheese with no more than 3 grams of fat per ounce. Be sure to check the label, since the lower the fat content of the cheese, the more it takes to equal about 90 calories.
Cottage cheese—½ cup low-fat or nonfat
Frozen dairy dessert—⅓ to ½ cup low-fat or nonfat. Be sure to check the label, since low-fat frozen dairy desserts vary in the amount that provides about 90 calories.
Milk—1 cup of skim, ½%, or 1% low-fat milk
Yogurt, plain—1 cup of nonfat (skim or fat-free), ½%, or 1% low-fat yogurt

Food Sections in *The Living Heart Brand Name Shopper's Guide* where foods from this group can be found include:

Dairy Products and Dairy Substitutes (page 167)
Frozen Desserts (page 217). Only those prepared with milk count as a serving of dairy products. Frozen desserts that are primarily fruit, juice, and water (i.e., sorbet) do not provide calcium and are part of the Optional group (on page 51).

★ *Fats and Oils*
Fats and oils provide much of the visible fat (the fats we can easily see) in our diets. Since any type of fat contributes over twice the calories (9 calories per gram) of carbohydrate (sugar and starch at 4 calories per gram) and protein (4 calories per gram), consuming a large amount of fat—even the ones recommended for a cholesterol-lowering diet—results in an eating pattern too high in calories and fat. All fats used in a cholesterol-lowering eating pattern should be low in saturated fat.
One serving of fats and oils provides about:

45 calories
5 grams of fat
1 gram of saturated fatty acids
Little or no cholesterol

The average size of one serving is:

Avocado—⅛ of an average avocado

Margarine—1 to 2 teaspoons. Check the label since the lower the fat, the more margarine it takes to equal about 45 calories. For example, 1 teaspoon regular margarine provides about 35 calories, and 1 teaspoon diet or light margarine provides about 17 calories (therefore, 2 teaspoons = 1 serving of fat).

Nuts—1 tablespoon chopped

Oil—1 teaspoon

Olives—10 small or 5 large

Peanut butter—2 teaspoons

Salad dressing—1 tablespoon of regular dressing or 2 teaspoons mayonnaise. The calorie level of salad dressings varies; check the label for the amount equal to about 45 calories. Those with less than 10 calories per tablespoon can be used as "free" foods.

Seeds—1 tablespoon

Food Sections in *The Living Heart Brand Name Shopper's Guide* where foods from this group can be found are:

Fats and Oils (page 210)
Salad Dressings and Sandwich Spreads (page 308)

★ *Bread, Cereal, Pasta, and Starchy Vegetables*

Many breads, cereals, pasta, and starchy vegetables are naturally low in fat. They are the primary sources of complex carbohydrates; the whole-grain or enriched products provide B vitamins and iron.

One serving from this group provides about:

80 calories
1 gram of fat
Negligible saturated fat
Negligible cholesterol

It is recommended that quick breads, such as biscuits, pancakes, and waffles, be made with margarine or oil and with skim, ½%, or 1% low-fat milk. Since there is a great deal of variation in the average serving sizes of these foods, it is especially important to check the calories in *The Living Heart Brand Name Shopper's Guide* or the nutrition information on the food label. Remember, calories listed in the Food Sections of this Guide are for the manufacturer's serving size. You may need to adjust the serving size to obtain a serving providing about 80 calories. One serving of bread, cereal, pasta, and starchy vegetables is:

Breads—1 average slice of bread; 2 slices diet or light bread (35 to 40 calories per slice); or ½ bagel, English muffin, or hamburger bun

Cereal—½ cup of cooked cereal (after cooking) and 1 ounce of ready-to-eat cereal (check individual labels; the volume equal to an ounce can vary from about ¼ to 1 cup)

Corn—½ cup

Crackers and pretzels—the amount equal to about 80 calories

Graham crackers—3 squares (each 2½")

Pasta—½ cup (after cooking)

Peas, green—½ cup

Popcorn—3 cups popped without fat

Potatoes—1 medium (3-ounce) baked potato; ½ cup mashed potato or ⅓ cup sweet potato or yam (no sugar added)

Rice—⅓ cup (after cooking)

Soup—¾ to 1 cup

Food Sections in *The Living Heart Brand Name Shopper's Guide* where foods from this group can be found include:

Breads and Bread Products (page 99)
Cereals (page 120)
Crackers (page 148)
Pasta, Rice, and Other Grain Products (page 299)
Snack Foods (page 340)
Soups (page 349)
Vegetables (page 377)—Vegetables that fit in the starchy vegetables category are dried beans and peas, potatoes, corn, hominy, and English peas.

★ *Vegetables*

Most vegetables are low in calories; all vegetables are naturally very low in fat and saturated fat and contain no cholesterol. They are also an excellent source of fiber. Eating a wide variety of vegetables helps insure an adequate intake of several vitamins and minerals, including fat-soluble vitamins A, E, and K; water-soluble vitamins, such as vitamin C, riboflavin, folacin, and biotin; and minerals, such as calcium, magnesium, potassium, iron, and various trace minerals.

One serving of vegetables provides about:

> 25 calories
> Negligible fat
> Negligible saturated fat
> No cholesterol

The average serving size for vegetables is about 1 cup raw or ½ cup cooked or ½ cup vegetable juice. A vegetable product that includes a sauce is usually higher in fat. Count part of a serving of fat for vegetables with fat or sauce. A good rule of thumb is to allow ½ teaspoon fat per ½ cup of vegetables. Check the calories in *The Living Heart Brand Name Shopper's Guide* or the nutrition information on the food label to estimate the amount of a vegetable that provides about 25 calories. Vegetables with less than 20 calories per cup can be eaten as desired (any number of servings per day).

Food Sections in *The Living Heart Brand Name Shopper's Guide* where foods from this group can be found include:

> Vegetables (page 377)
> Juices (page 266)

★ *Fruits*

Fruits are a good source of fiber and provide vitamins A and C, biotin, and potassium. Fruit products do not usually contain fat. However, the fat content of a fruit dessert increases if you add whipped topping, sour cream, or nuts. Avocados and olives, which are high in fat but relatively low in saturated fat, are in the fats and oils food group.

One serving of fruits provides about:

> 60 calories
> Negligible fat
> Negligible saturated fat
> No cholesterol

Check the values in *The Living Heart Brand Name Shopper's Guide* for the calories in fruit. One serving of fruit is:

Fresh apple, peach, pear, orange, kiwi—1 average piece
Banana, grapefruit, mango—½ piece
Strawberries (whole), watermelon—1¼ cups
Canned, unsweetened fruit—½ cups
Dried fruit—2 tablespoons to ¼ cup
Fruit juice, unsweetened—⅓ to ½ cup

Food Sections in *The Living Heart Brand Name Shopper's Guide* where foods from this group can be found include:

> Fruits, except avocado (page 239)
> Juices (page 266)

★ *Optional Foods*
This food group includes those "extras" that are not really necessary in the diet but add variety and increase enjoyment. Many of them are higher in calories than foods from the other food groups because they are prepared with fat and sugar (examples include cake, pie, and cookies). Since these foods supply calories without being important sources of needed nutrients, they are limited in a lower-calorie eating pattern.

One serving of sweets and modified-fat desserts provides about:

> 120 calories
> 0 to 3 grams of fat
> 0 to 1 gram of saturated fat
> 0 to 10 milligrams of cholesterol

This food group contains two different types of food—sweets and modified-fat desserts. "Sweets" refers to those foods that contain mostly sugar and little or no fat. Examples include regular soft drinks; angel food cake; "fat-free" cakes, cookies, and other baked goods; pudding made with skim milk; flavored gelatin; fruit ices; jelly; and hard candy. Chocolate and other candies high in fat and saturated fat are not included in this food group.

"Modified-fat desserts" refers to pastries and baked desserts that contain limited amounts of fat, saturated fat, and/or cholesterol. Both commercial products that contain little or no fat (see page 186) and modified-fat desserts made at home with appropriate ingredients (see page 401) are included in the optional foods group.

Use the information in *The Living Heart Brand Name Shopper's Guide* or nutrition information on the food label to estimate the amount of a "sweet" or "modified-fat dessert" that provides about 120 calories. Of course, the selection of a "sweet" will result in a lower fat intake than the selection of a modified-fat dessert.

Food Sections in *The Living Heart Brand Name Shopper's Guide* where foods from this group can be found include:

> Beverages and Beverage Flavorings (page 79)
> Desserts (page 186)
> Frozen Desserts (page 217)
> Sweets (page 367)

★ *Free Foods*

Foods that contain very little or no fat, saturated fat, or cholesterol and are very low in calories are called "free" foods. Most of these foods provide less than 20 calories per average serving and don't have to be limited. A few of the following foods list a serving size. If you use more than the serving size listed for these foods, you can calculate the calories consumed from label information or from values found in the Food Sections in this Guide.

- *Beverages and Beverage Flavorings*
  Bitters
  Carbonated drinks, sugar-free
  Carbonated water
  Club soda
  Coffee or tea (no sugar or creamer)
  Drink mixes, sugar-free
  Tonic water, sugar-free
- *Condiments*
  Catsup (1 tablespoon)
  Horseradish
  Hot sauce
  Mustard
  Picante sauce
  Pickles, dill, unsweetened
  Soy sauce
  Taco sauce
  Vinegar
  Worcestershire sauce

- *Fruits*
  Cranberries, unsweetened (½ cup)
  Lemon
  Lime
  Rhubarb, unsweetened (½ cup)
- *Ingredients*
  Cocoa powder, unsweetened (1 tablespoon)
  Flavoring essence (maple, vanilla, butter-flavored, etc.)
  Liquid smoke
  Rennet tablets
  Spices and herbs
  Sugar substitutes*
  Vinegar
- *Salad Dressings*
  Salad dressing, oil-free
  Salad dressing, low-calorie
- *Sweets*
  Candy, hard, sugar-free
  Gelatin, sugar-free
  Gum, sugar-free
  Jam or jelly, sugar-free (2 teaspoons)
  Pancake syrup, sugar-free
- *Soups*
  Bouillon, fat-free
  Broth, fat-free
  Consommé, fat-free
- *Vegetables*
  Chicory
  Chinese cabbage
  Endive
  Escarole
  Lettuce
  Parsley
  Radishes
  Watercress

*Subject to current warnings about sugar substitutes.

GRAMS OF FAT METHOD

The Grams of Fat Method provides precision in monitoring the grams of fat and saturated fat in the food you eat. It simply involves adding up the grams of fat and saturated fat in the foods eaten each day to be sure that the total of each is under the goal set for it. To determine your goal, the first step is to determine how many calories you need each day (see "Determining Your Calorie Level" on page 40). Once you know your approximate calorie needs, find the closest calorie level in the following table. From that you can determine your goal for grams of fat (equal to 30% of calories) and grams of saturated fat (equal to 10% of calories) in your food each day. Select your foods so that the levels of fat and saturated fat in your diet each day are under your goal.

CALORIE LEVELS: GRAMS OF FAT AND SATURATED FAT

Calorie Levels	Fat* g	Saturated Fat* g
1,200	40	13
1,300	43	14
1,400	47	16
1,500	50	17
1,600	53	18
1,700	57	19
1,800	60	20
1,900	63	21
2,000	67	22
2,100	70	23
2,200	73	24
2,300	77	26
2,400	80	27
2,500	83	28
2,600	87	29
2,700	90	30
2,800	93	31
2,900	97	32
3,000	100	33

*Grams of fat equal to 30% of calories and grams of saturated fat equal to 10% of calories.

The Living Heart Brand Name Shopper's Guide can be used to determine the number of grams of fat and saturated fat in many of the foods you eat. However, since most brand name foods listed in the Guide are low in fat and saturated fat, you will need to use food labels or find another reference to obtain values for foods that are high in fat. An excellent reference is Table 2, page 338, in the back of our book The Living Heart Diet (New York: Simon & Schuster, 1984). For this method to work effectively, it is important that you determine the grams of fat and satu-rated fat in each food you eat. Of course, some foods such as plain fruits and vegetables do not contain fat.

If you do not find your calorie level in the table, use the following formula to estimate the grams of fat and grams of saturated fat for your calorie level:

To determine grams of fat (30% of calories) and saturated fat (10% of calories) at the 1,650-calorie level:

1. Multiply calorie level (1,650) × .30 (30%) = 495 calories from fat.
2. Divide calories from fat (495) by 9 (calories in 1 gram of fat) = 55 grams of fat (equal to 30% of 1,650 calories from fat).
3. Divide the grams of fat representing 30% of 1,650 calories (55) by 3 = 18 grams of saturated fat (grams of saturated fatty acids equal to 10%, or ⅓ of 30%, of 1,650 calories).

On a 1,650-calorie plan, a *maximum* of 55 grams of fat and 18 grams of saturated fat is allowed each day. If you eat a food high in fat, you will need to select lower-fat foods during the remainder of the day to compen-sate for it. Remember, the total should not go over 55 grams of fat per day at the 1,650-calorie level. This method can help insure that your intake of fat will be no more than 30% of calories and your saturated fat will provide less than 10% of calories per day. A sample food record for someone requiring about 1,600 calories shows how this method works (shown below). A blank food record, which you can copy and use, is on the following page.

FOOD RECORD

Name _Joe Doe_ GOALS: __53__ grams Fat
Day _Mon._ Date _9/24_ __18__ grams Sat. Fat

Write ONE food on each line.

Time & Place	Amount	Food—How Prepared	Fat g	Sat. Fat g
7 A.M.	½ cup	Orange juice	0	0
Home	1 cup	Corn flakes	0	0
	1 cup	1% low-fat milk	2.6	1.6
	2 sl.	Toast	1.8	.4
	2 tsp.	Margarine, stick	7.3	1.3
12 noon		Sandwich:		
Cafe	2 sl.	Rye bread	.6	.2
	2 oz.	Lean roast beef	4.0	1.6
	1 tbsp.	Mayonnaise, low-calorie	5.0	1.0
	1 sl.	American cheese	4.0	2.0
	2 cups	Tossed salad	0	0
	2 tbsp.	French dressing, low-calorie	2.0	0
	1 cup	Frozen yogurt, low-fat	4.0	2.0
7 P.M.	4 oz.	Steak—fat trimmed off	6.4	2.5
Home	1	Baked potato	0	0
	2 tbsp.	Sour cream, light	2.0	1.0
	2 tsp.	Margarine, stick	7.3	1.3
	1 cup	Chopped fresh fruit	0	0
		Totals for day	47.0	14.9

FOOD RECORD

Name_____ GOALS: _____ grams Fat
Day_____ Date_____   _____ grams Sat. Fat

Write ONE food on each line.

Time & Place	Amount	Food—How Prepared	Fat g	Sat. Fat g
		Totals for day		

Chapter 5

Understanding Food Labels

Reading food labels is often very confusing. The confusion is primarily in the areas of: (1) the exact meanings of descriptive terms used on labels, (2) differences in serving sizes, and (3) health claims being made for some types of foods.

Have you ever picked up a product in the supermarket and wondered what "light" (or "lite") on the label really means? At the present time, this term has no legal meaning. Depending on the particular product, "light" can mean lower in calories, fat, or salt; lighter in color or texture; milder in flavor—or any combination of the above. The term "cholesterol free" has long been a source of confusion for consumers. It suggests that products with "cholesterol free" on their label once contained cholesterol that has been removed. Although cholesterol is present only in animal foods, "cholesterol free" has been used on all-vegetable products, such as salad oil, that would not be expected to contain cholesterol.

The current lack of standard serving sizes on food labels makes it difficult for consumers to compare calories and fat in different brands of similar products. It is not easy to compare nutrition information on different brands of cookies, for example, when serving sizes may be given as ½ ounce, 1 ounce, 1 cookie, or 6 cookies. Consumers also find it confusing when the serving size used by the manufacturer for nutrition information differs from the serving size they consider logical. Sliced cheese, for example, commonly comes in ¾-ounce slices, and yet the nutrition information given on the label is for 1 ounce.

THE NUTRITION LABELING AND EDUCATION ACT

In the fall of 1990, President Bush signed the Nutrition Labeling and Education Act (NLEA) to overhaul nutrition labeling of food. The NLEA represents a major effort by the government to improve the format and content of food labels. The Food and Drug Administration (FDA) published several proposals for the new regulations in July 1990. The revised proposals, which were released in November 1991, were accompanied by similar proposals from the Food Safety and Inspection Service (FSIS) of the United States Department of Agriculture (USDA). The last set of proposals will be released by November 1992 and will become effective in May 1993.

The FSIS approves labels for meat, poultry, and food products containing at least 2% poultry or 3% meat. The FDA is responsible for the labeling of non-meat products and foods containing less than 2% poultry or 3% meat. Both government agencies require specific information on the labels of foods under their jurisdiction. FDA and FSIS worked together to make their 1991 proposals similar so that consumers will find it easier to read all food labels. With the new proposals, FDA and FSIS will continue to require the following on the labels of foods under their jurisdiction.

FSIS REQUIREMENTS ON FOOD LABELS FOR MEAT AND POULTRY

Product name
List of ingredients
Weight of product
Official USDA inspection stamp
Producer's or distributor's name and address
Instructions for handling perishable food products

FDA REQUIREMENTS ON FOOD LABELS

Product name
Amount of food in the container, either as net volume (usually fluid ounces) or net weight (in ounces and often also in grams), including the weight of any liquid in canned food
Name and location of food manufacturer, packer, or distributor

Most food labels must also include a complete list of ingredients, identified by their usual names. Information about labeling of ingredients begins on page 64 of this chapter.

The 1991 proposals require nutrition labeling for processed food (FDA) and for pre-cooked and processed meat and poultry products (FSIS). Labeling of fresh produce, seafood, and single-ingredient raw meat and poultry is voluntary. For both FDA and FSIS, nutrition labels will state the serving size and the number of servings in each container. In addition, the new label will list the amount of the following present in one serving:

- Calories
- Calories from fat

- Total fat
- Saturated fat
- Cholesterol
- Total carbohydrate (not including dietary fiber)
- Complex carbohydrate
- Sugars
- Dietary fiber
- Protein
- Sodium
- Percent of Daily Value of vitamin A, vitamin C, calcium, iron, and any other vitamin or mineral added to a food as a nutrient supplement or when a claim is made about it

Under the proposed changes, some information on nutrition labels will continue to be voluntary. Food manufacturers will be allowed to include or not include in their nutrition labeling the amount in one serving of the following:

- Calories from saturated and unsaturated fat, total carbohydrate, and protein
- Unsaturated fat or polyunsaturated and monounsaturated fats (unless a claim is made about fatty acid or cholesterol content)
- Insoluble and soluble fiber (unless a claim is made)
- Protein as a percent of RDI (Reference Daily Intake—a proposed revision of the U.S. Recommended Dietary Allowances) for foods, except infant foods (unless a claim is made)
- Potassium, thiamin, riboflavin, niacin, and other vitamins and minerals

DESCRIPTIVE TERMS ON FOOD LABELS

Descriptors are terms commonly found on food labels that describe something special about a product. For example, "low fat," "low sodium," or "low cholesterol" on a label suggests that the product differs from similar products by containing less fat, less sodium, or less cholesterol. Partly because of the confusion caused by use of these descriptors in the past, the FDA and FSIS have proposed significant changes in the regulations for using descriptors on food labels. The following table contains simplified definitions of descriptive terms as proposed in 1991.

DESCRIPTIVE TERMS ON LABELS

TERMS REFERRING TO CALORIES:

Calorie Free: The food contains less than 5 calories per serving.

Low Calorie: The food contains a maximum of 40 calories per serving and per 100 grams. Meal-type products contain 105 calories per 100 grams of the product.

Sugar Free: The food contains less than 0.5 gram of all sugar sources combined per serving and no sugar has been deliberately added. Other label terms meaning the same as "sugar free" and having the same definition include "sugarless" and "no sugar."

No Added Sugar: No type of sugar was added to the food during processing and packaging.

Reduced Calorie: The calories in the reference food are reduced by one-third.

TERMS REFERRING TO CHOLESTEROL:

Cholesterol Free: The food contains less than 2 milligrams of cholesterol and 2 grams or less of saturated fat per serving. Terms meaning the same as "cholesterol free" include "zero cholesterol," "free of cholesterol," "no cholesterol," "trivial source of cholesterol," "negligible source of cholesterol," and "dietarily insignificant source of cholesterol."

Low Cholesterol: The food contains 20 milligrams or less of cholesterol per serving and per 100 grams of food and 2 grams or less of saturated fat per serving. A low-cholesterol meal-type product must contain 20 milligrams or less of cholesterol per 100 grams of the product. Terms meaning the same as "low cholesterol" include "contains a small amount of cholesterol" and "low in cholesterol."

Reduced Cholesterol: Cholesterol has been reduced by 50% or more when compared to the cholesterol in the comparison food, with a minimum reduction of more than 20 milligrams of cholesterol per serving of the comparison food.

Less Cholesterol: Cholesterol has been reduced by 25% or more, with a minimum reduction of 20 milligrams per serving of a comparison food.

TERMS REFERRING TO FAT AND SATURATED FAT:

Fat Free: The food contains less than 0.5 gram of fat per serving, and no fat or oil has been added as an ingredient. The "fat free" claim cannot be made on labels of foods normally free of fat unless the label clearly states this information. Other label terms meaning the same as "fat free" include "free of fat," "no fat," "nonfat," "zero fat," "trivial source of fat," "negligible source of fat," and "dietarily insignificant source of fat."

Low Fat: The food contains 3 grams or less of fat per serving and per 100 grams of food. Meal-type products must contain 3 grams or less of fat per

100 grams. Other label terms meaning the same as "low fat" include "low in fat," "contains a small amount of fat," "low source of fat," and "little fat."

Reduced Fat: The fat content of the food is no more than half the amount in a comparison food, with a minimum reduction of 3 grams of fat per serving. Other terms meaning the same as "reduced fat" include "reduced in fat" and "fat reduced."

Percent Fat Free: This term may be used only to describe products meeting the definition of "low fat."

Less Fat: The food contains at least 25% less fat than the food with which it is compared, with a minimum reduction of more than 3 grams of fat per serving.

Low in Saturated Fat: The food contains 1 gram or less of saturated fat per serving and not more than 15% of calories from saturated fat. Meal-type products contain 1 gram or less of saturated fat per 100 grams of the product.

Reduced Saturated Fat: The term describes a food containing no more than 50% of the saturated fat in the food with which it is compared, with a minimum reduction of more than 1 gram of saturated fat per serving.

Less Saturated Fat: The saturated fat has been reduced by 25% or more when compared to the comparison food; there is a minimum reduction of 1 gram of saturated fat per serving.

TERMS REFERRING TO MEAT AND POULTRY:

Lean: This term can be used to label meat and poultry containing less than 10.5 grams of fat, less than 3.5 grams of saturated fat, and less than 94.5 milligrams of cholesterol per 100 grams cooked (about 3½ ounces).

Extra Lean: This term can be used to label meat and poultry containing less than 4.9 grams of fat, less than 1.8 grams of saturated fat, and less than 94.5 milligrams of cholesterol per 100 grams cooked.

TERMS REFERRING TO SODIUM: (Consumers often use the terms "sodium" and "salt" interchangeably; salt is made up of 40% sodium and 60% chloride.)

Sodium Free and Salt Free: The food contains less than 5 milligrams of sodium per serving.

Very Low Sodium: The food contains less than 35 milligrams of sodium per serving and per 100 grams of food.

Low Sodium: The food contains less than 140 milligrams of sodium per serving and per 100 grams of food.

Reduced Sodium: The food contains no more than 50% of the sodium present in the comparison food.

OTHER TERMS:

Light or Lite: Food contains at least one-third less calories than a comparable product. When "light" is used in any other way, this must be clearly stated. For example, a label might read "light in color" or "light in texture."

More: Used to show that a food contains more of a desirable nutrient, such as fiber or potassium, than does a comparable food. A food must contain at least 10% more of the desired nutrient than the comparable food.

FAT FACTS—CALORIES FROM FAT, PERCENT OF CALORIES FROM FAT, AND PERCENT FAT

Does "calories from fat," "percent of calories from fat," or "percent fat" tell you what you want to know about a food? Each of these numbers tells you something a little different about the amount of fat in a particular food, and this information can be useful in different ways.

★ Calories from Fat

"Calories from fat" refers to the actual number of calories provided by fat in one serving of a food. The "calories from fat" value is calculated by multiplying the number of grams of fat in one serving by 9, since each gram of fat provides 9 calories. For example, a 570-calorie slice of cheesecake that contains 40 grams of fat provides 360 calories from fat ($40 \times 9 = 360$). The FDA has proposed that manufacturers print the calories from fat on food labels; currently, this is not required.

★ Percent of Calories from Fat

"Percent of calories from fat" is a way of showing what percent of the total calories come from fat. This value is calculated by dividing the calories from fat by the total calories in the food. Using the same example presented above, the slice of cheesecake provides 360 calories from fat and 570 total calories. When you divide 360 by 570 (and multiply by 100 to get percent), the percent of calories from fat in the cheesecake is 63%.

It is important to note that "percent of calories from fat" should not be used to evaluate whether individual foods are appropriate in a cholesterol-lowering eating plan. You may have heard people say that you should eat only foods with less than 30% of calories from fat. The dietary guideline of consuming no more than 30% of calories from fat is often misused. (Other guidelines include eating a diet with 15% to 20% of calories from protein and 50% to 55% of calories from carbohydrate.) The guideline of

30% of calories from fat refers to the total food eaten in a day and not to individual foods or meals. If "30% of calories from fat" is applied to single foods in an attempt to evaluate them, it will cause many foods that are often included in a well-balanced cholesterol-lowering eating plan to be excluded. Examples of these foods include oil and margarine (100% of calories from fat), eggs (64% of calories from fat), regular salad dressing (85% to 100% of calories from fat), dark chicken meat without the skin (43% of calories from fat), and salmon (36% of calories from fat). Even turkey ham, which is considered a lower-fat meat, seems artificially high, with its 34% of calories from fat.

★ *Percent Fat*

"Percent fat" is often confused with "percent of calories from fat." Percent fat simply means the amount of fat by weight (in grams) in a specified amount (100 grams) of a food. "Percent fat" is used only to describe the amount of fat in a single food. For example, "2% fat milk" means that 2% of the weight of milk is fat. In other words, each 100 grams of milk (a little less than ½ cup) contains 2 grams of fat. Other common examples of foods for which "percent fat" is often given are 10% fat meat and 4% fat cottage cheese. Another way to state the fat content by weight is by listing "percent fat free." When a label states that a product is 90% fat-free, this is the same as saying that it is 10% fat by weight. Both ways of stating percent fat are accurate.

INGREDIENTS LISTED ON FOOD LABELS

The first ingredient shown in the ingredient list on a food label is the one present in the largest amount by weight, the second ingredient is the next largest, and so on. Labels must list ingredients by their common or usual names. Some of the ingredients listed on food labels are actually additives, such as preservatives and stabilizers that help foods stay fresh and retain their flavor.

Previously, certain foods were considered standardized, ones for which the FDA had adopted "standards of identity," and didn't have to list all of the ingredients on the label. The standard of identity was a list of ingredients that must be present in any food being called "jelly" or "mayonnaise," for example; it also spelled out what other ingredients might be added. In June 1991 the FDA proposed requiring the listing of all ingredients in standardized foods.

The following table identifies some of the ingredients most commonly found listed on food labels.

INGREDIENTS COMMONLY APPEARING ON FOOD LABELS

BHA and BHT are common antioxidants that help keep fats and oils from becoming rancid and delay or prevent the discoloration of such foods as peeled potatoes and apples.

Diglycerides are commonly used as emulsifiers, substances that help oil and water to mix. They are mainly added to foods such as bread, margarine, chocolate, peanut butter, and cake.

Fructose is a type of simple sugar found in fruit. Although it provides the same number of calories per gram as regular white or brown sugar, it tastes sweeter. Therefore, a smaller amount of fructose is needed to produce the same amount of sweetening power as sugar.

Hydrogenated and Partially Hydrogenated refer to the process of changing a liquid oil to a more solid form that is usually higher in saturated and monounsaturated fatty acids. This process changes the physical properties of a fat so that it is less likely to spoil. Shortening and margarine are two common foods resulting from the hydrogenation of liquid oil.

Hydrolyzed refers to splitting a compound into simpler substances by adding the elements of water (hydrogen and oxygen) to it.

Monoglycerides are emulsifiers that are similar to diglycerides.

Monosodium Glutamate is a sodium compound used in many foods as a flavor enhancer.

Sodium Nitrite and Nitrate are sodium compounds that are commonly used as preservatives in cured meats.

Sucrose is the chemical name for "table" sugar.

Vegetable Shortening is a solid fat made by hydrogenating unsaturated vegetable oils.

OTHER INFORMATION ON FOOD LABELS

The Nutrition Labeling and Education Act of 1990 allows food labels to carry claims about the relationship between the food and specific health conditions or diseases. This was not allowed previously. Four relationships between nutrients and the risk of disease are being proposed initially: calcium and osteoporosis, sodium and hypertension, fat and cardiovascular disease, and fat and cancer.

Reading (and understanding) nutrition labels can be more complicated when you are shopping for a mix or "helper-type" product that requires added ingredients in its preparation. Although many food labels clearly list the calories and other nutrients in one serving "as prepared" or for a serving of the product both "as packaged" and "as prepared," some do not. For example, if you are checking the calories and amount of fat in one serving of a dry rice mix, be aware that values (calories, fat, etc.) given on the nutrition label may or may not include the margarine you are instructed to add in the package directions.

"Helper-type" products that require the addition of one or more ingredients in preparation must clearly state on the package what other ingredients are added to prepare the dish. For example, the label on a package of a "helper-type" mix must state "you must add ground beef to complete the recipe."

Other information that *may* appear on a food label includes:

- *Grade.* The USDA grades meat and poultry and the National Marine Fisheries Service grades fish products based on the quality of their taste, texture, and appearance. Beef, for example, is graded based on its fat content. Individual states grade milk, based on sanitary standards for producing and processing milk products; the standards have been recommended by the FDA. Grades for meat, poultry, fish, and milk are not based on the nutritional content of the food product.
- *Product date.* Consumers may use the "sell date" or "use-by date" listed on food products to judge freshness. Some stores use a "pull date" to tell them when to remove a food from the shelf. The "pack date" tells you when the food was packed.
- *Code date.* Federal law requires a code date on most canned foods. Code dating is commonly used on foods with a long shelf life and is not usually used by the consumer. It provides information about where and when the food was packaged and is primarily used to identify a particular lot of food in case it needs to be recalled.
- *Universal product code (UPC).* Most products now carry universal product codes that are used with computerized check-out equipment to provide an automatic inventory system.
- *Letter symbols.* "R" on a food label indicates that the trademark on the label is registered with the U.S. Patent Office, and "C" means that any written or artistic content of the label is covered by U.S. copyright laws. "U" inside the letter "O" indicates that the food complies with Jewish dietary laws; "K" inside the letter "O" means that the food is kosher.

Chapter 6

How to Use
The Living Heart
Brand Name Shopper's Guide

The purpose of *The Living Heart Brand Name Shopper's Guide* is to identify supermarket products low in saturated fat that can be used to help meet the dietary recommendations for a cholesterol-lowering diet, such as *The Living Heart Diet*. The recommendation to limit the amount of total fat eaten helps people who are following a cholesterol-lowering eating pattern restrict their intake of saturated fat. Decreasing saturated fat intake is the most important factor in a diet designed to lower blood cholesterol; it is followed in importance by decreasing dietary cholesterol. Since at the present time most manufacturers do not list saturated fat content on food labels, the authors primarily used the amount of total fat in a food to identify products that qualify for the Guide. However, cutoff points for three values—fat, saturated fat, and cholesterol—were used to evaluate foods for the Guide. The Guide lists the amount of these nutrients, plus values for calories and sodium, for each food. It includes information on:

- Numerous commercial brand name products that are low in fat, saturated fat, and cholesterol
- Products where "most brands" are low in fat, saturated fat, and cholesterol (such as skim milk, coffee, and fruit juice)
- Generic products that do not have brand names—fresh fruit, vegetables, meat, poultry, and fish—that are low in fat, saturated fat, and cholesterol
- Fats (oil, margarine, salad dressing, nuts, and seeds) that are low in saturated fat

Use of these foods may help add variety to your cholesterol-lowering diet. Most supermarkets currently sell approximately 30,000 food and non-food items. The large number of available food items often makes it difficult for consumers to identify foods low in saturated fat and cholesterol. Inclusion of a food in this Guide does not imply an endorsement and is not meant to classify any food as good or bad.

All foods listed in this Guide are low in saturated fat. Some foods—such as oil, margarine, salad dressing, nuts, and seeds—that are high in total fat can be used in limited amounts in a cholesterol-lowering eating plan if they are low enough in saturated fat. These foods can be used with *The Living Heart Diet* and other eating plans that recommend an eating pattern providing:

- Less than 10% of calories from saturated fatty acids
- No more than 30% of calories from total fat
- Less than 300 mg of cholesterol per day

More information about dietary recommendations and lowering blood cholesterol is found in chapter 1.

EVALUATING FOODS FOR THE GUIDE

Two pieces of information were used to evaluate each food listed in *The Living Heart Brand Name Shopper's Guide*—cutoff points and serving sizes.

CUTOFF POINTS

Foods are included in this Guide if one serving of that food contains no more than a specified level—called a cutoff point—of fat, saturated fat,

CUTOFF POINTS PER SERVING OF FOOD

	Fat (g)	Saturated Fat (g)	Cholesterol (mg)
All Foods (except Meat, Dairy, Single-Serving Entrées and Dinners, Oil, Margarine, Salad Dressing, Nuts, and Seeds)	3	1	10
Meat			
Fresh, Lean (3 oz cooked)	9	3	80
Processed/Luncheon, Lean (1 oz)	3	1	27
Dairy Products	3	2	10
Single-Serving Entrées and Dinners	9	3	80
Oil, Margarine, Salad Dressing, Nuts, and Seeds	*	2	10

No cutoff point; since oil, margarine, salad dressing, nuts, and seeds are naturally high in fat, the level of saturated fat is used as the cutoff point.

and cholesterol. A cutoff point is the *upper limit* of fat, saturated fat, or cholesterol that can be present in one serving of a food for it to be included in the Guide.

SERVING SIZES

In order to treat all foods fairly, cutoff points must be applied to a stated amount of each type of food that is considered one serving for purposes of evaluation. Although the serving sizes used in this Guide differ for each type of food, they are the same for all brands of the same food. For example, for all brands of yogurt, the cutoff points were applied to a serving size of 8 ounces; cutoff points were applied to a serving size of 4 fluid ounces (or ½ cup) for all brands of frozen yogurt.

Since food manufacturers do not always use the same serving size in labeling different brands of similar foods, it is difficult for consumers to compare nutrient information for similar products. For example, although 4 fluid ounces (½ cup) is the most common serving size listed on frozen dessert labels, many manufacturers use a 3-fluid-ounce serving. In many cases, manufacturers' serving sizes are the same as those used in this Guide. However, when manufacturer's servings and the serving sizes used for evaluating foods for the Guide were different, the amount of fat, saturated fat, and cholesterol in one serving, as specified in the Guide, was calculated and compared to the cutoff points to determine if the food could be listed in the Guide. If the fat, saturated fat, and cholesterol in one serving of the food did not exceed the cutoff points, it was included in the Food Sections of the Guide. The amount of each food considered to be one serving for purposes of evaluation for the Guide is listed in the introductory page of each food category in the Food Sections of the Guide. The amounts of calories, fat, saturated fat, cholesterol, and sodium printed in the Guide are for the manufacturer's serving size, which appears in parentheses next to each food.

Most of the serving sizes used to evaluate foods for this Guide are the "standard" serving sizes that were proposed by the Food and Drug Administration (FDA) in July 1990 and by the U.S. Department of Agriculture (USDA) and the FDA in November 1991. Although some of them may be changed again in the proposals that will be published in November 1992, the serving sizes adopted at that time will become law in 1993. Future editions of the Guide will reflect the new serving sizes.

HOW SERVING SIZES ARE USED

The cutoff points used to evaluate foods for the Guide are always stated as the upper limit of fat, saturated fat, and cholesterol in one serving of food. For example, the cutoff points for cookies are 3 grams of fat, 1 gram of saturated fat, and 10 milligrams of cholesterol *in 1 ounce of cookies.*

A couple of examples will make it easier to see how these serving sizes are used to evaluate foods for the Guide. One serving of yogurt used to evaluate foods for the Guide is 8 ounces. Most supermarkets sell a variety of single-serving containers of yogurt, including 4.4 ounces, 6 ounces, and 8 ounces. The calories, grams of fat, grams of saturated fat, milligrams of cholesterol, and milligrams of sodium in each 4.4-ounce and 6-ounce container were first converted to the values for 8 ounces. These values were then compared to the cutoff points—3 grams of fat, 2 grams of saturated fat, and 10 milligrams of cholesterol—for one 8-ounce serving of yogurt.

Example of Nutrition Label		*Conversion Factor**	*One Serving*	*Cutoff Points*
Berry Low-Fat Yogurt (1% Milk Fat)				
Nutrition Information per Serving				
Serving Size = 4.4 oz		× 1.8	8 oz	
Calories	140			
Protein	5 g			
Carbohydrate	27 g			
Fat	1 g	× 1.8	1.8 g	3 g
Saturated fat**	(0.6 g)	× 1.8	1.1 g	2 g
Cholesterol	5 mg	× 1.8	9.0 mg	10 mg
Sodium	70 mg			

*See calculation of conversion factor in step 1 below.
**Value calculated based on information from "Composition of Foods: Dairy and Egg Products," Agriculture Handbook No. 8-1, 1976.*

In order to calculate the values for 8 ounces of this yogurt, the following steps were used:

1. The 8-ounce size was divided by the manufacturer's serving size to get the comparison between the two. Therefore, 8 ounces divided by 4.4 ounces = 1.8; the serving size used for evaluation in the Guide is 1.8 times the manufacturer's serving size.

2. Since the nutrition information on this yogurt label does not include saturated fat, information from the USDA handbook on dairy products was used to calculate the amount of saturated fat in 4.4 ounces of yogurt as 0.6 gram.

3. Then, all the values for 4.4 ounces were multiplied by 1.8 to get the values for 8 ounces of yogurt.

4. Finally, the values for 8 ounces of yogurt were compared to the cutoff points. This yogurt qualifies for the Guide, since an 8-ounce serving contains *less* fat, saturated fat, and cholesterol than the cutoff points.

In the second example, the manufacturer's serving size for Brand X cookies is 0.4 ounce, and the serving size used for evaluation in the Guide is 1 ounce.

Example of Nutrition Label		Conversion Factor*	One Serving	Cutoff Points
Cookies				
Nutrition Information per Serving				
Serving Size = 1 cookie (0.4 oz)		× 2.5	1 oz	
Calories	30			
Protein	0 g			
Carbohydrate	6 g			
Fat	1 g	× 2.5	2.5 g	3 g
Saturated Fat	0.2 g	× 2.5	0.5 g	1 g
Cholesterol	0 mg	× 2.5	0	10 mg
Sodium	90 mg			

See calculation of conversion factor in step 1 below.

In order to compare this cookie to the cutoff points, the authors:

1. Divided the 1-ounce serving size by the manufacturer's serving size to get the comparison between the two. Therefore, 1 ounce divided by 0.4 ounce = 2.5; 1 serving, as used for evaluation in the Guide, is 2.5 times the manufacturer's serving size.

2. Multiplied all the values for 0.4 ounce of cookies by 2.5 to get the values for 1 ounce of cookies.

3. Compared these values for 1 ounce of cookies to the cutoff points. Brand X cookies qualify for the Guide, since 1 ounce does not provide more than the cutoff points for fat, saturated fat, and cholesterol.

The values printed in the Guide are for the serving size used by the manufacturer on the label, not for one serving as used to evaluate foods for the Guide.

You can use the serving sizes and cutoff points listed in the introductory page of each food category in the Food Section in the same way as in the examples to evaluate new products for your cholesterol-lowering diet.

There are several foods—such as eggs, oil, margarine, salad dressing, nuts, and seeds—that are high in fat or cholesterol but that, in limited amounts, can play a role in an eating pattern to lower blood cholesterol. Two grams of saturated fat in one serving was used as the only cutoff point to evaluate foods that are primarily fat (oil, margarine, salad dressing, nuts, and seeds). The amount of saturated fat was chosen as the cutoff point since a low intake of saturated fat is a very important factor in lowering blood cholesterol. Although all types of oil have the same amount of fat in one tablespoon, they differ widely in the amount of saturated fat they provide. For example, one tablespoon of both corn and cottonseed oils contains 13.6 grams of fat, but corn oil has 1.7 grams of saturated fat and cottonseed oil has 3.5 grams—more than twice as much.

Whole eggs and foods containing large amounts of egg yolk are not included in the Guide because they provide more cholesterol than the cutoff point for cholesterol in one serving. Each egg yolk adds 213 milligrams of cholesterol to a product. If a product with one egg yolk as its only source of cholesterol is divided into four servings, each serving provides 53 milligrams of cholesterol (about the same amount as in two ounces of beef or chicken), which is above the cutoff point. The recommended level of dietary cholesterol is less than 300 milligrams per day. Three egg yolks per week can be included in a cholesterol-lowering diet. When fewer meat and dairy products are consumed, egg yolks can be increased to four per week.

FOODS NOT INCLUDED IN THE GUIDE

There are several possible reasons why a food not appearing in the Guide may not have been included:

- Some foods have more fat, saturated fat, and/or cholesterol in one serving than the cutoff points on page 69.
- Nutrition information for some foods is not available from the manufacturer, or the food company may not have given the authors permission to include information in the Guide.
- Some foods are too new to have been evaluated by the authors.
- Some foods were just missed. Let us know about these foods, and we will evaluate them for the next edition of the Guide. See the form on page 413.

Some foods low enough in fat, saturated fat, and cholesterol to meet the cutoff points in the Guide may contain ingredients that are high in these nutrients. These ingredients include egg yolk, butter, cream, palm kernel oil, coconut oil, beef fat, and lard. However, such small amounts of these ingredients are present in the food that it still qualifies for the Guide.

FOOD PREPARATION

Although many foods in the Guide are ready to eat just as they are sold, some food products require preparation before they can be eaten. In most cases, the values printed in the Guide are for the food when prepared as directed on the package. Some products requiring preparation contain more fat, saturated fat, and/or cholesterol than the cutoff points because of ingredients added when following package directions. Examples include cake mixes and pancake mixes that require the addition of eggs, oil, and whole milk in preparation. These ingredients make the completed product higher than the cutoff points for fat and cholesterol. If the amount of oil is decreased and egg white or egg substitute and skim milk are substituted for the ingredients listed on the package, the finished product will be lower in fat and cholesterol.

As a rule, the Guide does not include products requiring preparation if the ingredients added when following package directions do not yield a completed product low in fat, saturated fat, and cholesterol. In a few cases, however, the Guide lists specific instructions for preparation. For example, the values for pudding printed in the Guide are for the dry mix combined with skim milk instead of the whole milk that may be part of the package directions.

USING THE GUIDE

For easy use and to make comparing foods more convenient, this Guide is divided into sections similar to the way foods are grouped in most supermarkets. For example, fresh meat, poultry, and fish are grouped together; frozen dinners are grouped together; and crackers are grouped together. The Table of Contents at the front is a complete list of the sections in the Guide.

This Guide can be useful in several ways. You can use it to identify foods low in calories, fat, saturated fat, cholesterol, and/or sodium. This will help add more variety to your eating pattern. The Guide can also provide specific brand name information for "food guides" or lists of "allowed foods" in books like *The Living Heart Diet,* which deal with cholesterol-lowering diets. If you are seeing a registered dietitian or other health professional for help in lowering your blood cholesterol, triglycerides, weight, or blood pressure, that person can help you adapt the information in this Guide to your eating plan.

The Guide can be helpful in making out your grocery shopping list. Planning your purchases before you go to the supermarket may help reduce impulse buying. (More information about saving time and money when shopping for food is found in chapter 3.) Since the Guide may not include all of the products low in fat, saturated fat, and cholesterol available in your supermarkets, use the cutoff points printed on page 69 and at the beginning of each category to evaluate new products. If one serving of a food, as listed in the Guide, contains no more than the cutoff points for fat, saturated fat, and cholesterol, you may wish to add it to your Guide in the space provided on page 411.

CONTENTS OF THE GUIDE

The following information is provided for each food in the Guide:

Product Name. The first column of the Guide shows the name of the food as it appears on the label. In the Guide, foods are divided into categories (Bread, Cereal, etc.) that are further divided into sub-categories. The Bread category, for example, is divided into sub-categories for Breadsticks, English Muffins, etc. These foods are then printed in alphabetical order—either by brand name or by the type of product. For example, the Guide lists single-serving entrées and dinners alphabetically by brand name and canned vegetables alphabetically by type (asparagus, corn, etc.).

Brand Names. Foods are identified in the Guide in three ways—by specific brand name, as "most brands," or as foods without brands for which information from the USDA handbooks is used.

• Specific brand names are shown for individual products when some brands qualify for the Guide and others do not. For example, brands of crackers listed in the Guide contain no more than the cutoff points for fat, saturated fat, and cholesterol. Specific brand names are also shown when several similar items meet the cutoff points but all of them have different analyses. For example, different brands of corn flakes contain different amounts of sodium.

Although brand names have been used in the Guide, the authors have not included information on the status of brand names as registered trademarks.

- "Most brands" is used when all of the brand name foods in a category contain approximately the same amount of calories, fat, saturated fat, and cholesterol. For example, specific brand names for coffee, plain low-fat cottage cheese, and skim milk are not used in the Guide, since all brands have about the same analysis.

- Generic information about fresh meat (beef, veal, pork, and lamb), poultry (chicken, turkey, and other fowl), and fish (finfish and shellfish) is from the USDA Handbook No. 8 series. These handbooks are also the source of information for most fresh fruits and vegetables.

Serving Size. The serving size used by the manufacturer on the package appears in parentheses beside each food. The calorie, fat, saturated fat, cholesterol, and sodium values in the Guide are for the manufacturer's serving size as listed beside the food. (The Guide's serving sizes, used only to evaluate products, are discussed on page 68.) The conversion tables on page 404 show how to change teaspoons to tablespoons, grams to ounces, etc.

Calorie Column. The calorie column shows the calories in the serving of food as it is listed in the Guide. A cutoff point is not used for calories. Some of the foods in the Guide are high in calories and others are low. If you need to decrease your calorie level, the Guide can help you compare the calories in similar food products to find those lowest in calories. Be sure that you are using the same serving size when comparing calories between similar foods.

Fat Column. The fat column shows the grams of fat in the serving of food that is printed in the Guide.

Saturated Fat Column. The saturated fat column shows the grams of saturated fat in the serving of food listed in the Guide. At present, values for saturated fat often are not available either from the package label or from the manufacturer. When these values were not available, they were estimated and appear in parentheses. The method used to estimate missing values is discussed in "Estimated Values," below.

Cholesterol Column. The cholesterol column shows the milligrams of cholesterol in the serving of food that is printed in the Guide. When cholesterol values were not available, they were estimated (see "Estimated Values," below).

Sodium Column. The sodium column shows the milligrams of sodium in a serving of food. This Guide does not use a cutoff point for sodium. Both foods that are high and those that are low in sodium are included as long as they are not over the cutoff points for fat, saturated fat, or cholesterol. If you need to limit your sodium intake, you will find the information on sodium values in this Guide useful in identifying foods low in sodium. For example, the Guide can help you identify cheeses and frozen dinners low in fat and also low in sodium.

ESTIMATED VALUES

Most of the nutrient information in this Guide came from food manufacturers, from the label on the package, or from USDA handbooks (for fresh fruits and vegetables, meat, poultry, fish, and oil). When information on saturated fat, cholesterol, or sodium was not available from any of these sources, the values were estimated. The authors based these estimates on analyses of similar products, such as those listed in the USDA handbooks, and the list of ingredients (including ingredients to be added during preparation) on the package. Estimated values in this Guide appear in parentheses. In future editions of the Guide, estimated values will be replaced by the actual values as they become available.

UPDATING THE GUIDE

The Living Heart Brand Name Shopper's Guide will be updated frequently. Please use page 415 in the Guide to send us your name and address so that you can be added to our mailing list for the updated Guide. If you have questions about a new product, please send us the name of the product and the manufacturer's name and address so that we can evaluate the food for the next edition of the Guide.

Between revisions of the Guide, use the table on page 69 and the information at the beginning of each category of food in the Food Sections to evaluate new products. When one serving of the new product, as stated in the Guide, provides no more fat, saturated fat, and cholesterol than the cutoff points for that food, use page 411 to add it to the Guide.

FOOD SECTIONS

BEVERAGES AND
BEVERAGE FLAVORINGS

Most of the foods in this category contain very little or no fat. Beverages were evaluated the way they will be consumed—*as purchased*, when *prepared according to package directions*, or when *prepared with skim milk* (as indicated next to the individual food in the Guide). A serving of the foods in this section of the Guide does not exceed the cutoff points for fat, saturated fat, and cholesterol listed below.

CUTOFF POINTS FOR BEVERAGES AND BEVERAGE FLAVORINGS

Fat (grams)	Saturated Fat (grams)	Cholesterol (milligrams)
3	1	10

SERVINGS

Food	Serving Sizes
Alcoholic Beverages, except wine coolers	Serving varies
Carbonated Beverages	12 fluid ounces
Cocoa Mixes, prepared	8 fluid ounces
Coffee and Tea, prepared	8 fluid ounces
Fruit-Flavored Beverages, prepared	12 fluid ounces
Instant Breakfast Mixes, prepared	8 fluid ounces
Milk Beverage Mixes, prepared	8 fluid ounces
Milk Shakes, prepared	12 fluid ounces
Wine Coolers	12 fluid ounces

Instant Breakfast Mixes. Calories and other values given in the Guide are for the prepared product (as it will be consumed). In order to qualify for the Guide, instant breakfast mixes must be prepared with skim milk, as directed next to each entry. Some instant breakfast mixes not listed in the Guide may not exceed the cutoff points for fat, saturated fat, and cholesterol if skim milk is substituted for the whole milk listed in the directions on the package.

Coffee, Tea, and Fruit-Flavored Beverages. These products normally do not contain fat. However, flavored coffees containing chocolate and/or creamer (both of which contain fat) may be too high in fat and saturated fat to qualify for the Guide.

The following abbreviations are used in the Food Sections: oz = ounce; fl oz = fluid ounce; pkg = package; pkt = packet; env = envelope; g = gram; prep (w/ . . .) = prepared with; < = less than; and tr = trace.

Alcholic Beverages	Calories	Fat g	Saturated Fat g	Choles- terol mg	Sodium mg
ALCOHOLIC BEVERAGES					
Beer, Light—Most Brands (12 fl oz)	100	0.0	0.0	0	10
Beer, Regular—Most Brands (12 fl oz)	146	0.0	0.0	0	19
Gin—Most Brands (1-1/2 fl oz)	110	0.0	0.0	0	1
Liqueur, Coffee—Most Brands (1-1/2 fl oz)	174	0.1	0.1	0	4
Liqueur, Creme de Menthe—Most Brands (1-1/2 fl oz)	186	0.1	0.0	0	3
Rum—Most Brands (1-1/2 fl oz)	97	0.0	0.0	0	0
Vodka—Most Brands (1-1/2 fl oz)	97	0.0	0.0	0	0
Whiskey—Most Brands (1-1/2 fl oz)	105	0.0	0.0	0	0
Wine, Dessert—Most Brands (2 fl oz)	90	0.0	0.0	0	5
Wine, Table—Most Brands (3-1/2 fl oz)	72	0.0	0.0	0	8
CARBONATED BEVERAGES					
Barq's Root Beer, Diet (6 fl oz)	2	0.2	(0.0)	(0)	35
Bel Air Seltzer: Lemon, Lime or Orange-Flavored (6 fl oz)	0	0.0	0.0	0	20
Club Soda—Most Brands (12 fl oz)	0	0.0	0.0	0	75
Cola—Most Brands (12 fl oz)	151	0.0	0.0	0	14
Cragmont Soda, Cherry Cola (6 fl oz)	79	0.0	0.0	0	35
Cragmont Soda, Cherry, Lemon-Lime, or Grapefruit, Diet (6 fl oz)	0	0.0	0.0	0	65
Cragmont Soda, Grapefruit (6 fl oz)	84	0.0	0.0	0	35
Cragmont Soda, Lemon (6 fl oz)	0	0.0	0.0	0	45
Cragmont Soda, Orange, Diet (6 fl oz)	0	0.0	0.0	0	65
Cragmont Soda, Root Beer, Diet (6 fl oz)	0	0.0	0.0	0	35

Carbonated Beverages (continued)	Calories	Fat g	Saturated Fat g	Choles-terol mg	Sodium mg
Cragmont Soda, Sparkling Punch (6 fl oz)	89	0.0	0.0	0	35
Cream Soda—Most Brands (12 fl oz)	191	0.0	0.0	0	43
Diet Cola (Sweetened with Aspartame)—Most Brands (12 fl oz)	2	0.0	0.0	0	21
Giant Seltzer, Lemon, Lemon-Lime, Lime, Mandarin Orange, Plain, or Raspberry (8 fl oz)	0	0.0	0.0	0	10
Giant Soda, Bitter Lemon (8 fl oz)	110	0.0	0.0	0	5
Giant Soda, Black Cherry (8 fl oz)	120	0.0	0.0	0	0
Giant Soda, Mandarin Orange (8 fl oz)	130	0.0	0.0	0	30
Ginger Ale—Most Brands (12 fl oz)	124	0.0	0.0	0	25
Grape Soda—Most Brands (12 fl oz)	161	0.0	0.0	0	57
Hansen's Natural Soda, Cherry (12 fl oz)	149	0.6	(0.0)	(0)	<10
Hansen's Natural Soda, Grapefruit (12 fl oz)	152	0.4	(0.0)	(0)	<10
Hansen's Natural Soda, Mandarin Lime (12 fl oz)	152	0.4	(0.0)	(0)	<10
Hansen's Natural Soda, Raspberry (12 fl oz)	149	0.6	(0.0)	(0)	<10
IGA Black Cherry (6 fl oz)	78	0.0	0.0	0	(35)
IGA Cherry Cola (6 fl oz)	82	0.0	0.0	0	(35)
IGA Ginger Ale, Diet (6 fl oz)	2	0.0	0.0	0	(33)
IGA Grape, Diet (6 fl oz)	0	0.0	0.0	0	(80)
IGA Punch (6 fl oz)	88	1.5	(0.0)	0	(35)
IGA Red Pop (6 fl oz)	84	0.0	0.0	0	(22)
Lemon-Lime Soda—Most Brands (12 fl oz)	149	0.0	0.0	0	41
Orange Soda—Most Brands (12 fl oz)	177	0.0	0.0	0	46
Pepper-Type Cola—Most Brands (12 fl oz)	151	0.4	0.0	0	38
Root Beer—Most Brands (12 fl oz)	152	0.0	0.0	0	49

Carbonated Beverages (continued)	Calories	Fat g	Saturated Fat g	Choles- terol mg	Sodium mg
Schweppes Bitter Lemon (6 fl oz)	82	0.0	0.0	0	13
Schweppes Flavored Seltzer, Black Cherry (6 fl oz)	0	0.0	0.0	0	<5
Schweppes Flavored Seltzer, Lemon (6 fl oz)	0	0.0	0.0	0	<5
Schweppes Flavored Seltzer, Lime (6 fl oz)	0	0.0	0.0	0	<5
Schweppes Flavored Seltzer, Orange (6 fl oz)	0	0.0	0.0	0	<5
Schweppes Flavored Seltzer, Peaches 'N Cream (6 fl oz)	0	0.0	0.0	0	<5
Schweppes Flavored Seltzer, Wild Raspberry (6 fl oz)	0	0.0	0.0	0	<5
Schweppes Ginger Ale, Raspberry (6 fl oz)	65	0.0	0.0	0	10
Schweppes Ginger Ale, Raspberry, Diet (6 fl oz)	2	0.0	0.0	0	55
Schweppes Ginger Ale, Sugar Free (6 fl oz)	2	0.0	0.0	0	39
Schweppes Ginger Beer (6 fl oz)	70	0.0	0.0	0	30
Schweppes Lemon Sour (6 fl oz)	79	0.0	0.0	0	12
Schweppes Seltzer Water, Sodium Free (6 fl oz)	0	0.0	0.0	0	<5
Schweppes Seltzer Water, Very Low Sodium (6 fl oz)	0	0.0	0.0	0	7
Tonic Water—Most Brands (12 fl oz)	125	0.0	0.0	0	15
COCOA MIXES					
Carnation Hot Cocoa Mix with Chocolate Marshmallows (1 env)	110	1.0	1.0	2	120
Carnation Hot Cocoa Mix with Marshmallows (1 env)	110	1.0	0.9	1	120
Carnation Hot Cocoa Mix, 70-Calorie (1 env)	70	<1.0	0.2	1	135
Carnation Hot Cocoa Mix, Chocolate Fudge (1 env)	110	1.0	1.0	1	130
Carnation Hot Cocoa Mix, Milk Chocolate (1 env)	110	1.0	0.9	1	130
Carnation Hot Cocoa Mix, Rich Chocolate (1 env)	110	1.0	1.0	1	130

Cocoa Mixes (continued)	Calories	Fat g	Saturated Fat g	Choles- terol mg	Sodium mg
Carnation Sugar Free Hot Cocoa Mix, Diet (1 env)	25	<1.0	0.2	0	150
Carnation Sugar Free Hot Cocoa Mix, Mocha (1 env)	50	<1.0	0.2	2	140
Carnation Sugar Free Hot Cocoa Mix, Rich Chocolate (1 env)	50	<1.0	0.2	3	160
Featherweight Sugar Free Hot Cocoa Mix (1 env)	50	1.0	(0.6)	0	110
Featherweight Sugar Free Hot Cocoa Mix, Mint (1 env)	50	1.0	(0.6)	0	110
Giant Cocoa Mix, Milk Chocolate, prep (w/water) (6 fl oz)	110	1.0	<1.0	0	125
Giant Cocoa Mix, Mini Marshmallow, prep (w/water) (6 fl oz)	110	1.0	<1.0	0	140
Lucerne Sugar Free Cocoa Mix, prep (w/water) (6 fl oz)	50	1.0	(<1.0)	0	155
Nestle Hot Cocoa Mix, Rich Chocolate Flavor with Marshmallows, prep (w/skim milk) (6 fl oz)	190	1.0	(0.6)	(2)	200
Nestle Hot Cocoa Mix, Rich Chocolate Flavor, prep (w/skim milk) (6 fl oz)	180	1.0	(0.6)	(2)	200
Swiss Miss Cocoa Mix, Diet, prep (w/water) (6 oz)	20	<1.0	(0.0)	2	180
Swiss Miss Cocoa Mix, Sugar Free, prep (w/water) (6 oz)	50	<1.0	(0.0)	2	190
Swiss Miss Lite Cocoa Mix, prep (w/water) (6 oz)	70	<1.0	(0.0)	1	180
Swiss Miss Sugar Free Cocoa with Sugar Free Marshmallows, prep (w/water) (6 oz)	50	<1.0	(0.0)	2	180
Weight Watchers Hot Cocoa Mix, Milk Chocolate and Marshmallow Flavored (1 env)	60	0.0	0.0	(0)	160

COFFEE AND TEA

	Calories	Fat g	Saturated Fat g	Choles- terol mg	Sodium mg
Cafix Instant Beverage, prep (w/water) (1 cup)	6	0.0	0.0	(0)	3
Coffee, Brewed, Regular or Decaffeinated, Unsweetened— Most Brands (1 cup)	5	0.0	0.0	0	5

Coffee and Tea (continued)	Calories	Fat g	Saturated Fat g	Choles- terol mg	Sodium mg
Coffee, Instant, Regular or Decaffeinated, prep (w/water) —Most Brands (1 cup)	5	0.0	0.0	0	8
Lipton Instant Tea, Raspberry Flavored (8 fl oz)	3	0.0	0.0	0	1
Nestea Ice Teasers, Wild Cherry, Orange, Citrus, Lemon or Tropical (8 fl oz)	6	0.0	0.0	0	0
Postum Instant Hot Beverage (6 fl oz)	12	0.0	0.0	0	0
Postum Instant Hot Beverage, Coffee Flavor (6 oz)	12	0.0	0.0	0	0
Tea, Brewed or Instant, Regular or Herbal, Unsweetened—Most Brands (8 fl oz)	3	0.0	0.0	0	2–8
Tea, Instant, Regular or Decaffeinated, Presweetened with Artificial Sweetener, Dry—Most Brands (2 tsp)	5	0.0	0.0	0	17
Tea, Instant, Regular or Decaffeinated, Presweetened with Sugar, prep (w/water)— Most Brands (8 fl oz)	87	0.0	0.0	0	0
Worthington Kaffree Roma (8 fl oz)	6	0.0	0.0	(0)	(10)
FLAVORED MILK BEVERAGES					
Carnation Malted Milk, Chocolate (3 heaping tsp)	80	1.0	0.5	1	55
Carnation Malted Milk, Original (3 heaping tsp)	90	2.0	(0.9)	4	105
Kraft Instant Malted Milk, Chocolate (3 tsp)	90	1.0	0.6	(0)	45
Nestle Quik Strawberry Flavor, dry (2-1/2 tsp)	80	0.0	0.0	(0)	0
Nestle Quik Sugar Free Chocolate Flavor, prep (w/skim milk) (8 fl oz)	104	1.0	(<1.0)	(4)	(160)
Nestle Quik Syrup, Strawberry Flavor (1-2/3 tbsp)	100	0.0	0.0	(0)	0
Nestle Quik, Chocolate Flavor, dry (2-1/2 heaping tsp)	90	1.0	(0.6)	(0)	25
Weight Watchers Shake Mix, Chocolate Fudge (1 env)	70	1.0	(<1.0)	(0)	170

Flavored Milk Beverages (continued)	Calories	Fat g	Saturated Fat g	Choles- terol mg	Sodium mg
Weight Watchers Shake Mix, Orange Sherbet (1 env)	70	0.0	0.0	0	210

FRUIT-FLAVORED BEVERAGES

	Calories	Fat g	Saturated Fat g	Choles- terol mg	Sodium mg
Bama Fruit Punch Drink (with 10% fruit juice) (8.45 fl oz)	130	0.0	0.0	(0)	15
Bama Grape Drink (with 10% fruit juice) (8.45 fl oz)	120	0.0	0.0	(0)	25
Bama Orange Drink (with 10% fruit juice) (8.45 fl oz)	120	0.0	0.0	(0)	60
Betty Crocker Squeezit: Apple, Orange, Red Punch, or Wild Berry (6.75 oz)	110	<1.0	(0.0)	(0)	5
Betty Crocker Squeezit: Cherry or Grape (6.75 oz)	110	<1.0	(0.0)	(0)	30
Bright & Early Breakfast Beverage (6 fl oz)	90	0.2	(0.0)	(0)	18
Citrus Fruit Juice Drink—Most Brands (6 fl oz)	84	0.0	0.0	0	6
Country Time Drink Mix (sugar-sweetened), Lemonade Punch (8 fl oz)	80	0.0	0.0	0	15
Country Time Drink Mix (sugar-sweetened), Pink Lemonade or Lemonade (8 fl oz)	80	0.0	0.0	0	20
Country Time Drink Mix Sugar Free Drink Mix (sweetened with Nutrasweet) (8 fl oz)	4	0.0	0.0	0	0
Cragmont Presweetened Drink Mix, Orange (8 fl oz)	90	0.0	0.0	0	40
Cragmont Presweetened Drink Mix: Cherry, Grape, Lemonade, Punch or Strawberry (8 fl oz)	90	0.0	0.0	0	15
Cragmont Sugar Free Drink Mix, Pink Punch or Lemonade (8 fl oz)	4	0.0	0.0	0	0
Cranberry Juice Cocktail—Most Brands (6 fl oz)	102	0.0	0.0	0	6
Crystal Light Sugar Free Drink Mix (sweetened with Nutrasweet), Lemon-Lime, prep (w/water) (8 fl oz)	4	0.0	0.0	0	0

Fruit-Flavored Beverages (continued)	Calories	Fat g	Saturated Fat g	Choles- terol mg	Sodium mg
Crystal Light Sugar Free Drink Mix (sweetened with Nutrasweet), Lemonade, prep (w/water) (8 fl oz)	4	0.0	0.0	0	0
Crystal Light Sugar Free Drink Mix (sweetened with Nutrasweet), Berry Blend, Citrus Blend, or Fruit Punch, prep (w/water) (8 fl oz)	4	0.0	0.0	0	0
Five Alive To-Go Box, Citrus (8.45 fl oz)	123	0.0	0.0	(0)	32
Five Alive, Berry Citrus (6 fl oz)	88	0.1	(0.0)	(0)	21
Five Alive, Citrus, prep (from frozen) (6 fl oz)	87	0.0	0.0	(0)	6
Five Alive, Tropical Citrus (6 fl oz)	85	0.1	(0.0)	(0)	19
Giant Cranberry Apple Juice Cocktail, prep (from frozen) (6 fl oz)	130	0.0	0.0	0	10
Giant Cranberry Raspberry Juice Cocktail, prep (from frozen) (6 fl oz)	110	0.0	0.0	0	10
Giant Fruit Punch, Green, prep (from frozen) (6 fl oz)	150	0.0	0.0	0	10
Giant Fruit Punch, Red, prep (from frozen) (6 fl oz)	150	0.0	0.0	0	10
Giant Fruit Punch, chilled (6 fl oz)	90	0.0	0.0	0	10
Giant Lemon Limeade, chilled (6 fl oz)	80	0.0	0.0	0	5
Giant Lemonade, chilled (6 fl oz)	80	0.0	0.0	0	5
Giant Lemonade, prep (from frozen) (6 fl oz)	80	0.0	0.0	0	0
Giant Orangeade, chilled (6 fl oz)	80	0.0	0.0	0	20
Giant Pink Grapefruit Cocktail, prep (from frozen) (6 fl oz)	80	0.0	0.0	0	15
Giant Pink Lemonade, prep (from frozen) (6 fl oz)	80	0.0	0.0	0	0
Giant Sugar Sweetened Powdered Drink Mix, Cherry, prep (w/water) (6 fl oz)	70	0.0	0.0	0	10

Fruit-Flavored Beverages (continued)	Calories	Fat g	Saturated Fat g	Cholesterol mg	Sodium mg
Giant Sugar Sweetened Powdered Drink Mix, Fruit Punch, prep (w/water) (6 fl oz)	70	0.0	0.0	0	40
Giant Sugar Sweetened Powdered Drink Mix, Grape, prep (w/water) (6 fl oz)	70	0.0	0.0	0	0
Giant Sugar Sweetened Powdered Drink Mix, Lemonade, prep (w/water) (6 fl oz)	70	0.0	0.0	0	15
Giant Sugar Sweetened Powdered Drink Mix, Orangeade, prep (w/water) (6 fl oz)	70	0.0	0.0	0	0
Hi-C Fruit Drink, Boppin' Berry (6 fl oz)	90	0.0	0.0	(0)	20
Hi-C Fruit Drink, Cherry (6 fl oz)	100	0.1	(0.0)	(0)	17
Hi-C Fruit Drink, Double Fruit Cooler (6 fl oz)	93	0.0	0.0	(0)	18
Hi-C Fruit Drink, Ecto Cooler (6 fl oz)	95	0.0	0.0	(0)	17
Hi-C Fruit Drink, Fruit Punch (6 fl oz)	96	0.0	0.0	(0)	17
Hi-C Fruit Drink, Grape (6 fl oz)	96	0.1	(0.0)	(0)	17
Hi-C Fruit Drink, Hula Cooler (6 fl oz)	97	0.0	0.0	(0)	17
Hi-C Fruit Drink, Hula Punch (6 fl oz)	87	0.0	0.0	(0)	17
Hi-C Fruit Drink, Jammin' Apple (6 fl oz)	86	0.0	0.0	(0)	16
Hi-C Fruit Drink, Orange (6 fl oz)	95	0.0	0.0	(0)	17
Hi-C Fruit Drink, Peach (6 fl oz)	101	0.0	0.0	(0)	18
Hi-C Fruit Drink, Wild Berry (6 fl oz)	92	0.1	(0.0)	(0)	17
Hi-C Fruit Punch, prep (from frozen) (6 fl oz)	95	0.4	(0.0)	(0)	10
Hi-C Powder Drink Mixes, Cherry, prep (w/water) (6 fl oz)	75	0.0	0.0	(0)	25
Hi-C Powder Drink Mixes, Fruit Punch, prep (w/water) (6 fl oz)	76	0.0	0.0	(0)	0

Fruit-Flavored Beverages (continued)	Calories	Fat g	Saturated Fat g	Choles- terol mg	Sodium mg
Hi-C Powder Drink Mixes, Grape, prep (w/water) (6 fl oz)	76	0.0	0.0	(0)	0
Hi-C Powder Drink Mixes Lemonade (pink or white), prep (w/water) (6 fl oz)	74	0.0	0.0	(0)	5
Hi-C Powder Drink Mixes, Light Fruit Punch, prep (w/water) (6 fl oz)	3	0.0	0.0	(0)	7
Hi-C Powder Drink Mixes, Light Lemon, prep (w/water) (6 fl oz)	7	0.0	0.0	(0)	3
Hi-C Powder Drink Mixes, Orange, prep (w/water) (6 fl oz)	75	0.0	0.0	(0)	0
Hi-C Powder Drink Mixes, Peach, prep (w/water) (6 fl oz)	76	0.0	0.0	(0)	20
Hi-C Powder Drink Mixes, Whipped Orange, prep (w/water) (6 fl oz)	92	0.0	0.0	(0)	30
Hi-C Powder Drink Mixes, Whipped Strawberry, prep (w/water) (6 fl oz)	91	0.0	0.0	(0)	30
Hi-C To-Go Box, Candy Apple Cooler (8.45 fl oz)	132	0.0	0.0	(0)	25
Hi-C To-Go Box, Cherry (8.45 fl oz)	141	0.1	(0.0)	(0)	24
Hi-C To-Go Box, Double Fruit Cooler (8.45 fl oz)	131	0.0	0.0	(0)	25
Hi-C To-Go Box, Fruit Punch (8.45 fl oz)	135	0.0	0.0	(0)	24
Hi-C To-Go Box, Grape (8.45 fl oz)	136	0.1	(0.0)	(0)	24
Hi-C To-Go Box, Lemonade (8.45 fl oz)	109	0.1	(0.0)	(0)	73
Hi-C To-Go Box, Orange (8.45 fl oz)	134	0.0	0.0	(0)	24
Hi-C To-Go Box, Wild Berry (8.45 fl oz)	129	0.1	(0.0)	(0)	24
IGA Apple Cherry Berry (6 fl oz)	100	0.0	0.0	0	(20)
IGA Cranberry Apple Drink (6 fl oz)	120	0.0	0.0	0	(10)
IGA Cranberry Cocktail (6 fl oz)	100	0.0	0.0	0	(10)
IGA Fruit Punch (6 fl oz)	90	0.0	0.0	0	(35)

Fruit-Flavored Beverages (continued)	Calories	Fat g	Saturated Fat g	Choles- terol mg	Sodium mg
IGA Grape Drink (6 fl oz)	100	0.0	0.0	0	(20)
IGA Orange Banana Drink (6 fl oz)	100	0.0	0.0	0	(5)
IGA Papaya Punch (6 fl oz)	90	0.0	0.0	0	(20)
IGA Pineapple Orange Drink (6 fl oz)	90	0.0	0.0	0	(20)
IGA Pink Grapefruit Cocktail (6 fl oz)	90	0.0	0.0	0	(10)
IGA Tropical Punch (6 fl oz)	90	0.0	0.0	0	(20)
Kern's Islander Punch (8 fl oz)	120	0.0	0.0	(0)	40
Knox Drinking Gelatin with Nutrasweet, Orange Flavored (1 env)	39	0.1	(0.0)	0	17
Kool-Aid Koolers Juice Drink, Cherry (8.45 fl oz)	140	0.0	0.0	0	10
Kool-Aid Koolers Juice Drink, Grape (8.45 fl oz)	140	0.0	0.0	0	10
Kool-Aid Koolers Juice Drink, Mountain Berry Punch (8.45 fl oz)	140	0.0	0.0	0	10
Kool-Aid Koolers Juice Drink, Orange (8.45 fl oz)	110	0.0	0.0	0	10
Kool-Aid Koolers Juice Drink, Rainbow Punch (8.45 fl oz)	130	0.0	0.0	0	10
Kool-Aid Koolers Juice Drink, Tropical Punch (8.45 fl oz)	130	0.0	0.0	0	10
Kool-Aid Soft Drink Mix (sugar-sweetened), Berry Blue or Purplesaurus Rex, prep (w/water) (8 fl oz)	80	0.0	0.0	0	5
Kool-Aid Soft Drink Mix (sugar-sweetened), Grape or Raspberry, prep (w/water) (8 fl oz)	80	0.0	0.0	0	25
Kool-Aid Soft Drink Mix (sugar sweetened), Mountain Berry Punch, prep (w/water) (8 fl oz)	80	0.0	0.0	0	15
Kool-Aid Soft Drink Mix (sugar-sweetened), Rainbow Punch, prep (w/water) (8 fl oz)	80	0.0	0.0	0	20
Kool-Aid Soft Drink Mix (sugar-sweetened), Sharkleberry Fin or Tropical Punch (8 fl oz)	80	0.0	0.0	0	0

Fruit-Flavored Beverages (continued)	Calories	Fat g	Saturated Fat g	Cholesterol mg	Sodium mg
Kool-Aid Soft Drink Mix (sugar-sweetened), Cherry, Lemonade, Orange, or Strawberry, prep (w/water) (8 fl oz)	80	0.0	0.0	0	0
Kool-Aid Soft Drink Mix (unsweetened), Mountain Berry Punch, prep (w/sugar and water) (8 fl oz)	100	0.0	0.0	0	15
Kool-Aid Soft Drink Mix (unsweetened), Purplesaurus Rex, prep (w/sugar and water) (8 fl oz)	100	0.0	0.0	0	5
Kool-Aid Soft Drink Mix (unsweetened), Berry Blue, Black Cherry, Cherry, Grape, Lemonade, Lemon-Lime, Orange, Pink Lemonade, Rainbow Punch, Sharkleberry Fin, or Tropical Punch, prep (w/sugar and water) (8 fl oz)	100	0.0	0.0	0	0
Kool-Aid Soft Drink Mix (unsweetened), Raspberry, Strawberry, or Surfin Berry Punch, prep (w/sugar and water) (8 fl oz)	100	0.0	0.0	0	25
Kool-Aid Sugar Free Soft Drink Mix (sweetened with Nutrasweet), Berry Blue or Purplesaurus Rex, prep (w/water) (8 fl oz)	4	0.0	0.0	0	5
Kool-Aid Sugar Free Soft Drink Mix (sweetened with Nutrasweet), Mountain Berry Punch, prep (w/water) (8 fl oz)	4	0.0	0.0	0	35
Kool-Aid Sugar Free Soft Drink Mix (sweetened with Nutrasweet), Surfin' Berry Punch, prep (w/water) (8 fl oz)	4	0.0	0.0	0	25
Kool-Aid Sugar Free Soft Drink Mix (sweetened with Nutrasweet), Tropical Punch, prep (w/water) (8 fl oz)	4	0.0	0.0	0	10
Kool-Aid Sugar Free Soft Drink Mix (sweetened with Nutrasweet), Cherry, Grape, Lemonade, or Sharkleberry Fin, prep (w/water) (8 fl oz)	4	0.0	0.0	0	0

Fruit-Flavored Beverages (continued)	Calories	Fat g	Saturated Fat g	Choles- terol mg	Sodium mg
Libby's Juice Drink, Fruit Medley (6 fl oz)	80	0.0	0.0	(0)	0
Libby's Juice Drink, Grape Medley (6 fl oz)	90	0.0	0.0	(0)	0
Libby's Lemonade (6 fl oz)	80	0.0	0.0	(0)	10
McCain Apple Peach (3/4 cup)	78	0.1	0.0	0	11
McCain Pineapple Grapefruit (8 fl oz = 1 box)	115	0.2	0.1	0	8
Minute Maid Juices and Punches, Concord Punch (11.5 fl oz = 1 can)	178	0.1	(0.0)	(0)	74
Minute Maid Juices and Punches, Fruit Punch (11.5 fl oz = 1 can)	174	0.1	(0.0)	(0)	33
Minute Maid Juices and Punches, Pink Grapefruit Juice Cocktail (11.5 fl oz = 1 can)	163	0.2	(0.0)	(0)	34
Minute Maid Juices and Punches, Tropical Punch (11.5 fl oz = 1 can)	176	0.0	0.0	(0)	33
Minute Maid On-The-Go Bottle, Concord Punch (10 fl oz)	155	0.1	(0.0)	(0)	29
Minute Maid On-The-Go Bottle, Fruit Punch (10 fl oz)	152	0.1	(0.0)	(0)	29
Minute Maid On-The-Go Bottle, Orange (10 fl oz)	155	0.6	(0.0)	(0)	32
Minute Maid Punches, Apple, prep (from frozen) (6 fl oz)	90	0.0	0.0	(0)	0
Minute Maid Punches, Citrus, prep (from frozen) (6 fl oz)	93	0.0	0.0	(0)	18
Minute Maid Punches, Fruit, prep (from frozen) (6 fl oz)	91	0.1	(0.0)	(0)	17
Minute Maid Punches, Grape, prep (from frozen) (6 fl oz)	89	0.0	0.0	(0)	3
Minute Maid To-Go Box, Concord Punch (8.45 fl oz)	131	0.1	(0.0)	(0)	25
Minute Maid To-Go Box, Fruit Punch (8.45 fl oz)	128	0.1	(0.0)	(0)	24
Minute Maid To-Go Box, Tropical Punch (8.45 fl oz)	130	0.0	0.0	(0)	24
Newman's Own Roadside Virgin Lemonade (8 fl oz)	100	<1.0	(0.0)	0	0

Fruit-Flavored Beverages (continued)	Calories	Fat g	Saturated Fat g	Choles- terol mg	Sodium mg
Newman's Own Roadside Virgin Lemonade, Honey (8 fl oz)	100	<1.0	(0.0)	0	0
Ocean Spray Cran*Blueberry Blueberry Cranberry Drink (6 fl oz)	120	0.0	0.0	(0)	10
Ocean Spray Cran*Grape Grape Cranberry Drink (6 fl oz)	130	0.0	0.0	(0)	5
Ocean Spray Cran*Raspberry Raspberry Cranberry Drink (6 fl oz)	110	0.0	0.0	(0)	5
Ocean Spray Cran*Raspberry Raspberry Cranberry Drink, Low Calorie (6 fl oz)	40	0.0	0.0	(0)	10
Ocean Spray Cran*Strawberry (6 fl oz)	110	0.0	0.0	(0)	10
Ocean Spray Cran*Tastic Blended Juice Drink (6 fl oz)	110	0.0	0.0	(0)	15
Ocean Spray Cranapple Cranberry Apple Drink (6 fl oz)	130	0.0	0.0	(0)	10
Ocean Spray Cranapple Cranberry Apple Juice Drink, Low Calorie (6 fl oz)	40	0.0	0.0	(0)	5
Ocean Spray Cranberry Juice Cocktail, Low Calorie (6 fl oz)	40	0.0	0.0	(0)	10
Ocean Spray Cranicot Cranberry Apricot Juice Drink (6 fl oz)	110	0.0	0.0	(0)	5
Ocean Spray Mauna La'i Hawaiian Guava Fruit Drink (6 fl oz)	100	0.0	0.0	(0)	10
Ocean Spray Mauna La'i Hawaiian Guava*Passion Fruit Drink (6 fl oz)	100	0.0	0.0	(0)	5
Ocean Spray Pineapple Grapefruit Juice Cocktail (6 fl oz)	110	0.0	0.0	(0)	5
Ocean Spray Pink Grapefruit Juice Cocktail (6 fl oz)	80	0.0	0.0	(0)	15
Sundance Natural Juice Sparklers, Apple (10 oz)	119	0.0	0.0	0	23
Sundance Natural Juice Sparklers, Black Currant (10 oz)	119	0.0	0.0	0	12

Fruit-Flavored Beverages (continued)	Calories	Fat g	Saturated Fat g	Choles- terol mg	Sodium mg
Sundance Natural Juice Sparklers, Cranberry (10 oz)	133	0.0	0.0	0	48
Sundance Natural Juice Sparklers, Kiwi Lime (10 oz)	119	0.0	0.0	0	34
Sundance Natural Juice Sparklers, Raspberry (10 oz)	128	0.0	0.0	0	35
Sundance Natural Juice Sparklers, Sour Cherry (10 oz)	133	0.0	0.0	0	20
Sundance Natural Juice Sparklers, Tropical Lemon (10 oz)	126	0.0	0.0	0	23
Tang Breakfast Beverage Crystals, prep (w/water) (6 fl oz)	90	0.0	0.0	0	0
Tang Fruit Box Juice Drink, Cherry (8.45 fl oz)	120	0.0	0.0	0	10
Tang Fruit Box Juice Drink, Grape (8.45 fl oz)	130	0.0	0.0	0	10
Tang Fruit Box Juice Drink, Mixed Fruit (8.45 fl oz)	140	0.0	0.0	0	10
Tang Fruit Box Juice Drink, Orange (8.45 fl oz)	130	0.0	0.0	0	10
Tang Fruit Box Juice Drink, Strawberry (8.45 fl oz)	120	0.0	0.0	0	10
Tang Fruit Box Juice Drink, Tropical Orange (8.45 fl oz)	150	0.0	0.0	0	10
Tang Sugar Free Breakfast Beverage Crystals (sweetened with Nutrasweet), prep (w/water) (6 fl oz)	6	0.0	0.0	0	0
Town House Juice Drink, Cranraspberry (6 fl oz)	110	0.0	0.0	0	10
Treehouse Beverages, Apple Cherry (6 fl oz)	66	0.0	0.0	0	8
Treehouse Beverages, Apple Cranberry (8.3 fl oz = 1 drinking box)	131	0.1	0.0	0	7
Treehouse Beverages, Grape Raspberry (6 fl oz)	72	0.0	0.0	0	6
Treehouse Beverages, Orange Banana (6 fl oz)	73	0.0	0.0	0	5
Treehouse Beverages, Orange Peach (6 fl oz)	70	0.0	0.0	0	5

Fruit-Flavored Beverages (continued)	Calories	Fat g	Saturated Fat g	Choles- terol mg	Sodium mg
Treehouse Beverages, Pineapple Tangerine (8.3 fl oz = 1 drinking box)	113	0.1	0.0	0	6
Welch's Grape Juice, Red (6 fl oz)	120	0.0	0.0	0	15
Welch's Grape Juice, White (6 fl oz)	120	0.0	0.0	0	15
Welch's Juice Cocktail, Apple Cranberry (6 fl oz)	110	0.0	0.0	0	20
Welch's Juice Cocktail, Apple Grape Cherry (6 fl oz)	120	0.0	0.0	0	20
Welch's Juice Cocktail, Apple Grape Raspberry (6 fl oz)	120	0.0	0.0	0	20
Welch's Juice Cocktail, Apple-Orange-Pineapple (6 fl oz)	120	0.0	0.0	0	20
Welch's Juice Cocktail, Apple-Orange-Pineapple, prep (from frozen) (6 fl oz)	110	0.0	0.0	0	0
Welch's Juice Cocktail, Cranberry Apple, prep (from frozen) (6 fl oz)	120	0.0	0.0	0	0
Welch's Juice Cocktail, Cranberry Cherry, prep (from frozen) (6 fl oz)	110	0.0	0.0	0	0
Welch's Juice Cocktail, Cranberry Orange, prep (from frozen) (6 fl oz)	110	0.0	0.0	0	0
Welch's Juice Cocktail, Cranberry Raspberry, no sugar added, prep (from frozen) (6 fl oz)	40	0.0	0.0	0	0
Welch's Juice Cocktail, Cranberry Raspberry, prep (from frozen) (6 fl oz)	110	0.0	0.0	0	0
Welch's Juice Cocktail, Cranberry, no sugar added, prep (from frozen) (6 fl oz)	40	0.0	0.0	0	5
Welch's Juice Cocktail, Fruit Punch (6 fl oz)	110	0.0	0.0	0	20
Welch's Juice Cocktail, Grape (6 fl oz)	110	0.0	0.0	0	20
Welch's Juice Cocktail, Grape, no sugar added, prep (from frozen) (6 fl oz)	40	0.0	0.0	0	0

Fruit-Flavored Beverages (continued)	Calories	Fat g	Saturated Fat g	Choles- terol mg	Sodium mg
Welch's Juice Cocktail, Tropical (6 fl oz)	110	0.0	0.0	0	20
Welch's Orchard Juice Cocktail, Apple Grape (bottle) (6 fl oz)	110	0.0	0.0	0	20
Welch's Orchard Juice Cocktail, Apple-Grape, prep (from frozen) (6 fl oz)	110	0.0	0.0	0	0
Welch's Orchard Juice Cocktail, Apple-Grape-Cherry, prep (from frozen) (6 fl oz)	110	0.0	0.0	0	0
Welch's Orchard Juice Cocktail, Apple-Grape-Raspberry, prep (from frozen) (6 fl oz)	110	0.0	0.0	0	0
Welch's Orchard Juice Cocktail, Apple-Orange-Pineapple (6 fl oz)	110	0.0	0.0	0	20
Welch's Orchard Juice Cocktail, Fruit Harvest Punch, prep (from frozen) (6 fl oz)	110	0.0	0.0	0	0
Welch's Orchard Juice Cocktail, Grape (6 fl oz)	110	0.0	0.0	0	20
Welch's Orchard Juice Cocktail, Harvest Blend (6 fl oz)	110	0.0	0.0	0	20
Welch's Orchard Juice Cocktail, Harvest Blend, prep (from frozen) (6 fl oz)	110	0.0	0.0	0	0
Welch's Orchard Tropical Drink, Passion Fruit (6 fl oz)	100	0.0	0.0	0	20
Welch's Tropical Drinks, Pineapple Banana (6 fl oz)	100	0.0	0.0	0	20
Wyler's Big Squeeze, Grape (8 fl oz)	95	0.0	0.0	(0)	21
Wyler's Big Squeeze, Orange (8 fl oz)	92	0.0	0.0	(0)	21
Wyler's Flavor Crystals, Tropical Punch (8 fl oz)	85	0.1	(0.0)	(0)	18
Wyler's Flavor Crystals, Wild Strawberry (8 fl oz)	85	0.3	(0.0)	(0)	43
Wyler's Fruit Punch (6 fl oz)	84	0.1	(0.0)	(0)	8
Wyler's Unsweetened Drink Mix, Citrus Burst Punch (1 pkt)	4	0.0	0.0	(0)	0

Fruit-Flavored Beverages (continued)	Calories	Fat g	Saturated Fat g	Choles- terol mg	Sodium mg
Wyler's Unsweetened Drink Mix, Fruit Punch (1 pkt)	3	0.0	0.0	(0)	27
Wyler's Unsweetened Drink Mix, Grape (1 pkt)	1	0.0	0.0	(0)	13
Wyler's Unsweetened Drink Mix, Lemonade (1 pkt)	5	0.0	0.0	(0)	18
Wyler's Unsweetened Drink Mix, Berry Burst Punch, Cherry, Black Cherry, or Raspberry (1 pkt)	2	0.0	0.0	(0)	0

INSTANT BREAKFAST MIXES

	Calories	Fat g	Saturated Fat g	Choles- terol mg	Sodium mg
Carnation Diet Instant Breakfast, Chocolate Malt, prep (w/8 fl oz skim milk) (1 env)	156	1.6	1.1	6	261
Carnation Diet Instant Breakfast, Chocolate, prep (w/8 fl oz skim milk) (1 env)	156	1.2	0.8	6	241
Carnation Diet Instant Breakfast, Strawberry, prep (w/8 fl oz skim milk) (1 env)	156	0.6	0.5	7	246
Carnation Diet Instant Breakfast, Vanilla, prep (w/8 fl oz skim milk) (1 env)	156	0.6	0.4	7	246
Carnation Instant Breakfast, Chocolate Malt, prep (w/8 fl oz skim milk) (1 env)	216	1.7	1.0	7	286
Carnation Instant Breakfast, Chocolate, prep (w/8 fl oz skim milk) (1 env)	216	1.3	0.8	6	261
Carnation Instant Breakfast, Coffee, prep (w/8 fl oz skim milk) (1 env)	216	0.6	0.4	7	276
Carnation Instant Breakfast, Strawberry, prep (w/8 fl oz skim milk) (1 env)	216	0.6	0.4	7	336
Carnation Instant Breakfast, Vanilla, prep (w/8 fl oz skim milk) (1 env)	216	0.6	0.4	7	261
Giant Instant Breakfast, Chocolate Malt, prep (w/skim milk) (8 fl oz)	210	1.0	(0.8)	5	260
Giant Instant Breakfast, Chocolate, prep (w/skim milk) (8 fl oz)	210	1.0	(0.8)	5	310

Instant Breakfast Mixes (continued)	Calories	Fat g	Saturated Fat g	Choles- terol mg	Sodium mg
Giant Instant Breakfast, Coffee, prep (w/skim milk) (8 fl oz)	220	1.0	(0.8)	5	270
Giant Instant Breakfast, Strawberry, prep (w/skim milk) (8 fl oz)	220	1.0	(0.4)	10	300
Giant Instant Breakfast, Vanilla, prep (w/skim milk) (8 fl oz)	220	1.0	(0.4)	5	290
Lucerne Instant Breakfast, Chocolate, prep (w/skim milk) (8 fl oz)	216	1.4	(0.9)	(7)	306
Lucerne Instant Breakfast, Coffee, prep (w/skim milk) (8 fl oz)	216	0.4	(0.3)	(7)	266
Lucerne Instant Breakfast, Strawberry, prep (w/skim milk) (8 fl oz)	216	0.4	(0.3)	(7)	296
Lucerne Instant Breakfast, Vanilla, prep (w/skim milk) (8 fl oz)	216	0.4	(0.3)	(7)	286
Pillsbury Instant Breakfast, Chocolate Malt, prep (w/skim milk) (8 fl oz)	216	<1.0	(<1.0)	(8)	346
Pillsbury Instant Breakfast, Chocolate, prep (w/skim milk) (8 fl oz)	216	<1.0	(<1.0)	(8)	326
Pillsbury Instant Breakfast, Strawberry, prep (w/skim milk) (8 fl oz)	216	<1.0	(<1.0)	(8)	306
Pillsbury Instant Breakfast, Vanilla, prep (w/skim milk) (8 fl oz)	226	<1.0	(<1.0)	(8)	336

MIXERS

	Calories	Fat g	Saturated Fat g	Choles- terol mg	Sodium mg
Bacardi Frozen Concentrated Tropical Fruit Mixers, Banana Daiquiri, prep (w/water only) (8 fl oz)	104	0.8	(0.2)	(0)	17
Bacardi Frozen Concentrated Tropical Fruit Mixers, Margarita Mix, prep (w/water only) (8 fl oz)	99	0.0	0.0	(0)	20
Bacardi Frozen Concentrated Tropical Fruit Mixers, Peach Daiquiri, prep (w/water only) (8 fl oz)	131	0.0	0.0	(0)	21

Mixers (continued)	Calories	Fat g	Saturated Fat g	Choles-terol mg	Sodium mg
Bacardi Frozen Concentrated Tropical Fruit Mixers, Raspberry Daiquiri, prep (w/water only) (8 fl oz)	187	0.0	0.0	(0)	20
Bacardi Frozen Concentrated Tropical Fruit Mixers, Strawberry Daiquiri, prep (w/water only) (8 fl oz)	139	0.0	0.0	(0)	20
Cragmont Collins Mix (6 fl oz)	58	0.0	0.0	(0)	35
Cragmont Tonic Mix, Diet (6 fl oz)	0	0.0	0.0	(0)	35
Libby's Bloody Mary Mix (6 fl oz)	40	0.0	0.0	(0)	1120

BREAD AND BREAD PRODUCTS

Bread products included in this section of the Guide are low in fat, saturated fat, and cholesterol *as purchased* or when *prepared according to package directions*. The levels of fat, saturated fat, and cholesterol in a serving of these foods, as listed below, do not exceed the following cutoff points.

CUTOFF POINTS FOR BREAD AND
BREAD PRODUCTS

Fat (grams)	Saturated Fat (grams)	Cholesterol (milligrams)
3	1	10

SERVINGS

Food	Serving Sizes
Breads:	
Bread	2 ounces
Breadsticks	1 ounce
English Muffin	2 ounces
Hamburger and Hot Dog Buns	2 ounces
Pita Bread	2 ounces
Tortilla	2 ounces
Bread Products:	
Bagel	2 ounces
Biscuit	2 ounces
Bread Crumbs and Coatings	1 ounce
Bread Mix, prepared	2 ounces
Cornbread	2 ounces
Croutons	⅓ ounce
Pancakes and French Toast	4 ounces*
Waffles	3 ounces*
Rolls, Dinner	2 ounces
Stuffing Mix, prepared	⅔ cup

*When the weight of a prepared product was not available for comparison to the stated serving size, the calories, fat, cholesterol, and sodium values for 1 serving as listed on the package were used for comparison.

Bread. Since so many brands of bread are low in fat, "most brands" is used for many of the entries in this section. The serving size used in the Guide for bread is 2 ounces. The number of slices equal to 2 ounces may vary from 1 thick slice to 2 "regular" slices to 4 or 5 very thin slices of bread. Some brands of bread are very light in weight, and it may take 4 to 5 slices of these breads to equal 2 ounces. Since the calories in a slice of bread depend on the size of the slice, 2 slices of a "diet" or "light" bread often contain the same number of calories as 1 regular slice of bread.

Bagels. Fresh or frozen bagels are usually low in fat. However, fillings or spreads added to bagels can increase their fat content. A wide variety of flavors is available in specialty shops, bakeries, and supermarkets.

Biscuits. Biscuits are usually high in fat because of the shortening, lard, or margarine used to prepare them. Biscuit mixes are either "complete" or "incomplete." Complete dry mixes contain fat and usually require only the addition of water to the mix. Incomplete mixes, which require the addition of fat, eggs, and/or milk during preparation, are usually preferred, since they allow you to use skim milk, egg white or egg substitute, and less oil (see page 214) or margarine (see page 211) in preparation. Reducing the amount of fat added to a mix may change the texture of the finished product.

Bread Mixes. Dry bread mixes containing little or no fat can be used to prepare a product that is low in fat by adding skim milk and less margarine (see page 211) or oil (see page 214) in preparation. A list of ingredients low in fat that can be substituted for ingredients containing more fat appears on page 401.

Bread Crumbs. Both dry and soft bread crumbs are included in the Guide if 1 ounce contains no more than the cutoff points for fat and saturated fat.

Breading Mixes. Although most plain varieties contain little fat, some seasoned breading mixes contain more fat than the cutoff point.

Cornbread. At the time of printing this Guide, no cornbread mixes have been identified that, when prepared according to package directions, are low enough in fat, saturated fat, and cholesterol to qualify for the Guide. A serving of cornbread often exceeds the cutoff point for cholesterol because of egg added to the mix. However, if egg substitute or egg white, skim milk, and less oil (see page 214) or margarine (see page 211) are used to prepare a mix that is low in fat, the prepared product may qualify for the Guide.

Croutons. Although many brands of croutons are sprayed with oil, some are low enough in fat not to exceed the cutoff points for fat and saturated fat listed in the Guide.

Pancakes, Waffles, and French Toast. When you prepare "incomplete" pancake and waffle mixes using egg substitute or egg white, skim milk, and oil or margarine, the prepared product is usually lower in fat, saturated fat, and cholesterol than in "complete" mixes, which call only for adding water. Some dry pancake and waffle mixes not listed in this Guide may not exceed the cutoff points if ingredients low in fat and cholesterol are used in preparation (page 401). Reducing the amount of fat added to a mix may change the texture of these products. A serving of frozen French toast included in the Guide does not exceed the stated cutoff points for fat, saturated fat, and cholesterol.

Rolls (dinner). French rolls and hard rolls contain little or no fat and are included in the Guide. Many ready-to-eat rolls not listed in the Guide are too high in fat because of the shortening, butter, lard, margarine, oil, and/or whole milk they contain and the butter or margarine used to brush their tops.

Stuffing Mixes. At the time of printing this Guide, no stuffing mixes have been identified that, when prepared according to package directions, are low enough in fat, saturated fat, and cholesterol to qualify for the Guide. When products that are lower in fat become available, they will be listed in revisions of the Guide. Some mixes low in fat that are not listed in the Guide may not exceed the cutoff points if the added fat called for in the package directions is reduced or omitted; this reduction may result in a different texture.

The following abbreviations are used in the Food Sections: oz = ounce; fl oz = fluid ounce; pkg = package; pkt = packet; env = envelope; g = gram; prep (w/ . . .) = prepared with; < = less than; and tr = trace.

Bread	Calories	Fat g	Saturated Fat g	Choles- terol mg	Sodium mg
BREAD					
BREAD					
Arnold Cinnamon Raisin Bread (1 slice)	67	1.4	(0.4)	2	86
Arnold Oatmeal Raisin Bread (1 slice)	58	0.7	(0.2)	0	91
B & M Brown Bread, Plain (1.6 oz)	92	0.0	0.0	0	345
B & M Brown Bread, Raisin (1.6 oz)	94	0.0	0.0	0	320
Beefsteak Rye Bread, Hearty (9/10 oz = 1 slice)	60	1.0	<1.0	0	170
Beefsteak Rye Bread, Onion (9/10 oz = 1 slice)	60	1.0	<1.0	0	170
Bran Bread—Most Brands (1 oz = 1 slice)	69	0.9	0.2	1	249
Bread Du Jour Austrian Wheat (1 oz = 1 slice)	70	1.0	<1.0	0	140
Bridgeford Bread Dough, Honey Wheat (1 oz)	80	1.0	(0.2)	0	150
Bridgeford Bread Dough, White (1 oz)	80	1.0	(0.3)	0	160
Brownberry Bran'nola Nutty Grains Bread (1 slice)	85	1.6	(0.3)	0	144
Brownberry Natural Oatmeal Bread (1 slice)	63	1.1	(0.3)	0	144

Bread (continued)	Calories	Fat g	Saturated Fat g	Choles- terol mg	Sodium mg
Brownberry Orange Raisin Bread (1 slice)	67	1.2	(0.3)	0	83
Brownberry Raisin Bran Bread (1 slice)	61	1.3	(0.3)	0	108
Brownberry Raisin Cinnamon Bread (1 slice)	66	1.3	(0.3)	0	107
Cinnamon Bread—Most Brands (1 oz = 1 slice)	77	0.9	0.2	1	144
Colonial Bread, Family Recipe Honey Buttered Split Top Wheat (1 oz = 1 slice)	70	1.0	(0.2)	0	150
Colonial Bread, Family Recipe Honey Buttered Split Top White (1 oz = 1 slice)	80	1.0	(0.3)	0	150
Colonial Bread, Family Recipe Honey Grain (1 oz = 1 slice)	70	1.0	(0.2)	0	180
Country Harvest Bread, Oat 'N' Honey (1 slice)	106	1.4	0.2	0	(195)
Country Harvest Bread, Oat Bran (2 slices)	186	3.2	0.8	0	(335)
Country Harvest Bread, Prairie Bran (1 slice)	83	1.4	0.2	0	(180)
Country Hearth Bread, Bran 'N Honey (1 oz = 1 slice)	70	1.0	(0.2)	(2)	160
Country Hearth Bread, European Butter Sesame (1 oz = 1 slice)	70	1.0	(0.3)	(2)	190
Country Hearth Bread, Grainola (1 oz = 1 slice)	70	1.0	(0.2)	(0)	240
Country Hearth Bread, Honey & Oat (1 oz = 1 slice)	70	1.0	(0.3)	(1)	180
Country Hearth Bread, Old Fashioned Buttermilk (1 oz = 1 slice)	70	1.0	(0.3)	(2)	190
Country Hearth Bread, Wheat Berry (1 oz = 1 slice)	70	1.0	(0.2)	(2)	160
Dicarlo's Parisian French (1 oz = 1 slice)	70	1.0	< 1.0	0	170
Diet Bread—Most Brands (1.2 oz = 2 slices)	92	1.1	0.3	1	172
Earth Grains Bread, Dill Rye (1 oz = 1 slice)	80	1.0	0.4	0	190
Earth Grains Bread, Extra Sour Rye (1 oz = 1 slice)	70	1.0	0.3	0	200

Bread (continued)	Calories	Fat g	Saturated Fat g	Choles- terol mg	Sodium mg
Earth Grains Bread, Honey Oat Bran (1 oz = 1 slice)	80	1.0	(0.3)	0	105
Earth Grains Bread, Honey Oatberry (1 oz = 1 slice)	70	1.0	(0.2)	0	135
Earth Grains Bread, Honey Wheat Berry (1 oz = 1 slice)	70	1.0	(0.2)	0	160
Earth Grains Bread, Salt Free Sandwich (1 oz = 1 slice)	80	1.0	(0.3)	0	20
French Bread—Most Brands (1 oz = 1 slice)	82	0.9	0.2	0	162
Giant Bakery Bread, Buttermilk (2 oz = 2 slices)	150	2.0	(0.5)	0	360
Giant Bakery Bread, English Raisin (1 slice)	130	2.0	(0.5)	0	100
Giant Bakery Bread, Oat Bran (2 oz = 2 slices)	160	3.0	(0.9)	0	290
Giant Bakery Bread, Raisin, No Salt Added (2 oz = 2 slices)	150	2.0	(0.5)	0	20
Giant Bakery Bread, Sourdough French Style (2 oz = 2 slices)	140	1.0	(0.2)	0	240
Giant Bakery Bread, Vienna (2 oz = 2 slices)	140	1.0	(0.2)	0	255
Giant Bakery Hearty Grain Bread, Granola (2 oz = 2 slices)	160	3.0	(0.6)	0	270
Giant Bakery Hearty Grain Bread, Honey Oatmeal (2 oz = 2 slices)	150	3.0	(0.9)	0	290
Grant's Farm Bread, Buttermilk (1 oz = 1 slice)	80	1.0	(0.3)	0	190
Grant's Farm Bread, Honey Cracked Rye (1 oz = 1 slice)	70	1.0	(0.4)	0	190
Grant's Farm Bread, Honey Wheat Bran (1 oz = 1 slice)	70	1.0	(0.2)	0	120
Grant's Farm Bread, Wheatberry (1 oz = 1 slice)	70	1.0	(0.2)	0	150
Home Pride Honey Buttertop Wheat Bread (1-3/10 oz = 1 slice)	100	2.0	< 1.0	< 5	210
Italian Bread—Most Brands (1 oz = 1 slice)	77	0.2	0.0	(0)	(164)
Kilpatrick's Bread, Family Recipe Honey Buttered Split Top Wheat (1 oz = 1 slice)	70	1.0	(0.2)	0	150

Bread (continued)	Calories	Fat g	Saturated Fat g	Choles- terol mg	Sodium mg
Kilpatrick's Bread, Family Recipe Honey Buttered Split Top White (1 oz = 1 slice)	80	1.0	(0.3)	0	150
Kilpatrick's Bread, Family Recipe Honey Grain (1 oz = 1 slice)	70	1.0	(0.2)	0	180
Kilpatrick's Bread, Honey Grain (1 oz = 1 slice)	70	1.0	(0.2)	0	170
Light, Lite, Thin, Very Thin-Type Bread—Most Brands (1.2 oz = 2 slices)	92	1.1	0.3	1	172
Mrs. Wright's Onion Hot Bread (2 oz = 2 sections)	160	3.0	(0.8)	(2)	220
Multi-Grain and 7-Grain Bread—Most Brands (1 oz = 1 slice)	69	0.9	0.2	1	149
Oatmeal Goodness Light, Bran (8/10 oz = 1 slice)	40	<1.0	<1.0	0	95
Oatmeal Goodness Light, Wheat (8/10 oz = 1 slice)	40	<1.0	<1.0	0	90
Oatmeal Goodness, Oatmeal/Bran (1-2/10 oz = 1 slice)	80	1.0	<1.0	0	150
Oatmeal Goodness, Oatmeal/Sunflower Seeds (1-2/10 oz = 1 slice)	80	1.0	<1.0	0	150
Oatmeal Goodness, Oatmeal/Wheat (1-2/10 oz = 1 slice)	80	1.0	<1.0	0	150
Pepperidge Farm Bread, Honey Bran (1 slice)	90	1.0	(0.2)	0	160
Pepperidge Farm Bread, Sesame Wheat Bread (2 slices)	190	3.0	1.0	0	340
Pepperidge Farm Hearth Bread, Brown 'N Serve Italian Enriched (1 oz)	80	1.0	1.0	0	150
Pepperidge Farm Hearth Bread, Vienna Thick Sliced Enriched (1 slice)	70	1.0	0.0	0	125
Pepperidge Farm Light Style Bread, Vienna (1 slice)	45	0.0	0.0	0	100
Pepperidge Farm Light Style, Oatmeal (1 slice)	45	0.0	0.0	0	95

Bread (continued)	Calories	Fat g	Saturated Fat g	Choles- terol mg	Sodium mg
Pumpernickel Bread—Most Brands (1 oz = 1 slice)	69	0.4	0.1	(0)	159
Rainbo Bread, Family Recipe Honey Buttered Split Top Wheat (1 oz = 1 slice)	70	1.0	(0.2)	0	150
Rainbo Bread, Family Recipe Honey Buttered Split Top White (1 oz = 1 slice)	80	1.0	(0.3)	0	150
Rainbo Bread, Family Recipe Honey Grain (1 oz = 1 slice)	70	1.0	(0.2)	0	180
Raisin Bread—Most Brands (1 oz = 1 slice)	68	0.8	0.2	1	102
Rubschlager 100% Stone Ground Whole Wheat (1 oz = 1 slice)	70	1.0	(0.2)	0	130
Rubschlager Danish Pumpernickel (1 oz = 1 slice)	70	< 1.0	(0.0)	0	140
Rubschlager German Style Kommissbrot (1 oz = 1 slice)	70	1.0	(0.1)	0	150
Rubschlager Raisin Pumpernickel (3/4 oz = 1 slice)	60	< 1.0	(0.0)	0	105
Rubschlager Swedish Limpa Rye (3/4 oz = 1 slice)	60	1.0	(0.1)	0	95
Rubschlager Westphalian Pumpernickel (1 oz = 1 slice)	70	< 1.0	(0.0)	0	130
Rye Bread—Most Brands (1 oz = 1 slice)	68	0.3	(0.1)	(0)	156
Sourdough Bread—Most Brands (1 oz = 1 slice)	78	0.3	0.1	0	166
Stonehouse Farm Bread, Honey Bran (1 slice)	91	1.4	(0.3)	(0)	(185)
Stonehouse Farm Bread, Oat 'N' Fibre (1 slice)	97	1.3	0.4	0	(170)
Stonehouse Farm Bread, Potato Scone (1 slice)	90	0.8	(0.2)	(0)	(195)
White Bread—Most Brands (1 oz = 1 slice)	76	0.9	0.2	(1)	142
Whole-Grain Bread—Most Brands (1 oz = 1 slice)	68	0.9	0.1	1	148
Wonder Light, Italian (8/10 oz = 1 slice)	40	0.0	0.0	0	115
Wonder Light, Sourdough (8/10 oz = 1 slice)	40	0.0	0.0	0	115

Bread (continued)	Calories	Fat g	Saturated Fat g	Choles- terol mg	Sodium mg
BREADSTICKS					
Angonoa Breadsticks, Cheese (1 oz)	110	2.0	(1.0)	0	210
Angonoa Breadsticks, Garlic (1 oz)	120	2.0	(1.0)	0	160
Angonoa Breadsticks, Italian (1 oz)	120	2.0	(1.0)	0	240
Angonoa Breadsticks, Mini Cheese (1 oz)	110	2.0	(1.0)	0	160
Angonoa Breadsticks, Mini Pizza (1 oz)	120	2.0	(1.0)	0	220
Barbara's Bakery Breadsticks (1 oz = 8 sticks)	120	3.0	(1.5)	0	(220)
Breadsticks—Most Brands, 7-3/4" × 3/4" diam (5 breadsticks)	69	0.2	0.0	0	146
Fattorie & Pandea Grissini Breadsticks, Pizza (1/2 oz = 3 sticks)	59	1.0	(0.1)	(0)	100
Fattorie & Pandea Grissini Breadsticks, Sesame (1/2 oz = 3 sticks)	65	2.0	(0.3)	(0)	100
Fattorie & Pandea Grissini Breadsticks, Traditional (1/2 oz = 3 sticks)	60	1.0	(0.1)	(0)	100
Fattorie & Pandea Grissini Breadsticks, Whole Wheat (1/2 oz = 3 sticks)	57	1.0	(0.1)	(0)	100
Giant Breadsticks, Sesame (.5 oz = 3 sticks)	60	<1.0	<1.0	0	(60)
Pillsbury Breadsticks (1 breadstick)	100	2.0	<1.0	0	230
Roman Meal Breadsticks, Refrigerated (1 breadstick)	117	3.9*	1.2	0	274
ENGLISH MUFFINS					
Amana English Muffins, Apple Cinnamon (1/2 muffin)	41	0.0	0.0	(0)	105
Amana English Muffins, Blueberry (1/2 muffin)	56	0.0	0.0	(0)	105
Amana English Muffins, Honey Wheat (1/2 muffin)	47	0.0	0.0	(0)	105
Arnold Extra Crisp Muffins (1 muffin)	122	1.4	(0.2)	0	233

*The value printed for fat is higher than the cutoff point because the manufacturer's serving size is larger than the standard serving size used in evaluating the food.

Bread (continued)	Calories	Fat g	Saturated Fat g	Choles- terol mg	Sodium mg
Arnold Raisin Muffins (1 muffin)	149	1.4	(0.2)	0	222
Arnold Sourdough Muffins (1 muffin)	124	1.3	(0.2)	0	247
Crystal Farms English Muffins, Oat Bran (2 oz)	130	0.8	(0.1)	(0)	260
Crystal Farms English Muffins, Raisin (2 oz)	130	<1.0	(0.0)	(0)	100
Earth Grains English Muffins, Oat Bran (2 oz=1 muffin)	120	1.0	0.4	0	410
Earth Grains English Muffins, Plain or Sourdough (2 oz=1 muffin)	120	1.0	0.2	0	390
Earth Grains English Muffins, Raisin (2.3 oz=1 muffin)	160	2.0	0.3	0	300
Earth Grains English Muffins, Wheatberry (2.3 oz=1 muffin)	140	1.0	0.4	0	470
Earth Grains English Muffins, Whole Wheat (2.3 oz=1 muffin)	130	1.0	0.4	0	420
English Muffins, Plain—Most Brands (1 muffin)	137	1.1	0.2	1	298
Giant Bakery English Muffins, Honey Bran (2.5 oz=1 muffin)	150	0.0	0.0	0	250
Giant Bakery English Muffins, Oat Bran (2 oz=1 muffin)	110	0.0	0.0	0	190
Giant Bakery English Muffins, Raisin (2.6 oz=1 muffin)	190	2.0	(0.3)	0	235
Giant Bakery English Muffins, Regular (2 oz=1 muffin)	130	1.0	(0.1)	0	210
Giant Bakery English Muffins, Sourdough (2 oz=1 muffin)	190	2.0	(0.2)	0	240
IGA English Muffins (2 oz)	130	1.0	(0.1)	0	(290)
IGA English Muffins, Oat Bran (2 oz)	120	1.0	(0.2)	0	(150)
Oatmeal Goodness English Muffins, Cinnamon Raisin (1 muffin)	140	2.0	<1.0	0	190
Oatmeal Goodness English Muffins, Honey and Oatmeal (1 muffin)	140	2.0	<1.0	0	210

Bread (continued)	Calories	Fat g	Saturated Fat g	Choles- terol mg	Sodium mg
Pepperidge Farm English Muffins, Cinnamon Apple (1 muffin)	140	1.0	0.0	0	210
Pepperidge Farm English Muffins, Cinnamon Chip (1 muffin)	160	3.0	0.0	0	180
Pepperidge Farm English Muffins, Cinnamon Raisin (1 muffin)	150	2.0	0.0	0	200
Pepperidge Farm English Muffins, Plain (1 muffin)	140	1.0	0.0	0	220
Pepperidge Farm English Muffins, Sourdough (1 muffin)	135	1.0	0.0	0	260
Roman Meal English Muffins, Honey Nut & Oat Bran, Refrigerated (1/2 muffin)	81	1.3	0.2	0	114
Roman Meal English Muffins, Original (1 muffin)	126	0.7	0.1	0	294
Roman Meal English Muffins, Refrigerated (1/2 muffin)	71	0.5	0.1	0	88
Sun Maid English Muffins, Raisin (2.5 oz = 1 muffin)	160	1.0	0.4	0	180
Thomas' English Muffins, Honey Wheat (1 muffin)	128	1.4	(0.2)	(<1)	199
Thomas' English Muffins, Oat Bran (1 muffin)	116	1.2	(0.2)	0	192
Thomas' English Muffins, Raisin with Cinnamon (1 muffin)	151	1.3	(0.2)	(<1)	183
Thomas' English Muffins, Regular (1 muffin)	130	1.3	(0.2)	(<1)	206
Thomas' English Muffins, Sour Dough (1 muffin)	131	1.3	(0.2)	(<1)	210
Wolferman's Crumpets, Brown Sugar Cinnamon (1 crumpet)	110	2.0	(0.3)	0	220
Wolferman's Crumpets, Buttermilk (1 crumpet)	100	<1.0	(0.0)	0	230
Wolferman's Deluxe English Muffins (1/2 muffin)	120	1.0	(0.1)	0	219
Wolferman's Deluxe English Muffins, Apple Strudel (1/2 muffin)	110	2.0	(0.3)	0	220

Bread (continued)	Calories	Fat g	Saturated Fat g	Choles- terol mg	Sodium mg
Wolferman's Deluxe English Muffins, Cinnamon Raisin (1/2 muffin)	110	<1.0	(0.0)	0	229
Wolferman's Deluxe English Muffins, Sourdough (1/2 muffin)	110	<1.0	(0.0)	0	281
Wonder English Muffins, Sourdough (1 muffin)	120	1.0	<1.0	0	240
HAMBURGER AND HOT DOG BUNS					
Arnold Bran'nola Natural Buns (1 bun)	99	0.8	(0.2)	0	164
Giant Hamburger Buns, Wheat (1.3 oz = 1 bun)	100	2.0	(0.5)	0	160
Hamburger Bun, Small, 3″ diam—Most Brands (1.4 oz = 1 bun)	119	2.2	0.5	(1)	202
Hot Dog Bun, Small, 3-3/4″ long—Most Brands (1.4 oz = 1 bun)	119	2.2	0.5	(1)	202
Pepperidge Farm Frankfurter Rolls with Poppy Seeds (1 roll)	130	2.0	1.0	0	280
Pepperidge Farm Sandwich Rolls, Onion, Sliced Sandwich Buns with Poppy Seeds (1 roll)	150	3.0	1.0	0	260
Wonder Buns, Honey Wheat (1 bun)	130	2.0	<1.0	0	230
Wonder Buns, Light Hamburger (1 bun)	80	1.0	<1.0	0	210
Wonder Buns, Light Hot Dog (1 bun)	80	1.0	<1.0	0	210
PITA BREAD					
Athens Mini Pita Hi Fiber (1 pita)	70	0.0	0.0	(<3)	105
Athens Mini Pita Onion (1 pita)	80	0.0	0.0	(<3)	90
Athens Mini Pita Sourdough (1 pita)	80	0.0	0.0	(<3)	105
Giant Pita Pocket, Cinnamon Raisin (2 oz = 2 mini pitas)	160	0.0	0.0	0	240
Giant Pita Pocket, Onion (2 oz = 2 mini pitas)	140	0.0	0.0	0	200

Bread (continued)	Calories	Fat g	Saturated Fat g	Choles- terol mg	Sodium mg
Giant Pita Pocket, White Salt Free (2 oz = 2 mini pitas)	160	0.0	0.0	0	0
White Pita, Large, 6-1/2" diam—Most Brands (3 oz = 1 pita)	240	0.8	0.1	0	405
White Pita, Medium, 5-1/4" diam—Most Brands (1.6 oz = 1 pita)	127	0.4	0.1	0	215
White Pita, Small, 4" diam—Most Brands (1 oz = 1 pita)	79	0.3	0.0	0	134
Whole Wheat or Seasoned Pita, Large, 6-1/2" diam—Most Brands (3 oz = 1 pita)	236	1.3	0.2	0	480
Whole Wheat or Seasoned Pita, Medium, 5-1/4" diam—Most Brands (1.6 oz = 1 pita)	125	0.7	0.1	0	254
Whole Wheat or Seasoned Pita, Small, 4" diam—Most Brands (1 oz = 1 pita)	78	0.4	0.1	0	158
TORTILLAS					
Tortilla, Corn—Most Brands (.8 oz = 1 tortilla)	38	0.7	0.1	(0)	30

BREAD PRODUCTS

	Calories	Fat g	Saturated Fat g	Choles- terol mg	Sodium mg
BAGELS					
Bagels, Plain—Most Brands (1 small)	150	1.4	0.2	(0)	206
Food Club Bagels, Cinnamon Raisin with Honey (1 bagel)	200	1.0	(0.2)	0	310
Food Club Bagels, Egg (1 bagel)	160	1.0	(0.1)	5	330
Food Club Bagels, Onion (1 bagel)	150	1.0	(0.2)	0	330
Food Club Bagels, Plain (1 bagel)	150	1.0	(0.2)	0	330
Giant Bagelette, Plain, frozen (1.8 oz = 2 bagels)	140	1.0	(0.2)	0	340
Lender's Bagelettes, Cinnamon'n Raisin (.9 oz)	70	1.0	(0.2)	0	115
Lender's Bagelettes, Onion (.9 oz)	70	<1.0	(0.0)	0	110

Bread Products (continued)	Calories	Fat g	Saturated Fat g	Choles- terol mg	Sodium mg
Lender's Bagelettes, Plain (.9 oz)	70	< 1.0	(0.0)	0	130
Lender's Bagels, Blueberry (2.5 oz)	190	2.0	(0.3)	0	320
Lender's Bagels, Cinnamon'n Raisin (2.5 oz)	190	2.0	(0.3)	0	310
Lender's Bagels, Egg (2 oz)	150	1.0	(0.1)	0	310
Lender's Bagels, Garlic (2 oz)	140	1.0	(0.2)	0	280
Lender's Bagels, Oat Bran (2 oz)	170	2.0	(0.4)	0	300
Lender's Bagels, Onion (2 oz)	150	1.0	(0.2)	0	300
Lender's Bagels, Plain (2 oz)	150	1.0	(0.2)	0	320
Lender's Bagels, Poppy Seed (2 oz)	140	1.0	(0.2)	0	290
Lender's Bagels, Pumpernickel (2 oz)	140	1.0	(0.1)	0	330
Lender's Bagels, Rye (2 oz)	140	1.0	(0.1)	0	320
Lender's Bagels, Sesame Seed (2 oz)	150	1.0	(0.2)	0	280
Lender's Bagels, Soft Original (2 oz)	200	3.0	(0.5)	10	340
Lender's Big'n Crusty Bagels, Cinnamon'n Raisin (3 oz)	230	2.0	(0.3)	0	330
Lender's Big'n Crusty Bagels, Egg (3 oz)	210	1.0	(0.1)	0	400
Lender's Big'n Crusty Bagels, Garlic (3 oz)	210	1.0	(0.2)	0	420
Lender's Big'n Crusty Bagels, Onion (3 oz)	210	1.0	(0.2)	0	410
Lender's Big'n Crusty Bagels, Plain (3 oz)	210	2.0	(0.3)	0	430
Sara Lee Bagels, Cinnamon Raisin (1 bagel)	200	2.0	(0.3)	0	230
Sara Lee Bagels, Egg (1 bagel)	200	2.0	(0.2)	15	360
Sara Lee Bagels, Oat Bran (1 bagel)	180	1.0	(0.2)	0	360
Sara Lee Bagels, Onion (1 bagel)	190	1.0	(0.2)	0	450
Sara Lee Bagels, Plain (1 bagel)	190	1.0	(0.2)	0	460
Sara Lee Bagels, Poppy Seed (1 bagel)	190	1.0	(0.2)	0	450

Bread Products (continued)	Calories	Fat g	Saturated Fat g	Choles- terol mg	Sodium mg
Sara Lee Bagels, Sesame Seed (1 bagel)	190	1.0	(0.2)	0	440
Sara Lee Deli Style Bagels, Cinnamon Raisin (1 bagel)	240	2.0	(0.2)	0	280
Sara Lee Deli Style Bagels, Onion (1 bagel)	230	1.0	(0.2)	0	630
Sara Lee Deli Style Bagels, Plain (1 bagel)	230	1.0	(0.2)	0	540
Sara Lee Deli Style Bagels, Poppy Seed (1 bagel)	230	1.0	(0.2)	0	580
Sara Lee Deli Style Bagels, Sesame Seed (1 bagel)	260	3.0	(0.5)	0	570

BISCUITS

	Calories	Fat g	Saturated Fat g	Choles- terol mg	Sodium mg
Ballard Extra Lights Ovenready Biscuits (1 biscuit)	50	< 1.0	0.0	0	180
Ballard Extra Ready Ovenready Buttermilk Biscuits (1 biscuit)	50	< 1.0	0.0	0	180
Hungry Jack Extra Rich Buttermilk Biscuits (1 biscuit)	50	1.0	0.0	0	180
IGA Buttermilk Biscuits (2 biscuits)	100	1.0	(0.3)	0	(340)
IGA Homestyle Biscuits (2 biscuits)	100	1.0	(0.3)	0	(340)
Pillsbury Butter Biscuits (1 biscuit)	50	< 1.0	0.0	0	180
Pillsbury Buttermilk Biscuits (1 biscuit)	50	1.0	0.0	0	180
Pillsbury Country Biscuits (1 biscuit)	50	1.0	0.0	0	180
Pillsbury Tender Layer Buttermilk Biscuits (1 biscuit)	50	1.0	0.0	0	170
Roman Meal Biscuits, Mixed Grain, refrigerated (2 biscuits)	180	3.8	0.9	0	456

BREAD CRUMBS AND COATINGS

	Calories	Fat g	Saturated Fat g	Choles- terol mg	Sodium mg
A&P Bread Crumbs, Flavored (1/2 oz)	50	1.0	(0.2)	(0)	244
A&P Bread Crumbs, Plain (1/2 oz)	50	1.0	(0.3)	(1)	104
Contadina Bread Crumbs, Seasoned (1 tbsp)	35	< 1.0	(< .3)	1	250
Devonsheer Bread Crumbs, Plain (1 oz)	108	1.4	(0.4)	0	272

Bread Products (continued)	Calories	Fat g	Saturated Fat g	Choles- terol mg	Sodium mg
Giant Bread Crumbs, Plain (1/2 oz)	50	1.0	<1.0	0	130
IGA Bread Crumbs, Italian Style (.5 oz)	50	1.0	(0.3)	(<1)	(105)
IGA Bread Crumbs, Plain (.5 oz)	50	1.0	(0.3)	(<1)	(105)
Kellogg's Corn Flakes Crumbs (1 oz)	100	0.0	0.0	0	290
Kellogg's Croutettes (.7 oz)	70	0.0	0.0	0	260
Mrs. Dash, Crispy Coating Mix (17 g)	(60)	0.1	(0.0)	0	3
Old London Bread Crumbs, Italian Style (1/2 oz)	50	<1.0	0.0	0	200
Old London Bread Crumbs, Plain (1/2 oz)	50	<1.0	0.0	0	80
Progresso Bread Crumbs, Italian Style (2 tbsp)	60	<1.0	(0.0)	0	240
Progresso Bread Crumbs, Plain (2 tbsp)	60	<1.0	(0.0)	0	110
Shake 'N Bake Seasoning Mixture, Original Barbecue Recipe for Pork (1/8 pouch)	40	1.0	(0.3)	0	350
Shake 'N Bake Seasoning Mixture, Original Recipe for Chicken (1/4 pouch)	80	2.0	(0.5)	0	450
Shake 'N Bake Seasoning Mixture, Original Recipe for Fish (1/4 pouch)	70	1.0	(0.3)	0	410
Shake 'N Bake Seasoning Mixture, Original Recipe for Pork (1/8 pouch)	40	1.0	(0.3)	0	310
Tone's Bread Crumbs, Italian (1 tsp)	8	0.1	0.0	0	15
Tone's Bread Crumbs, plain (1 tsp)	8	0.1	0.0	0	15
Tone's Cajun Chicken Batter (1 tsp)	12	0.1	0.0	0	75
Tone's Cajun Fish Batter (1 tsp)	12	0.1	0.0	0	49
Tone's Corn Flake Crumbs (1 tsp)	2	<1.0	0.0	0	6
CROUTONS					
Arnold Crispy Croutons, Cheese Garlic (1/2 oz)	60	2.2	(1.9)	1	133

Bread Products (continued)	Calories	Fat g	Saturated Fat g	Choles- terol mg	Sodium mg
Arnold Crispy Croutons, Fine Herbs (1/2 oz)	53	0.8	(0.7)	0	151
Brownberry Croutons, Caesar Salad (1/2 oz)	60	3.0	(0.4)	0	170
Brownberry Croutons, Cheese & Garlic (1/2 oz)	60	3.0	(0.4)	0	160
Brownberry Croutons, Onion and Garlic (1/2 oz)	60	2.2	(1.9)	1	190
Brownberry Croutons, Ranch (1/2 oz)	60	2.0	(0.3)	0	180
Brownberry Croutons, Seasoned (1/2 oz)	59	2.2	(1.9)	1	155
Brownberry Croutons, Toasted (1/2 oz)	56	1.4	(1.2)	0	145
Giant Crouton Cubes, Plain (1/2 oz)	50	< 1.0	< 1.0	0	125
Giant Crouton Cubes, Seasoned (1/2 oz)	50	< 1.0	< 1.0	0	125
Giant Croutons, Seasoned (1/2 oz)	60	2.0	< 1.0	0	180
Keebler Croutons, Herb Seasoned (1/2 oz)	59	2.2	(1.9)	1	155
Pepperidge Farm Croutons, Cheddar and Romano Cheese (1/2 oz)	60	2.0	0.0	0	200
Pepperidge Farm Croutons, Cheese and Garlic (1/2 oz)	70	3.0	1.0	0	180
Pepperidge Farm Croutons, Onion and Garlic (1/2 oz)	70	3.0	0.0	0	160
Pepperidge Farm Croutons, Seasoned (1/2 oz)	70	3.0	1.0	0	180
Pepperidge Farm Croutons, Seasoned (1/2 oz)	70	3.0	1.0	0	210
Pepperidge Farm Croutons, Sour Cream and Chive (1/2 oz)	70	3.0	1.0	0	170
Pepperidge Farm Home Style Croutons, Classic Caesar (1/2 oz)	70	3.0	1.0	0	180
Pepperidge Farm Home Style Croutons, Sourdough Cheese (1/2 oz)	70	2.0	1.0	< 5	160
Pepperidge Farm Home Style Croutons, Zesty Italian (1/2 oz)	70	3.0	1.0	0	170

Bread Products (continued)	Calories	Fat g	Saturated Fat g	Choles- terol mg	Sodium mg
PANCAKES, WAFFLES, AND FRENCH TOAST					
Aunt Jemima Lite Healthy Waffles, frozen (1 waffle)	60	1.0	(0.1)	0	240
Aunt Jemima Pancake Mix, Lite Buttermilk Complete (3 4" pancakes)	130	2.0	(0.3)	10	570
Featherweight Complete Pancake Mix, prep (w/water) (3 4" pancakes)	140	2.0	(0.3)	5	90
Hungry Jack Pancake Mixes, Buttermilk Complete, prep (w/water) (3 4" pancakes)	180	1.0	<1.0	5	720
Kellogg's Special K Waffles, Fat Free, Cholesterol Free (1 waffle)	80	0.0	0.0	0	200
Krusteaz Pancake Mix, Buttermilk, prep (w/water) (3 4" pancakes)	200	3.0	(0.5)	(5)	770
Krusteaz Pancake Mix, Oat Bran Lite Complete, prep (w/water) (3 4" pancakes)	130	1.0	(0.2)	0	370
Krusteaz Pancake Mix, Whole Wheat and Honey, prep (w/water) (3 4" pancakes)	215	1.0	(0.3)	(5)	630
Pillsbury Extra Lights Complete Pancake Mix prep (w/water) (3 4" pancakes)	180	3.0	0.0	0	730
Pillsbury Extra Lights Pre-Measured Packets Pancake Mix prep (w/water) (3 4" pancakes)	180	3.0	<1.0	0	650
Weight Watchers Pancakes with Blueberry Topping (4.75 oz)	200	3.0	1.0	10	300
Weight Watchers Pancakes with Strawberry Topping (4.75 oz)	200	3.0	1.0	10	360
ROLLS					
Arnold Francisco Kaiser Rolls (1 roll)	184	2.9	(0.7)	5	338
Arnold Soft Sandwich Rolls (1 roll)	110	2.3	(0.6)	1	194
Bread Du Jour Rolls, Bavarian Wheat (1 roll)	80	1.0	<1.0	0	180

Bread Products (continued)	Calories	Fat g	Saturated Fat g	Choles- terol mg	Sodium mg
Bread Du Jour Rolls, Crusty Italian (1 roll)	80	1.0	< 1.0	0	190
Dicarlo's Rolls, French (1 roll)	180	2.0	< 1.0	0	390
Dicarlo's Rolls, Sourdough (1 roll)	200	3.0	< 1.0	0	310
Earth Grains Rolls, French (1 roll)	100	1.0	(0.2)	0	270
Earth Grains Rolls, Kaiser (1 roll)	190	2.0	(0.5)	0	520
Earth Grains Rolls, Onion (1 roll)	490	2.0	(0.3)	0	53
Earth Grains Rolls, Sourdough French (1 roll)	100	1.0	(0.2)	0	160
Earth Grains Rolls, Submarine (1 roll)	180	1.0	(0.3)	0	500
Earth Grains Rolls, Wheat (1 roll)	110	1.0	(0.2)	0	260
Francisco International French Rolls (1.4 oz = 1 roll)	108	1.5	(0.2)	0	285
Francisco International French Rolls (2.3 oz = 1 roll)	183	2.6	(0.4)	0	484
Giant Bakery Rolls, Blunt Hard (1 roll)	120	1.0	(0.3)	0	280
Giant Rolls, Caddies (1 roll)	110	1.0	(0.3)	0	210
Giant Rolls, Cloverleaf Brown 'N Serve (2 rolls)	140	2.0	(0.6)	5	320
Giant Rolls, Dinner Party (1.3 oz = 2 rolls)	100	2.0	(0.5)	5	190
Giant Rolls, Hard (2 oz = 1 roll)	150	2.0	(0.6)	0	250
Giant Rolls, Oat Bran (1.3 oz = 1 roll)	90	2.0	(0.4)	0	95
Giant Rolls, Party Flake Brown 'N Serve (2 rolls)	140	2.0	(0.6)	5	320
Giant Rolls, Potato (1.3 oz = 1 roll)	100	2.0	(0.6)	0	180
Giant Rolls, Sesame Seed (1.3 oz = 1 roll)	90	2.0	(0.5)	0	190
Giant Rolls, Sourdough Club (1 roll)	100	1.0	(0.2)	0	180
Giant Rolls, Sourdough French (1/2 roll)	160	2.0	(< 1.0)	0	320
Giant Rolls, Split Top (2 rolls)	200	2.0	(0.5)	0	280

Bread Products (continued)	Calories	Fat g	Saturated Fat g	Choles- terol mg	Sodium mg
Giant Rolls, Twist (1.5 oz = 1 roll)	110	2.0	(0.5)	0	160
Giant Rolls, Twist with Poppy Seeds (1.5 oz = 1 roll)	110	2.0	(0.5)	0	150
Giant Rolls, Wheat Brown 'N Serve (2 rolls)	140	2.0	(0.4)	0	260
Levy's Old Country Deli Rolls, Egg (1 roll)	146	2.8	(0.9)	11	431
Levy's Old Country Deli Rolls, Kaiser (1 roll)	170	2.7	(0.7)	5	312
Levy's Old Country Deli Rolls, Onion (1 roll)	153	1.9	(0.5)	11	380
Levy's Old Country Deli Rolls, Sub (1 roll)	163	2.3	(0.6)	0	388
Mrs. Wright's Blunt Rolls (1 roll)	150	2.0	(0.5)	(3)	(295)
Mrs. Wright's Brown and Serve Rolls, Sesame Seeds (1 roll)	90	1.0	(0.3)	0	160
Mrs. Wright's Deli Krisp Rolls (1 roll)	120	2.0	(0.5)	(2)	(196)
Mrs. Wright's Enriched Banquet Rolls (1 roll)	90	1.0	(0.3)	0	160
Mrs. Wright's French Rolls, Sesame (2 oz)	145	3.0	(0.5)	(1)	145
Mrs. Wright's Italian Rolls (1 roll)	150	2.0	(0.3)	(1)	(355)
Mrs. Wright's Junior Sub Rolls (1 roll)	220	3.0	(0.8)	(3)	335
Mrs. Wright's Kaiser Rolls, all varieties (1 roll)	150	2.0	(0.5)	(2)	(355)
Mrs. Wright's Old Fashioned Potato Rolls (1 roll)	100	1.0	(0.3)	0	190
Mrs. Wright's Seeded Steak Rolls (1 roll)	220	2.0	(0.5)	(4)	(366)
Mrs. Wright's Soft Sandwich Rolls (1 roll)	110	2.0	(0.5)	(1)	196
Mrs. Wright's Split Top Dinner Rolls (1 roll)	80	1.0	(0.3)	(2)	(165)
Mrs. Wright's Sub Rolls (1 roll)	310	4.0*	(1.0)	(4)	(560)
Mrs. Wright's Tea Rolls (1 roll)	70	1.0	(0.3)	0	150

*The value printed for fat is higher than the cutoff point because the manufacturer's serving size is larger than the standard serving size used in evaluating the food.

Bread Products (continued)	Calories	Fat g	Saturated Fat g	Choles- terol mg	Sodium mg
Mrs. Wright's Wheat Berry Rolls (1 roll)	150	2.0	(0.5)	0	340
Pepperidge Farm Deli Classic Rolls, French Style Enriched (4/pkg) (1.3 oz = 1/2 roll)	120	2.0	(0.0)	(0)	250
Pepperidge Farm Deli Classic Rolls, French Style Enriched (9/pkg) (1.3 oz = 1 roll)	100	1.0	0.0	0	230
Pepperidge Farm Deli Classic Rolls, Sourdough Style French Enriched (1.3 oz = 1 roll)	100	1.0	0.0	0	240
Pepperidge Farm Deli Classic Rolls, Brown 'N Serve, Hearth Enriched (.7 oz = 1 roll)	50	1.0	0.0	0	100
Pepperidge Farm Deli Classic Rolls, Brown 'N Serve, French Enriched (2/pkg) (2.5 oz = 1/2 roll)	180	2.0	1.0	0	380
Pepperidge Farm Deli Classic Rolls, Brown 'N Serve, French Enriched (3/pkg) (1.7 oz = 1/2 roll)	120	1.0	0.0	0	250
Pepperidge Farm Deli Classic Rolls, Brown 'N Serve, Club Enriched (1.3 oz = 1 roll)	100	1.0	0.0	0	190
Pepperidge Farm Dinner Rolls, Soft Family Enriched (1.2 oz = 1 roll)	100	2.0	1.0	0	190
Pepperidge Farm Dinner Rolls, Country Style Classic (.7 oz = 1 roll)	50	1.0	0.0	0	90
Pepperidge Farm Dinner Rolls, Parker House, Enriched (.6 oz = 1 roll)	60	1.0	0.0	5	80
Rolls, Hard, 3-3/4" diameter × 2" high—Most Brands (1 roll)	156	1.6	0.4	(2)	313
Roman Meal Dinner Rolls, Original (2 rolls)	151	3.1	0.1	0	280
Rubschlager Dinner Rolls, Honey Whole Grain (1 roll)	80	1.0	(0.2)	0	160
Rubschlager Dinner Rolls, Original Recipe (1 roll)	70	1.0	(0.3)	0	170
Rubschlager Dinner Rolls, Pumpernickel (1 roll)	90	2.0	(0.2)	0	210

Bread Products (continued)	Calories	Fat g	Saturated Fat g	Choles- terol mg	Sodium mg
Rubschlager Dinner Rolls, Rye (1 roll)	80	2.0	(0.2)	0	220
Rubschlager Dinner Rolls, Wheat (1 roll)	90	1.0	(0.2)	0	180
Wonder Bakery Style Rolls, Original (1 roll)	140	2.0	< 1.0	0	280
Wonder Bakery Style Rolls, Sourdough (1 roll)	150	2.0	< 1.0	0	300
Wonder Bakery Style Rolls, Wheat (1 roll)	150	2.0	< 1.0	0	300
Wonder Pan Rolls, Bisquit (1 roll)	80	1.0	< 1.0	0	140
Wonder Pan Rolls, Dinner (1 roll)	80	1.0	< 1.0	0	140
Wonder Rolls, Brown 'N Serve (1 roll)	70	1.0	< 1.0	0	135
Wonder Rolls, Brown 'N Serve with Buttermilk (1 roll)	70	1.0	< 1.0	0	135

CEREALS

Many cereals naturally contain a small amount of fat. Adding nuts, coconut, or seeds to cereal or spraying it with a fat-based coating (to help it stay crisp) increases the fat content. Cooked and ready-to-eat cereals included in this section of the Guide are low in fat, saturated fat, and cholesterol either *as purchased* or when *prepared according to package directions*. A serving of the cereals included in the Guide does not exceed the cutoff points listed below.

Cereal is usually eaten with milk; the recommended types include skim milk and ½% to 1% low-fat milks, which are low in fat, saturated fat, and cholesterol.

CUTOFF POINTS FOR CEREALS

Fat (grams)	Saturated Fat (grams)	Cholesterol (milligrams)
3	1	10

SERVINGS

Food	Serving Sizes
Bran	½ ounce
Cereal, cooked	1½ ounces (dry weight)
Cereal, ready-to-eat	1 ounce
Wheat Germ	½ ounce

Refer to page 402 for the yield after cooking of some cereals.

The following abbreviations are used in the Food Sections: oz = ounce; fl oz = fluid ounce; pkg = package; pkt = packet; env = envelope; g = gram; prep (w/ . . .) = prepared with; < = less than; and tr = trace.

Cooked Cereals	Calories	Fat g	Saturated Fat g	Choles- terol mg	Sodium mg
COOKED CEREALS					
Albers Hominy Quick Grits, dry (.7 oz = 1/4 cup)	150	0.0	(0.0)	0	0
Arrowhead Mills Cereal, Bear Mush, dry (1 oz)	100	0.0	0.0	0	1
Arrowhead Mills Cereal, Bulgur Wheat, dry (2 oz)	200	1.0	(0.2)	0	0
Arrowhead Mills Cereal, Cracked Wheat, dry (2 oz)	180	1.0	(0.2)	0	2
Arrowhead Mills Cereal, Four Grain, dry (2 oz)	94	1.0	(0.2)	0	1
Arrowhead Mills Cereal, Oat Bran, dry (1 oz)	110	1.0	(0.2)	0	2
Arrowhead Mills Cereal, Seven Grain, dry (1 oz)	100	1.0	(0.2)	0	1
Arrowhead Mills Corn Grits, White or Yellow, dry (2 oz)	200	1.0	(0.1)	0	1
Arrowhead Mills Instant Oatmeal, Apple Spice, dry (1 oz)	130	2.0	(0.3)	0	5
Arrowhead Mills Instant Oatmeal, Regular, dry (1 oz)	100	2.0	(0.3)	0	0
Arrowhead Mills Oatmeal, Steel Cut, dry (2 oz)	220	4.0*	(0.6)	0	1
Aunt Jemima Enriched Hominy Grits, Regular or Quick, White, dry (1 oz = 3 tbsp)	101	0.2	0.0	(0)	0
Buckwheat Groats (Kasha), Roasted, cooked, prep (w/water)—Most Brands (1/4 cup)	91	0.6	(0.1)	(0)	4
Corn Grits, Regular & Quick, cooked—Most Brands (1 cup)	146	0.5	0.1	0	0
Elam's Cereal, Cracked Wheat, dry (1.3 oz)	130	<1.0	(0.0)	(0)	4
Elam's Cereal, Miller's Bran, dry (.4 oz)	16	<1.0	(0.0)	(0)	2
Elam's Oatmeal, Steel Cut, dry (1.6 oz)	180	3.0	(0.5)	(0)	3
Elam's Oatmeal, Stone Ground or Scotch Style, dry (1 oz)	110	2.0	(0.3)	(0)	3
Elam's Wheat Germ, dry (.5 oz)	60	1.0	(0.2)	(0)	3

The value printed for fat is higher than the cutoff point because the manufacturer's serving size is larger than the standard serving size used in evaluating the food.

Cooked Cereals (continued)	Calories	Fat g	Saturated Fat g	Choles- terol mg	Sodium mg
Erewhon Barley Plus (1 oz = 1/3 cup dry)	110	1.0	(0.2)	0	0
Erewhon Brown Rice Cream (1 oz = 1/3 cup dry)	110	1.0	(0.3)	(0)	20
Erewhon Instant Oatmeal, Apple Raisin (1 pkt)	150	3.0	(0.5)	(0)	100
Erewhon Oat Bran with Toasted Wheat Germ (1 oz = 1/3 cup dry)	115	2.0	(0.4)	0	15
Farina, Cooked (1 cup)	116	0.2	0.0	0	1
General Mills Wheat Hearts, dry (1 oz = 3-1/3 tbsp)	110	1.0	(0.2)	0	0
Giant Hominy Quick Grits, prep (w/water and no salt) (3/4 cup)	100	0.0	0.0	0	0
Giant Instant Oatmeal, Apple & Cinnamon (1 pkt)	140	2.0	(0.4)	0	200
Giant Instant Oatmeal, Plain (1 pkt)	110	2.0	(0.3)	0	220
Giant Instant Oatmeal, Strawberry & Cream (1 pkt)	140	2.0	(0.3)	0	150
Giant Oat Bran (1 oz dry)	90	2.0	(<1.0)	0	5
Giant Oatmeal, Quick Oats, prep (w/water and no salt) (2/3 cup)	100	2.0	(0.3)	0	0
IGA Instant Oatmeal, Apples and Cinnamon (1-1/4 oz)	140	2.0	(0.4)	0	(130)
IGA Instant Oatmeal, Maple Brown Sugar (1-1/2 oz)	170	2.0	(0.4)	0	(320)
IGA Instant Oatmeal, Peaches and Cream (1-1/4 oz)	140	2.0	(0.8)	0	(180)
IGA Instant Oatmeal, Regular Flavor (1 oz)	100	2.0	(0.3)	0	(270)
IGA Instant Oatmeal, Strawberries and Cream (1-1/4 oz)	150	2.0	(1.1)	0	(205)
Malt-O-Meal, 40% Oat Bran Plus, dry (1.3 oz)	128	1.7	(<1.0)	(0)	1
Malt-O-Meal, Chocolate Flavored, dry (1 oz)	99	0.3	0.1	0	0
Malt-O-Meal, Quick, dry (1 oz)	100	0.4	0.1	0	1

Cooked Cereals (continued)	Calories	Fat g	Saturated Fat g	Choles- terol mg	Sodium mg
Mother's Oat Bran, cooked (1 oz dry=2/3 cup cooked)	92	2.1	0.2	0	1
Mother's Whole Wheat Hot Natural Cereal, cooked (2/3 cup)	92	0.6	0.1	0	1
Nabisco Cream of Rice, dry (1 oz=2-1/2 tbsp)	100	0.0	0.0	0	0
Nabisco Mix 'n Eat Cream of Wheat, Apple and Cinna- mon, dry (1-1/4 oz=1 pkt)	130	0.0	0.0	0	250
Nabisco Mix 'n Eat Cream of Wheat, Brown Sugar Cinna- mon, dry (1-1/4 oz=1 pkt)	130	0.0	0.0	0	230
Nabisco Mix 'n Eat Cream of Wheat, Maple Brown Sugar, dry (1-1/4 oz=1 pkt)	130	0.0	0.0	0	180
Nabisco Mix 'n Eat Cream of Wheat, Original, dry (1-1/4 oz=1 pkt)	100	0.0	0.0	0	170
Nabisco, Cream of Wheat, Instant, dry (1 oz=2-1/2 tbsp)	100	<1.0	<1.0	<5	0
Nabisco, Cream of Wheat, Quick, dry (1 oz=2-1/2 tbsp)	100	<1.0	<1.0	<5	80
Nabisco, Cream of Wheat, Regular, dry (1 oz=2-1/2 tbsp)	100	0.0	0.0	0	0
Oat Bran, cooked—Most Brands (1/2 cup)	44	1.0	0.2	0	1
Oatmeal Swirlers, Apple Cinnamon, dry (1.7 oz)	160	2.0	(0.3)	0	120
Oatmeal Swirlers, Cherry, dry (1.7 oz)	150	2.0	(0.3)	0	130
Oatmeal Swirlers, Cinnamon Spice, dry (1.6 oz)	160	2.0	(0.3)	0	100
Oatmeal Swirlers, Maple Brown Sugar, dry (1.6 oz)	160	2.0	(0.3)	0	100
Oatmeal Swirlers, Milk Chocolate, dry (1.7 oz)	170	2.0	(0.3)	0	100
Oatmeal Swirlers, Strawberry, dry (1.6 oz)	150	2.0	(0.3)	0	120
Oatmeal, Regular, cooked—Most Brands (1 cup)	145	2.4	0.4	0	1

Cooked Cereals (continued)	Calories	Fat g	Saturated Fat g	Choles- terol mg	Sodium mg
Perky's Quick 'N Creamy Hot Rice Cereal, dry (1 oz)	100	(<1.0)	(0.0)	(0)	<2
Pillsbury Farina, cooked, prep (w/water) (2/3 cup)	80	<1.0	(0.0)	(0)	270
Pritikin Hot Cereal, Apple/Raisin/Spice, dry (1.64 oz)	160	2.0	0.3	0	2
Pritikin Multigrain Hot Cereal (1.57 oz)	140	1.3	0.2	0	2
Quaker Enriched Hominy Grits, Quick or Regular, White or Yellow, dry (1 oz = 3 tbsp)	101	0.2	0.0	(0)	0
Quaker Extra Fortified Instant Oatmeal, Apples & Spice (1 pkt)	133	1.9	0.3	0	191
Quaker Extra Fortified Instant Oatmeal, Raisins & Cinnamon (1 pkt)	129	1.9	0.3	0	119
Quaker Extra Fortified Instant Oatmeal, Regular (1 pkt)	95	2.0	0.2	0	219
Quaker Instant Grits White Hominy Product (1 pkt)	79	0.1	0.0	(0)	440
Quaker Instant Grits with Imitation Bacon Bits (1 pkt)	101	0.4	0.0	(0)	590
Quaker Instant Grits with Imitation Ham Bits (1 pkt)	99	0.3	0.0	0	800
Quaker Instant Grits with Real Cheddar Cheese Flavor (1 pkt)	104	1.0	1.0	0	700
Quaker Instant Oatmeal, Apples & Cinnamon (1 pkt)	118	1.5	0.3	0	128
Quaker Instant Oatmeal, Cinnamon & Spice (1 pkt)	164	2.1	0.4	0	322
Quaker Instant Oatmeal, Maple & Brown Sugar (1 pkt)	152	2.1	0.4	0	320
Quaker Instant Oatmeal, Peaches & Cream Flavor (1 pkt)	129	2.2	0.9	0	179
Quaker Instant Oatmeal, Raisins & Spice (1 pkt)	149	2.0	0.3	0	266
Quaker Instant Oatmeal, Regular, dry (1 pkt)	94	2.0	0.3	0	270
Quaker Instant Oatmeal, Strawberries & Cream (1 pkt)	129	2.0	1.1	0	204

Cooked Cereals (continued)	Calories	Fat g	Saturated Fat g	Choles- terol mg	Sodium mg
Quaker Oat Bran, dry (1 oz dry = 2/3 cup cooked)	92	2.1	0.2	0	1
Quaker Oats, Quick and Old Fashioned, dry (1 oz dry = 2/3 cup)	99	2.0	0.3	0	1
Quaker Whole Wheat Hot Natural Cereal, dry (1 oz dry = 2/3 cup cooked)	92	0.6	0.1	0	1
Ralston High Fiber Hot Cereal, dry (1 oz = 1/3 cup)	90	1.0	(0.2)	0	0
Roman Meal Cereal, Cream of Rye, cooked (1/3 cup)	112	1.0	0.1	0	0
Roman Meal Cereal, Original, cooked (1/3 cup)	82	0.6	0.1	0	1
Safeway Old Fashion Oatmeal, dry (1 oz)	100	2.0	(0.3)	0	0
Safeway Quick Oats, dry (1 oz)	100	2.0	(0.3)	0	5
Skinner's Oat Bran (1 oz = 1/3 cup)	110	2.0	(0.4)	0	5
Tone's Grits, dry (1-1/2 oz)	142	0.4	0.1	0	0
Tone's Rolled Oats, dry (1-1/2 oz)	163	2.7	0.5	0	0
Total Instant Oatmeal, Apple Cinnamon, dry (1.5 oz)	150	2.0	(0.3)	0	105
Total Instant Oatmeal, Maple Brown Sugar, dry (1.6 oz)	160	2.0	(0.3)	0	150
Total Instant Oatmeal, Raisin Cinnamon, dry (1.8 oz)	170	2.0	(0.3)	0	130
Total Instant Oatmeal, Regular, dry (1.2 oz)	110	2.0	(0.3)	0	220
Total Oatmeal, Quick, dry (1 oz)	90	2.0	(0.3)	0	0

READY-TO-EAT CEREALS

	Calories	Fat g	Saturated Fat g	Choles- terol mg	Sodium mg
A&P 40% Bran Flakes (1 oz = 2/3 cup)	90	0.0	0.0	0	200
A&P Corn Flakes (1 oz = 1 cup)	110	0.0	0.0	0	270
A&P Crispy Rice (1 oz = 1 cup)	110	0.0	0.0	0	280
A&P Fruit Rings (1 oz = 1 cup)	110	1.0	(0.2)	0	125

Ready-to-Eat Cereals (continued)	Calories	Fat g	Saturated Fat g	Choles- terol mg	Sodium mg
A&P Honey & Nut Sweetened Toasted Oats (1 oz=3/4 cup)	110	1.0	(0.7)	(0)	230
A&P Raisin Bran (1.4 oz=3/4 cup)	120	1.0	(0.2)	0	200
A&P Rice Puffs (1/2 oz=1 cup)	50	<1.0	(0.0)	0	<10
A&P Sugar Frosted Flakes (1 oz=3/4 cup)	110	0.0	0.0	0	180
A&P Toasted Oats (1 oz=1-1/4 cups)	110	2.0	(0.4)	(0)	300
A&P Wheat Puffs (1/2 oz=1 cup)	50	0.0	0.0	0	0
A&P Wheat Puffs, Sweetened (1 oz=7/8 cup)	110	0.0	0.0	0	25
Arrowhead Mills Apple Corns (1 oz)	100	1.0	(0.2)	0	70
Arrowhead Mills Arrowhead Crunch (1 oz)	120	3.0	(0.5)	0	40
Arrowhead Mills Barley Flakes (2 oz=1-1/4 cups)	200	1.0	(0.2)	0	1
Arrowhead Mills Bran Flakes (1 oz)	100	1.0	(0.2)	0	4
Arrowhead Mills Corn Flakes (1 oz)	110	1.0	(0.1)	0	15
Arrowhead Mills Maple Corns (1 oz)	100	1.0	(0.2)	0	75
Arrowhead Mills Nature O's (1 oz)	110	1.0	(0.2)	0	14
Arrowhead Mills Oat Bran Flakes (1 oz)	110	2.0	(0.4)	0	30
Arrowhead Mills Oat Flakes (2 oz=1-1/3 cups)	220	4.0*	(0.7)	0	1
Arrowhead Mills Puffed Corn (1/2 oz)	50	0.0	0.0	0	1
Arrowhead Mills Puffed Millet (1/2 oz)	50	0.0	0.0	0	1
Arrowhead Mills Puffed Rice (1/2 oz)	50	0.0	0.0	0	1
Arrowhead Mills Puffed Wheat (1/2 oz)	50	0.0	0.0	0	1
Arrowhead Mills Rye Flakes (2 oz=1 cup)	190	1.0	(0.2)	0	1

*The value printed for fat is higher than the cutoff point because the manufacturer's serving size is larger than the standard serving size used in evaluating the food.

Ready-to-Eat Cereals (continued)	Calories	Fat g	Saturated Fat g	Choles- terol mg	Sodium mg
Arrowhead Mills Wheat Bran (2 oz)	50	2.0	(0.3)	0	5
Arrowhead Mills Wheat Flakes (1 oz)	110	1.0	(0.2)	0	15
Barbara's Bakery Breakfast O's (1 oz = 1-1/4 cups)	120	2.0	(0.4)	(0)	(63)
Barbara's Bakery Brown Rice Crisps (1.1 oz = 1 cup)	120	1.0	(0.1)	(0)	(118)
Barbara's Bakery Corn Flakes (1 oz = 1 cup)	110	0.0	0.0	(0)	(122)
Barbara's Bakery Raisin Bran (1 oz = 1 cup)	170	1.0	(0.2)	0	(101)
Erewhon Apple Stroodles (1 oz = 1 cup)	90	0.0	0.0	0	15
Erewhon Aztec (1 oz = 1 cup)	100	0.0	0.0	0	85
Erewhon Crispy Brown Rice Cereal (1 oz = 1 cup)	110	1.0	(0.1)	(0)	185
Erewhon Crispy Brown Rice Cereal, Low Sodium (1 oz = 1 cup)	110	1.0	(0.1)	(0)	5
Erewhon Fruit'n Wheat (1 oz = 1/2 cup)	100	1.0	(0.2)	0	75
Erewhon Poppets (1 oz = 1 cup)	110	1.0	(0.1)	(0)	10
Erewhon Raisin Bran (1 oz = 1/2 cup)	100	0.0	0.0	0	80
Erewhon Right Start (1 oz = 1/3 cup)	90	0.0	0.0	0	80
Erewhon Right Start with Raisins (1 oz = 1/3 cup)	90	0.0	0.0	0	80
Erewhon Super-O's (1 oz = 3/4 cup)	110	0.0	0.0	0	5
Erewhon Wheat Flakes (1 oz = 1/2 cup)	110	0.0	0.0	0	75
Featherweight Cereal, Corn Flakes (1 oz = 1-1/4 cups)	110	0.0	0.0	0	35
Featherweight Cereal, Crisp Rice (1 oz = 1 cup)	110	0.0	0.0	0	35
General Mills Body Buddies, Natural Fruit (1 oz = 1 cup)	110	1.0	(0.2)	0	280
General Mills Booberry (1 oz = 1 cup)	110	1.0	(0.2)	0	210
General Mills Cheerios (1 oz = 1-1/4 cups)	110	2.0	(0.4)	0	290

Ready-to-Eat Cereals (continued)	Calories	Fat g	Saturated Fat g	Cholesterol mg	Sodium mg
General Mills Cheerios, Apple Cinnamon (1 oz = 3/4 cup)	110	2.0	(0.4)	0	180
General Mills Cheerios, Honey Nut (1 oz = 3/4 cup)	110	1.0	(0.7)	0	250
General Mills Cinnamon Toast Crunch (1 oz = 3/4 cup)	120	3.0	(0.5)	0	220
General Mills Cocoa Puffs (1 oz = 1 cup)	110	1.0	(0.2)	0	170
General Mills Count Chocula (1 oz = 1 cup)	110	1.0	(0.2)	0	210
General Mills Country Corn Flakes (1 oz = 1 cup)	110	<1.0	0.0	0	280
General Mills Crispy Wheats 'n Raisins (1 oz = 3/4 cup)	100	1.0	(0.2)	0	140
General Mills Fiber One (1 oz = 1/2 cup)	60	1.0	(0.2)	0	140
General Mills Frankenberry (1 oz = 1 cup)	110	1.0	(0.2)	0	210
General Mills Fruity Yummy Mummy (1 oz = 1 cup)	110	1.0	(0.2)	0	160
General Mills Golden Grahams (1 oz = 3/4 cup)	110	1.0	(0.2)	0	280
General Mills Kaboom (1 oz = 1 cup)	110	1.0	(0.2)	0	290
General Mills Kix (1 oz = 1-1/2 cups)	110	1.0	(0.6)	0	260
General Mills Lucky Charms (1 oz = 1 cup)	110	1.0	(0.2)	0	180
General Mills Oatmeal Crisp (1 oz = 1 cup)	110	2.0	(0.4)	0	180
General Mills Total (1 oz = 1 cup)	100	1.0	(0.2)	0	140
General Mills Total Corn Flakes (1 oz = 1 cup)	110	1.0	(0.1)	0	280
General Mills Total Raisin Bran (1.5 oz = 1 cup)	140	1.0	(0.2)	0	190
General Mills Trix (1 oz = 1 cup)	110	1.0	(0.2)	0	140
General Mills Wheaties (1 oz = 1 cup)	100	1.0	(0.1)	0	200
Giant 40% Bran Flakes (2/3 cup)	90	0.0	0.0	0	200

Ready-to-Eat Cereals (continued)	Calories	Fat g	Saturated Fat g	Choles- terol mg	Sodium mg
Giant Bite Size Shredded Wheat (2/3 cup)	110	1.0	(0.2)	0	0
Giant Corn Flakes (1 cup)	110	0.0	0.0	0	270
Grainfield's Brown Rice (1 oz)	110	0.5	(0.1)	0	4
Grainfield's Corn Flakes (1 oz = 1-1/4 cups)	110	0.1	(0.0)	0	2
Grainfield's Raisin Bran (1 oz = 2/3 cup)	90	0.4	(0.1)	0	4
Grainfield's Wheat Flakes (1 oz = 1 cup)	100	0.6	(0.1)	0	2
Grainfield's Crisp Rice (1 oz)	112	0.1	(0.0)	0	3
Health Valley Blue Corn Flakes (1 oz = 1/2 cup)	90	<1.0	(0.0)	0	10
Health Valley Fiber 7 Flakes (1 oz = 1/2 cup)	90	<1.0	(0.0)	0	0
Health Valley Oat Bran Flakes (1 oz = 1/2 cup)	90	<1.0	(0.0)	0	0
Health Valley Oat Bran Flakes, Almonds and Dates (1 oz = 1/2 cup)	90	1.0	(0.1)	0	0
Health Valley Oat Bran Flakes, Raisins (1 oz = 1/2 cup)	90	<1.0	(0.0)	0	0
Health Valley Oat Bran O's (1 oz = 1/2 cup)	90	<1.0	(0.0)	0	0
Health Valley Oat Bran O's, Fruit & Nut (1 oz = 3/4 cup)	110	3.0	(0.3)	0	3
Health Valley Raisin Bran Flakes (1 oz = 1/2 cup)	90	<1.0	(0.0)	0	5
IGA Bran Flakes (1 oz)	100	0.0	0.0	0	(240)
IGA Corn Flakes (1 oz)	110	0.0	0.0	0	(290)
IGA Crispy Rice (1 oz)	110	0.0	0.0	0	(290)
IGA Honey Nut Toasted Oats (1 oz)	110	1.0	(0.2)	0	(135)
IGA Popped Wheat (1/2 oz)	50	0.0	0.0	0	(1)
IGA Raisin Bran (1.3 oz)	120	1.0	(0.2)	0	(185)
IGA Sugar Frosted Flakes (1 oz)	110	0.0	0.0	0	(200)
IGA Sweetened Popped Wheat (1 oz)	110	0.0	0.0	0	(200)
Kashi, Lightly Puffed (3/4 oz = 1 cup)	74	0.5	(0.1)	0	2

Ready-to-Eat Cereals (continued)	Calories	Fat g	Saturated Fat g	Choles- terol mg	Sodium mg
Kellogg's All-Bran (1 oz = 1/3 cup)	70	1.0	(0.2)	0	260
Kellogg's All-Bran with Extra Fiber (1 oz = 1/2 cup)	50	0.0	0.0	0	140
Kellogg's Apple Jacks (1 oz = 1 cup)	110	0.0	0.0	0	125
Kellogg's Apple Raisin Crisp (1 oz = 2/3 cup)	130	0.0	0.0	0	230
Kellogg's Bigg Mixx (1 oz = 1/2 cup)	110	2.0	(0.3)	0	190
Kellogg's Bigg Mixx with Raisins (1oz = 1/2 cup)	140	2.0	(0.3)	0	190
Kellogg's Bran Buds (1 oz = 1/3 cup)	70	1.0	(0.2)	0	170
Kellogg's Bran Flakes (1 oz = 2/3 cup)	90	0.0	0.0	0	220
Kellogg's Cocoa Krispies (1 oz = 3/4 cup)	110	0.0	0.0	0	190
Kellogg's Common Sense Oat Bran (1 oz = 1/2 cup)	100	1.0	(0.2)	0	270
Kellogg's Common Sense Oat Bran with Raisins (1 oz = 1/2 cup)	120	1.0	(0.2)	0	250
Kellogg's Corn Flakes (1 oz = 1 cup)	100	0.0	0.0	0	290
Kellogg's Corn Pops (1 oz = 1 cup)	110	0.0	0.0	0	90
Kellogg's Crispix (1 oz = 1 cup)	110	0.0	0.0	0	220
Kellogg's Froot Loops (1 oz = 1 cup)	110	1.0	(0.2)	0	125
Kellogg's Frosted Flakes (1 oz = 3/4 cup)	110	0.0	0.0	0	200
Kellogg's Frosted Krispies (1 oz = 3/4 cup)	110	0.0	0.0	0	220
Kellogg's Frosted Mini Wheats Biscuits (1 oz = 4 biscuits)	100	0.0	0.0	0	0
Kellogg's Frosted Mini Wheats Bite Size Biscuits (1 oz = 1/2 cup)	100	0.0	0.0	0	0
Kellogg's Fruitful Bran (1 oz = 2/3 cup)	110	0.0	0.0	0	230

Ready-to-Eat Cereals (continued)	Calories	Fat g	Saturated Fat g	Choles- terol mg	Sodium mg
Kellogg's Fruity Marshmallow Krispies (1 oz = 1-1/4 cups)	140	0.0	0.0	0	210
Kellogg's Heartwise (1 oz = 2/3 cup)	90	1.0	(0.2)	0	140
Kellogg's Honey Smacks (1 oz = 3/4 cup)	110	1.0	(0.2)	0	70
Kellogg's Just Right with Fiber Nuggets (1 oz = 2/3 cup)	100	1.0	(0.2)	0	200
Kellogg's Just Right with Fruit and Nuts (1 oz = 3/4 cup)	140	1.0	(0.2)	0	190
Kellogg's Kenmei Rice Bran (1 oz = 3/4 cup)	110	1.0	(0.2)	0	250
Kellogg's Kenmei Rice Bran, Almond and Raisin (1 oz = 3/4 cup)	150	2.0	(0.3)	0	240
Kellogg's Mueslix, Crispy Blend (1 oz = 2/3 cup)	160	2.0	(0.3)	0	150
Kellogg's Mueslix, Golden Crunch (1 oz = 1/2 cup)	120	2.0	(0.3)	0	170
Kellogg's Nut & Honey Crunch (1 oz = 2/3 cup)	110	1.0	(0.1)	0	200
Kellogg's Nut & Honey Crunch O's (1 oz = 2/3 cup)	110	2.0	(0.3)	0	190
Kellogg's Nutri-Grain, Almond Raisin (1 oz = 2/3 cup)	140	2.0	(0.3)	0	220
Kellogg's Nutri-Grain, Raisin Bran (1 oz = 1 cup)	130	1.0	(0.2)	0	200
Kellogg's Nutri-Grain, Wheat (1 oz = 2/3 cup)	100	0.0	0.0	0	170
Kellogg's Oatbake, Honey Bran (1 oz = 1/3 cup)	110	3.0	1.0	0	180
Kellogg's Oatbake, Raisin Nut (1 oz = 1/3 cup)	110	3.0	1.0	0	190
Kellogg's Product 19 (1 oz = 1 cup)	100	0.0	0.0	0	320
Kellogg's Raisin Bran (1 oz = 3/4 cup)	120	1.0	(0.7)	0	230
Kellogg's Rice Krispies (1 oz = 1 cup)	110	0.0	0.0	0	290
Kellogg's Shredded Wheat Squares, Apple Cinnamon (1 oz = 1/2 cup)	90	0.0	0.0	0	5

	Calories	Fat g	Saturated Fat g	Choles- terol mg	Sodium mg
Kellogg's Shredded Wheat Squares, Blueberry (1 oz = 1/2 cup)	90	0.0	0.0	0	5
Kellogg's Shredded Wheat Squares, Raisin (1 oz = 1/2 cup)	90	0.0	0.0	0	0
Kellogg's Shredded Wheat Squares, Strawberry (1 oz = 1/2 cup)	90	0.0	0.0	0	5
Kellogg's Special K (1 oz = 1 cup)	110	0.0	0.0	0	230
Kohl's Corn Flakes (1 oz = 1 cup)	110	0.0	0.0	0	270
Kohl's Fruit Rings (1 oz = 1 cup)	110	1.0	(0.2)	0	125
Kohl's Raisin Bran (1.4 oz = 3/4 cup)	120	1.0	(0.2)	0	200
Kohl's Sugar Frosted Flakes (1 oz = 3/4 cup)	110	0.0	0.0	0	180
Kretschmer Toasted Wheat Bran (1 oz = 1/3 cup)	57	2.3	0.2	0	2
Kretschmer Wheat Germ (1 oz = 1/4 cup)	103	3.4	0.5	0	2
Kretschmer Wheat Germ, Honey Crunch (1 oz = 1/4 cup)	105	2.8	0.4	0	2
Malt-O-Meal Bran Flakes (1 oz = 2/3 cup)	93	0.9	0.1	0	205
Malt-O-Meal Corn Flakes (1 oz)	106	0.2	0.0	0	268
Malt-O-Meal Crisp 'n Crackling Rice (1 oz = 1 cup)	108	0.3	0.1	0	252
Malt-O-Meal Honey & Nut Toasty O's (1 oz = 3/4 cup)	107	1.2	0.2	0	172
Malt-O-Meal Puffed Rice (1/2 oz = 1 cup)	54	0.2	0.0	0	0
Malt-O-Meal Puffed Rice, Unfortified (1/2 oz = 1 cup)	54	0.2	(0.0)	0	0
Malt-O-Meal Puffed Wheat (1/2 oz = 1 cup)	53	0.4	0.1	0	0
Malt-O-Meal Puffed Wheat, Unfortified (1/2 oz = 1 cup)	49	0.4	(0.0)	0	0
Malt-O-Meal Raisin Bran (1.4 oz = 3/4 cup)	129	1.7	(0.3)	0	199

Ready-to-Eat Cereals (continued)	Calories	Fat g	Saturated Fat g	Choles-terol mg	Sodium mg
Malt-O-Meal Sugar Frosted Corn Flakes (1 oz = 3/4 cup)	109	0.2	0.0	0	186
Malt-O-Meal Sugar Puffs (1 oz = 1 cup)	109	0.4	0.1	0	23
Malt-O-Meal Toasty O's (1 oz = 1-1/4 cups)	107	2.0	0.3	0	236
Malt-O-Meal Tootie Fruities (1 oz = 1 cup)	113	1.1	0.2	0	121
Nabisco 100% Bran (1 oz = 1/2 cup)	70	1.0	0.0	0	180
Nabisco Fruit Wheats, Apple (1 oz = 1/2 cup)	90	0.0	0.0	0	15
Nabisco Shredded Wheat 'n Bran (1 oz = 2/3 cup)	100	1.0	0.0	0	0
Nabisco Shredded Wheat (5/6 oz = 1 biscuit)	80	1.0	0.0	0	0
Nabisco Shredded Wheat with Oat Bran (1 oz = 2/3 cup)	100	0.0	0.0	0	0
Nabisco Spoon Size Shredded Wheat (1 oz = 2/3 cup)	90	1.0	0.0	0	0
Nabisco Team Flakes (1 oz = 1 cup)	110	1.0	(0.0)	0	180
Perky's Carob Flavored Crispy Brown Rice (1 oz = 3/4 cup)	110	1.0	(0.2)	(0)	5
Perky's Nutty Rice, Original (1 oz = 1/4 cup)	110	0.1	(0.0)	(0)	56
Post Alpha-Bits (1 oz = 5/6 cup)	110	1.0	(0.2)	0	190
Post Cocoa Pebbles (1 oz = 7/8 cup)	110	1.0	(0.8)	0	160
Post Fruit & Fibre, Dates, Raisins, Walnuts with Oat Clusters (1.25 oz = 5/8 cup)	120	2.0	(0.3)	0	170
Post Fruit & Fibre, Peaches, Raisins and Almonds (1.25 oz = 5/8 cup)	120	2.0	(0.3)	0	170
Post Fruit & Fibre, Tropical Fruit with Oat Clusters (1.25 oz = 5/8 cup)	120	3.0	(0.5)	0	170
Post Fruity Pebbles (1 oz = 7/8 cup)	110	1.0	(0.8)	0	160

Ready-to-Eat Cereals (continued)	Calories	Fat g	Saturated Fat g	Choles-terol mg	Sodium mg
Post Grape-Nuts Brand Cereal (1 oz = 1/4 cup)	110	0.0	0.0	0	170
Post Grape-Nuts Flakes (1 oz = 5/7 cup)	100	1.0	(0.2)	0	160
Post Honey Bunches of Oats, Honey Roasted (1 oz = 3/4 cup)	110	2.0	(0.4)	0	180
Post Honey Bunches of Oats, with Almonds (1 oz = 3/4 cup)	120	3.0	(0.5)	0	160
Post Honeycomb (1 oz = 1-1/3 cups)	110	0.0	(0.0)	0	170
Post Natural Bran Flakes (1 oz = 2/3 cup)	90	0.0	(0.0)	0	240
Post Natural Raisin Bran (1.4 oz = 5/8 cup)	120	1.0	(0.4)	0	200
Post Oat Flakes (1 oz = 2/3 cup)	110	1.0	(0.2)	0	130
Post Raisin Grape-Nuts (1 oz = 1/4 cup)	100	0.0	(0.0)	0	140
Post Smurf-Magic Berries (1 oz = 1 cup)	120	1.0	(0.5)	0	60
Post Super Golden Crisp (1 oz = 7/8 cup)	110	0.0	(0.0)	0	45
Post Toasties Corn Flakes (1 oz = 1-1/4 cups)	110	0.0	(0.0)	0	310
Quaker Cap'n Crunch Cereal (1 oz = 3/4 cup)	113	1.7	0.8	(0)	241
Quaker Cap'n Crunch's Crunchberries Cereal (1 oz = 3/4 cup)	113	1.7	0.9	(0)	247
Quaker Cap'n Crunch's Peanut Butter Crunch Cereal (1 oz = 3/4 cup)	119	3.0	0.9	(0)	281
Quaker Crunchy Bran Cereal (1 oz = 2/3 cup)	89	1.3	0.4	(0)	316
Quaker King Vitamin Cereal (1 oz = 1-1/2 cups)	110	1.0	0.0	(0)	280
Quaker Life Cereal (1 oz = 2/3 cup)	101	1.7	(0.0)	(0)	186
Quaker Life Cereal, Cinnamon (1 oz = 2/3 cup)	101	1.7	(0.0)	(0)	182
Quaker Oat Bran (1 oz = 3/4 cup)	100	2.0	(0.4)	0	125

Ready-to-Eat Cereals (continued)	Calories	Fat g	Saturated Fat g	Choles- terol mg	Sodium mg
Quaker Oat Squares Cereal (1 oz = 1/2 cup)	105	1.6	(0.0)	(0)	159
Quaker Popeye Sweet Crunch Cereal (1 oz = 1 cup)	113	1.8	1.0	(0)	254
Quaker Puffed Rice (1/2 oz = 1 cup)	54	0.1	0.0	0	1
Quaker Puffed Wheat (1/2 oz = 1 cup)	50	0.2	0.0	0	1
Quaker Shredded Wheat (1.4 oz = 2 biscuits)	132	0.6	(0.0)	(0)	1
Quaker Unprocessed Bran (1/4 oz = 2 tbsp)	8	0.2	0.0	(0)	0
Ralston Almond Delight Cereal (1 oz = 3/4 cup)	110	2.0	(1.0)	0	200
Ralston Batman Cereal (1 oz = 1 cup)	110	1.0	(0.5)	0	140
Ralston Bill & Ted's Excellent Sweetened Cereal (1 oz = 1 cup)	110	1.0	0.2	0	160
Ralston Bran News Cereal, Cinnamon (1 oz = 3/4 cup)	100	0.0	0.0	0	160
Ralston Breakfast with Barbie Cereal (1 oz = 1 cup)	110	1.0	(0.5)	0	70
Ralston Chex Cereal, Corn (1 oz = 1 cup)	110	0.0	0.0	0	310
Ralston Chex Cereal, Double (1 oz = 2/3 cup)	100	0.0	0.0	0	190
Ralston Chex Cereal, Honey Graham (1 oz = 2/3 cup)	110	1.0	(0.8)	0	180
Ralston Chex Cereal, Honey Nut Oat (1 oz = 1/2 cup)	100	1.0	(0.8)	0	220
Ralston Chex Cereal, Multi-Bran (1 oz = 2/3 cup)	90	0.0	(0.0)	0	200
Ralston Chex Cereal, Rice (1 oz = 1-1/8 cups)	110	0.0	0.0	0	280
Ralston Chex Cereal, Wheat (1 oz = 2/3 cup)	100	0.0	0.0	0	230
Ralston Cookie-Crisp Cereal, Chocolate Chip (1 oz = 1 cup)	110	1.0	(0.6)	0	190
Ralston Cookie-Crisp Cereal, Vanilla Wafer (1 oz = 1 cup)	110	1.0	(0.6)	0	220
Ralston Dinersaurs Cereal (1 oz = 1 cup)	110	1.0	(0.5)	0	70

Ready-to-Eat Cereals (continued)	Calories	Fat g	Saturated Fat g	Cholesterol mg	Sodium mg
Ralston Fruit Muesli Cereal, Apple Almond (1.5 oz = 1/2 cup)	150	2.0	(0.4)	0	140
Ralston Fruit Muesli Cereal, Date Almond (1.5 oz = 1/2 cup)	140	2.0	(0.4)	0	95
Ralston Fruit Muesli Cereal, Peach Pecan (1.5 oz = 1/2 cup)	150	3.0	(0.6)	0	95
Ralston Fruit Muesli Cereal, Cranberry Walnut (1.5 oz = 1/2 cup)	150	3.0	(0.6)	0	95
Ralston Hot Wheels Cereal (1 oz = 1 cup)	110	1.0	(0.5)	0	160
Ralston Morning Funnies Cereal (1 oz = 1 cup)	110	1.0	(0.5)	0	70
Ralston Nintendo Cereal System Sweetened Cereal (1 oz = 1 cup)	110	1.0	(0.5)	0	70
Ralston Options Cereal, Oat Bran (1.5 oz = 3/4 cup)	130	1.0	(0.2)	0	150
Ralston Options Cereal, Rice Bran (1.12 oz = 2/3 cup)	120	2.0	(0.4)	0	120
Ralston Slimer! and the Real Ghostbusters Cereal (1 oz = 1 cup)	110	1.0	(0.5)	0	115
Ralston Sunflakes Multi-Grain Cereal (1 oz = 1 cup)	100	1.0	(0.2)	0	240
Ralston Teenage Mutant Ninja Turtles Cereal (1 oz = 1 cup)	110	0.0	0.0	0	190
Ralston The Jetsons Sweetened Cereal (1 oz = 3/4 cup)	110	1.0	0.2	0	160
Safeway 40% Bran Flakes (1 oz = 2/3 cup)	90	0.0	0.0	0	285
Safeway Corn Flakes (1 cup)	110	0.0	0.0	0	290
Safeway Crispy Rice (1 oz = 1 cup)	110	0.0	0.0	0	270
Safeway Fruit Rings (1 oz = 1 cup)	110	1.0	(0.2)	0	125
Safeway Honey & Nut Tasteeos (1 cup)	110	1.0	(0.7)	(0)	210
Safeway Raisin Bran (1.5 oz = 3/4 cup)	110	1.0	(0.2)	0	240

Ready-to-Eat Cereals (continued)	Calories	Fat g	Saturated Fat g	Choles-terol mg	Sodium mg
Safeway Sugar Frosted Flakes (1 oz = 3/4 cup)	110	0.0	0.0	0	180
Safeway Toasted Oats (1 oz = 1-1/4 cups)	110	2.0	(0.4)	0	300
Skinner's Raisin Bran, Regular (1 oz = 1/2 cup)	110	2.0	(0.3)	(0)	45
Skinner's Toasted Oat Rings (1 oz = 1 cup)	90	1.0	(0.2)	0	290
Sunshine Shredded Wheat (1 biscuit)	80	0.6	(0.1)	0	0
Sunshine Shredded Wheat, Bite Size (1 oz = 2/3 cup)	90	0.7	(0.2)	0	0
Uncle Sam Cereal (1 oz = 1/2 cup dry)	110	1.0	(0.1)	0	65
Wheat Germ, Plain, Toasted—Most Brands (1 oz)	108	3.0	0.5	0	1
Wheetabix (1.2 oz = 2 biscuits)	100	0.6	(0.1)	0	106

CONDIMENTS

Most condiments contain little or no fat and cholesterol and are low in calories. The levels of fat, saturated fat, and cholesterol in a serving of the foods listed in this section do not exceed the cutoff points listed below. Since the calories, fat, saturated fat, cholesterol, and sodium are similar in different brands of some condiments (such as regular catsup and mustard and dill pickles), "most brands" is used instead of individual brand names for many of these products.

Although many condiments are high in sodium, several low-sodium condiments, such as catsup, mustard, and pickles, are included in the Guide for individuals trying to limit their sodium intake.

CUTOFF POINTS FOR CONDIMENTS

Fat (grams)	Saturated Fat (grams)	Cholesterol (milligrams)
3	1	10

SERVINGS

Food	Serving Sizes
Catsup and Steak Sauce	1 tablespoon
Cocktail Sauce	¼ cup
Chili Sauce	1 tablespoon
Enchilada Sauce	¼ cup
Horseradish Sauce	1 tablespoon
Hot Sauce	1 tablespoon
Mustard	1 tablespoon
Peppers	1 ounce
Picante Sauce, Salsa, and Taco Sauce	1 tablespoon
Pickles, dill or sour	2 ounces
Pickles, except dill or sour	1 ounce
Relishes	½ ounce
Soy Sauce	1 tablespoon

The following abbreviations are used in the Food Sections: oz = ounce; fl oz = fluid ounce; pkg = package; pkt = packet; env = envelope; g = gram; prep (w/ . . .) = prepared with; < = less than; and tr = trace.

Catsup and Steak Sauce	Calories	Fat g	Saturated Fat g	Choles- terol mg	Sodium mg
CATSUP AND STEAK SAUCE					
Catsup, Low Sodium—Most Brands (1 tbsp)	16	0.1	0.0	0	3
Catsup, Regular—Most Brands (1 tbsp)	16	0.1	0.0	0	156
Featherweight Catsup (1 tbsp)	6	0.0	0.0	0	5
Mrs. Dash Steak Sauce (1 tbsp)	(17)	0.1	(0.0)	0	10
COCKTAIL AND CHILI SAUCE					
El Molino Chile Sauce, Mild Green (2 tbsp)	10	0.0	0.0	0	210
Featherweight Chili Sauce (1 tbsp)	8	0.0	0.0	0	10
Giant Chili Sauce (1 tbsp)	18	0.0	0.0	0	160
IGA Chili Sauce (1 tbsp)	16	1.0	(0.0)	0	(200)
Kraft Sauceworks, Cocktail Sauce (1 tbsp)	14	0.0	0.0	0	170
McCormick Creamy Seafood Sauce, prep (as directed) (1/2 cup)	135	1.8	(0.9)	(17)	3016
ENCHILADA SAUCE					
El Molino Enchilada Sauce, Hot (2 tbsp)	16	1.0	(0.3)	(0)	100
Gebhardt Enchilada Sauce (3 tbsp)	25	1.0	0.7	<1	170
La Victoria Enchilada Sauce (1 tbsp)	5	<1.0	(0.0)	(0)	93
Old El Paso Enchilada Sauce, Green (2 tbsp)	11	0.0	0.0	0	200
Old El Paso Enchilada Sauce, Hot (1/4 cup)	30	1.0	(0.7)	0	250
Old El Paso Enchilada Sauce, Mild (1/4 cup)	25	1.0	(0.7)	0	250
Rosarita Enchilada Sauce, Hot (3 tbsp)	15	<1.0	(0.0)	0	150
Rosarita Enchilada Sauce, Mild (3 tbsp)	15	<1.0	0.0	0	150
HORSERADISH SAUCE					
Kraft Cream Style Prepared Horseradish (1 tbsp)	12	1.0	0.0	0	85

Horseradish Sauce (continued)	Calories	Fat g	Saturated Fat g	Choles- terol mg	Sodium mg
Kraft Prepared Horseradish (1 tbsp)	10	0.0	0.0	0	140
MUSTARD					
Escoffier Sauce, Diable (1 tsp)	20	0.0	0.0	0	160
Featherweight Mustard (1 tsp)	5	0.0	0.0	0	0
Grey Poupon Parisian Mustard (1 tsp)	6	0.0	0.0	0	55
Hain Stone Ground Mustard (1 tbsp)	14	1.0	(0.0)	0	185
Hain Stone Ground Mustard, No Salt Added (1 tbsp)	14	1.0	(0.0)	0	10
IGA Horseradish Mustard (1 tbsp)	11	1.0	0.0	0	(135)
IGA Salad Style Mustard (1 tbsp)	11	1.0	0.0	0	(180)
Kraft Horseradish Mustard (1 tbsp)	14	1.0	0.0	0	135
Mustard, Chinese—Most Brands (1 tsp)	4	0.2	0.0	0	63
Mustard, Horseradish—Most Brands (1 tsp)	2	tr	0.0	0	5
Mustard, Regular—Most Brands (1 tsp)	4	0.2	0.0	0	63
PEPPERS AND HOT SAUCE					
Gebhardt Hot Sauce (1/2 tsp)	< 1.0	(0.0)	(0.0)	0	55
Gedney Banana Peppers, Hot (1/2 oz)	2	0.0	0.0	(0)	170
Gedney Banana Peppers, Mild (1/2 oz)	2	0.0	0.0	(0)	170
Gedney Cherry Peppers, Hot (1/2 oz)	4	0.0	0.0	(0)	200
Gedney Cherry Peppers, Sweet (1/2 oz)	4	0.0	0.0	(0)	200
Gedney Pepper Rings, Hot (1/2 oz)	2	0.0	0.0	(0)	170
Gedney Pepper Rings, Mild (1/2 oz)	2	0.0	0.0	(0)	170
Giant Fresh Pack Hot Cherry Peppers (1 oz)	2	0.0	0.0	0	480

Peppers and Hot Sauce (continued)	Calories	Fat g	Saturated Fat g	Choles- terol mg	Sodium mg
Hot Chili Peppers, canned—Most Brands (1 pepper)	18	0.1	0.0	0	(3)
Hot Chili Peppers, raw—Most Brands (1 pepper)	18	0.1	0.0	0	3
Jalapeno Peppers, canned—Most Brands (1/2 cup)	17	0.4	0.0	0	995
La Victoria Marinated Jalapenos (1 tbsp)	4	<1.0	(0.0)	(0)	251
La Victoria Nacho Jalapenos (1 tbsp)	2	<1.0	(0.0)	(0)	335
Old El Paso Green Chilies, chopped (2 tbsp)	8	<1.0	(0.0)	(0)	70
Progresso Tuscan Peppers (1/2 cup)	20	0.0	0.0	0	5
Tabasco Brand Pepper Sauce (1/4 tsp)	<1.0	0.0	0.0	0	9
Vlasic Mild Greek Pepperoncini Salad Peppers (1 oz)	4	0.0	0.0	(0)	450
Vlasic Peppers, Hot Banana Pepper Rings (1 oz)	4	0.0	0.0	0	465
PICANTE, SALSA, AND TACO SAUCE					
Casa Del Pueblo Picante Sauce, Medium (2 tbsp)	15	0.0	0.0	0	280
Casa Del Pueblo Picante Sauce, Mild (2 tbsp)	15	0.0	0.0	0	280
El Molino Taco Sauce, Mild Red (2 tbsp)	10	0.0	0.0	0	170
Frito-Lay's Chunky Salsa Dip, Hot (1 oz)	12	0.0	0.0	0	180
Frito-Lay's Chunky Salsa Dip, Medium (1 oz)	12	0.0	0.0	0	150
Frito-Lay's Chunky Salsa Dip, Mild (1 oz)	12	0.0	0.0	0	200
Giant Taco Sauce, Hot (1 tbsp)	6	0.0	0.0	0	80
Giant Taco Sauce, Medium (1 tbsp)	6	0.0	0.0	0	80
Giant Taco Sauce, Mild (1 tbsp)	6	0.0	0.0	0	80

Picante, Salsa, and Taco Sauce (continued)	Calories	Fat g	Saturated Fat g	Cholesterol mg	Sodium mg
Guiltless Gourmet Picante Sauce, Hot (1 oz = 2 tbsp)	6	0.0	0.0	0	133
Guiltless Gourmet Picante Sauce, Medium (1 oz = 2 tbsp)	6	0.0	0.0	0	133
Guiltless Gourmet Picante Sauce, Mild (1 oz = 2 tbsp)	6	0.0	0.0	0	133
Hain Salsa, Hot (1/4 cup)	22	0.0	0.0	0	480
Hain Salsa, Mild (1/4 cup)	20	0.0	0.0	(0)	410
Hain Taco Dip and Sauce (4 tbsp)	25	1.0	(<1.0)	5	350
IGA Picante Sauce (2 tsp)	4	<1.0	(0.0)	0	(110)
IGA Salsa (2 tsp)	4	<1.0	(0.0)	0	(110)
IGA Taco Sauce (2 tsp)	4	<1.0	(0.0)	0	(110)
La Victoria Chili Dip (1 tbsp)	6	<1.0	(0.0)	(0)	90
La Victoria Green Chili Salsa (1 tbsp)	3	<1.0	(0.0)	(0)	44
La Victoria Salsa Brava (1 tbsp)	6	<1.0	(0.0)	(0)	100
La Victoria Salsa Casera (1 tbsp)	4	<1.0	(0.0)	(0)	80
La Victoria Salsa Jalapena, Green (1 tbsp)	4	<1.0	(0.0)	(0)	105
La Victoria Salsa Jalapena, Red (1 tbsp)	6	<1.0	(0.0)	(0)	95
La Victoria Salsa Picante (1 tbsp)	4	<1.0	(0.0)	(0)	80
La Victoria Salsa Ranchera (1 tbsp)	6	<1.0	(0.0)	(0)	85
La Victoria Salsa Suprema (1 tbsp)	4	<1.0	(0.0)	(0)	95
La Victoria Salsa Victoria (1 tbsp)	4	<1.0	(0.0)	(0)	80
La Victoria Taco Sauce, Green (1 tbsp)	4	<1.0	(0.0)	(0)	85
La Victoria Taco Sauce, Red (1 tbsp)	6	<1.0	(0.0)	(0)	85
Newman's Own Bandito Salsa, Hot (1 tbsp)	6	<1.0	(0.0)	0	120
Newman's Own Bandito Salsa, Medium (1 tbsp)	6	<1.0	(0.0)	0	70
Newman's Own Bandito Salsa, Mild (1 tbsp)	6	<1.0	(0.0)	0	60

Picante, Salsa, and Taco Sauce (continued)	Calories	Fat g	Saturated Fat g	Cholesterol mg	Sodium mg
Old El Paso Picante Salsa (2 tbsp)	10	<1.0	(0.0)	0	160
Old El Paso Picante Sauce (2 tbsp)	8	<1.0	(0.0)	0	310
Old El Paso Sauce, Chunky Picante (2 tbsp)	7	0.0	0.0	0	270
Old El Paso Taco Sauce (can) (2 tbsp)	15	0.0	0.0	0	300
Old El Paso Taco Sauce (jar) Mild, Medium, or Hot (2 tbsp)	10	<1.0	(0.0)	0	130
Old El Paso Thick 'n Chunky Salsa, Green Chili (2 tbsp)	3	0.0	0.0	0	270
Old El Paso Thick 'n Chunky Salsa, Mild, Medium, or Hot (2 tbsp)	6	<1.0	(0.0)	0	170
Old El Paso Thick 'n Chunky Salsa, Verde (2 tbsp)	10	<1.0	0.0	0	135
Ortega Green Chili Salsa, Hot (1/2 oz = 1 tbsp)	6	0.0	0.0	0	190
Ortega Green Chili Salsa, Medium (1/2 oz = 1 tbsp)	6	0.0	0.0	0	190
Ortega Green Chili Salsa, Mild (1/2 oz = 1 tbsp)	8	0.0	0.0	0	190
Ortega Thick and Smooth Taco Sauce, Hot (1/2 oz = 1 tbsp)	8	0.0	0.0	0	105
Ortega Thick and Smooth Taco Sauce, Medium (1/2 oz = 1 tbsp)	8	0.0	0.0	0	105
Ortega Thick and Smooth Taco Sauce, Mild (1/2 oz = 1 tbsp)	8	0.0	0.0	0	115
Pace Picante Sauce (2 tsp)	3	<1.0	(0.0)	(0)	111
Pace Thick & Chunky Salsa (2 tsp)	4	<1.0	(0.0)	(0)	102
Rosarita Chunky Salsa Dip, Hot (3 tbsp)	25	<1.0	(0.0)	0	300
Rosarita Chunky Salsa Dip, Medium (3 tbsp)	25	<1.0	(0.0)	0	350
Rosarita Chunky Salsa Dip, Mild (3 tbsp)	25	<1.0	(0.0)	0	340
Rosarita Picante Sauce, Hot Chunky (3 tbsp)	18	<1.0	(0.0)	0	515

Picante, Salsa, and Taco Sauce (continued)	Calories	Fat g	Saturated Fat g	Choles-terol mg	Sodium mg
Rosarita Picante Sauce, Medium Chunky (3 tbsp)	16	<1.0	(0.0)	0	650
Rosarita Picante Sauce, Mild Chunky (3 tbsp)	25	<1.0	(0.0)	0	630
Rosarita Taco Sauce, Medium Chunky (3 tbsp)	25	<1.0	(0.0)	0	310
Rosarita Taco Sauce, Mild (3 tbsp)	15	<1.0	(0.0)	0	310
Rosarita Taco Sauce, Mild Chunky (3 tbsp)	25	<1.0	(0.0)	0	300
Tree of Life Salsa, Medium (1 oz)	8	0.0	0.0	0	30
Wise Picante Sauce (2 tbsp)	12	0.0	0.0	(0)	130
PICKLES					
Bread and Butter Pickles—Most Brands (2 slices)	11	tr	0.0	0	101
Dill Pickles, Low Sodium—Most Brands (1 large = 3-3/4″ long)	12	0.1	0.0	0	12
Dill Pickles, Low Sodium—Most Brands (1 slice)	1	0.0	0.0	0	tr
Dill Pickles—Most Brands (1 large = 3-3/4″ long)	12	0.1	0.0	0	833
Featherweight Pickles, Sweet, sliced (3–4 slices)	24	0.0	0.0	0	5
Gedney Dill Pickles (1 oz)	4	0.0	0.0	(0)	280
Gedney Sweet Pantry Pickles (1 oz)	25	0.0	0.0	(0)	170
Giant Fresh Pack Sweet Spears (1 oz)	18	0.0	0.0	0	170
Giant Sweet Pack Cocktail Midgets (1 oz)	45	0.0	0.0	0	170
IGA Dill Salad Cubes (1 oz)	4	0.0	0.0	0	(360)
IGA Fresh Pack Baby Kosher Dill Pickles (1 oz)	4	0.0	0.0	0	(360)
IGA Fresh Pack Icicle Pickles (1 oz)	4	0.0	0.0	0	(360)
IGA Fresh Pack Kosher Dill Pickles (1 oz)	4	0.0	0.0	0	(360)
IGA Hamburger Kosher Pickles (1 oz)	4	0.0	0.0	0	(360)
IGA Kosher Chunk Pickles (1 oz)	4	0.0	0.0	0	(360)

Pickles (continued)	Calories	Fat g	Saturated Fat g	Choles-terol mg	Sodium mg
IGA Kosher Dill Gherkins (1 oz)	4	0.0	0.0	0	(360)
IGA Polish Dill Gherkins (1 oz)	4	0.0	0.0	0	(360)
IGA Polish Style Chunk Pickles (1 oz)	4	0.0	0.0	0	(360)
IGA Salad Picklettes (1 oz)	25	0.0	0.0	0	(200)
IGA Sweet Cucumber Slice Pickles (1 oz)	30	0.0	0.0	0	(200)
IGA Sweet Midget Pickles (1 oz)	35	0.0	0.0	0	(200)
IGA Sweet Mixed Pickles (1 oz)	35	0.0	0.0	0	(200)
IGA Sweet Pickle Chips (1 oz)	50	0.0	0.0	0	(200)
IGA Sweet Salad Cubes (1 oz)	25	0.0	0.0	0	(200)
IGA Whole Sweet Pickles (1 oz)	35	0.0	0.0	0	(200)
IGA Zesty Sweet Chunk Pickles (1 oz)	30	0.0	0.0	0	(200)
Pickled Cocktail Onions—Most Brands (1 onion)	12	0.0	0.0	0	5
Pickled Sweet Peppers—Most Brands (1 med)	8	0.0	0.0	0	26
Sour Pickles, Low Sodium—Most Brands (1 med = 3 3/4" long)	4	0.0	0.0	0	6
Sour Pickles—Most Brands (1 med = 3 3/4" long)	4	0.0	0.0	0	423
Sweet Gherkins—Most Brands (1 med)	18	0.0	0.0	0	141
Vlasic Kosher Pickles, Dill Gherkins (1 oz)	4	0.0	0.0	0	210
Vlasic No Garlic Dill Spears (1 oz)	4	0.0	0.0	0	210
Watermelon Rind Pickles—Most Brands (1 piece)	44	0.1	0.0	0	214

RELISH

Chow Chow, Sour—Most Brands (1 tbsp)	4	0.2	0.0	0	201
Chow Chow, Sweet—Most Brands (1 tbsp)	18	0.1	0.0	0	81
Chutney—Most Brands (1 tbsp)	21	0.1	0.0	0	9

Relish (continued)	Calories	Fat g	Saturated Fat g	Choles- terol mg	Sodium mg
Corn Relish—Most Brands (1 tbsp)	20	0.5	0.0	0	135
Hot Dog Relish—Most Brands (1 tbsp)	14	0.1	0.0	0	164
Old El Paso Jalapeno Relish (2 tbsp)	16	0.0	0.0	0	100
Pickle Relish, Hamburger (1 tbsp)	19	0.0	0.0	0	164
Pickle Relish, Sour—Most Brands (1 tbsp)	3	0.0	0.0	0	192
Pickle Relish, Sweet—Most Brands (1 tbsp)	19	0.1	0.0	0	122
Vlasic Relish, Hot Piccalilli (1 oz)	35	0.0	0.0	0	165
Vlasic Relish, India (1 oz)	30	0.0	0.0	0	205
SOY SAUCE					
Eden Double Brewed Shoyu Soy Sauce, Low Sodium (1/2 tsp)	2	0.0	0.0	0	80
Eden Naturally Brewed Tamari Soy Sauce, Wheat Free (1/2 tsp)	2	0.0	0.0	0	160
Eden Shoyu Soy Sauce, Naturally Brewed (1/2 tsp)	2	0.0	0.0	0	160
Eden Shoyu Soy Sauce, Traditional Japanese (1/2 tsp)	2	0.0	0.0	0	140
Eden Traditional Japanese Shoyu Soy Sauce, Organic (1/2 tsp)	2	0.0	0.0	0	140
Kikkoman Lite Soy Sauce (1 tbsp)	13	0.0	0.0	0	564
Kikkoman Soy Sauce (1 tbsp)	12	0.0	0.0	0	938
La Choy Lite Soy Sauce (1/2 tsp)	1	< 1.0	(0.0)	0	110
La Choy Soy Sauce (1/2 tsp)	2	< 1.0	(0.0)	0	230
OTHER CONDIMENTS					
Betty Crocker Bac*Os (2 tsp)	25	1.0	(< 1.0)	0	90
Dromedary Pimientos, all types (1 oz)	10	0.0	0.0	(0)	5
Giant Capers (1 tbsp)	10	< 1.0	< 1.0	0	300
Giant Pimientos, sliced (2 tbsp)	(6)	0.0	0.0	0	10

Other Condiments (continued)	Calories	Fat g	Saturated Fat g	Choles- terol mg	Sodium mg
Giant Pimientos, whole (2 tbsp)	(6)	0.0	0.0	0	10
La Choy Plum Sauce (2 tbsp)	40	0.0	0.0	0	8
La Choy Sauce, Hot & Spicy Szechwan (1 tbsp)	25	<1.0	(0.0)	0	70
La Choy Sauce, Mandarin Orange (1 tbsp)	25	<1.0	(0.0)	0	40
La Choy Sauce, Tangy Plum (1 tbsp)	25	<1.0	(0.0)	0	10
McCormick Bac 'N Pieces Chips (1/4 tsp)	7	0.1	(0.0)	0	51
Ocean Spray Cran*Fruit Sauce, Cranberry Strawberry, Cranberry Orange or Cranberry Raspberry (2 oz)	100	0.0	0.0	0	10
Talk O' Texas Crisp Okra Pickles (2 pods)	(8)	<0.1	(0.0)	0	244
Talk O' Texas Crisp Okra Pickles, Hot (2 pods)	(8)	<0.1	(0.0)	0	244
Tone's Bacon Bits (1 tsp)	7	0.3	0.0	0	59
Vlasic Hot & Spicy Cauliflower (1 oz)	4	0.0	0.0	0	435
Vlasic Hot & Spicy Garden Mix (1 oz)	4	0.0	0.0	0	380
Vlasic Lightly Spiced Cocktail Onions (1 oz)	4	0.0	0.0	(0)	365
Vlasic Sweet Cauliflower (1 oz)	35	0.0	0.0	0	225

CRACKERS

Crackers and cracker-like foods included in this section of the Guide are low in fat, saturated fat, and cholesterol. A serving of the products in this section, as specified below, does not exceed the cutoff points for these nutrients. Many cracker labels specify the number of crackers equal to one serving (usually ½ ounce). If this information is not provided, you may need to weigh several crackers to determine the number equal to ½ ounce.

CUTOFF POINTS FOR CRACKERS

Fat (grams)	Saturated Fat (grams)	Cholesterol (milligrams)
3	1	10

SERVINGS

Food	Serving Sizes
Crackers	½ ounce
Graham Crackers	see Cookies (page 192)
Rice Cakes, Popcorn Cakes, etc.	½ ounce
Sandwich Crackers	1 ounce

The following abbreviations are used in the Food Sections: oz = ounce; fl oz = fluid ounce; pkg = package; pkt = packet; env = envelope; g = gram; prep (w/ . . .) = prepared with; < = less than; and tr = trace.

Crackers	Calories	Fat g	Saturated Fat g	Choles- terol mg	Sodium mg
CRACKERS					
A&P Saltines (1/2 oz = 5 crackers)	60	2.0	(0.8)	(1)	160
A&P Snack & Party Crackers (1/2 oz = 4 crackers)	70	3.0	(0.8)	(1)	90
A&P Snack Bite-Size Snack Crackers (1/2 oz)	70	3.0	(<1.0)	(0)	90
A&P Snack Rich & Crisp Crackers (1/2 oz = 4 crackers)	70	3.0	(0.8)	(1)	100
A&P Snack Soup & Oyster Crackers (1/2 oz = 32 crackers)	60	2.0	(0.6)	(0)	190
A&P Unsalted Tops Crackers (1/2 oz = 5 crackers)	60	2.0	(0.8)	(1)	90
Barbara's Bakery Wheatine Bits (1/2 oz)	60	1.8	(0.4)	0	132
Barbara's Bakery Wheatines, Cracked Pepper (1/2 oz)	60	1.8	(0.4)	0	132
Barbara's Bakery Wheatines, Lightly Salted Tops (1/2 oz)	60	1.8	(0.4)	0	132
Barbara's Bakery Wheatines, Sesame (1/2 oz)	60	1.8	(0.4)	0	132
Barbara's Bakery Wheatines, Unsalted Tops (1/2 oz)	60	1.8	(0.4)	0	45
Bremner Wafers, Plain (1 oz = 12–14 crackers)	119	3.3	(1.3)	0	165
Cracklesnax (6 crackers)	35	<1.0	(0.0)	(0)	n/a
Cracottes Crackerbread (1 piece)	12	0.2	(0.0)	(0)	20
Crispini, Seeds and Spice (1 oz)	100	1.0	(0.5)	0	120
Crispini, Sesame (1 oz)	100	1.0	(0.5)	0	140
Crispini, Sesame with Garlic (1 oz)	100	1.0	(0.5)	0	140
Crispini, Stoned Ground Wheat (1 oz)	100	1.0	(0.5)	0	140
Delicious Crackers, Real Cheddar Cheese (1/2 oz)	70	3.0	(0.8)	(<2)	135
Delicious Snack Crackers, Crispy Bacon Flavored (1/2 oz = 5 crackers)	70	3.0	(0.8)	0	190
Delicious Snack Crackers, Onion (1/2 oz = 5 crackers)	70	3.0	(0.8)	0	180

Crackers (continued)	Calories	Fat g	Saturated Fat g	Choles- terol mg	Sodium mg
Devonsheer Melba Rounds, Garlic (1/2 oz=5 rounds)	56	1.2	(0.3)	0	132
Devonsheer Melba Rounds, Honey Bran (1/2 oz=5 rounds)	52	0.9	(0.1)	0	98
Devonsheer Melba Rounds, Onion (1/2 oz=5 rounds)	51	0.6	(0.3)	0	120
Devonsheer Melba Rounds, Plain (1/2 oz=5 rounds)	53	0.6	(0.1)	0	111
Devonsheer Melba Rounds, Plain, Unsalted (1/2 oz= 5 rounds)	52	0.6	(0.1)	0	<5
Devonsheer Melba Rounds, Rye (1/2 oz=5 rounds)	53	0.6	(0.3)	0	130
Devonsheer Melba Rounds, Sesame (1/2 oz=5 rounds)	57	1.8	(0.5)	0	131
Featherweight Crispbread, Garlic (1 slice)	25	0.0	0.0	0	40
Featherweight Crispbread, Rye (1 slice)	25	0.0	0.0	0	40
Finn Crisp Bread Cracker, Dark (.4 oz=2 slices)	38	0.0	0.0	(0)	130
Finn Crisp Bread Cracker, Dark with Caraway (.4 oz= 2 slices)	38	0.0	0.0	(0)	130
Fortts Bath Oliver (1 cracker)	8	1.8	(0.7)	(1)	53
Giant Oyster & Soup Crackers (1/2 oz=16 crackers)	60	1.0	<1.0	0	190
Giant Saltine Crackers (1/2 oz= 5 crackers)	60	2.0	1.0	0	210
Giant Saltine Crackers, Unsalted Tops (1/2 oz=5 crackers)	60	1.0	1.0	0	120
Grille French Crisp Toast/Biscottes (1 slice)	35	<1.0	(0.0)	0	35
Grissol Biscottes, 60% Whole Wheat (4 slices)	142	2.0	0.4	0	(79)
Grissol Biscottes, Müsli (4 slices)	147	3.0	1.3	0	(79)
Grissol Biscottes, No Salt Added (4 slices)	146	1.8	0.4	0	11

Crackers (continued)	Calories	Fat g	Saturated Fat g	Choles- terol mg	Sodium mg
Grissol Hors d'oeuvre Petite Biscotte Ronde, Aux Legumes (Vegetable Round Rusk) (10 slices)	126	1.6	0.4	0	(72)
Grissol Hors d'oeuvre Petite Biscotte Ronde, Reguliere (Regular Round Rusk) (10 slices)	127	1.7	0.4	0	(72)
Grissol Melba Toast, 60% Whole Wheat (7 slices)	137	1.4	0.1	0	(194)
Grissol Melba Toast, Double Fiber (7 slices)	137	1.3	0.3	0	(194)
Grissol Melba Toast, No Salt Added (7 slices)	140	1.1	0.2	0	11
Grissol Melba Toast, Regular (7 slices)	135	1.2	0.3	0	(194)
Grissol Melba Toast, Rye (7 slices)	138	1.3	0.3	0	(194)
Grissol Melba Toast, Sesame (7 slices)	140	2.1	0.4	0	(117)
Hain Crackers, Cheese (1 oz)	130	6.0*	(1.7)	(2)	180
Hain Crackers, Onion (1 oz)	130	6.0*	(1.5)	(9)	160
Hain Crackers, Onion, No Salt Added (1 oz)	130	6.0*	(1.5)	(9)	5
Hain Crackers, Rich (1 oz)	130	5.0*	(1.4)	(2)	160
Hain Crackers, Rich, No Salt Added (1 oz)	130	5.0*	(1.4)	(2)	15
Hain Crackers, Rye (1 oz)	120	4.0*	(1.0)	(9)	200
Hain Crackers, Rye, No Salt Added (1 oz)	120	4.0*	(1.0)	(9)	10
Hain Crackers, Sour Cream & Chive (1 oz)	130	6.0*	(1.5)	(9)	150
Hain Crackers, Sour Cream & Chive, No Salt Added (1 oz)	130	6.0*	(1.5)	(9)	25
Hain Crackers, Sourdough (1/2 oz)	65	3.0	(0.8)	(5)	100
Hain Crackers, Sourdough, Low Salt (1 oz)	130	5.0*	(1.3)	(9)	10
Hain Crackers, Vegetable (1 oz)	130	5.0*	(1.3)	(9)	180
Hain Crackers, Vegetable, No Salt Added (1 oz)	130	5.0*	(1.3)	(9)	50

*The value printed for fat is higher than the cutoff point because the manufacturer's serving size is larger than the standard serving size used in evaluating the food.

Crackers (continued)	Calories	Fat g	Saturated Fat g	Choles- terol mg	Sodium mg
Health Valley Stoned Wheat Crackers (1/2 oz)	55	2.0	(0.2)	0	80
Health Valley Stoned Wheat Crackers, Herb (1/2 oz)	55	2.0	(0.2)	0	80
Health Valley Stoned Wheat Crackers, Sesame (1/2 oz)	55	2.0	(0.2)	0	80
House of Aulsebrooks (see The House of Aulsebrooks)					
IGA Cheese Crackers (.5 oz)	70	3.0	(0.8)	1	(130)
IGA Saltines (.5 oz)	80	2.0	(0.8)	0	(180)
IGA Saltines, Unsalted (.5 oz)	60	2.0	(0.8)	0	(105)
IGA Snack Crackers (.5 oz)	70	3.0	(0.8)	0	(150)
IGA Soup & Oyster Crackers (.5 oz)	60	2.0	(0.6)	<1	(95)
IGA Wheat Snack Crackers (.5 oz)	70	3.0	(0.7)	0	(120)
Ideal Norwegian Crispbread, Extra Thins (3 slices)	48	0.0	0.0	(0)	191
Ideal Norwegian Crispbread, Fiber Thins (2 slices)	41	0.5	(0.1)	(0)	175
Interbake Cheddar Thins (1/2 oz = 7 crackers)	70	2.0	(0.6)	(1)	220
Interbake Double Cheddar (1/2 oz = 7 crackers)	70	2.0	(0.6)	(1)	220
Interbake Ham & Cheese Crispy Wafers (1/2 oz = 7 crackers)	70	2.0	(0.6)	(1)	160
Interbake Ocean Crisp (1/2 oz = 1 cracker)	60	2.0	<1.0	0	120
Interbake Sailor Boy Pilot Bread (1 cracker)	100	3.0	<1.0	0	125
Interbake Schooners (1/2 oz = 33 crackers)	60	2.0	<1.0	0	130
Interbake Sesame Crisp Crackers (1/2 oz = 1 cracker)	60	2.0	<1.0	0	120
Interbake Sesame Crisp Wafers (1/2 oz = 4 crackers)	60	2.0	<1.0	0	140
Interbake Stoned Wheat Wafers (1/2 oz = 4 single crackers)	60	1.0	<1.0	0	170
Interbake Wheat Crispy Wafers (1/2 oz = 6 crackers)	70	3.0	(0.7)	(0)	80
J. J. Flats Breadflats, Caraway (1 slice)	52	0.8	(0.4)	0	126

Crackers (continued)	Calories	Fat g	Saturated Fat g	Choles- terol mg	Sodium mg
J. J. Flats Breadflats, Caraway and Salt (1 slice)	51	0.8	(0.4)	0	213
J. J. Flats Breadflats, Cinnamon (1 slice)	53	0.7	(0.3)	0	126
J. J. Flats Breadflats, Flavorall (1 slice)	52	0.9	(0.4)	0	139
J. J. Flats Breadflats, Garlic (1 slice)	52	0.7	(0.3)	0	127
J. J. Flats Breadflats, Oat Bran (1 slice)	49	0.9	(0.4)	0	141
J. J. Flats Breadflats, Onion (1 slice)	53	0.7	(0.3)	0	140
J. J. Flats Breadflats, Plain (1 slice)	53	0.8	(0.4)	0	143
J. J. Flats Breadflats, Poppy (1 slice)	53	1.1	(0.5)	0	126
J. J. Flats Breadflats, Sesame (1 slice)	55	1.5	(0.7)	0	124
Jacobs Choice Grain Crackers (1 cracker)	13	0.9	(0.1)	(0)	72
Jacobs Cream Crackers (1 cracker)	13	1.1	(0.4)	(4)	42
Kavli Crispbread, All Natural Whole Grain (1 slice)	15	< 1.0	(0.0)	0	10
Kavli Crispbread, Muesli (1 slice)	30	0.0	0.0	0	30
Kavli Crispbread, Rye Bran (1 slice)	30	0.2	(0.0)	(0)	35
Kavli Crispy Thin (1 slice)	15	< 1.0	(0.0)	0	10
Kavli Norwegian Crispbread, Thin Style (2 wafers)	40	0.3	(0.0)	(0)	32
Keebler Club Crackers (1/2 oz = 4 crackers)	60	3.0	< 1.0	0	150
Keebler Harvest Wheats Wholegrain Wheat Crackers (1/2 oz = 4 crackers)	60	3.0	< 1.0	0	95
Keebler Munch 'Ems, Cheddar (1/2 oz)	70	3.0	< 1.0	0	220
Keebler Munch 'Ems, Original (1/2 oz)	70	3.0	< 1.0	0	230
Keebler Munch 'Ems, Seasoned Original (1/2 oz)	70	3.0	< 1.0	0	230
Keebler Munch 'Ems, Sour Cream & Onion (1/2 oz)	70	3.0	< 1.0	0	260

Crackers (continued)	Calories	Fat g	Saturated Fat g	Choles- terol mg	Sodium mg
Keebler Toasteds Crackers, Buttercrisp (1/2 oz = 4 crackers)	60	3.0	< 1.0	0	180
Keebler Toasteds Crackers, Wheat (1/2 oz = 4 crackers)	60	3.0	< 1.0	0	125
Keebler Wheatables Whole Wheat Snacks (1/2 oz = 12 crackers)	70	3.0	< 1.0	0	140
Keebler Zesta Saltines, Low Salt (1/2 oz = 5 crackers)	60	2.0	< 1.0	0	95
Keebler Zesta Saltines, Original (1/2 oz = 5 crackers)	60	2.0	< 1.0	0	190
Keebler Zesta Saltines, Wheat (1/2 oz = 5 crackers)	60	2.0	< 1.0	0	190
Keeblers Wheatables, Ranch Whole Wheat (1/2 oz = 11 crackers)	70	3.0	< 1.0	0	190
Krisp Crackers, Oat Bran (1/2 oz = 2 triple crackers)	60	3.0	(0.6)	0	140
LaVosh Hawaii 10-Grain Flatbread (1 piece)	45	1.0	0.0	0	115
LaVosh Hawaii Caraway & Rye (1 piece)	45	1.0	(0.3)	10	110
LaVosh Hawaii Classic Island (1 piece)	45	1.0	(0.3)	10	100
LaVosh Hawaii Slightly Onion (1 piece)	45	1.0	(0.3)	10	100
Lance Oyster Crackers (1/2 oz)	70	2.0	1.0	0	170
Lance Saltines, Slug Pack (1/3 oz = 4 crackers)	50	1.0	0.0	0	130
Lavasch Crisp Wafer Bread, Whole Wheat with Fruit Concentrate (1/2 oz)	59	1.4	(0.6)	0	52
Manischewitz American Matzos (1 board)	115	1.9	(0.4)	n/a	n/a
Manischewitz Dietetic Matzo Thins (1 board)	91	0.4	0.0	0	0
Manischewitz Egg n' Onion Matzos (1 board)	112	1.0	0.2	15	180
Manischewitz Matzo Cracker Miniatures (10 crackers)	90	< 1.0	0.0	0	< 10
Manischewitz Passover Egg Matzo Crackers (10 crackers)	108	2.0	(0.4)	20	< 10

Crackers (continued)	Calories	Fat g	Saturated Fat g	Choles- terol mg	Sodium mg
Manischewitz Passover Matzos (1 board)	129	0.4	0.0	0	<5
Manischewitz Thin Salted Matzos (1 board)	100	0.3	0.0	0	n/a
Manischewitz Thin Tea Matzos (Daily) (1 board)	103	0.3	0.0	0	1
Manischewitz Unsalted Matzos (Daily) (1 board)	110	0.3	0.0	0	1
Manischewitz Whole Wheat Matzos with Bran (1 board)	110	0.6	0.0	0	1
Nabisco American Classic, Dairy Butter (1/2 oz=4 crackers)	70	3.0	<1.0	<2	140
Nabisco American Classic, Golden Sesame (1/2 oz=4 crackers)	70	3.0	<1.0	0	120
Nabisco American Classic, Minced Onion (1/2 oz=4 crackers)	70	3.0	<1.0	0	120
Nabisco American Classic, Toasted Poppy (1/2 oz=4 crackers)	70	3.0	<1.0	0	140
Nabisco Bran Thins, Toasted (1/2 oz= 7 crackers)	60	3.0	<1.0	0	70
Nabisco Cheddar Wedges (1/2 oz=31 crackers)	70	3.0	<1.0	<2	240
Nabisco Crown Pilot (1/2 oz=1 cracker)	70	2.0	<1.0	0	70
Nabisco Dandy Soup and Oyster (1/2 oz=20 crackers)	60	2.0	<1.0	0	220
Nabisco Harvest Crisps, 5 Grain (1/2 oz=6 crackers)	60	2.0	<1.0	0	135
Nabisco Harvest Crisps, Oat (1/2 oz=6 crackers)	60	2.0	<1.0	0	135
Nabisco Harvest Crisps, Rice (1/2 oz=6 crackers)	60	2.0	<1.0	0	135
Nabisco Meal Mates Sesame Bread Wafers (1/2 oz=3 crackers)	70	3.0	<1.0	0	160
Nabisco Mr. Phipps Pretzel Chips, Lightly Salted (1/2 oz=8 crackers)	60	1.0	(<1.0)	0	240
Nabisco Mr. Phipps Pretzel Chips, Original (1/2 oz=8 chips)	60	1.0	(0.5)	0	380

Crackers (continued)	Calories	Fat g	Saturated Fat g	Choles- terol mg	Sodium mg
Nabisco Mr. Phipps Pretzel Chips, Sesame (1/2 oz = 8 chips)	60	2.0	< 1.0	0	350
Nabisco Nips Cheese (1/2 oz = 13 crackers)	70	3.0	< 1.0	< 2	130
Nabisco Oat Thins (1/2 oz = 8 crackers)	70	3.0	< 1.0	0	90
Nabisco Oysterettes, Soup & Oyster (1/2 oz = 18 crackers)	60	1.0	< 1.0	0	140
Nabisco Premium Bits (1/2 oz = 16 crackers)	70	3.0	< 1.0	0	160
Nabisco Premium Plus Saltine, Whole Wheat (1/2 oz = 5 crackers)	60	2.0	< 1.0	0	130
Nabisco Premium Saltine (1/2 oz = 5 crackers)	60	2.0	< 1.0	0	180
Nabisco Premium Saltine, Fat Free (1/2 oz = 5 crackers)	50	0.0	0.0	0	115
Nabisco Premium Saltine, Low Salt (1/2 oz = 5 crackers)	60	2.0	< 1.0	0	115
Nabisco Premium Saltine, Unsalted Tops (1/2 oz = 5 crackers)	60	2.0	< 1.0	0	135
Nabisco Ritz Crackers with Whole Wheat (1/2 oz = 5 crackers)	70	3.0	< 1.0	0	110
Nabisco Rounds, Plain (2 rounds)	20	0.2	(0.0)	0	37
Nabisco Royal Lunch (1/2 oz = 1 cracker)	60	2.0	< 1.0	< 2	80
Nabisco Sociables (1/2 oz = 6 crackers)	70	3.0	< 1.0	0	135
Nabisco Swiss Cheese (1/2 oz = 7 crackers)	70	3.0	< 1.0	< 2	170
Nabisco Swiss Cheese Naturally Flavored Snack Crackers (1/2 oz = 7 crackers)	70	3.0	< 1.0	< 2	170
Nabisco Triscuit Bits Wafers (1/2 oz = 8 crackers)	60	2.0	< 1.0	0	75
Nabisco Triscuit Wafers (1/2 oz = 3 crackers)	60	2.0	< 1.0	0	75
Nabisco Triscuit Wafers, Wheat 'n Bran (1/2 oz = 3 crackers)	60	2.0	< 1.0	0	75

Crackers (continued)	Calories	Fat g	Saturated Fat g	Choles- terol mg	Sodium mg
Nabisco Triscuit Wafers, low salt (1/2 oz = 3 crackers)	60	2.0	< 1.0	0	35
Nabisco Uneeda Biscuits Unsalted Tops (1/2 oz = 2 crackers)	60	2.0	< 1.0	0	100
Nabisco Waverly (1/2 oz = 4 crackers)	70	3.0	< 1.0	0	160
Nabisco Waverly, Low Salt (1/2 oz = 4 crackers)	70	3.0	< 1.0	0	80
Nabisco Wheat Thins (1/2 oz = 8 crackers)	70	3.0	< 1.0	0	120
Nabisco Wheat Thins, Low Salt (1/2 oz = 8 crackers)	70	3.0	< 1.0	0	60
Nabisco Wheatsworth, Stone Ground (1/2 oz = 4 crackers)	70	3.0	< 1.0	0	135
Nabisco Zings Snack Chips (1/2 oz = 15 pieces)	70	3.0	(< 1.0)	0	115
Nabisco Zwieback Toast (1/2 oz = 2 crackers)	60	1.0	< 1.0	< 2	20
Nejaimes Lavasch Crisp Sesame Wafer Bread, Dill & Garlic (1/2 oz)	58	1.1	(0.5)	(0)	57
Nejaimes Lavasch Crisp Sesame Wafer Bread, Garlic (1/2 oz)	58	1.1	(0.5)	(0)	57
Nejaimes Lavasch Crisp Sesame Wafer Bread, Poppy (1/2 oz)	58	1.1	(0.5)	(0)	57
Nejaimes Lavasch Crisp Wafer Bread, Sesame (1/2 oz)	58	1.1	(0.2)	(5)	57
O.T.C. (Original Trenton Cracker) Soup, Chowder and Oyster Crackers (10 gm)	40	1.0	(0.1)	0	5
O.T.C. (Original Trenton Cracker), Wine Crackers (1/2 oz)	60	1.5	(0.2)	0	25
Old London Cracker Bread, Wheat (1/2 oz = 3 slices)	50	< 1.0	(0.0)	0	70
Old London Melba Snacks, Bacon (1/2 oz = approx 5 rounds)	50	1.0	0.0	0	130
Old London Melba Snacks, Cheese (1/2 oz = approx 5 rounds)	50	1.0	0.0	0	120

Crackers (continued)	Calories	Fat g	Saturated Fat g	Choles- terol mg	Sodium mg
Old London Melba Snacks, Garlic (1/2 oz = approx 5 rounds)	50	1.0	0.0	0	105
Old London Melba Snacks, Onion (1/2 oz = approx 5 rounds)	50	1.0	0.0	0	120
Old London Melba Snacks, Rye (1/2 oz = approx 5 rounds)	50	1.0	0.0	0	130
Old London Melba Snacks, Sesame (1/2 oz = approx 5 rounds)	60	2.0	0.0	0	150
Old London Melba Snacks, White (1/2 oz = approx 5 rounds)	50	1.0	0.0	0	110
Old London Melba Snacks, Whole Grain (1/2 oz = approx 5 rounds)	50	1.0	0.0	0	100
Old London Melba Toast, Onion (1/2 oz = 3 slices)	50	<1.0	0.0	0	120
Old London Melba Toast, Rye (1/2 oz = 3 slices)	50	<1.0	0.0	0	130
Old London Melba Toast, Sesame (1/2 oz = 3 slices)	50	1.0	0.0	0	150
Old London Melba Toast, Sesame, Unsalted (1/2 oz = 3 slices)	50	1.0	0.0	0	0
Old London Melba Toast, Wheat (1/2 oz = 3 slices)	50	<1.0	0.0	0	120
Old London Melba Toast, White (1/2 oz = 3 slices)	50	<1.0	0.0	0	110
Old London Melba Toast, White, Unsalted (1/2 oz = 3 slices)	50	<1.0	0.0	0	0
Old London Melba Toast, Whole Grain (1/2 oz = 3 slices)	50	<1.0	0.0	0	120
Old London Melba Toast, Whole Grain, Unsalted (1/2 oz = 3 slices)	50	<1.0	0.0	0	0
Old London Rounds, Bacon (1/2 oz = 5 crackers)	53	1.0	(0.1)	0	126
Old London Rounds, Garlic (1/2 oz = 5 crackers)	56	1.2	(0.2)	0	132

Crackers (continued)	Calories	Fat g	Saturated Fat g	Choles- terol mg	Sodium mg
Old London Rounds, Onion (1/2 oz = 5 rounds)	52	0.8	(0.1)	0	121
Old London Rounds, Rye (1/2 oz = 5 rounds)	52	0.7	(0.4)	0	132
Old London Rounds, Sesame (1/2 oz = 5 rounds)	56	1.8	(0.5)	0	149
Old London Rounds, White (1/2 oz = 5 rounds)	48	0.6	(0.1)	0	111
Old London Rounds, Whole Grain (1/2 oz = 5 crackers)	54	1.2	(0.2)	0	102
Olof Sweden Crisp, Four Grain Rolls (1 crisp)	45	<1.0	(<.5)	(3)	35
Olof Sweden Crisp, Oat Bran Rolls (1 crisp)	44	1.2	0.2	(3)	32
Olof Sweden Crisp, Whole Grain Roll (1 crisp)	42	<1.0	(<.5)	(3)	75
Pepperidge Farm Distinctive Crackers, Butter Flavored Thins (1/2 oz = 4 crackers)	70	3.0	1.0	<5	115
Pepperidge Farm Distinctive Crackers, Cheese Goldfish Thins (1/2 oz = 4 crackers)	50	2.0	0.0	0	160
Pepperidge Farm Distinctive Crackers, Cracked Wheat (3 crackers)	100	4.0*	1.0	0	180
Pepperidge Farm Distinctive Crackers, English Water Biscuit (4 crackers)	70	1.0	0.0	0	100
Pepperidge Farm Distinctive Crackers, Hearty Wheat (4 crackers)	100	5.0*	1.0	0	140
Pepperidge Farm Distinctive Crackers, Sesame (4 crackers)	80	4.0*	1.0	0	140
Pepperidge Farm Distinctive Crackers, Symphony Cracker Assortment (see individual data for each variety)					
Pepperidge Farm Distinctive Crackers, Three Cracker Assortment (see individual data for each variety)					
Pepperidge Farm Distinctive Crackers, Toasted Wheat with Onion (4 crackers)	80	3.0	1.0	0	140

*The value printed for fat is higher than the cutoff point because the manufacturer's serving size is larger than the standard serving size used in evaluating the food.

Crackers (continued)	Calories	Fat g	Saturated Fat g	Choles-terol mg	Sodium mg
Pepperidge Farm Flutters, Garden Herb (3/4 oz)	100	4.0*	1.0	0	190
Pepperidge Farm Flutters, Original Butter (3/4 oz)	100	4.0*	1.0	5	150
Pepperidge Farm Tiny Goldfish Crackers, Cheddar Cheese (1 oz)	120	4.0*	1.0	5	230
Pepperidge Farm Tiny Goldfish Crackers, Cheddar Cheese Snack Pack (1/2 oz)	60	2.0	1.0	<5	115
Pepperidge Farm Tiny Goldfish Crackers, Low Salt Cheddar Cheese (1 oz)	120	4.0*	1.0	5	130
Pepperidge Farm Tiny Goldfish Crackers, Original (1 oz)	130	5.0*	1.0	0	190
Pepperidge Farm Tiny Goldfish Crackers, Parmesan Cheese (1 oz)	120	4.0*	1.0	<5	330
Pepperidge Farm Tiny Goldfish Crackers, Pizza Flavored (1 oz)	130	5.0*	1.0	<5	220
Pepperidge Farm Tiny Goldfish Crackers, Pretzel (1 oz)	110	3.0	0.0	0	160
Pepperidge Farm Tiny Goldfish Crackers, Smoked Flavor Cheddar Cheese Goldfish (45 Crackers)	130	5.0*	(1.0)	(<5)	470
Pepperidge Farm Wholesome Choice Crackers, Garden Vegetable Crackers (5 crackers)	60	2.0	0.0	0	125
Pepperidge Farm Wholesome Choice Crackers, Multi Grain Crackers (4 crackers)	70	2.0	0.0	0	130
Pepperidge Farm Wholesome Choice Crackers, Toasted Rice (4 crackers)	60	2.0	0.0	0	140
Pogen Krisprolls Original Swedish Toast (.4 oz = 1 toast)	38	1.0	(0.4)	0	(50)
Red Oval Farms Stoned Wheat Thins (1/2 oz = 9 crackers)	60	2.0	<1.0	0	140
Rickburn Pita Crisps, Caraway (1 oz)	100	2.0	(0.3)	0	210

*The value printed for fat is higher than the cutoff point because the manufacturer's serving size is larger than the standard serving size used in evaluating the food.

Crackers (continued)	Calories	Fat g	Saturated Fat g	Choles- terol mg	Sodium mg
Rickburn Pita Crisps, Plain (1 oz)	90	1.0	(0.1)	0	320
Rickburn Pita Crisps, Poppy (1 oz)	100	2.0	(0.3)	0	210
Rickburn Pita Crisps, Sesame (1 oz)	100	2.0	(0.3)	0	210
Rykrisp Crackers, Sesame (1/2 oz = 2 triple crackers)	50	2.0	(0.3)	0	105
Rykrisp Seasoned Crackers (1/2 oz = 2 triple crackers)	45	1.0	(0.5)	0	105
Rykrisp Seasoned Twindividuals Snack Crackers (1/2 oz = 2 triple crackers)	45	1.0	(0.5)	0	105
Rykrisp Snack Crackers, Natural (1/2 oz = 2 triple crackers)	40	0.0	0.0	0	75
Ryvita Crisp Bread, Dark Rye (1 cracker)	26	<1.0	0.0	0	35
Ryvita Crisp Bread, High Fiber (1 cracker)	23	<1.0	0.0	0	10
Ryvita Crisp Bread, Light Rye (1 cracker)	26	<1.0	0.0	0	20
Ryvita Crisp Bread, Toasted Sesame Rye (1 cracker)	31	<1.0	0.0	0	10
Ryvita Snackbread, High Fiber (1 cracker)	14	<1.0	0.0	0	25
Ryvita Snackbread, Original Wheat (1 cracker)	20	<1.0	0.0	0	20
Salerno Saltines, Multi-Grain (1/2 oz = 5 crackers)	60	2.0	(0.6)	0	80
Sunshine American Heritage, Wheat & Bran (1/2 oz = 4 crackers)	60	3.0	1.0	0	120
Sunshine American Heritage, Wheat Snack (1/2 oz = 4 crackers)	60	3.0	(1.0)	0	135
Sunshine Cheese Shuffles (1/2 oz = 18 crackers)	70	3.0	1.0	<2	140
Sunshine Hi Ho, Whole Wheat (1/2 oz = 4 crackers)	60	3.0	1.0	0	130
Sunshine Krispy Saltines (1/2 oz = 5 crackers)	60	1.0	<1.0	0	210
Sunshine Krispy Unsalted Tops (1/2 oz = 5 crackers)	60	1.0	(0.3)	0	120

Crackers (continued)	Calories	Fat g	Saturated Fat g	Choles-terol mg	Sodium mg
Sunshine Krispy Saltines, Whole Wheat (1/2 oz = 5 crackers)	60	1.0	< 1.0	0	130
Sunshine Oyster Crackers (1/2 oz = 16 crackers)	60	1.0	(0.3)	0	190
The House of Aulsebrooks Crispbread, Cracked Pepper (1 crispbread)	20	< 1.0	(0.0)	(0)	(20)
The House of Aulsebrooks Crispbread, Sesame (1 crispbread)	20	< 1.0	(0.0)	(0)	(20)
The House of Aulsebrooks Crispbread, Wheaten (1 crispbread)	20	< 1.0	(0.0)	(0)	(20)
Tuscany Toast, Pepato (1 oz)	90	2.0	(0.3)	0	400
Tuscany Toast, Pesto (1 oz)	100	2.0	(0.3)	3	300
Tuscany Toast, Plain (1 oz)	100	2.0	(0.3)	0	390
Tuscany Toast, Tomato-Onion (1 oz)	100	2.0	(0.3)	0	380
Valley Lahvosh Hearts (1/4 oz = 2 hearts)	28	0.4	(0.1)	(0)	44
Valley Lahvosh Rounds (.6 oz = 1 cracker)	70	1.1	(0.2)	(0)	117
Venus Armenian Cracker Bread (1/2 oz = 5 wafers)	60	< 1.0	(0.0)	0	90
Venus Crackers, Corn, Salt Free (1/2 oz = 5 wafers)	60	1.2	(0.2)	0	0
Venus Parak, A Crisp Original Lavash Wafer Bread (1/2 oz = 2 wafers)	60	1.0	0.2	0	90
Venus Parak, A Crisp Sesame Lavash Wafer Bread (1/2 oz = 2 wafers)	60	1.3	0.2	0	70
Venus Wafers, Bran, Salt Free (1/2 oz = 5 wafers)	60	0.7	(0.1)	0	0
Venus Wafers, Cracked Wheat, Salt Free (1/2 oz = 5 wafers)	60	1.3	(0.3)	0	0
Venus Wafers, Oat Bran (1/2 oz = 5 wafers)	60	1.4	(0.3)	0	105
Venus Wafers, Oat Bran, Salt Free (1/2 oz = 5 wafers)	60	1.2	(0.2)	0	0
Venus Wafers, Rye, Salt Free (1/2 oz = 5 wafers)	60	0.7	(0.3)	0	0

Crackers (continued)	Calories	Fat g	Saturated Fat g	Choles- terol mg	Sodium mg
Venus Wafers, Stoned Wheat (1/2 oz = 5 wafers)	60	1.5	(0.4)	0	180
Venus Wafers, Wheat (1/2 oz = 5 wafers)	60	1.5	(0.4)	0	120
Venus Wafers, Wheat, Salt Free (1/2 oz = 5 wafers)	60	1.2	(0.3)	0	0
Wasa Crisp Bread, Falu-Rye (1 slice)	30	0.0	0.0	0	50
Wasa Crisp Bread, Fiber-Plus (1 slice)	35	1.0	(0.3)	0	60
Wasa Crisp Bread, Golden Rye (1 slice)	30	0.0	0.0	0	50
Wasa Crisp Bread, Light Rye (1 slice)	25	0.0	0.0	0	40
Wasa Crisp Bread, Sesame Rye (1 slice)	30	1.0	(0.2)	0	45
Wasa Crisp Bread, Sesame Wheat (1/2 oz – 1 slice)	60	2.0	(0.3)	0	160
Wasa Crisp Bread, Toasted Wheat (1/2 oz = 1 slice)	50	1.0	(0.4)	0	70
Wasa Crispbread, Hearty Rye (1 slice)	50	0.0	0.0	0	75
Weight Watchers Crispbread, Garlic (2 wafers)	30	0.0	0.0	0	55
Weight Watchers Crispbread, Golden Wheat (2 wafers)	30	0.0	0.0	0	55
Weight Watchers Crispbread, Harvest Rice (2 wafers)	30	0.0	0.0	0	55
RICE CAKES					
Chico San Mini Rice Cakes, Apple Cinnamon (1/2 oz = 4 cakes)	60	1.0	(<1.0)	0	20
Chico San Mini Rice Cakes, Cheddar Cheese (1/2 oz = 6 cakes)	70	3.0	(0.5)	0	135
Chico San Mini Rice Cakes, Cinnamon Sugar (1/2 oz = 5 cakes)	50	0.0	0.0	0	0
Chico San Mini Rice Cakes, Honey Nut (1/2 oz = 4 cakes)	60	1.0	(<1.0)	0	35
Chico San Mini Rice Cakes, Sesame, Sodium Free (1/2 oz = 6 cakes)	50	0.0	0.0	0	0

Rice Cakes (continued)	Calories	Fat g	Saturated Fat g	Choles-terol mg	Sodium mg
Chico San Mini Rice Cakes, Sour Cream and Onion (1/2 oz = 4 cakes)	70	3.0	(0.5)	0	100
Chico San Popcorn Cakes, Cheddar Cheese (1 cake)	50	2.0	(1.2)	0	65
Chico San Popcorn Cakes, Lightly Salted (1 cake)	40	0.0	0.0	0	45
Chico San Popcorn Cakes, Lightly Salted (1/8 oz = 1 cake)	40	0.0	0.0	0	45
Chico San Popcorn Cakes, Natural Butter Flavor (1 cake)	40	0.0	0.0	0	45
Chico San Rice Cakes, Ranch Style (.4 oz = 1 cake)	50	2.0	(0.6)	0	50
Chico San Rice Cakes, Sesame, Sodium Free (1 cake)	35	0.0	0.0	0	30
Chico San Rice Cakes, Sesame, Very Low Sodium (.3 oz = 1 cake)	35	0.0	0.0	0	30
Hain Mini Rice Cakes, Apple Cinnamon (1/2 oz)	60	< 1.0	(0.0)	0	10
Hain Mini Rice Cakes, Barbecue (1/2 oz)	70	3.0	(0.8)	0	50
Hain Mini Rice Cakes, Cheese (1/2 oz)	60	2.0	(0.5)	< 5	100
Hain Mini Rice Cakes, Honey Nut (1/2 oz)	60	< 1.0	(0.0)	0	30
Hain Mini Rice Cakes, Nacho Cheese (1/2 oz)	70	2.0	(0.5)	< 5	90
Hain Mini Rice Cakes, Plain (1/2 oz)	60	< 1.0	(0.0)	0	20
Hain Mini Rice Cakes, Plain, No Salt Added (1/2 oz)	60	< 1.0	(0.0)	0	5
Hain Mini Rice Cakes, Ranch (1/2 oz)	70	3.0	(0.8)	0	90
Hain Mini Rice Cakes, Teriyaki (1/2 oz)	50	< 1.0	(0.0)	0	75
Hain Rice Cakes, 5-Grain (1 cake)	40	< 1.0	(0.0)	0	10
Hain Rice Cakes, Plain (1 cake)	40	< 1.0	(0.0)	0	10
Hain Rice Cakes, Plain, No Salt Added (1 cake)	40	< 1.0	(0.0)	0	< 5

Rice Cakes (continued)	Calories	Fat g	Saturated Fat g	Choles- terol mg	Sodium mg
Hain Rice Cakes, Sesame (1 cake)	40	<1.0	(0.0)	0	10
Hain Rice Cakes, Sesame, No Salt Added (1 cake)	40	<1.0	(0.0)	0	<5
Heart Lovers Rice Cakes, Plain, Lightly Salted (1 cake)	35	0.0	0.0	0	30
Heart Lovers Rice Cakes, Sesame, Lightly Salted (1 cake)	35	0.0	0.0	0	30
Mother's Rice Cakes, Barley & Oats (1 cake)	34	0.3	0.1	0	41
Mother's Rice Cakes, Buckwheat (unsalted) (1 cake)	35	0.3	0.1	0	0
Pacific Rice Crispy Cakes (1 cake)	20	0.2	(0.0)	0	1
Pacific Rice Mini Crispys Rice Cake Snacks (1 cake)	12	<1.0	(0.0)	0	10
Pacific Rice Mini Crispys Rice Cake Snacks, Apple Spice (1 cake)	30	<1.0	(0.0)	0	10
Pacific Rice Mini Crispys Rice Cake Snacks, Honey Almond (1 cake)	12	<1.0	(0.0)	0	7
Pacific Rice Mini Crispys Rice Cake Snacks, Honey Sesame (1 cake)	12	<1.0	(0.0)	0	5
Pacific Rice Mini Crispys Rice Cake Snacks, Teriyaki (1 cake)	12	<1.0	(0.0)	0	14
Pritikin Rice Cakes, Multi-Grain (1 cake)	35	0.4	0.1	(0)	29
Pritikin Rice Cakes, Multi-Grain, Salt-Free (1 cake)	35	0.4	0.1	0	0
Pritikin Rice Cakes, Plain (1 cake)	35	0.3	0.1	0	36
Pritikin Rice Cakes, Plain, Unsalted (1 cake)	35	0.3	0.1	0	0
Pritikin Rice Cakes, Sesame (1 cake)	35	0.3	0.1	0	36
Pritikin Rice Cakes, Sesame, Salt-Free (1 cake)	35	0.0	0.1	0	1
Quaker Grain Cakes, Corn (1 cake)	35	0.2	(0.0)	(0)	53
Quaker Grain Cakes, Rye (1 cake)	35	0.3	0.0	0	52

Rice Cakes (continued)	Calories	Fat g	Saturated Fat g	Choles- terol mg	Sodium mg
Quaker Grain Cakes, Wheat (1 cake)	34	0.3	0.1	0	52
Quaker Rice Cakes, Corn (1 cake)	35	0.3	0.1	0	31
Quaker Rice Cakes, Multigrain (1 cake)	34	0.4	0.1	(0)	29
Quaker Rice Cakes, Multigrain (unsalted) (1 cake)	35	0.4	0.1	0	0
Quaker Rice Cakes, Plain (1 cake)	35	0.3	0.1	0	36
Quaker Rice Cakes, Plain (unsalted) (1 cake)	35	0.3	0.1	0	0
Quaker Rice Cakes, Rye (1 cake)	34	0.4	0.1	0	12
Quaker Rice Cakes, Sesame (1 cake)	35	0.3	0.1	0	36
Quaker Rice Cakes, Sesame (unsalted) (1 cake)	35	0.3	0.1	0	1

DAIRY PRODUCTS AND DAIRY SUBSTITUTES

The butterfat in "regular" dairy products is a major source of fat, saturated fat, and cholesterol in the typical American diet. The values for fat, saturated fat, and cholesterol in a serving of the dairy and non-dairy products included in this section of the Guide do not exceed the cutoff points shown below.

Note that the cutoff point for saturated fat in dairy products is 2 grams per serving (as listed below) instead of the 1 gram used for dairy substitutes in this section and for most other products in the Guide. Almost two-thirds of the fat in dairy products is saturated. However, dairy products are an excellent source of calcium and protein. A cutoff point of 2 grams of saturated fat in a serving of dairy products allows inclusion in the Guide of a greater variety of calcium-rich foods, which are important to health. The meal patterns (page 45) include dairy products with 2 grams of saturated fat per serving and still provide less than 10% of total calories from saturated fat per day.

CUTOFF POINTS FOR DAIRY PRODUCTS AND DAIRY SUBSTITUTES

	Fat (grams)	Saturated Fat (grams)	Cholesterol (milligrams)
Dairy Products	3	2	10
Dairy Substitutes	3	1	10

SERVINGS

Food	Serving Sizes
Dairy Products:	
Cheese	1 ounce
Cottage Cheese	4 ounces
Evaporated Milk	½ cup
Milk and Buttermilk	8 fluid ounces
Sour Cream	2 tablespoons
Yogurt	8 ounces
Dairy Substitutes:	
Coffee Creamers: Powdered	2 teaspoons
Liquid	2 tablespoons
Sour Cream	2 tablespoons
Whipped Topping, Prepared	2 tablespoons

Cheese. Most varieties of regular cheese (cheddar, Swiss, and American) provide from 8 to 9 grams of fat and from 5 to 6 grams of saturated fat per ounce. In this Guide, varieties of cheese either with no fat or containing 3 grams or less of fat and 2 grams or less of saturated fat per ounce are listed alphabetically according to type. Although the amount of calcium in different types and brands of cheese varies, cheeses that are lower in fat provide about as much calcium as cheeses containing more fat. Be aware that pre-sliced cheese often weighs ⅔ of an ounce or ¾ of an ounce per slice but the nutrition labeling on the package is for 1 ounce. It takes 1½ of the ⅔-ounce slices and 1⅓ of the ¾-ounce slices to equal 1 ounce of cheese.

Cottage Cheese. All brands labeled nonfat, 1%, or 1½% low-fat cottage cheese are low enough in fat and saturated fat not to exceed the cutoff points. Most types of cottage cheese in the Guide are listed as "most brands." However, specific brand names are listed for products that have added ingredients, such as fruit, vegetables, or flavorings.

Milk. The Guide does not include each brand of milk containing 1% or less butterfat (skim, ½%, and 1% low-fat milk), since this would entail listing identical products from hundreds of local dairies. The majority of milk products are listed as "most brands." However, specific brand names are listed for a few types of milk that are more unusual.

Non-dairy Coffee Creamers. These products can be powdered or liquid. Remember that even though 1 serving (2 teaspoons) of some powdered coffee creamers provides only 2 grams of fat, using that amount in each of 5 cups of coffee adds 10 grams of fat to your day's intake.

Sour Cream and Sour Cream Substitutes. Although some sour cream substitutes included in the Guide may contain oils high in saturated fat (coconut, palm kernel, and palm oil), the total fat and saturated fat in a serving, as listed, do not exceed the cutoff points.

Whipped Topping. Even though some non-dairy whipped toppings included in the Guide may contain oils high in saturated fat (coconut, palm kernel, and palm oil), the total fat and saturated fat in a serving do not exceed the cutoff points.

Yogurt. Many brands of yogurt that are low in fat and all nonfat yogurt qualify for the Guide. Yogurt containing fruit or vegetables may appear to be lower in fat than plain yogurt because part of the volume is filled with these fat-free ingredients. Single-serving containers of yogurt come in many sizes, including 4 ounces, 4.4 ounces, 6 ounces, and 8 ounces. When comparing the nutrition information on the labels of different brands of yogurt, be sure that the values are for the same size serving. See page 70 for an example of how to convert the values for a 4.4-ounce serving of yogurt to values for the 8-ounce serving size used for evaluating yogurt. (For frozen yogurt, see page 218 in the Frozen Desserts section.)

The following abbreviations are used in the Food Sections: oz = ounce; fl oz = fluid ounce; pkg = package; pkt = packet; env = envelope; g = gram; prep (w/ . . .) = prepared with; < = less than; and tr = trace.

Cheese	Calories	Fat g	Saturated Fat g	Choles- terol mg	Sodium mg
CHEESE					
AMERICAN CHEESE					
Borden Lite-Line Pasteurized Process Cheese Product Singles, American Flavor, Yellow and White (2/3 oz)	35	2.0	(1.3)	5	280
Borden Lite-Line Pasteurized Process Cheese Product, Low Sodium (2/3 oz)	35	2.0	(1.3)	5	90
Count Down Imitation Cheese (1 oz)	40	<1.0	(<1.0)	2	(439)
Heart Beat Slices, American (2/3 oz)	35	2.0	<1.0	0	180
IGA Sliced Pasteurized Processed Cheese Product (1 oz)	60	3.0	(1.9)	8	(420)
Kraft Free Singles Nonfat Pasteurized Process Cheese Product (1 oz)	45	0.0	0.0	5	420
Tasty-Lo Cheese, American (1 oz)	50	2.0	(1.3)	10	200
Weight Watcher's Cheese Slices, American Flavor (2/3 oz = 1 slice)	35	1.0	(0.6)	5	270
Weight Watchers Slices, American, White or Yellow (1 oz)	50	2.0	1.0	5	400
Weight Watchers Slices, Low Sodium American, White or Yellow (1 oz)	50	2.0	1.0	5	120
CHEDDAR CHEESE					
Alpine Lace Free N'Lean Pasteurized Process Skim Milk Cheese, All Varieties (1 oz)	35	0.0	0.0	5	290
Alpine Lace Free N'Lean Skim Milk Cheese (1 oz)	40	0.0	0.0	5	120
Borden Lite-Line Pasteurized Process Cheese Product, Mild Cheddar Flavor (2/3 oz)	35	2.0	(1.3)	5	300
Borden Lite-Line Pasteurized Process Cheese Product Singles, Sharp Cheddar Flavor (2/3 oz)	35	2.0	(1.3)	5	300
County Line Advantage Cheddar Cheese (1 oz)	70	3.0	1.9	13	50

Cheese (continued)	Calories	Fat g	Saturated Fat g	Choles- terol mg	Sodium mg
County Line Light Reduced Fat/Sodium Cheddar Cheese (1 oz)	80	4.0	2.0	12	90
Heart Beat Slices, Sharp Cheddar Cheese Flavor (2/3 oz)	35	2.0	<1.0	0	210
Lifetime Fat Free Cheese, Cheddar (1 oz)	40	0.0	0.0	3	200
Lifetime Natural Cheese, Mild Cheddar (1 oz)	70	3.0	(2.0)	9	60
Mrs. Margareten's Parvemage Cheese Alternative, Cheddar (1 oz)	60	3.0	<1.0	0	120
Weight Watchers Slices, Sharp Cheddar (1 oz)	50	2.0	1.0	5	400
COTTAGE CHEESE					
Borden Dry Curd Cottage Cheese, 0.5% Milkfat (1/2 cup)	80	1.0	(0.6)	(8)	20
Borden Lite-Line Lowfat Cottage Cheese, 1-1/2% Milkfat (1/2 cup)	90	2.0	(1.3)	(7)	400
Borden Lite-Line Nonfat Cottage Cheese (1/2 cup)	70	0.0	0.0	5	430
Breakstone's Cottage Cheese, Dry Curd (4 oz)	90	0.0	0.0	10	65
Cottage Cheese, 1% Fat—Most Brands (1/2 cup)	82	1.2	0.7	5	459
Cottage Cheese, 2% Fat—Most Brands (1/2 cup)	101	2.2	1.4	9	459
Cottage Cheese, Dry Curd—Most Brands (1/2 cup)	62	0.3	0.2	5	10
Friendship Lactose Reduced Lowfat Cottage Cheese, 1% Milk Fat (4 oz)	90	1.0	(0.6)	5	350
Friendship Large Curd Pot Style Lowfat Cottage Cheese, 2% Milk Fat (4 oz)	100	2.0	(1.3)	9	405
Friendship Lowfat Cottage Cheese, 1% Milk Fat (4 oz)	90	1.0	(0.6)	5	350
Friendship Lowfat Cottage Cheese, 1% Milk Fat, No Salt Added (4 oz)	90	1.0	(0.6)	5	31

Cheese (continued)	Calories	Fat g	Saturated Fat g	Choles- terol mg	Sodium mg
Friendship Lowfat Cottage Cheese with Pineapple, 1% Milk Fat (4 oz)	110	1.0	(0.6)	5	300
Friendship Nonfat Cottage Cheese (1/2 cup)	70	0.0	0.0	0	350
Giant Lowfat Cottage Cheese, Lite One, 1% Milkfat (1/2 cup)	90	1.0	< 1.0	5	285
Giant Lowfat Cottage Cheese, No Salt Added, 1% Milkfat (1/2 cup)	90	1.0	< 1.0	5	35
Kemps Lite Cottage Cheese (4 oz)	90	1.0	(0.6)	(5)	490
Knudsen Lowfat Cottage Cheese, 2% Milkfat, with Fruit Cocktail (4 oz)	130	2.0	2.0	10	330
Knudsen Lowfat Cottage Cheese, 2% Milkfat, with Mandarin Orange (4 oz)	110	2.0	2.0	10	320
Knudsen Lowfat Cottage Cheese, 2% Milkfat, with Pear (4 oz)	110	2.0	2.0	10	320
Knudsen Nonfat Cottage Cheese (4 oz)	70	0.0	0.0	5	420
Light 'N Lively Free Nonfat Cottage Cheese (4 oz)	90	0.0	0.0	10	400
Light N' Lively Lowfat Cottage Cheese, 1% Milkfat, Garden Salad (4 oz)	80	2.0	1.0	10	350
Light N' Lively Lowfat Cottage Cheese, 1% Milkfat, with Peach and Pineapple (4 oz)	100	1.0	1.0	10	320
Nancy's Lowfat Cottage Cheese (4 oz)	82	1.0	(0.6)	5	353
Viva Nonfat Cottage Cheese (1/2 cup)	70	0.0	0.0	5	430
CREAM CHEESE					
Mrs. Margareten's Parvemage Cream Cheese (1 oz)	60	3.0	< 1.0	0	120
Weight Watchers Creamed Cheese (1 oz)	35	2.0	(1.3)	(6)	40

Cheese (continued)	Calories	Fat g	Saturated Fat g	Choles- terol mg	Sodium mg
MONTEREY JACK CHEESE					
Borden Lite-Line Pasteurized Process Cheese Product, Monterey Jack (2/3 oz)	35	2.0	(1.3)	5	245
County Line Advantage Monterey Jack Cheese (1 oz)	70	3.0	1.9	13	50
Lifetime Natural Cheese, Monterey Jack (1 oz)	70	3.0	(1.9)	9	60
Mrs. Margareten's Parvemage Cheese Alternative, Monterey Jack (1 oz)	60	3.0	<1.0	0	120
MOZZARELLA CHEESE					
County Line Advantage Mozzarella Cheese (1 oz)	60	2.0	1.3	8	70
County Line Light Reduced Fat/Sodium Mozzarella Cheese (1 oz)	70	3.0	1.0	10	70
Frigo Lite Low Moisture Part Skim Mozzarella (1 oz)	60	2.0	2.0	8	140
Frigo Shredded Pizza Cheese (1 oz)	65	3.0	(1.9)	10	150
Lifetime Natural Cheese, Mozzarella (1 oz)	60	2.0	(1.3)	7	50
Mrs. Margareten's Parvemage Cheese Alternative, Mozzarella (1 oz)	60	3.0	<1.0	0	120
Polly-O Free Natural Nonfat Cheese, Mozzarella or Shredded Mozzarella (1 oz)	40	0.0	0.0	5	240
Polly-O Lite Cheese, Mozzarella (1 oz)	60	3.0	2.0	10	240
Sargento Preferred Light, Fancy Shredded Reduced Fat Mozzarella (1 oz)	60	3.0	1.9	10	150
Sargento Preferred Light, Sliced Mozzarella (1 oz)	60	3.0	(1.9)	10	150
PARMESAN AND ROMANO CHEESE					
Sargento Preferred Light, Grated Parmesan (1/3 oz)	43	1.0	(0.6)	(5)	95
RICOTTA CHEESE					
Crystal Farm's Lite Ricotta Cheese (1 oz)	20	1.0	(0.6)	14	20

Cheese (continued)	Calories	Fat g	Saturated Fat g	Choles- terol mg	Sodium mg
Frigo Low Fat Low Salt Ricotta (1 oz)	30	1.0	(0.6)	5	10
Frigo Part Skim Ricotta (1 oz)	40	3.0	(1.9)	10	30
Frigo Truly Lite No Fat Ricotta (1 oz)	20	1.0	0.0	3	15
Giant Ricotta, Part Skim (1 oz)	40	3.0	(1.9)	10	55
Maggio Ricotta Cheese, Non Fat (1 oz)	20	<0.5	<0.2	<2	50
Maggio Ricotta Cheese, Part Skim (2 oz)	80	5.0*	3.1	10	105
Miceli Ricotta, Natural Lite (1 oz)	25	1.0	(0.6)	14	20
Polly-O Free Natural Nonfat Cheese, Ricotta (1 oz)	25	0.0	0.0	0	35
Ricotta, Part Skim Milk—Most Brands (1 oz)	39	2.2	1.4	9	35
Sargento Ricotta Lite (1 oz)	24	0.8	(0.5)	4	23
STRING CHEESE					
Frigo Lite String Cheese (1 oz)	60	2.0	2.0	8	140
Sargento MooTown Snackers Light String Cheese, Mozzarella (1 oz)	40	2.0	(1.3)	10	125
SWISS CHEESE					
Borden Lite-Line Pasteurized Process Cheese Product Singles, Swiss Flavor (1 oz)	50	2.0	(1.3)	(6)	380
County Line Advantage Swiss Cheese (1 oz)	80	3.0	1.9	12	8
Lifetime Fat Free Cheese, Swiss (1 oz)	40	0.0	0.0	3	200
Mrs. Margareten's Parvemage Cheese Alternative, Swiss (1 oz)	60	3.0	<1.0	0	120
Swiss Knight Light (1 oz)	45	2.0	(1.2)	5	370
OTHER TYPES OR FLAVORS OF CHEESE					
Borden Lite-Line Pasteurized Process Cheese Product, Colby (2/3 oz)	35	2.0	(1.3)	5	240
Borden Lite-Line Pasteurized Process Cheese Product, Muenster (2/3 oz)	35	2.0	(1.3)	5	245

*The value printed for fat is higher than the cutoff point because the manufacturer's serving size is larger than the standard serving size used in evaluating the food.

Cheese (continued)	Calories	Fat g	Saturated Fat g	Choles- terol mg	Sodium mg
County Line Advantage Colby Cheese (1 oz)	70	3.0	(1.9)	13	50
Friendship Farmer Cheese (4 oz)	160	12.0*	(1.9)	40	356
Friendship Farmer Cheese, No Salt Added (4 oz = 1/2 cup)	160	12.0*	(1.9)	40	8
Laughing Cow Lite Soft Cheese Spread, Original Flavor (1 oz)	45	2.0	(1.2)	5	250
Laughing Cow Reduced Calorie Cheesebits (1/6 oz)	8	0.4	(0.2)	(2)	55
Laughing Cow Reduced Calorie Wedges (1 oz)	50	3.0	(1.9)	10	370
Lifetime Fat Free Cheese, Garden Vegetable (1 oz)	40	0.0	0.0	3	200
Lifetime Fat Free Cheese, Mild Mexican (1 oz)	40	0.0	0.0	3	200
Mrs. Margareten's Parvemage Cheese Alternative, Jalapeno (1 oz)	60	3.0	< 1.0	0	120
Tasty-Lo Cheese, Dill (1 oz)	50	2.0	(1.3)	10	299
Tasty-Lo Cheese, Garlic (1 oz)	50	2.0	(1.3)	10	299
Tasty-Lo Cheese, Onion (1 oz)	50	2.0	(1.3)	10	299
Tasty-Lo Cheese, Pepper (1 oz)	50	2.0	(1.3)	10	299
CHEESE SPREADS					
Koched Kase High Protein Dairy Spread (1 oz)	25	0.0	0.0	0	260
Koched Kase High Protein Dairy Spread, Caraway (1 oz)	25	0.0	0.0	0	260
Sargento Pot Cheese (1 oz)	26	0.2	(0.1)	(2)	1
Tupper Pot Cheese Diet Dairy Spread (1 oz)	25	0.0	0.0	0	185
Weight Watchers Cheese Cup, Port Wine (1 oz)	70	3.0	2.0	10	190
Weight Watchers Cheese Cup, Sharp Cheddar (1 oz)	70	3.0	2.0	10	190

*The value printed for fat is higher than the cutoff point because the manufacturer's serving size is larger than the standard serving size used in evaluating the food.

Coffee Creamers	Calories	Fat g	Saturated Fat g	Choles- terol mg	Sodium mg
COFFEE CREAMERS					
LIQUID					
Carnation Coffee-Mate Lite Non-Dairy Creamer, Liquid (1 tbsp)	10	<1.0	0.0	0	10
Carnation Coffee-Mate Non-Dairy Creamer, Liquid (1 tbsp)	16	1.0	0.3	0	5
Mocha Mix Lite Non-Dairy Creamer (1 tbsp)	9	0.8	0.1	0	4
Mocha Mix Lite Non-Dairy Creamer (1 tbsp)	10	<1.0	0.0	0	0
Mocha Mix Non-Dairy Creamer (1 tbsp)	19	1.6	0.3	0	(7)
POWDER					
Carnation Coffee-Mate Lite Non-Dairy Creamer, Powder (1 tsp)	8	<1.0	0.3	0	0
Carnation Coffee-Mate Non-Dairy Creamer, Powder (1 tsp)	10	<1.0	0.7	0	<5
Carnation Lite Non-Dairy Creamer (1 tbsp)	10	<1.0	(0.0)	0	10
Morning Blend Non-Dairy Creamer (2 tbsp)	30	3.0	0.0	0	10
Swiss Miss N'Rich Coffee Cream (1 tsp)	10	<1.0	0.3	0	0
Weight Watchers Dairy Creamer Instant Non-Fat Dry Milk (1 pkt)	10	0.0	0.0	0	15
MILK SUBSTITUTES					
Edensoy Natural Soy Beverage, Vanilla (8.45 fl oz)	150	3.0	0.4	0	140
Second Nature Lowfat Milk Alternative, Lactose Free (8 oz)	100	3.0	<1.0	0	5
MILK AND BUTTERMILK					
Borden Lowfat Milk, 1% Milkfat with L. Acidophilus Culture Added (1 cup)	100	2.0	(1.2)	(10)	130
Buttermilk, Cultured—Most Brands (1 cup)	99	2.2	1.3	9	257

Milk and Buttermilk (continued)	Calories	Fat g	Saturated Fat g	Choles- terol mg	Sodium mg
Carnation Evaporated Lowfat Milk (1/2 cup)	110	3.0	2.0	8	12
Carnation Evaporated Skim Milk (1/2 cup)	100	<1.0	0.2	9	4
Evaporated Skim Milk, canned—Most Brands (1/2 cup)	99	0.3	0.2	5	147
Golden Daisy Nonfat Milk (1 cup)	100	<1.0	0.0	0	100
Lactaid Lactose Reduced Nonfat Milk (1 cup)	90	0.0	0.0	(4)	125
Milk, 1% Fat—Most Brands (1 cup)	102	2.6	1.6	10	123
Milk, 1/2% Fat—Most Brands (1 cup)	94	1.0	1.0	7	125
Milk, Nonfat Dry—Most Brands (1/4 cup)	109	<1.0	0.0	0	161
Milk, Skim or Nonfat—Most Brands (1 cup)	86	0.4	0.3	4	126
SOUR CREAM					
Borden Lite-Line Lowfat Sour Cream, 9% (1 oz = 2 tbsp)	40	2.0	(1.2)	10	30
Friendship Light Sour Cream (1 oz)	35	2.0	(1.3)	8	25
Kemps Lite Sour Cream (1 oz = 2 tbsp)	30	2.0	(1.2)	(8)	35
King Cholesterol Free Non-Butterfat Sour Cream Alternative (1 oz)	40	3.0	<1.0	0	20
King Sour Non-Butterfat Sour Dressing (1 oz)	40	3.0	(<1.0)	0	15
Knudsen Light Sour Cream (2 tbsp)	35	2.0	(1.2)	10	20
Land O'Lakes Light Sour Cream (2 tbsp)	40	2.0	1.0	5	35
Land O'Lakes Light Sour Cream, Chives (2 tbsp)	40	2.0	1.0	5	150
Light N' Lively Free Nonfat Sour Cream Alternative (1/2 oz)	8	0.0	0.0	0	10
Lucerne Light Sour Cream (2 tbsp)	45	3.0	(1.9)	(12)	20
Neilson Light Sour Cream (2 tbsp)	32	1.7	1.1	5	(25)

Sour Cream (continued)	Calories	Fat g	Saturated Fat g	Choles- terol mg	Sodium mg
Ralph's Lite n' Lean Sour Cream (4 tbsp)	80	6.0*	(3.7)	(22)	50
Sour Lean (2 tbsp)	40	2.0	(1.2)	(10)	16
Viva Light Sour Cream (1 tbsp)	20	1.0	(0.6)	(4)	15
Viva Lite Lowfat Sour Cream, 9% (1 oz = 2 tbsp)	40	2.0	(1.2)	10	30
Weight Watchers Light Sour Cream (2 tbsp)	35	2.0	(1.3)	(7)	40
WHIPPED TOPPING					
A&P Handi Whip Non-Dairy Whipped Topping (1 tbsp)	14	1.0	(<1.0)	(0)	0
Cool Whip Lite Whipped Topping (1 tbsp)	8	<1.0	(<1.0)	0	0
Dream Whip Whipped Topping Mix, prep (w/whole milk) (1 tbsp)	10	0.0	0.0	0	0
Featherweight Whipped Topping (1 tbsp)	4	0.0	0.0	0	5
Flav-O-Rite Non Dairy Whipped Topping (1 tbsp)	12	1.0	(0.9)	0	5
Giant Whipped Topping (1 tbsp)	14	1.0	(0.4)	0	0
IGA Whipped Topping (1/2 cup)	70	2.0	(1.7)	0	(28)
La Creme (1 tbsp)	16	1.0	(<1.0)	<1	5
Pet Whip (1 tbsp)	14	1.0	(<1.0)	(<1)	0
Reddi Wip Lite Whipped Topping (1 tbsp)	6	<0.5	(0.0)	0	2
Valu Time Non Dairy Frozen Whipped Topping (1 tbsp)	14	1.0	(0.9)	(0)	0
YOGURT					
Altadena Nonfat Yogurt, Black Cherry (1 cup)	190	<1.0	(0.0)	(0)	128
Altadena Nonfat Yogurt, Mixed Berries (1 cup)	200	<1.0	(0.0)	(0)	128
Altadena Nonfat Yogurt, Plain (1 cup)	100	<1.0	(0.0)	(0)	160
Altadena Nonfat Yogurt, Strawberry (1 cup)	190	<1.0	(0.0)	(0)	128
Altadena Nonfat Yogurt, Vanilla (1 cup)	170	<1.0	(0.0)	(0)	140

*The value printed for fat is higher than the cutoff point because the manufacturer's serving size is larger than the standard serving size used in evaluating the food.

Yogurt (continued)	Calories	Fat g	Saturated Fat g	Choles- terol mg	Sodium mg
Borden Lite-Line Lowfat Yogurt, Cherry Vanilla (1 cup)	240	2.0	(1.2)	(10)	150
Borden Lite-Line Lowfat Yogurt, Peach (1 cup)	230	2.0	(1.2)	(10)	150
Borden Lite-Line Lowfat Yogurt, Strawberry (1 cup)	240	2.0	(1.2)	(10)	150
Breyer's Lowfat Yogurt, 1% Milkfat, Black Cherry (8 oz)	260	3.0	1.0	10	120
Breyer's Lowfat Yogurt, 1% Milkfat, Blueberry (8 oz)	250	2.0	1.0	10	120
Breyer's Lowfat Yogurt, 1% Milkfat, Mixed Berry (8 oz)	250	2.0	1.0	10	120
Breyer's Lowfat Yogurt, 1% Milkfat, Peach (8 oz)	250	2.0	1.0	10	120
Breyer's Lowfat Yogurt, 1% Milkfat, Pineapple (8 oz)	250	2.0	1.0	10	120
Breyer's Lowfat Yogurt, 1% Milkfat, Red Raspberry (8 oz)	250	2.0	1.0	10	120
Breyer's Lowfat Yogurt, 1% Milkfat, Strawberry (8 oz)	250	2.0	1.0	10	120
Breyer's Lowfat Yogurt, 1% Milkfat, Strawberry Banana (8 oz)	250	2.0	1.0	10	120
Colombo Nonfat Lite Minipack, all flavors (4.4 oz)	100	0.0	0.0	0	70
Colombo Nonfat Lite Yogurt, Vanilla (8 oz)	160	< 1.0	(0.0)	5	140
Colombo Nonfat Yogurt, Fruit on the Bottom, all flavors (8 oz)	190	< 1.0	(0.0)	5	140
Continental Light Nonfat Yogurt with Nutrasweet, Strawberry-Banana (7 oz)	80	0.0	0.0	0	100
Continental Light Nonfat Yogurt with Nutrasweet, Peach (7 oz)	80	0.0	0.0	0	100
Continental Light Nonfat Yogurt with Nutrasweet, Strawberry (7 oz)	80	0.0	0.0	0	100
Continental Light Nonfat Yogurt with Nutrasweet, Wild Berry (7 oz)	80	0.0	0.0	0	100
Dannon Blended Fat Free Yogurt, Blueberry (6 oz)	150	0.0	0.0	< 5	110

Yogurt (continued)	Calories	Fat g	Saturated Fat g	Choles- terol mg	Sodium mg
Dannon Blended Fat Free Yogurt, Peach (6 oz)	150	0.0	0.0	<5	110
Dannon Blended Fat Free Yogurt, Raspberry (6 oz)	150	0.0	0.0	<5	110
Dannon Blended Fat Free Yogurt, Strawberry (6 oz)	150	0.0	0.0	<5	110
Dannon Blended Fat Free Yogurt, Strawberry-Banana (6 oz)	150	0.0	0.0	<5	110
Dannon Lowfat Fruit on Bottom Mini-6 Pack (1% Milkfat), Blueberry/Raspberry (4.4 oz)	120	1.0	(0.6)	5	65
Dannon Lowfat Fruit on Bottom Yogurt Mini-6 Pack (1% Milkfat), Strawberry-Banana/Cherry (4.4 oz)	120	1.0	(0.6)	5	65
Dannon Lowfat Fruit on Bottom Yogurt Mini-6 Pack (1% Milkfat), Strawberry/Blueberry (4.4 oz)	120	1.0	(0.6)	5	65
Dannon Lowfat Fruit on Bottom Yogurt Mini-6 Pack (1% Milkfat), Strawberry/Mixed Berries (4.4 oz)	120	1.0	(0.6)	5	65
Dannon Lowfat Fruit on Bottom Yogurt, Banana (8 oz)	240	3.0	(1.9)	10	120
Dannon Lowfat Fruit on Bottom Yogurt, Blueberry (8 oz)	240	3.0	(1.9)	10	120
Dannon Lowfat Fruit on Bottom Yogurt, Boysenberry (8 oz)	240	3.0	(1.9)	10	120
Dannon Lowfat Fruit on Bottom Yogurt, Cherry (8 oz)	240	3.0	(1.9)	10	120
Dannon Lowfat Fruit on Bottom Yogurt, Dutch Apple (8 oz)	240	3.0	(1.9)	10	120
Dannon Lowfat Fruit on Bottom Yogurt, Exotic Fruit (8 oz)	240	3.0	(1.9)	10	120
Dannon Lowfat Fruit on Bottom Yogurt, Mixed Berries (8 oz)	240	3.0	(1.9)	10	120
Dannon Lowfat Fruit on Bottom Yogurt, Peach (8 oz)	240	3.0	(1.9)	10	120

Yogurt (continued)	Calories	Fat g	Saturated Fat g	Choles- terol mg	Sodium mg
Dannon Lowfat Fruit on Bottom Yogurt, Pina-Colada (8 oz)	240	3.0	(1.9)	10	120
Dannon Lowfat Fruit on Bottom Yogurt, Raspberry (8 oz)	240	3.0	(1.9)	10	120
Dannon Lowfat Fruit on Bottom Yogurt, Strawberry (8 oz)	240	3.0	(1.9)	10	120
Dannon Lowfat Fruit on Bottom Yogurt, Strawberry-Banana (8 oz)	240	3.0	(1.9)	10	120
Dannon Lowfat Yogurt, Coffee (8 oz)	200	3.0	(1.9)	10	120
Dannon Lowfat Yogurt, Lemon (8 oz)	200	3.0	(1.9)	10	120
Dannon Lowfat Yogurt, Vanilla (8 oz)	200	3.0	(1.9)	10	120
Dannon Nonfat Blended Yogurt, Blueberry (6 oz)	140	0.0	0.0	<5	105
Dannon Nonfat Blended Yogurt, Peach (6 oz)	140	0.0	0.0	<5	105
Dannon Nonfat Blended Yogurt, Raspberry (6 oz)	140	0.0	0.0	<5	105
Dannon Nonfat Blended Yogurt, Strawberry (6 oz)	140	0.0	0.0	<5	105
Dannon Nonfat Blended Yogurt, Strawberry-Banana (6 oz)	140	0.0	0.0	<5	105
Dannon Nonfat Light Yogurt with Aspartame, Cherry Vanilla (8 oz)	100	0.0	0.0	<5	130
Dannon Nonfat Light Yogurt with Aspartame, Peach (8 oz)	100	0.0	0.0	<5	130
Dannon Nonfat Light Yogurt with Aspartame, Raspberry (8 oz)	100	0.0	0.0	<5	130
Dannon Nonfat Light Yogurt with Aspartame, Strawberry (8 oz)	100	0.0	0.0	<5	130
Dannon Nonfat Light Yogurt with Aspartame, Strawberry Fruit Cup (8 oz)	100	0.0	0.0	<5	130

Yogurt (continued)	Calories	Fat g	Saturated Fat g	Choles- terol mg	Sodium mg
Dannon Nonfat Light Yogurt with Aspartame, Strawberry-Banana (8 oz)	100	0.0	0.0	<5	130
Dannon Nonfat Light Yogurt with Aspartame, Vanilla (8 oz)	100	0.0	0.0	<5	130
Dannon Nonfat Light with Aspartame, Blueberry (8 oz)	100	0.0	0.0	<5	130
Danone Fresh Flavors Yogurt, Banana (6.2 oz)	160	2.6	(1.7)	7	103
Danone Fresh Flavors Yogurt, Cafe Au Lait (6.2 oz)	160	2.6	(1.7)	7	103
Danone Fresh Flavors Yogurt, Lemon (6.2 oz)	160	2.6	(1.7)	7	103
Danone Fresh Flavors Yogurt, Vanilla (6.2 oz)	160	2.6	(1.7)	7	103
Danone Yogurt, Lowfat (6.2 oz)	105	2.6	(1.7)	7	134
Danone Yogurt, Nofat (6.2 oz)	86	0.3	(0.1)	1	136
Giant Nonfat Yogurt, Plain (8 oz)	120	0.0	0.0	5	170
Jerseymaid Light Yogurt with Aspartame, Mixed Berry (6 oz)	90	0.0	0.0	<5	110
Jerseymaid Light Yogurt with Aspartame, Peach (6 oz)	90	0.0	0.0	<5	110
Jerseymaid Light Yogurt with Aspartame, Strawberry Banana (6 oz)	90	0.0	0.0	<5	110
Jerseymaid Light Yogurt, Plain Nonfat (6 oz)	98	0.0	0.0	<1	140
Jerseymaid Light Yogurt with Aspartame, Raspberry (6 oz)	90	0.0	0.0	<5	110
Jerseymaid Light Yogurt with Aspartame, Strawberry (6 oz)	90	0.0	0.0	<5	110
Kemp's Lite Nonfat Yogurt (6 oz)	80	<0.5	(<0.3)	(0)	(131)
Kemp's Yogurt Jr.'s (4 oz)	130	1.0	(0.6)	(5)	(80)
Knudsen Cal 70 Nonfat Yogurt with Aspartame Sweetener, Black Cherry (6 oz)	70	0.0	0.0	5	75
Knudsen Cal 70 Nonfat Yogurt with Aspartame Sweetener, Blueberry (6 oz)	70	0.0	0.0	5	80

Yogurt (continued)	Calories	Fat g	Saturated Fat g	Choles- terol mg	Sodium mg
Knudsen Cal 70 Nonfat Yogurt with Aspartame Sweetener, Lemon (6 oz)	70	0.0	0.0	0	125
Knudsen Cal 70 Nonfat Yogurt with Aspartame Sweetener, Peach (6 oz)	70	0.0	0.0	0	95
Knudsen Cal 70 Nonfat Yogurt with Aspartame Sweetener, Pineapple (6 oz)	70	0.0	0.0	0	125
Knudsen Cal 70 Nonfat Yogurt with Aspartame Sweetener, Red Raspberry (6 oz)	70	0.0	0.0	5	80
Knudsen Cal 70 Nonfat Yogurt with Aspartame Sweetener, Strawberry (6 oz)	70	0.0	0.0	0	85
Knudsen Cal 70 Nonfat Yogurt with Aspartame Sweetener, Strawberry Banana (6 oz)	70	0.0	0.0	0	80
Knudsen Cal 70 Nonfat Yogurt with Aspartame Sweetener, Strawberry Fruit Basket (6 oz)	70	0.0	0.0	5	75
Knudsen Cal 70 Nonfat Yogurt with Aspartame Sweetener, Vanilla (6 oz)	70	0.0	0.0	0	90
Light N' Lively 100 Calorie Nonfat Yogurt with Aspartame Sweetener, Black Cherry (8 oz)	100	0.0	0.0	0	100
Light N' Lively 100 Calorie Nonfat Yogurt with Aspartame Sweetener, Blueberry (8 oz)	90	0.0	0.0	0	110
Light N' Lively 100 Calorie Nonfat Yogurt with Aspartame Sweetener, Lemon (8 oz)	100	0.0	0.0	5	150
Light N' Lively 100 Calorie Nonfat Yogurt with Aspartame Sweetener, Peach (8 oz)	100	0.0	0.0	5	115
Light N' Lively 100 Calorie Nonfat Yogurt with Aspartame Sweetener, Red Raspberry (8 oz)	90	0.0	0.0	0	105

Yogurt (continued)	Calories	Fat g	Saturated Fat g	Choles- terol mg	Sodium mg
Light N' Lively 100 Calorie Nonfat Yogurt with Aspartame Sweetener, Strawberry (8 oz)	90	0.0	0.0	5	105
Light N' Lively 100 Calorie Nonfat Yogurt with Aspartame Sweetener, Strawberry Banana (8 oz)	100	0.0	0.0	0	105
Light N' Lively 100 Calorie Nonfat Yogurt with Aspartame Sweetener, Strawberry Fruit Cup (8 oz)	90	0.0	0.0	0	100
Light N' Lively Free Nonfat Yogurt with Aspartame Sweetener, Blueberry (4.4 oz)	50	0.0	0.0	0	60
Light N' Lively Free Nonfat Yogurt with Aspartame Sweetener, Red Raspberry (4.4 oz)	50	0.0	0.0	0	60
Light N' Lively Free Nonfat Yogurt with Aspartame Sweetener, Strawberry (4.4 oz)	50	0.0	0.0	0	60
Light N' Lively Free Nonfat Yogurt with Aspartame Sweetener, Strawberry Banana (4.4 oz)	50	0.0	0.0	0	55
Light N' Lively Lowfat Yogurt, 1% Milkfat, Blueberry (4.4 oz)	130	1.0	1.0	5	70
Light N' Lively Lowfat Yogurt, 1% Milkfat, Blueberry (8 oz)	240	2.0	1.0	10	130
Light N' Lively Lowfat Yogurt, 1% Milkfat, Cherry (4.4 oz)	140	1.0	1.0	5	70
Light N' Lively Lowfat Yogurt, 1% Milkfat, Peach (8 oz)	240	2.0	1.0	15	120
Light N' Lively Lowfat Yogurt, 1% Milkfat, Pineapple (4.4 oz)	130	1.0	1.0	5	65
Light N' Lively Lowfat Yogurt, 1% Milkfat, Pineapple (8 oz)	230	2.0	1.0	10	120

Yogurt (continued)	Calories	Fat g	Saturated Fat g	Choles- terol mg	Sodium mg
Light N' Lively Lowfat Yogurt, 1% Milkfat, Red Raspberry (4.4 oz)	130	1.0	1.0	5	70
Light N' Lively Lowfat Yogurt, 1% Milkfat, Red Raspberry (8 oz)	230	2.0	1.0	10	130
Light N' Lively Lowfat Yogurt, 1% Milkfat, Strawberry (4.4 oz)	130	1.0	1.0	10	70
Light N' Lively Lowfat Yogurt, 1% Milkfat, Strawberry Banana (4.4 oz)	140	1.0	1.0	5	65
Light N' Lively Lowfat Yogurt, 1% Milkfat, Strawberry Banana (8 oz)	260	2.0	1.0	10	120
Lucerne Nonfat Yogurt, all flavors (8 oz)	180	0.0	0.0	4	150
Nancy's Lowfat Yogurt, Maple (8 oz)	200	3.0	(1.9)	(10)	148
Nancy's Nonfat Yogurt (8 oz)	130	<1.0	<1.0	5	174
Nancy's Nonfat Yogurt—to Drink, Blueberry (8 oz)	179	<1.0	(<1.0)	5	147
Nancy's Nonfat Yogurt—to Drink, Boysenberry (8 oz)	176	<1.0	(<1.0)	5	145
Nancy's Nonfat Yogurt—to Drink, Cherry (8 oz)	185	<1.0	(<1.0)	5	145
Nancy's Nonfat Yogurt—to Drink, Raspberry (8 oz)	176	<1.0	(<1.0)	5	145
Nancy's Nonfat Yogurt—to Drink, Strawberry (8 oz)	168	<1.0	(<1.0)	5	145
Weight Watchers Nonfat Fruited (8 oz = 1 cup)	150	<1.0	(0.0)	5	120
Weight Watchers Ultimate 90 (8 oz = 1 cup)	90	0.0	0.0	5	120
Well's Blue Bunny Lite 85 Nonfat Yogurt, Orange (6 oz)	80	<1.0	(<1.0)	(0)	110
Well's Blue Bunny Reduced Calorie Sugar-Free Nonfat Yogurt, Black Cherry (6 oz)	85	0.0	0.0	0	110
Well's Blue Bunny Reduced Calorie Sugar-Free Nonfat Yogurt, Blueberry (6 oz)	85	0.0	0.0	0	110
Well's Blue Bunny Reduced Calorie Sugar-Free Nonfat Yogurt, Cherry Vanilla (6 oz)	85	0.0	0.0	0	110

Yogurt (continued)	Calories	Fat g	Saturated Fat g	Choles- terol mg	Sodium mg
Well's Blue Bunny Reduced Calorie Sugar-Free Nonfat Yogurt, Mixed Berry (6 oz)	85	0.0	0.0	0	110
Well's Blue Bunny Reduced Calorie Sugar-Free Nonfat Yogurt, Peach (6 oz)	85	0.0	0.0	0	110
Well's Blue Bunny Reduced Calorie Sugar-Free Nonfat Yogurt, Pineapple (6 oz)	85	0.0	0.0	0	110
Well's Blue Bunny Reduced Calorie Sugar-Free Nonfat Yogurt, Raspberry (6 oz)	85	0.0	0.0	0	110
Well's Blue Bunny Reduced Calorie Sugar-Free Nonfat Yogurt, Strawberry (6 oz)	85	0.0	0.0	0	110
Well's Blue Bunny Reduced Calorie Sugar-Free Nonfat Yogurt, Strawberry Banana (6 oz)	85	0.0	0.0	0	110
White Mountain Nonfat Bulgarian Yogurt with Live Acidophilus (8 oz)	93	0.4	(0.3)	5	138
Yoplait Fat Free Fruit on the Bottom, Cherry (6 oz)	160	0.0	0.0	5	105
Yoplait Fat Free Fruit on the Bottom, Peach (6 oz)	160	0.0	0.0	5	105
Yoplait Fat Free Fruit on the Bottom, Raspberry (6 oz)	160	0.0	0.0	5	105
Yoplait Fat Free Fruit on the Bottom, Strawberry (6 oz)	160	0.0	0.0	5	105
Yoplait Light Yogurt, Fruit Flavors (4 oz)	60	0.0	0.0	<5	65
Yoplait Light Yogurt, Fruit Flavors (6 oz)	80	0.0	0.0	<5	80
Yoplait Nonfat Yogurt, Plain (8 oz)	120	0.0	0.0	10	170
Yoplait Nonfat Yogurt, Vanilla (8 oz)	180	0.0	0.0	10	160

DESSERTS

The desserts included in this section of the Guide are low in fat, saturated fat, and cholesterol *as purchased,* when *prepared according to package directions,* or when *prepared with skim milk.* The levels of fat, saturated fat, and cholesterol in a serving of these foods, as specified in the Guide, do not exceed the cutoff points listed below.

Analysis of each product "as it will be eaten" was used to determine if it qualified for the Guide. For example, if a product requires preparation (such as cake or muffin mix), the dry mix plus the added ingredients must not exceed the cutoff points for it to qualify. Some package directions list the addition of an ingredient, such as whole milk, that is high in fat. For some of these products, simply substituting skim for whole milk allows the product to qualify for the Guide. In these cases, "prepared with skim milk" is clearly indicated next to the food in the Guide. A list of ingredients containing less fat that can be substituted for ingredients that are higher in fat appears on page 401.

CUTOFF POINTS FOR DESSERTS

Fat (grams)	Saturated Fat (grams)	Cholesterol (milligrams)
3	1	10

SERVINGS

Food	Serving Sizes
Bakery Products:	
Brownies	2 ounces
Cakes and Cupcakes:	
With icing, prepared	3½ ounces*
Without icing, prepared	2 ounces*
Frosting	3 tablespoons
Cheesecake	4 ounces
Cookies and Graham Crackers	1 ounce
Fruit and Nut Bread	2½ ounces
Muffins	2 ounces*
Pie Filling, Fruit	3 ounces
Sweet Rolls and Coffeecake	2½ ounces
Other Bakery Products	1 ounce
Chilled Desserts:	
Gelatin	½ cup
Mousse	½ cup
Pudding and Cream Pie Filling (prepared with skim milk)	½ cup

When the weight of a prepared product was not available for comparison to the serving size, the calories, fat, cholesterol, and sodium values for 1 serving as listed on the package were used for comparison.

Cake Mixes. Some brands that are low in fat in the dry form do not qualify for the Guide because directions on the package call for the addition of enough shortening, butter, margarine, oil, sour cream, cream cheese, and/or eggs to make the prepared cake higher in fat, saturated fat, and cholesterol than the cutoff points for one serving of cake. For dry mixes not listed in the Guide, you may wish to decrease the amount of fat added during preparation; however, the finished product may have a slightly different texture.

Cake Frostings. Brands listed in this Guide do not exceed the cutoff points *as purchased* or when *prepared according to package directions.*

Cookies. When cookies are made from packaged dry mix, either the fat may already be in the package or the directions may call for its addition during preparation. Only cookies that do not exceed the cutoff points *as purchased* or when *prepared according to package directions* are included in the Guide. For dry mixes low in fat that are not in the Guide, you may wish to decrease the amount of fat added during preparation; however, the finished product may have a slightly different texture.

Fruit and Nut Breads. These products are usually high in fat because of the margarine, oil, shortening, egg, whole milk, and nuts used to make them. Only fruit and nut breads that do not exceed the cutoff points *as purchased* or when *prepared according to package directions* are included in the Guide. For dry mixes not in the Guide, you may wish to decrease the amount of fat added during preparation; however, the finished product may have a slightly different texture.

Muffins. Several brands of ready-to-eat muffins and muffin mixes are included in this section of the Guide. The cutoff points apply to muffins *as purchased* or when *prepared according to package directions.*

Pies. Pie is usually high in fat because of the shortening, butter, lard, oil, or margarine in the crust, filling, and topping. The Guide includes some new commercial frozen pies that are low enough in fat that they do not exceed the cutoff points.

Pie Crust or Pastry. At the time of printing this Guide, any commercial pie crusts that do not exceed the cutoff point for fat have not been identified. Until acceptable products become available, you may wish to make crust from the recipes using margarine and oil found on pages 214 and 215 of *The Living Heart Diet* (by the same authors).

Pie Filling (fruit). Several prepared fruit fillings are included in the Guide. You can make your own fruit pie fillings using fresh, frozen, canned, or dried fruit and leaving fat out of the recipe.

Sweet Rolls and Coffeecake. Several products that provide no more than the cutoff points for fat and saturated fat are included in the Guide.

Gelatin Desserts. Most brands consist primarily of sugar and contain no fat or cholesterol. However, gelatin desserts can become high in fat when ingredients such as whipped cream, cream cheese, whipped topping, cheese, sour cream, or nuts are added. If you want to restrict your sugar intake, you may wish to use sugar-free gelatin desserts, which are lower in calories than regular flavored gelatin.

Pudding and Cream Pie Filling. Although the dry mixes are low in fat, the finished product may be high in fat and saturated fat if whole milk is added during preparation. For example, a ½-cup serving of pudding contains about ½ cup of milk; ½ cup of whole milk contains 4 grams of fat, while the same amount of skim milk contains about .25 gram of fat. The Guide includes pudding and cream pie filling mixes that do not exceed the cutoff points when *prepared with skim milk.* If you need to decrease your sugar intake, you may enjoy using sugar-free pudding mixes.

Frozen desserts, such as ice milk, frozen yogurt, sherbet, and sorbet, can be found in the Frozen Desserts section, beginning on page 217.

The following abbreviations are used in the Food Sections: oz = ounce; fl oz = fluid ounce; pkg = package; pkt = packet; env = envelope; g = gram; prep (w/ . . .) = prepared with; < = less than; and tr = trace.

Bakery Products	Calories	Fat g	Saturated Fat g	Choles-terol mg	Sodium mg
BAKERY PRODUCTS					
BROWNIES					
Betty Crocker Light Fudge Brownie Mix, prep (w/water) (1/24 of a recipe)	100	1.0	<1.0	0	90
Pillsbury Lovin' Lites, Fudge Brownie Mix, prep (w/egg whites) (1/24 of a pan)	100	2.0	<1.0	0	85
CAKES AND CUPCAKES					
Angel Food Cake, Plain or Flavored—Most Brands (1/12 of a cake)	137	0.0	0.0	0	77
Betty Crocker Angel Food Cake Mixes, Confetti (1/12 of a cake)	150	0.0	0.0	0	300
Betty Crocker Angel Food Cake Mixes, Lemon Custard (1/12 of a cake)	150	0.0	0.0	0	300
Betty Crocker Angel Food Cake Mixes, Traditional (1/12 of a cake)	130	0.0	0.0	0	170

Bakery Products (continued)	Calories	Fat g	Saturated Fat g	Choles- terol mg	Sodium mg
Betty Crocker Angel Food Cake Mixes, White (1/12 of a cake)	150	0.0	0.0	0	300
Betty Crocker Super Moist Light, Devils Food, prep (w/egg whites or egg substitute) (1/12 of a cake)	180	3.0	1.0	0	370
Betty Crocker Super Moist Light, White Cake, prep (w/egg whites and water) (1/12 of a cake)	180	3.0	1.0	0	330
Betty Crocker Supermoist Cake Mix, Cherry Chip, prep (w/egg whites) (1/12 of a cake)	190	3.0	1.0	0	270
Betty Crocker Supermoist Cake Mix, Sour Cream White, prep (w/egg whites) (1/12 of a cake)	180	3.0	1.0	0	300
Dromedary Gingerbread Mix, prep (according to recipe on package) (2″ × 2″)	100	2.0	(0.9)	(9)	190
Entenmann's Fat Free and Cholesterol Free Cakes, Apple Spice (1 oz)	80	0.0	0.0	0	80
Entenmann's Fat Free and Cholesterol Free Cakes, Banana Crunch (1 oz)	80	0.0	0.0	0	90
Entenmann's Fat Free and Cholesterol Free Cakes, Banana Loaf (1.3 oz)	90	0.0	0.0	0	125
Entenmann's Fat Free and Cholesterol Free Cakes, Blueberry Crunch (1 oz)	70	0.0	0.0	0	85
Entenmann's Fat Free and Cholesterol Free Cakes, Chocolate Crunch (1 oz)	70	0.0	0.0	0	130
Entenmann's Fat Free and Cholesterol Free Cakes, Chocolate Loaf (1 oz)	70	0.0	0.0	0	130
Entenmann's Fat Free and Cholesterol Free Cakes, Fudge Iced Chocolate (1.3 oz)	90	0.0	0.0	0	125
Entenmann's Fat Free and Cholesterol Free Cakes, Fudge Iced Golden (1.3 oz)	90	0.0	0.0	0	100

Bakery Products (continued)	Calories	Fat g	Saturated Fat g	Choles- terol mg	Sodium mg
Entenmann's Fat Free and Cholesterol Free Cakes, Golden Loaf (1 oz)	70	0.0	0.0	0	100
Entenmann's Fat Free and Cholesterol Free Cakes, Louisiana Crunch (1 oz)	80	0.0	0.0	0	100
Entenmann's Fat Free and Cholesterol Free Cakes, Marble Loaf (1 oz)	70	0.0	0.0	0	115
Entenmann's Fat Free and Cholesterol Free Cakes, Pineapple Crunch (1 oz)	70	0.0	0.0	0	105
Giant Bakery Angel Food Cake, Cherry Ring (1/12 of a cake)	60	0.0	0.0	0	(71)
Giant Bakery Angel Food Cake, Lemon Ring (1/12 of a cake)	60	0.0	0.0	0	(71)
Giant Bakery Angel Food Cake, Orange Ring (1/12 of a cake)	60	0.0	0.0	0	(71)
Giant Bakery Angel Food Cake, Strawberry Ring (1/12 of a cake)	60	0.0	0.0	0	(71)
Giant Bakery No Fat No Cholesterol Cake, Apple Crunch (1/16 of a cake)	60	0.0	0.0	0	190
Giant Bakery No Fat No Cholesterol Cake, Banana Crunch (1/16 of a cake)	70	0.0	0.0	0	170
Giant Bakery No Fat No Cholesterol Cake, Blueberry Crunch (1/14 of a cake)	70	0.0	0.0	0	170
Hostess Grizzly Chomps (1-1/4 oz = 1 cake)	110	1.0	(0.2)	0	160
Hostess Lights, Light Chocolate Cupcakes with Creme Filling (1.5 oz = 1 cake)	130	2.0	< 1.0	0	190
Hostess Lights, Light Chocolate Cupcakes with Vanilla Pudding (1 cake)	130	1.0	< 1.0	0	180
Lean Line Cheesecake, Marble (4 oz)	160	< 1.0	(< 1.0)	(1)	313
Lean Line Cheesecake, Plain (4 oz)	160	< 1.0	(< 1.0)	(1)	313

Bakery Products (continued)	Calories	Fat g	Saturated Fat g	Choles- terol mg	Sodium mg
Pepperidge Farm Fat Free Golden Pound Cake (1 oz)	70	0.0	0.0	0	80
Pepperidge Farm 98% Fat Free Pound Cake, Chocolate (1 oz)	70	1.0	<1.0	0	85
Pillsbury Lovin' Lites Cake Mix, Devil's Food, prep (w/egg whites) (1/12 of a cake)	160	2.0	<1.0	0	380
Pillsbury Lovin' Lites Cake Mix, White, prep (w/egg whites) (1/12 of a cake)	170	2.0	<1.0	0	310
Pillsbury Lovin' Lites Cake Mix, Yellow, prep (w/egg whites) (1/12 of a cake)	170	2.0	<1.0	0	310
Pillsbury Plus Cake Mix, Lemon, prep (w/egg whites) (1/12 of a cake)	180	3.0	1.0	0	280
Ralph's Fat Free Cholesterol Free Loaf Cake, Chocolate (1 oz)	60	<1.0	(0.0)	0	130
Ralph's Fat Free Cholesterol Free Loaf Cake, Golden (1 oz)	60	<1.0	(0.0)	0	125
Ralph's Fat Free Cholesterol Free Loaf Cake, Marble (1 oz)	60	<1.0	(0.0)	0	160
Sara Lee Free and Light, Chocolate Cake (1/8 of a cake)	110	0.0	0.0	0	140
Sara Lee Free and Light, Pound Cake (1/10 of a cake)	70	0.0	0.0	0	90
Sara Lee Lights, Apple Crisp Cake (1 cake)	150	2.0	(0.4)	5	105
Sara Lee Lights, Strawberry French Cheesecake (1 cheesecake)	150	2.0	(0.4)	5	65
Sweet N Low Cake Mix, Banana (1/10 of a cake)	90	2.0	(0.6)	<5	40
Sweet N Low Cake Mix, Chocolate (1/10 of a cake)	90	2.0	(0.6)	<5	40
Sweet N Low Cake Mix, Lemon (1/10 of a cake)	90	2.0	(0.6)	<5	40
Sweet N Low Cake Mix, White (1/10 of a cake)	90	2.0	(0.6)	<5	40
Sweet N Low Cake Mix, Yellow (1/10 of a cake)	90	2.0	(0.6)	<5	40

Bakery Products (continued)	Calories	Fat g	Saturated Fat g	Choles- terol mg	Sodium mg
CAKE FROSTING					
Betty Crocker Fluffy Frosting Mix, White, prep (as directed) (1/12 mix)	70	0.0	0.0	0	40
Cake Frosting, White Boiled—Most Brands (3 tbsp)	56	0.0	0.0	0	25
Pillsbury Frosting Mix, Fluffy White (.6 oz = 1/12 mix)	60	0.0	0.0	0	65
Pillsbury Frosting Mix, Frost It Hot, Chocolate (.5 oz = 1/8 of mix)	50	0.0	0.0	0	50
Pillsbury Frosting Mix, Frost It Hot, Fluffy White (.5 oz = 1/8 of mix)	50	0.0	0.0	0	50
Pillsbury Lovin' Lites Frosting, Chocolate Fudge (1/12 of a can)	120	2.0	< 1.0	0	90
Pillsbury Lovin' Lites Frosting, Milk Chocolate (1/12 of a can)	130	2.0	< 1.0	0	95
Pillsbury Lovin' Lites Frosting, Vanilla (1/12 of a can)	130	2.0	< 1.0	0	70
COOKIES					
A Whale of a Snack Fruit Bars, Apple (2 oz = 1 bar)	210	4.0*	(1.6)	0	80
A Whale of a Snack Fruit Bars, Blueberry (2 oz = 1 bar)	210	3.0	(1.2)	0	90
A Whale of a Snack Fruit Bars, Fig (2 oz = 1 bar)	210	4.0*	(1.4)	0	160
Archway Apple Filled Oatmeal (1 cookie)	100	3.0	1.0	5	110
Archway Apple Oatmeal Bran (1 cookie)	105	3.0	0.5	5	115
Archway Apricot Filled (1 cookie)	100	3.0	1.2	5	80
Archway Apricot Oatmeal Bran (1 cookie)	105	2.0	0.5	5	115
Archway Blueberry Filled (1 cookie)	100	3.0	1.3	5	90
Archway Blueberry Oatmeal Bran (1 cookie)	105	3.0	0.6	5	110
Archway Cherry Filled (1 cookie)	100	3.0	1.2	5	90

*The value printed for fat is higher than the cutoff point because the manufacturer's serving size is larger than the standard serving size used in evaluating the food.

Bakery Products (continued)	Calories	Fat g	Saturated Fat g	Choles- terol mg	Sodium mg
Archway Cinnamon Apple (1 cookie)	110	3.0	0.6	5	140
Archway Date Filled Oatmeal (1 cookie)	100	3.0	0.6	5	100
Archway Dutch Cocoa (1 cookie)	100	3.0	0.6	0	95
Archway Fruit N' Honey (1 cookie)	100	3.0	0.5	5	120
Archway Lemon Drop (1 cookie)	85	2.0	0.5	5	110
Archway Molasses (1 cookie)	110	3.0	1.0	10	160
Archway Oatmeal (1 cookie)	110	3.0	1.0	5	100
Archway Oatmeal Raisin Bran (1 cookie)	110	3.0	1.0	0	85
Archway Old Fashioned Molasses (1 cookie)	120	3.0	1.0	5	140
Archway Raspberry Filled (1 cookie)	100	3.0	0.6	5	80
Archway Raspberry Oatmeal Bran (1 cookie)	105	3.0	0.5	5	110
Archway Soft Sugar Drop (1 cookie)	90	3.0	1.0	5	90
Archway Strawberry Filled (1 cookie)	100	3.0	1.2	5	90
Archway Sugar (1 cookie)	100	3.0	1.0	5	130
Austin Iced Oatmeal Spice Cookies (2.75 oz = 1 pkg)	320	7.0*	1.0	0	310
Barbara's Bakery California Lemon (1/3 oz = 2 cookies)	39	1.0	(0.2)	(4)	(30)
Barbara's Bakery Fruit & Nut Cookies (1 oz = 2 cookies)	125	2.0	(0.3)	0	(70)
Barbara's Bakery Fruit & Nut Cookies (1.4 oz = 2 cookies)	169	2.7	(0.4)	(0)	(95)
Barbara's Bakery Oatmeal Raisin Cookies (1 oz = 2 cookies)	102	2.0	(0.8)	0	(85)
Barbara's Bakery Tropical Coconut Cookies (1/2 oz = 2 cookies)	64	2.0	(0.5)	0	(85)
Betty Crocker Classic Dessert Mixes, Date Bar (1 bar)	60	2.0	1.0	0	35
Entenmann's Fat Free and Cholesterol Free Cookies, Fruit and Honey (2 cookies)	80	0.0	0.0	0	110

*The value printed for fat is higher than the cutoff point because the manufacturer's serving size is larger than the standard serving size used in evaluating the food.

Bakery Products (continued)	Calories	Fat g	Saturated Fat g	Choles- terol mg	Sodium mg
Entenmann's Fat Free and Cholesterol Free Cookies, Homestyle Apple (2 cookies)	70	0.0	0.0	0	125
Entenmann's Fat Free and Cholesterol Free Cookies, Oatmeal Raisin (2 cookies)	80	0.0	0.0	0	120
Entenmann's Fat Free and Cholesterol Free Cookies, Raisin (2 cookies)	70	0.0	0.0	0	100
Giant Animal Crackers (1 oz = 10 crackers)	120	3.0	(1.0)	0	135
Giant Bakery Cookie, Oat Bran (1 oz = 1/2 cookie)	80	2.0	< 1.0	0	70
Giant Fig Bars (1 oz = 2 cookies)	90	2.0	1.0	0	65
Grandma's Big Cookies, Old Time Molasses (2.75 oz = 2 cookies)	320	9.0*	(3.3)	5	520
Health Valley 100% Natural Fruit Bars, Apple Bakes (.9 oz = 1 bar)	100	3.0	(0.3)	0	25
Health Valley 100% Natural Fruit Bars, Date Bakes (.9 oz = 1 bar)	100	3.0	(0.3)	0	25
Health Valley 100% Natural Fruit Bars, Raisin Bakes (.9 oz = 1 bar)	100	3.0	(0.3)	0	20
Health Valley Fat-Free Cookies, Apple Spice (3 cookies)	75	< 1.0	(0.0)	0	40
Health Valley Fat-Free Cookies, Apricot Delight (3 cookies)	75	< 1.0	(0.0)	0	40
Health Valley Fat-Free Cookies, Date Delight (3 cookies)	75	< 1.0	(0.0)	0	40
Health Valley Fat-Free Cookies, Hawaiian Fruit (3 cookies)	75	< 1.0	(0.0)	0	40
Health Valley Fat-Free Cookies, Raisin Oatmeal (3 cookies)	75	< 1.0	(0.0)	0	40
Health Valley Fat-Free Fruit Bars, Apple (1.5 oz = 1 bar)	140	< 1.0	(0.0)	0	10
Health Valley Fat-Free Fruit Bars, Apricot (1.5 oz = 1 bar)	140	< 1.0	(0.0)	0	10

*The value printed for fat is higher than the cutoff point because the manufacturer's serving size is larger than the standard serving size used in evaluating the food.

Bakery Products (continued)	Calories	Fat g	Saturated Fat g	Choles- terol mg	Sodium mg
Health Valley Fat-Free Fruit Bars, Date (1.5 oz = 1 bar)	140	<1.0	(0.0)	0	10
Health Valley Fat-Free Fruit Bars, Raisin (1.5 oz = 1 bar)	140	<1.0	(0.0)	0	10
Health Valley Fat-Free Jumbo Fruit Cookies, Apple Raisin (1 cookie)	70	<1.0	(0.0)	0	35
Health Valley Fat-Free Jumbo Fruit Cookies, Raisin Raisin (1 cookie)	70	<1.0	(0.0)	0	35
Health Valley Fat-Free Jumbo Fruit Cookies, Raspberry (1 cookie)	70	<1.0	(0.0)	0	35
Health Valley Fruit & Nut Jumbo Fruit Bars, Oat Bran (1.5 oz = 1 bar)	140	2.0	(0.2)	0	10
Health Valley Jumbo Fruit Bars, Oat Bran Fruit and Nut (1-1/2 oz = 1 bar)	140	2.0	(0.2)	0	10
Interbake Oatmeal Apple Bars (1 bar)	70	2.0	<1.0	0	55
Interbake Oatmeal Raisin Bars (1 bar)	70	2.0	<1.0	0	40
Interbake Oatmeal Raspberry Bars (1 bar)	70	2.0	<1.0	0	50
Interbake Trolley Cakes Devils Food (2 cookies)	120	2.0	(0.7)	(3)	80
La Choy Fortune Cookies (1 cookie)	15	0.1	(0.0)	0	1
Lance Apple Oatmeal Bar (1.8 oz = 1 pkg)	200	5.0*	1.0	10	210
Lance Fig Bar (1 1/2 oz = 1 pkg)	150	2.0	1.0	0	85
Lance Fig Cake (2 1/8 oz = 1 pkg)	210	3.0	1.0	0	90
Little Debbie Figaroos (1.5 oz)	160	4.0*	1.0	<2	105
Mother's Fig Bars (1 oz = 1.6 bars)	100	2.0	(0.7)	<2	75
Mother's Fig Bars, Whole Wheat (1 oz = 1.6 bars)	90	2.0	(0.7)	<2	80
Nabisco Devil's Food Cakes (3/4 oz = 1 cookie)	70	1.0	<1.0	0	40
Nabisco Newtons, Apple (3/4 oz = 1 cookie)	70	2.0	<1.0	0	70

*The value printed for fat is higher than the cutoff point because the manufacturer's serving size is larger than the standard serving size used in evaluating the food.

Bakery Products (continued)	Calories	Fat g	Saturated Fat g	Choles- terol mg	Sodium mg
Nabisco Newtons, Fig (1/2 oz = 1 cookie)	60	1.0	< 1.0	0	60
Nabisco Newtons, Raspberry (3/4 oz = 1 cookie)	70	2.0	< 1.0	0	70
Nabisco Newtons, Strawberry (3/4 oz = 1 cookie)	70	2.0	< 1.0	0	70
Nabisco Newtons, Variety Pack (1 cookie)	120	3.0	1.0	0	110
Pepperidge Farm Wholesome Choice Cookies, Carrot Walnut (1/2 oz = 1 cookie)	60	1.0	< 1.0	0	45
Pepperidge Farm Wholesome Choice Cookies, Oatmeal Raisin (1/2 oz = 1 cookie)	60	1.0	< 1.0	0	50
R.W. Frookie, Apple Spice (.52 oz = 1 cookie)	50	0.0	0.0	0	80
R.W. Frookie, Oatmeal Raisin (.52 oz = 1 cookie)	50	0.0	0.0	0	75
Sunbelt Baked Apple Bar (1.31 oz)	130	2.0	1.0	< 1	130
Sunshine Golden Fruit (1/2 oz = 1 cookie)	70	1.0	< 1.0	< 2	40
Tom's Fig Bar (2 oz = 1 pkg)	200	2.0	(0.7)	(22)	180
Weight Watchers Apple Raisin Bar (1 oz = 1 bar)	100	3.0	(0.4)	(0)	115
Weight Watchers Oatmeal Spice Cookies (1 pkt = 3 cookies)	80	2.0	(0.4)	(0)	75
Weight Watchers Shortbread Cookies (1 pkt = 3 cookies)	80	2.0	(0.4)	(0)	95
FRUIT AND NUT BREADS					
Dromedary Date Nut Roll (1/2″ slice)	80	2.0	(0.5)	(4)	160
Pillsbury Quick Bread Mix, Date, prep (w/oil and egg substitute) (1/12 of a loaf)	160	3.0	< 1.0	0	150
GRAHAM CRACKERS					
Mother's Mini Dinosaur Grrrahams, Original (1/2 oz = 7 cookies)	60	1.0	(0.4)	0	40
Nabisco Honey Maid Grahams, Cinnamon (1/2 oz = 2 cookies)	60	1.0	< 1.0	0	85

Bakery Products (continued)	Calories	Fat g	Saturated Fat g	Choles- terol mg	Sodium mg
Nabisco Honey Maid Grahams, Honey (1/2 oz = 2 cookies)	60	1.0	< 1.0	0	90
MUFFINS					
Betty Crocker Light Muffin Mix, Wild Blueberry, prep (w/egg white or egg substitute and water) (1 muffin)	70	< 1.0	(0.0)	0	140
Betty Crocker Muffin Mix, Apple Cinnamon, prep (w/egg white and skim milk) (1 muffin)	110	3.0	1.0	0	140
Betty Crocker Muffin Mix, Oatmeal Raisin, prep (w/egg white and skim milk) (1 muffin)	130	3.0	1.0	0	125
Betty Crocker Muffin Mix, Wild Blueberry, prep (w/egg white and skim milk) (1 muffin)	110	3.0	< 1.0	0	150
Duncan Hines Muffin Mix, Blueberry, prep (according to package directions) (1 muffin)	120	3.0	(0.9)	8	185
Entenmann's Fat Free and Cholesterol Free Muffins, Blueberry (1 muffin)	150	0.0	0.0	0	140
Entenmann's Fat Free and Cholesterol Free Muffins, Cinnamon Apple Raisin Muffins (1 muffin)	160	0.0	0.0	0	140
Giant Bakery Gourmet Muffins, Bran (2.3 oz = 1/2 muffin)	170	3.0	(< 1.0)	0	325
Hain Muffin Mix, Apple Cinnamon Oat Bran (1 muffin)	140	3.0	(1.2)	0	200
Hain Muffin Mix, Raspberry Spice Oat Bran (1 muffin)	140	3.0	(1.2)	0	190
Health Valley Fat-Free Muffins, Apple Spice (1 muffin)	130	< 1.0	(0.0)	0	100
Health Valley Fat-Free Muffins, Raisin Spice (1 muffin)	140	< 1.0	(0.0)	0	100

Bakery Products (continued)	Calories	Fat g	Saturated Fat g	Choles- terol mg	Sodium mg
Health Valley Fat-Free Oat Bran Fancy Fruit Muffins, Almonds and Dates (1 muffin)	140	< 1.0	(0.0)	0	80
Health Valley Fat-Free Oat Bran Fancy Fruit Muffins, Blueberry (1 muffin)	140	< 1.0	(0.0)	0	100
Health Valley Fat-Free Oat Bran Fancy Fruit Muffins, Raisin (1 muffin)	140	< 1.0	(0.0)	0	90
Hostess Breakfast Muffins, Apple Streusel (1 1/4 oz = 1 muffin)	100	1.0	(0.3)	0	160
Hostess Breakfast Muffins, Blueberry (1 1/4 oz)	100	1.0	(0.3)	0	160
Pillsbury Lovin' Lites Muffin Mix, Blueberry, prep (w/egg whites) (1 muffin)	100	1.0	0.0	0	160
Sara Lee Free and Light, Blueberry Muffin (1 muffin)	150	3.0	(1.3)	0	140

PIES

Sara Lee Free and Light, Strawberry Yogurt Dessert (1/10 of a pie)	120	1.0	(< 1.0)	0	90

PIE FILLINGS

Apples, sweetened, sliced—Most Brands (1/2 cup)	68	0.5	0.1	0	3
Giant Pie Filling, Apple (1/6 of filling)	90	0.0	0.0	0	40
Libby's Pumpkin Pie Mix (1 cup)	260	0.3	(0.0)	(0)	440
None Such Mincemeat, Brandy and Rum, Ready-to-Use (1/3 cup)	220	2.0	(0.8)	(< 1)	260
None Such Mincemeat, Ready-to-Use (1/3 cup)	200	1.0	(0.4)	(< 1)	260
Pumpkin Pie Mix—Most Brands (1/2 cup)	141	0.2	0.1	0	280

SWEET ROLLS AND COFFEECAKE

Entenmann's Fat Free and Cholesterol Free Danish, Apricot Twist (1.1 oz)	90	0.0	0.0	0	80

Bakery Products (continued)	Calories	Fat g	Saturated Fat g	Choles-terol mg	Sodium mg
Entenmann's Fat Free and Cholesterol Free Danish, Bavarian Creme Pastry (1.3 oz)	80	0.0	0.0	0	95
Entenmann's Fat Free and Cholesterol Free Danish, Cheese Filled Crumb Pastry (1.2 oz)	90	0.0	0.0	0	95
Entenmann's Fat Free and Cholesterol Free Danish, Cherry Cheese Pastry (1.3 oz)	90	0.0	0.0	0	85
Entenmann's Fat Free and Cholesterol Free Danish, Cherry Filled Coffee Cake (1.3 oz)	90	0.0	0.0	0	80
Entenmann's Fat Free and Cholesterol Free Danish, Cinnamon Apple Coffee Cake (1.3 oz)	90	0.0	0.0	0	90
Entenmann's Fat Free and Cholesterol Free Danish, Cinnamon Apple Twist (1.1 oz)	90	0.0	0.0	0	75
Entenmann's Fat Free and Cholesterol Free Danish, Cinnamon Ring (1 oz)	80	0.0	0.0	0	75
Entenmann's Fat Free and Cholesterol Free Danish, Cinnamon Twist (1 oz)	80	0.0	0.0	0	75
Entenmann's Fat Free and Cholesterol Free Danish, Lemon Twist (1.1 oz)	90	0.0	0.0	0	80
Entenmann's Fat Free and Cholesterol Free Danish, Orange Twist (1.1 oz)	90	0.0	0.0	0	70
Entenmann's Fat Free and Cholesterol Free Danish, Pineapple Cheese Pastry (1.3 oz)	90	0.0	0.0	0	85
Entenmann's Fat Free and Cholesterol Free Danish, Raspberry Twist (1.1 oz)	90	0.0	0.0	0	75
Hostess Breakfast Cinnamon Crumb Coffee Cake (1 oz)	80	1.0	(0.3)	0	95
Hostess Snack Cakes, Light Apple Spice (1 cake)	130	1.0	< 1.0	0	150

Bakery Products (continued)	Calories	Fat g	Saturated Fat g	Choles- terol mg	Sodium mg
Hostess Snack Cakes, Light Crumb Cakes (1 cake)	80	1.0	< 1.0	0	95
Ralph's Fat Free Cholesterol Free Coffee Cake, Cherry Cheese (1 oz)	60	< 1.0	(0.0)	0	120
Ralph's Fat Free Cholesterol Free Coffee Cake, Cinnamon Apple (1 oz)	70	< 1.0	(0.0)	0	125
Ralph's Fat Free Cholesterol Free Coffee Cake, Raspberry Twist (1 oz)	70	< 1.0	(0.0)	0	125
Sara Lee Free and Light, Apple Danish (1/8 of a cake)	130	0.0	0.0	0	120
OTHER BAKERY PRODUCTS					
Hostess Snack Cakes, Light Twinkies (1 cake)	110	2.0	< 1.0	0	160

CHILLED DESSERTS

CHILLED DESSERTS

	Calories	Fat g	Saturated Fat g	Choles- terol mg	Sodium mg
Pepperidge Farm Dessert Light, Apple 'N Spice Bake (4-1/4 oz)	170	2.0	0.0	10	105
GELATIN					
Gelatin Sweetened with Nutrasweet, all flavors, prep (w/water)—Most Brands (1/2 cup)	8	0.0	0.0	0	(4)
Gelatin Sweetened with Saccharin, all flavors, prep (w/water)—Most Brands (1/2 cup)	8	0.0	0.0	0	(2)
Gelatin Sweetened with Sugar, all flavors, prep (w/water)—Most Brands (1/2 cup)	71	0.0	0.0	0	(61)
MOUSSE					
Lite Whip Mousse Instant Dessert Mix, Chocolate, prep (w/skim milk) (1/2 cup)	70	2.0	(0.7)	0	55
Lite Whip Mousse Instant Dessert Mix, Lemon, prep (w/skim milk) (1/2 cup)	60	2.0	(0.9)	0	55

Chilled Desserts (continued)	Calories	Fat g	Saturated Fat g	Choles- terol mg	Sodium mg
Lite Whip Mousse Instant Dessert Mix, Strawberry, prep (w/skim milk) (1/2 cup)	60	2.0	(0.9)	0	55
Lite Whip Mousse Instant Dessert Mix, Vanilla, prep (w/skim milk) (1/2 cup)	60	2.0	(0.9)	0	55
Sans Sucre de Paris Mousse Mix, Cheesecake, prep (w/skim milk) (1/2 cup)	73	1.0	(0.4)	1	180
Sans Sucre de Paris Mousse Mix, Chocolate Cheesecake, prep (w/skim milk) (1/2 cup)	73	1.0	(0.3)	1	180
Weight Watchers Mousse Mix, Cheesecake, prep (w/skim milk) (1/2 cup)	60	2.0	(1.1)	(2)	75

PUDDINGS AND
PIE FILLINGS

	Calories	Fat g	Saturated Fat g	Choles- terol mg	Sodium mg
D-Zerta Reduced Calorie Pudding, Butterscotch, prep (w/skim milk) (1/2 cup)	70	0.0	0.0	0	65
D-Zerta Reduced Calorie Pudding, Chocolate, prep (w/skim milk) (1/2 cup)	60	0.0	0.0	0	70
D-Zerta Reduced Calorie Pudding, Vanilla, prep (w/skim milk) (1/2 cup)	70	0.0	0.0	0	65
Del Monte Light Snack Cups, Chocolate (4.25 oz)	100	1.0	0.0	0	85
Del Monte Light Snack Cups, Vanilla (4.25 oz)	100	1.0	0.0	0	200
Del Monte Light Snack Pudding Cup, Vanilla (4-1/2 oz)	100	1.0	0.0	0	200
Featherweight Custard, Lemon, prep (w/skim milk) (1/2 cup)	40	0.0	0.0	0	40
Featherweight Custard, Vanilla, prep (w/skim milk) (1/2 cup)	40	0.0	0.0	0	40
Featherweight Instant Pudding, Butterscotch, prep (w/skim milk) (1/2 cup)	100	0.0	0.0	5	190
Featherweight Instant Pudding, Chocolate, prep (w/skim milk) (1/2 cup)	110	0.0	0.0	5	190

Chilled Desserts (continued)	Calories	Fat g	Saturated Fat g	Choles- terol mg	Sodium mg
Featherweight Instant Pudding, Vanilla, prep (w/skim milk) (1/2 cup)	100	0.0	0.0	5	190
Featherweight Ready-to-Serve Pudding, Butterscotch (1/2 cup)	100	1.0	(0.4)	0	160
Featherweight Ready-to-Serve Pudding, Chocolate (1/2 cup)	100	1.0	(0.3)	0	110
Featherweight Ready-to-Serve Pudding, Vanilla (1/2 cup)	100	2.0	(0.9)	0	150
Giant Instant Pudding and Pie Filling, Butterscotch, prep (w/skim milk) (1/2 cup)	150	< 1.0	< 1.0	5	335
Giant Instant Pudding and Pie Filling, Chocolate, prep (w/skim milk) (1/2 cup)	170	< 1.0	< 1.0	5	370
Giant Instant Pudding and Pie Filling, Lemon, prep (w/skim milk) (1/2 cup)	150	< 1.0	< 1.0	5	250
Giant Instant Pudding and Pie Filling, Vanilla, prep (w/skim milk) (1/2 cup)	150	< 1.0	< 1.0	5	260
Giant Pudding and Pie Filling, Chocolate, prep (w/skim milk) (1/2 cup)	150	< 1.0	< 1.0	5	190
Giant Pudding and Pie Filling, Dark Fudge, prep (w/skim milk) (1/2 cup)	150	< 1.0	< 1.0	5	195
Giant Pudding and Pie Filling, Tapioca, prep (w/skim milk) (1/2 cup)	140	< 1.0	< 1.0	5	205
Giant Pudding and Pie Filling, Vanilla, prep (w/skim milk) (1/2 cup)	140	< 1.0	< 1.0	5	200
Hunt's Snack Pack Lite Pudding, Chocolate (4 oz)	100	2.0	0.3	1	120
Hunt's Snack Pack Lite Pudding, Tapioca (4 oz)	100	2.0	0.4	1	105
Jell-O Americana Rice Pudding, prep (w/skim milk) (1/2 cup)	143	0.2	(0.1)	2	158
Jell-O Americana Tapioca Pudding, prep (w/skim milk) (1/2 cup)	133	0.2	(0.1)	0	173

Chilled Desserts (continued)	Calories	Fat g	Saturated Fat g	Choles- terol mg	Sodium mg
Jell-O Instant Pudding and Pie Filling, Banana Cream, prep (w/skim milk) (1/2 cup)	133	0.2	(0.1)	2	413
Jell-O Instant Pudding and Pie Filling, Butter Pecan, prep (w/skim milk) (1/2 cup)	143	1.2	(0.4)	2	413
Jell-O Instant Pudding and Pie Filling, Butterscotch, prep (w/skim milk) (1/2 cup)	133	0.2	(0.1)	2	453
Jell-O Instant Pudding and Pie Filling, Chocolate Fudge, prep (w/skim milk) (1/2 cup)	143	1.2	(0.4)	2	443
Jell-O Instant Pudding and Pie Filling, Coconut Cream, prep (w/skim milk) (1/2 cup)	143	2.2	(1.9)	2	323
Jell-O Instant Pudding and Pie Filling, French Vanilla, prep (w/skim milk) (1/2 cup)	133	0.2	(0.1)	2	413
Jell-O Instant Pudding and Pie Filling, Lemon, prep (w/skim milk) (1/2 cup)	133	0.2	(0.1)	2	363
Jell-O Instant Pudding and Pie Filling, Milk Chocolate, prep (w/skim milk) (1/2 cup)	143	1.2	(0.4)	2	473
Jell-O Instant Pudding and Pie Filling, Pistachio, prep (w/skim milk) (1/2 cup)	143	1.2	(0.4)	2	413
Jell-O Instant Pudding and Pie Filling, Vanilla, prep (w/skim milk) (1/2 cup)	133	0.2	(0.1)	2	413
Jell-O Light Pudding Snacks, Chocolate (4 oz)	100	2.0	(0.3)	5	125
Jell-O Light Pudding Snacks, Chocolate Fudge (4 oz)	100	1.0	(0.2)	5	125
Jell-O Light Pudding Snacks, Chocolate Vanilla Combo (4 oz)	100	2.0	(0.3)	5	125
Jell-O Light Pudding Snacks, Vanilla (4 oz)	100	2.0	(0.3)	5	130
Jell-O Microwave Pudding, Banana Cream, prep (w/skim milk) (1/2 cup)	123	0.2	0.1	2	223
Jell-O Microwave Pudding, Butterscotch, prep (w/skim milk) (1/2 cup)	133	0.2	0.1	2	183

Chilled Desserts (continued)	Calories	Fat g	Saturated Fat g	Choles- terol mg	Sodium mg
Jell-O Microwave Pudding, Chocolate, prep (w/skim milk) (1/2 cup)	133	1.2	(0.4)	2	193
Jell-O Microwave Pudding, Milk Chocolate, prep (w/skim milk) (1/2 cup)	133	1.2	(0.4)	2	193
Jell-O Microwave Pudding, Vanilla, prep (w/skim milk) (1/2 cup)	123	0.2	0.1	2	183
Jell-O Pudding and Pie Filling, Butterscotch, prep (w/skim milk) (1/2 cup)	133	0.2	0.1	2	193
Jell-O Pudding and Pie Filling, Chocolate Fudge, prep (w/skim milk) (1/2 cup)	133	0.2	0.1	2	173
Jell-O Pudding and Pie Filling, Chocolate, prep (w/skim milk) (1/2 cup)	133	0.2	0.1	2	173
Jell-O Pudding and Pie Filling, Flan, prep (w/skim milk) (1/2 cup)	123	0.2	0.1	2	68
Jell-O Pudding and Pie Filling, French Vanilla, prep (w/skim milk) (1/2 cup)	133	0.2	0.1	2	188
Jell-O Pudding and Pie Filling, Milk Chocolate, prep (w/skim milk) (1/2 cup)	133	0.2	0.1	2	173
Jell-O Pudding and Pie Filling, Vanilla, prep (w/skim milk) (1/2 cup)	123	0.2	0.1	2	203
Jell-O Sugar Free Instant Pudding and Pie Filling, Banana, prep (w/skim milk) (1/2 cup)	68	0.2	0.1	2	393
Jell-O Sugar Free Instant Pudding and Pie Filling, Butterscotch, prep (w/skim milk) (1/2 cup)	68	0.2	0.1	2	393
Jell-O Sugar Free Instant Pudding and Pie Filling, Chocolate Fudge, prep (w/skim milk) (1/2 cup)	78	1.2	(0.4)	2	333
Jell-O Sugar Free Instant Pudding and Pie Filling, Chocolate, prep (w/skim milk) (1/2 cup)	73	0.2	0.1	2	383

Chilled Desserts (continued)	Calories	Fat g	Saturated Fat g	Choles- terol mg	Sodium mg
Jell-O Sugar Free Instant Pudding and Pie Filling, Pistachio, prep (w/skim milk) (1/2 cup)	73	1.2	(0.4)	2	393
Jell-O Sugar Free Instant Pudding and Pie Filling, Vanilla, prep (w/skim milk) (1/2 cup)	68	0.2	0.1	2	393
Jell-O Sugar Free Pudding and Pie Filling, Chocolate, prep (w/skim milk) (1/2 cup)	73	0.2	0.1	2	163
Jell-O Sugar Free Pudding and Pie Filling, Vanilla, prep (w/skim milk) (1/2 cup)	63	0.2	0.1	2	203
My-T-Fine Pudding & Pie Filling, Lemon Flavored, prep (w/skim milk) (1 serving)	133	0.2	0.1	2	233
My-T-Fine Pudding, Butterscotch, prep (w/skim milk) (1/2 cup)	133	0.2	0.1	2	253
My-T-Fine Pudding, Chocolate Almond, prep (w/skim milk) (1/2 cup)	143	1.2	(0.4)	2	198
My-T-Fine Pudding, Chocolate Fudge, prep (w/skim milk) (1/2 cup)	143	0.2	0.1	2	203
My-T-Fine Pudding, Chocolate, prep (w/skim milk) (1/2 cup)	143	0.2	0.1	2	198
My-T-Fine Pudding, Vanilla Tapioca, prep (w/skim milk) (1/2 cup)	123	0.2	0.1	2	223
My-T-Fine Pudding, Vanilla, prep (w/skim milk) (1/2 cup)	133	0.2	0.1	2	183
Royal Custard Dessert Mix, prep (w/skim milk) (1/2 cup)	103	0.2	0.1	2	138
Royal Dark 'N' Sweet Pudding and Pie Filling, Chocolate, prep (w/skim milk) (1/2 cup)	133	0.2	0.1	2	158
Royal Flan Caramel Custard, prep (w/skim milk) (1/2 cup)	103	0.2	0.1	2	118
Royal Instant Dark 'N' Sweet Pudding, prep (w/skim milk) (1/2 cup)	153	0.2	0.1	2	523

Chilled Desserts (continued)	Calories	Fat g	Saturated Fat g	Choles- terol mg	Sodium mg
Royal Instant Pudding and Pie Filling, Banana Cream, prep (w/skim milk) (1/2 cup)	133	0.2	0.1	2	453
Royal Instant Pudding and Pie Filling, Butterscotch, prep (w/skim milk) (1/2 cup)	133	0.2	0.1	2	463
Royal Instant Pudding and Pie Filling, Cherry Vanilla, prep (w/skim milk) (1/2 cup)	133	0.2	0.1	2	363
Royal Instant Pudding and Pie Filling, Chocolate Almond, prep (w/skim milk) (1/2 cup)	163	1.2	(0.4)	2	503
Royal Instant Pudding and Pie Filling, Chocolate Chocolate Chip, prep (w/skim milk) (1/2 cup)	153	1.2	(0.4)	2	453
Royal Instant Pudding and Pie Filling, Chocolate Peanut Butter Chip, prep (w/skim milk) (1/2 cup)	153	1.2	(0.4)	2	543
Royal Instant Pudding and Pie Filling, Chocolate, prep (w/skim milk) (1/2 cup)	153	0.2	0.1	2	513
Royal Instant Pudding and Pie Filling, Lemon, prep (w/skim milk) (1/2 cup)	133	0.2	0.1	2	383
Royal Instant Pudding and Pie Filling, Pistachio, prep (w/skim milk) (1/2 cup)	133	1.2	(0.4)	2	423
Royal Instant Pudding and Pie Filling, Strawberry, prep (w/skim milk) (1/2 cup)	143	0.2	0.1	2	393
Royal Instant Pudding and Pie Filling, Toasted Coconut, prep (w/skim milk) (1/2 cup)	143	2.2	(0.7)	2	513
Royal Instant Pudding and Pie Filling, Vanilla Chocolate Chip, prep (w/skim milk) (1/2 cup)	133	1.2	(0.4)	2	413
Royal Instant Pudding and Pie Filling, Vanilla, prep (w/skim milk) (1/2 cup)	133	0.2	0.1	2	388
Royal Pie Filling, Key Lime, prep (w/skim milk) (1/2 cup)	93	0.2	0.1	2	183

Chilled Desserts (continued)	Calories	Fat g	Saturated Fat g	Choles- terol mg	Sodium mg
Royal Pie Filling, Lemon, prep (w/skim milk) (1 serving)	93	0.2	0.1	2	183
Royal Pudding and Pie Filling, Banana Cream, prep (w/skim milk) (1/2 cup)	123	0.2	0.1	2	173
Royal Pudding and Pie Filling, Butterscotch, prep (w/skim milk) (1/2 cup)	133	0.2	0.1	2	243
Royal Pudding and Pie Filling, Chocolate, prep (w/skim milk) (1/2 cup)	133	0.2	0.1	2	153
Royal Pudding and Pie Filling, Vanilla, prep (w/skim milk) (1 serving)	123	0.2	0.1	2	223
Royal Sugar Free Instant Pudding and Pie Filling, Chocolate, prep (w/skim milk) (1/2 cup)	93	0.2	0.1	2	483
Sweet N Low Custard Mix, Chocolate, prep (w/skim milk) (1/2 cup)	70	<1.0	0.0	5	115
Sweet N Low Custard Mix, Lemon, prep (w/skim milk) (1/2 cup)	70	<1.0	0.0	5	145
Sweet N Low Custard Mix, Vanilla, prep (w/skim milk) (1/2 cup)	70	<1.0	0.0	5	145
Swiss Miss Light Pudding, Chocolate (4 oz)	100	1.0	0.3	1	120
Swiss Miss Light Pudding, Chocolate Fudge (4 oz)	100	1.0	0.3	1	120
Swiss Miss Light Pudding, Vanilla (4 oz)	100	1.0	0.3	<1	105
Swiss Miss Light Pudding, Vanilla/Chocolate Parfait (4 oz)	100	1.0	0.3	<1	110
Ultra Slim-Fast Pudding, Butterscotch (4 oz)	100	<1.0	(0.0)	0	230
Ultra Slim-Fast Pudding, Chocolate (4 oz)	100	<1.0	(0.0)	0	240
Ultra Slim-Fast Pudding, Vanilla (4 oz)	100	<1.0	(0.0)	0	230
Weight Watchers Pudding Mix, Butterscotch, prep (w/skim milk) (1/2 cup)	90	0.0	0.0	(2)	460

Chilled Desserts (continued)	Calories	Fat g	Saturated Fat g	Choles- terol mg	Sodium mg
Weight Watchers Pudding Mix, Chocolate, prep (w/skim milk) (1/2 cup)	90	1.0	(0.3)	(2)	420
Weight Watchers Pudding Mix, Vanilla, prep (w/skim milk) (1/2 cup)	90	0.0	0.0	(2)	510

EGG SUBSTITUTES

The egg substitutes included in this section of the Guide are low in fat, saturated fat, and cholesterol. A serving of these foods does not exceed the cutoff points shown below.

CUTOFF POINTS FOR
EGG SUBSTITUTES

Fat (grams)	Saturated Fat (grams)	Cholesterol (milligrams)
3	1	10

SERVINGS

Food	Serving Size
Egg Substitute	2 ounces

The following abbreviations are used in the Food Sections: oz = ounce; fl oz = fluid ounce; pkg = package; pkt = packet; env = envelope; g = gram; prep (w/ . . .) = prepared with; < = less than; and tr = trace.

Egg Substitutes	Calories	Fat g	Saturated Fat g	Choles-terol mg	Sodium mg
Ballas Egg Whites (2 tbsp)	50	<1.0	(0.0)	0	150
Egg White, raw (1)	16	0.0	0.0	0	50
Fleishmann's Egg Beaters (1/4 cup)	25	0.0	0.0	0	80
Fleishmann's Egg Beaters Omelette Mix, Vegetable (1/2 cup)	50	0.0	0.0	0	170
Healthy Choice Cholesterol Free Egg Product (1/4 cup)	30	<1.0	0.0	0	90
Morningstar Farms Scramblers (1/4 cup)	60	3.0	0.0	0	130
Second Nature Egg Substitute (2 fl oz = 1/4 cup)	60	2.0	<1.0	0	90
Sunny Fresh Free (2 fl oz = 1/4 cup = 1 egg)	30	0.0	0.0	0	51

FATS AND OILS

Foods that are high in total fat but that are low in saturated fat and cholesterol can be included (in limited amounts) in a cholesterol-lowering diet, such as our *Living Heart Diet* (1984). Therefore, levels of saturated fat and cholesterol were used as the only cutoff points to evaluate avocado, margarine, nuts, oils, olives, and seeds; a cutoff point for fat was not used. Since these foods are naturally high in fat, the quantity eaten needs to be limited; please refer to chapter 4 for the amount suggested per day. Values for most of these foods, except margarine, are from USDA handbooks and are listed as "most brands."

This section of the Guide also includes butter and margarine substitutes and cooking sprays. To be listed in the Guide, a serving of these products, as specified by the manufacturer, does not exceed the cutoff points for fat, saturated fat, and cholesterol listed below.

Salad dressing, another food that can be high in fat, is in the Salad Dressings and Sandwich Spreads section, beginning on page 308.

CUTOFF POINTS FOR FATS AND OILS

	Fat (grams)	Saturated Fat (grams)	Cholesterol (milligrams)
Avocado, Margarine, Nuts, Nut Butters, Oil, Olives, and Seeds	*	2	10
Butter and Margarine Substitutes and Cooking Sprays	3	1	10

*No cutoff point; these foods are naturally high in fat.

SERVING SIZES

Food	Serving Sizes
Butter and Margarine Substitutes	1 serving as listed by manufacturer
Fats and Oils:	
Avocado	⅛ of whole
Cooking Spray	1 serving as listed by manufacturer
Margarine	1 tablespoon
Nut Butters	2 tablespoons
Nuts and Seeds	1½ ounces
Oil	1 tablespoon
Olives	½ ounce

The following abbreviations are used in the Food Sections: oz = ounce; fl oz = fluid ounce; pkg = package; pkt = packet; env = envelope; g = gram; prep (w/ . . .) = prepared with; < = less than; and tr = trace.

Butter and Margarine Substitutes	Calories	Fat g	Saturated Fat g	Choles- terol mg	Sodium mg
BUTTER AND MARGARINE SUBSTITUTES					
Butter Buds Mix (1 tbsp)	6	0.0	0.0	0	85
Butter Buds Sprinkles (1/2 tsp)	4	0.0	0.0	0	65
Molly McButter Sprinkles, Butter Flavor (1/2 tsp)	4	0.0	0.0	0	90
COOKING SPRAYS					
Baker's Joy Vegetable Oil and Flour Baking Spray (1/10 of 8″ 2-layer cake)	4	<1.0	(0.0)	0	0
Mazola No Stick Cooking Spray (2.5 second spray)	2	0.2	tr	0	0
Weight Watchers Buttery Spray (1 second spray)	2	<1.0	(0.0)	(0)	0
Weight Watchers Cooking Spray (1 second spray)	2	1.0	(0.0)	(0)	0
Wesson Lite Cooking Spray (.3 g)	0.4	<1.0	(0.0)	0	0
MARGARINE					
Blue Bonnet Margarine, Soft (1 tbsp)	100	11.0	2.0	0	95
Blue Bonnet Margarine, Stick (1 tbsp)	100	11.0	2.0	0	95
Blue Bonnet Margarine, Stick, Whipped (1 tbsp)	70	7.0	1.0	0	70
Blue Bonnet Spread, Soft, Better Blend, 76% fat (1 tbsp)	90	11.0	2.0	0	95
Blue Bonnet Spread, Stick, Better Blend, 76% fat (1 tbsp)	90	11.0	2.0	0	95
Blue Bonnet Spread, Stick, Better Blend, Unsalted (1 tbsp)	90	11.0	1.0	0	0
Blue Bonnet Spread, whipped, 60% oil (1 tbsp)	80	8.0	1.0	0	100
Canola Sunrise Margarine, stick (1 tbsp)	100	11.0	1.0	0	95
Canola Sunrise Spread, soft (1 tbsp)	70	7.0	<1.0	0	95
Chiffon Margarine, Soft Unsalted (1 tbsp)	90	10.0	2.0	0	0
Chiffon Margarine, stick (1 tbsp)	100	11.0	2.0	0	105
Chiffon Margarine, Soft, tub (1 tbsp)	90	10.0	1.0	0	95

Margarine (continued)	Calories	Fat g	Saturated Fat g	Cholesterol mg	Sodium mg
Chiffon Margarine, Whipped (1 tbsp)	70	8.0	1.0	0	80
Fleischmann's Margarine, Diet, Reduced Calorie (1 tbsp)	50	6.0	1.0	0	50
Fleischmann's Margarine, Soft (1 tbsp)	100	11.0	2.0	0	95
Fleischmann's Margarine, Soft, Sweet Unsalted (1 tbsp)	100	11.0	2.0	0	0
Fleischmann's Margarine, Stick (1 tbsp)	100	11.0	2.0	0	95
Fleischmann's Margarine, Stick, Sweet, Unsalted (1 tbsp)	100	11.0	2.0	0	0
Fleishmann's Margarine, Whipped, Lightly Salted (1 tbsp)	70	7.0	2.0	0	60
Fleischmann's Margarine, Whipped, Unsalted (1 tbsp)	70	7.0	2.0	0	0
Fleishmann's Spread, Extra Light Corn Oil, 40% oil (1 tbsp)	50	6.0	1.0	0	55
Fleishmann's Spread, Soft, Light Corn Oil, 60% oil (1 tbsp)	80	8.0	1.0	0	70
Fleishmann's Spread, Stick, Light Corn Oil, 60% oil (1 tbsp)	80	8.0	1.0	0	70
Giant Corn Oil Margarine, soft (1 tbsp)	100	11.0	2.0	0	110
Giant Corn Oil Margarine, stick (1 tbsp)	100	11.0	2.0	0	115
Giant Margarine, soft (1 tbsp)	90	10.0	2.0	0	105
Giant Margarine, stick (1 tbsp)	100	11.0	2.0	0	130
Giant Spread, soft (1 tbsp)	60	7.0	2.0	0	105
Giant Spread, stick (1 tbsp)	60	7.0	1.0	0	110
Hain Safflower Margarine, Soft (1 tbsp)	100	11.0	2.0	0	170
Hain Safflower Margarine, Unsalted (1 tbsp)	100	11.0	2.0	0	<5
Hain Safflower Margarine, stick (1 tbsp)	100	11.0	2.0	0	170
Heartlight Margarine, soft (1 tbsp)	100	11.0	1.0	0	109
Hollywood Safflower Margarine (1 tbsp)	100	11.0	2.0	0	130

Margarine (continued)	Calories	Fat g	Saturated Fat g	Choles- terol mg	Sodium mg
Hollywood Safflower Margarine, Sweet Unsalted (1 tbsp)	100	11.0	2.0	0	2
I Can't Believe It's Not Butter! Spread, Soft (1 tbsp)	90	10.0	2.0	0	90
I Can't Believe It's Not Butter! Spread, Stick (1 tbsp)	90	10.0	2.0	0	95
I Can't Believe It's Not Butter! Spread, Stick, Sweet Unsalted (1 tbsp)	90	10.0	2.0	0	0
Kraft Touch of Butter Spread, stick (1 tbsp)	90	10.0	2.0	0	110
Kraft Touch of Butter Spread, tub (1 tbsp)	50	6.0	1.0	0	110
Lucerne Corn Oil Margarine (1 tbsp)	100	11.0	2.0	0	120
Mazola Corn Oil Diet Reduced Calorie Margarine (1 tbsp)	50	5.5	0.9	0	130
Mazola Corn Oil Margarine (1 tbsp)	100	11.0	1.9	0	100
Mazola Corn Oil Margarine, Unsalted (1 tbsp)	100	11.0	2.0	0	1
Mazola Light Corn Oil Spread (1 tbsp)	50	5.6	1.0	0	100
Miracle Brand Margarine, Whipped, stick (1 tbsp)	70	7.0	1.0	0	65
Miracle Brand Margarine, Whipped, tub (1 tbsp)	60	7.0	1.0	0	70
Parkay Margarine, Soft (1 tbsp)	100	11.0	2.0	0	105
Parkay Margarine, Soft Diet Reduced Calorie (1 tbsp)	50	6.0	1.0	0	110
Parkay Margarine, Whipped, stick (1 tbsp)	70	7.0	1.0	0	65
Parkay Margarine, Whipped, tub (1 tbsp)	70	7.0	1.0	0	70
Parkay Spread (1 tbsp)	60	7.0	1.0	0	110
Parkay Squeeze Spread (1 tbsp)	90	10.0	2.0	0	110
Promise Extra Light Margarine, tub (1 tbsp)	50	6.0	1.0	0	50
Promise Spread, tub (1 tbsp)	90	10.0	1.0	0	90
Tree of Life Canola Soy Margarine (1 tbsp)	100	11.0	2.0	0	110

Margarine (continued)	Calories	Fat g	Saturated Fat g	Choles- terol mg	Sodium mg
Tree of Life Canola Soy Margarine, Salt Free (1 tbsp)	100	11.0	2.0	0	<2
Tree of Life Soy Margarine (1 tbsp)	100	11.0	2.0	0	110
Tree of Life Soy Margarine, Salt Free (1 tbsp)	100	11.0	2.0	0	<2
Weight Watchers Margarine, Reduced Calorie, stick (1 tbsp)	60	7.0	1.0	(0)	130
Weight Watchers Margarine, Reduced Calorie, tub (1 tbsp)	50	6.0	1.0	(0)	130
Weight Watchers Margarine, Sweet Unsalted, tub (1 tbsp)	50	6.0	1.0	(0)	(0)

OILS

	Calories	Fat g	Saturated Fat g	Choles- terol mg	Sodium mg
Canola Oil—Most Brands (1 tbsp)	120	13.6	0.8	0	0
Corn Oil—Most Brands (1 tbsp)	120	13.6	1.7	0	0
Eden Hot Pepper Sesame Oil (1 tbsp)	120	14.0	2.0	(0)	0
Eden Toasted Sesame Oil (1 tbsp)	120	14.0	2.0	(0)	0
Hain Almond Oil (1 tbsp)	120	14.0	1.0	0	0
Hain Apricot Kernel Oil (1 tbsp)	120	14.0	1.0	0	0
Hain Avocado Oil (1 tbsp)	120	14.0	1.0	0	0
Hain Safflower Oil, Hi-Oleic (1 tbsp)	120	14.0	1.0	0	0
Hain Walnut Oil (1 tbsp)	120	14.0	2.0	0	0
Olive Oil—Most Brands (1 tbsp)	119	13.5	1.8	0	0
Peanut Oil—Most Brands (1 tbsp)	119	13.5	2.3	0	0
Safflower Oil—Most Brands (1 tbsp)	120	13.6	1.2	0	0
Sesame Oil—Most Brands (1 tbsp)	120	13.6	1.9	0	0
Soybean Oil—Most Brands (1 tbsp)	120	13.6	2.0	0	0
Soybean and Cottonseed Oil—Most Brands (1 tbsp)	120	13.6	2.4	0	0
Sunflower Oil—Most Brands (1 tbsp)	120	13.6	1.4	0	0

Other Fats	Calories	Fat g	Saturated Fat g	Choles- terol mg	Sodium mg
OTHER FATS					
AVOCADO					
Avocado, California, raw (3 tbsp puree)	76	7.5	1.1	0	5
NUTS, SEEDS, AND NUT BUTTERS					
Beer Nuts, Almonds (1 oz)	170	14.0	1.0	0	65
Blue Diamond Almonds, Barbecue (1 oz)	160	16.0	1.0	0	220
Blue Diamond Almonds, Blanched, Sliced (1 oz)	150	13.0	1.0	0	0
Blue Diamond Almonds, Blanched, Whole (1 oz)	150	13.0	1.0	0	0
Blue Diamond Almonds, Chopped (1 oz)	150	13.0	1.0	0	0
Blue Diamond Almonds, Honey Roasted (1 oz)	140	12.0	1.0	0	40
Blue Diamond Almonds, Lightly Salted (1 oz)	150	13.0	1.0	0	140
Blue Diamond Almonds, Natural (1 oz)	150	13.0	1.0	0	0
Blue Diamond Almonds, Sliced (1 oz)	150	13.0	1.0	0	0
Blue Diamond Almonds, Slivered (1 oz)	150	13.0	1.0	0	0
Blue Diamond Almonds, Smokehouse (1 oz)	150	14.0	1.0	0	170
Blue Diamond Almonds, Sour Cream and Onion (1 oz)	150	14.0	1.0	0	140
Blue Diamond Almonds, Toasted, No Salt (1 oz)	150	13.0	1.0	0	0
Chestnuts, Roasted—Most Brands (6 tbsp)	102	0.5	0.2	0	2
Dole Almonds, Blanched, Slivered (1 oz)	170	14.0	(1.3)	(0)	4
Dole Almonds, Blanched, Whole (1 oz)	170	14.0	(1.3)	(0)	4
Dole Almonds, Natural, Chopped (1 oz)	170	14.0	(1.3)	(0)	4
Dole Almonds, Natural, Sliced (1 oz)	170	14.0	(1.3)	(0)	4
Dole Almonds, Natural, Whole (1 oz)	170	14.0	(1.3)	(0)	4

Other Fats (continued)	Calories	Fat g	Saturated Fat g	Choles- terol mg	Sodium mg
Dole Pistachios, Natural (1 oz)	90	7.0	(0.9)	(0)	250
Erewhon Almond Butter (1 tbsp)	90	8.0	(0.8)	0	18
Erewhon Peanut Butter, Chunky, Salted (2 tbsp)	190	14.0	(1.9)	(0)	75
Erewhon Peanut Butter, Chunky, Unsalted (2 tbsp)	190	14.0	(1.9)	(0)	10
Erewhon Peanut Butter, Creamy, Salted (2 tbsp)	190	14.0	(1.9)	(0)	75
Erewhon Peanut Butter, Creamy, Unsalted (2 tbsp)	190	14.0	(1.9)	(0)	10
Erewhon Sesame Butter (2 tbsp)	190	17.0	(2.4)	0	20
Erewhon Sunflower Butter (2 tbsp)	200	18.0	(1.9)	0	0
Fisher Almonds, Raw (1 oz)	170	15.0	1.0	0	0
Frito-Lay Sunflower Seeds (1 oz)	160	14.0	(1.5)	(0)	265
Hain Almond Butter, Natural, Raw (2 tbsp)	190	18.0	2.0	0	5
Hain Almond Butter, Toasted, Blanched (2 tbsp)	210	19.0	2.0	0	5
IGA Butter Toffee Peanuts (1 oz)	150	7.0	(1.0)	5	(120)
Lance Almonds, Smoke Flavored (3/4 oz = 1 pkg)	120	11.0	1.0	0	130
Party Pride Almonds, Sliced (1 oz)	170	15.0	(1.4)	0	0
Party Pride Almonds, Slivered (1 oz)	170	15.0	(1.4)	0	0
OLIVES					
Olives, Green—Most Brands (5 small)	17	1.8	0.2	0	343
Olives, Ripe—Most Brands (2 extra large)	15	1.6	0.2	0	96

FROZEN DESSERTS

Many of the products low in fat that are included in this section of the Guide have been developed as substitutes for ice cream. For example, ice milk and frozen yogurt are much lower in fat and saturated fat than ice cream. Note that the cutoff point for saturated fat for frozen desserts that are primarily milk-based, such as frozen yogurt, is 2 grams. Frozen desserts that are not milk-based, such as sorbet, have a cutoff point for saturated fat of 1 gram, the same as is used for most foods in the Guide. Values for fat, saturated fat, and cholesterol in one serving of the foods included in this section of the Guide do not exceed the cutoff points listed below.

CUTOFF POINTS FOR FROZEN DESSERTS

	Fat (grams)	Saturated Fat (grams)	Cholesterol (milligrams)
Frozen Desserts, Milk-Based	3	2	10
Frozen Desserts, Not Milk-Based	3	1	10

SERVINGS

Food	Serving Sizes
Frozen Yogurt	½ cup
Ice Milk and Frozen Dairy Desserts	½ cup
Pops and Bars	½ cup
Popsicles, Frozen Fruit Bars	3 ounces
Sherbet and Sorbet	½ cup

The following abbreviations are used in the Food Sections: oz = ounce; fl oz = fluid ounce; pkg = package; pkt = packet; env = envelope; g = gram; prep (w/ . . .) = prepared with; < = less than; and tr = trace.

Frozen Yogurts	Calories	Fat g	Saturated Fat g	Choles- terol mg	Sodium mg
FROZEN YOGURTS					
Ben & Jerry's Lowfat Frozen Yogurt, Banana Strawberry (3 fl oz)	140	1.0	(0.7)	5	(43)
Ben & Jerry's Lowfat Frozen Yogurt, Blueberry Cheesecake (3 fl oz)	110	2.0	(1.3)	5	(43)
Ben & Jerry's Lowfat Frozen Yogurt, Chocolate (3 fl oz)	120	2.0	(1.3)	7	(43)
Ben & Jerry's Lowfat Frozen Yogurt, Raspberry (3 fl oz)	130	1.0	(0.7)	5	(43)
Blue Bell Lowfat Frozen Yogurt, Banana Strawberry (1/2 cup)	120	2.0	(1.3)	9	80
Blue Bell Lowfat Frozen Yogurt, Chocolate (1/2 cup)	130	2.0	(1.3)	9	90
Blue Bell Lowfat Frozen Yogurt, Peach (1/2 cup)	130	2.0	1.0	9	75
Blue Bell Lowfat Frozen Yogurt, Strawberry (1/2 cup)	120	2.0	(1.0)	9	75
Blue Bell Lowfat Frozen Yogurt, Vanilla (1/2 cup)	130	2.0	(1.0)	9	90
Blue Bell Nonfat Frozen Yogurt, Chocolate (1/2 cup)	100	0.5	(0.3)	0	55
Blue Bell Nonfat Frozen Yogurt, Fruit Yogurt (1/2 cup)	100	0.5	(0.3)	0	50
Blue Bell Nonfat Frozen Yogurt, Strawberry (1/2 cup)	100	0.5	(0.3)	0	45
Blue Bell Nonfat Frozen Yogurt, Vanilla (1/2 cup)	100	0.5	(0.3)	0	60
Carnation Frozen Yogurt, Strawberry (4 fl oz)	100	1.0	(0.6)	<5	80
Colombo Shoppe Style Soft Lowfat Frozen Yogurt, Old World Chocolate (3 fl oz)	90	1.0	(0.7)	<5	50
Colombo Shoppe Style Soft Lowfat Frozen Yogurt, Strawberry Cheesecake Twist (3 fl oz)	90	1.0	(0.7)	<5	40
Colombo Shoppe Style Soft Lowfat Frozen Yogurt, Vanilla Peach Twist (3 fl oz)	90	1.0	(0.7)	<5	40
Colombo Shoppe Style Soft Lowfat Frozen Yogurt, Wild Strawberry (3 fl oz)	90	1.0	(0.7)	<5	35

Frozen Yogurts (continued)	Calories	Fat g	Saturated Fat g	Choles- terol mg	Sodium mg
Dannon Lowfat Soft Frozen Yogurt, Softy Peanut Butter (4 fl oz)	130	3.0	(2.0)	5	70
Dannon Lowfat Soft Frozen Yogurt, Softy Plain (4 fl oz)	90	1.0	(0.6)	5	60
Dannon Lowfat Soft Frozen Yogurt, Softy Raspberry (4 fl oz)	100	0.0	0.0	0	60
Dannon Nonfat Soft Frozen Yogurt, Softy Chocolate (4 fl oz)	110	0.0	0.0	0	65
Dannon Nonfat Soft Frozen Yogurt, Softy Golden Vanilla (4 fl oz)	100	0.0	0.0	0	60
Dannon Nonfat Soft Frozen Yogurt, Softy Red Raspberry (4 fl oz)	110	2.0	(1.3)	5	65
Dannon Nonfat Soft Frozen Yogurt, Softy Rum Raisin (4 fl oz)	100	0.0	0.0	0	65
Dannon Nonfat Soft Frozen Yogurt, Softy Strawberry (4 fl oz)	100	0.0	0.0	0	60
Danone Frozen Yogurt, Black Cherry (4.2 fl oz)	109	2.9	2.0	7	(60)
Danone Frozen Yogurt, Mandarin Orange (4.2 fl oz)	108	2.9	2.0	7	(60)
Danone Frozen Yogurt, Raspberry (4.2 fl oz)	108	2.9	2.0	7	(60)
Danone Frozen Yogurt, Strawberry (4.2 fl oz)	101	2.8	1.9	7	(60)
Danone Frozen Yogurt, Vanilla (4.2 fl oz)	103	3.0	2.0	7	(60)
Dreyer's Frozen Yogurt Inspirations, Banana Strawberry (3 fl oz)	80	1.0	(0.7)	5	40
Dreyer's Frozen Yogurt Inspirations, Blueberry (3 fl oz)	80	1.0	(0.7)	5	40
Dreyer's Frozen Yogurt Inspirations, Cherry (3 fl oz)	80	1.0	(0.7)	5	40
Dreyer's Frozen Yogurt Inspirations, Chocolate (3 fl oz)	80	1.0	(0.7)	5	40
Dreyer's Frozen Yogurt Inspirations, Chocolate Chip (3 fl oz)	100	1.0	(0.7)	5	55

Frozen Yogurts (continued)	Calories	Fat g	Saturated Fat g	Choles- terol mg	Sodium mg
Dreyer's Frozen Yogurt Inspirations, Citrus Heights (3 fl oz)	80	1.0	(0.7)	5	40
Dreyer's Frozen Yogurt Inspirations, Cookies 'N' Cream (3 fl oz)	100	1.0	(0.7)	5	55
Dreyer's Frozen Yogurt Inspirations, Marble Fudge (3 fl oz)	100	1.0	(0.7)	5	55
Dreyer's Frozen Yogurt Inspirations, Perfectly Peach (3 fl oz)	80	1.0	(0.7)	5	40
Dreyer's Frozen Yogurt Inspirations, Raspberry (3 fl oz)	80	1.0	(0.7)	5	40
Dreyer's Frozen Yogurt Inspirations, Raspberry-Vanilla Swirl (3 fl oz)	80	1.0	(0.7)	5	45
Dreyer's Frozen Yogurt Inspirations, Strawberry (3 fl oz)	80	1.0	(0.7)	5	40
Dreyer's Frozen Yogurt Inspirations, Vanilla (3 fl oz)	80	1.0	(0.7)	5	50
Edy's Frozen Yogurt Inspirations, Banana Strawberry (3 fl oz)	80	1.0	(0.7)	5	40
Edy's Frozen Yogurt Inspirations, Blueberry (3 fl oz)	80	1.0	(0.7)	5	40
Edy's Frozen Yogurt Inspirations, Cherry (3 fl oz)	80	1.0	(0.7)	5	40
Edy's Frozen Yogurt Inspirations, Chocolate (3 fl oz)	80	1.0	(0.7)	5	40
Edy's Frozen Yogurt Inspirations, Chocolate Chip (3 fl oz)	100	1.0	(0.7)	5	55
Edy's Frozen Yogurt Inspirations, Citrus Heights (3 fl oz)	80	1.0	(0.7)	5	40
Edy's Frozen Yogurt Inspirations, Cookies 'N' Cream (3 fl oz)	100	1.0	(0.7)	5	55
Edy's Frozen Yogurt Inspirations, Marble Fudge (3 fl oz)	100	1.0	(0.7)	5	55
Edy's Frozen Yogurt Inspirations, Perfectly Peach (3 fl oz)	80	1.0	(0.7)	5	40

Frozen Yogurts (continued)	Calories	Fat g	Saturated Fat g	Choles- terol mg	Sodium mg
Edy's Frozen Yogurt Inspirations, Raspberry (3 fl oz)	80	1.0	(0.7)	5	40
Edy's Frozen Yogurt Inspirations, Raspberry-Vanilla Swirl (3 fl oz)	80	1.0	(0.7)	5	45
Edy's Frozen Yogurt Inspirations, Strawberry (3 fl oz)	80	1.0	(0.7)	5	40
Edy's Frozen Yogurt Inspirations, Vanilla (3 fl oz)	80	1.0	(0.7)	5	50
Giant Frozen Yogurt, Nonfat, all flavors (self-serve) (4 fl oz)	100	0.0	0.0	0	75
Giant Frozen Yogurt, Chocolate (4 fl oz)	150	2.0	(1.3)	(5)	75
Giant Frozen Yogurt, Strawberry (4 fl oz)	150	2.0	(1.3)	(5)	70
Giant Frozen Yogurt, Vanilla (4 fl oz)	140	2.0	(1.3)	(5)	70
Goldcup Frozen Yogurt, Blueberry (3 fl oz)	90	2.0	(1.3)	(7)	30
Goldcup Frozen Yogurt, Black Cherry (3 fl oz)	90	2.0	(1.3)	(7)	30
Goldcup Frozen Yogurt, Chocolate (3 fl oz)	90	2.0	(1.3)	(7)	30
Goldcup Frozen Yogurt, Peach (3 fl oz)	90	2.0	(1.3)	(7)	30
Goldcup Frozen Yogurt, Raspberry (3 fl oz)	90	2.0	(1.3)	(7)	30
Goldcup Frozen Yogurt, Strawberry (3 fl oz)	90	2.0	(1.3)	(7)	30
Goldcup Frozen Yogurt, Vanilla (3 fl oz)	90	2.0	(1.3)	(7)	30
Heidi's Light Nonfat Frozen Yogurt, Pecan n' Pralines (3 fl oz)	65	0.0	0.0	(0)	55
I Can't Believe It's Yogurt, Nonfat (6-3/4 fl oz = 1 small serving)	135	0.0	0.0	0	18
I Can't Believe It's Yogurt, Sugar Free (6-3/4 fl oz = 1 small serving)	115	0.0	0.0	0	18
Kemps Frozen Yogurt (4 oz)	100	1.0	(0.7)	7	50
Kemps Frozen Yogurt, Nonfat (4 oz)	90	0.0	0.0	0	60

Frozen Yogurts (continued)	Calories	Fat g	Saturated Fat g	Choles-terol mg	Sodium mg
Land O'Lakes Frozen Yogurt, Strawberry (4 fl oz)	110	3.0	2.0	10	60
Sealtest Free Nonfat Frozen Yogurt, Black Cherry (1/2 cup)	110	0.0	0.0	0	50
Sealtest Free Nonfat Frozen Yogurt, Chocolate (1/2 cup)	110	0.0	0.0	0	55
Sealtest Free Nonfat Frozen Yogurt, Peach (1/2 cup)	100	0.0	0.0	0	35
Sealtest Free Nonfat Frozen Yogurt, Red Raspberry (1/2 cup)	100	0.0	0.0	0	40
Sealtest Free Nonfat Frozen Yogurt, Strawberry (1/2 cup)	100	0.0	0.0	0	35
Sealtest Free Nonfat Frozen Yogurt, Vanilla (1/2 cup)	100	0.0	0.0	0	45
Tazzi Nonfat Gourmet Lite Frozen Yogurt, Apple Pie (3 fl oz)	73	0.0	0.0	(0)	48
Tazzi Nonfat Gourmet Lite Frozen Yogurt, Blueberry (3 fl oz)	73	0.0	0.0	(0)	48
Tazzi Nonfat Gourmet Lite Frozen Yogurt, Coffee Mocha (3 fl oz)	73	0.0	0.0	(0)	48
Tazzi Nonfat Gourmet Lite Frozen Yogurt, Lemon Chiffon (3 fl oz)	73	0.0	0.0	(0)	48
Tazzi Nonfat Gourmet Lite Frozen Yogurt, Peanut Chocolate (3 fl oz)	73	0.0	0.0	(0)	48
Tazzi Nonfat Gourmet Lite Frozen Yogurt, Pistachio (3 fl oz)	73	0.0	0.0	(0)	48
Tazzi Nonfat Gourmet Lite Frozen Yogurt, Praline Pecan (3 fl oz)	73	0.0	0.0	(0)	48
Tazzi Nonfat Gourmet Lite Frozen Yogurt, Raspberry Frappe (3 fl oz)	73	0.0	0.0	(0)	48
Tazzi Nonfat Gourmet Lite Frozen Yogurt, Rocky Road (3 fl oz)	73	0.0	0.0	(0)	48
TCBY Frozen Yogurt, Non-Fat (6 fl oz)	150	< 1.0	0.0	0	68

Frozen Yogurts (continued)	Calories	Fat g	Saturated Fat g	Choles- terol mg	Sodium mg
Well's Blue Bunny Lite Sugar-Free Lowfat Frozen Yogurt, Burgundy Cherry (3 fl oz)	50	1.0	(0.6)	5	40
Well's Blue Bunny Lite Sugar-Free Lowfat Frozen Yogurt, Chocolate (3 fl oz)	60	1.0	(0.6)	5	65
Well's Blue Bunny Lite Sugar-Free Lowfat Frozen Yogurt, Peach (3 fl oz)	50	1.0	(0.6)	5	40
Well's Blue Bunny Lite Sugar-Free Lowfat Frozen Yogurt, Strawberry (3 fl oz)	50	1.0	(0.6)	5	40
Well's Blue Bunny Lite Sugar-Free Lowfat Frozen Yogurt, Vanilla (3 fl oz)	60	1.0	(0.6)	5	45
Well's Blue Bunny Nonfat Frozen Yogurt, Burgundy Cherry (3 fl oz)	60	0.0	0.0	0	45
Well's Blue Bunny Nonfat Frozen Yogurt, Chocolate (3 fl oz)	60	0.0	0.0	0	50
Well's Blue Bunny Nonfat Frozen Yogurt, Peach (3 fl oz)	60	0.0	0.0	0	45
Well's Blue Bunny Nonfat Frozen Yogurt, Strawberry (3 fl oz)	60	0.0	0.0	0	45
Well's Blue Bunny Nonfat Frozen Yogurt, Vanilla (3 fl oz)	60	0.0	0.0	0	45
Yarnell's Lowfat Frozen Yogurt, Chocolate (3 oz)	90	1.0	(0.7)	7	45
Yarnell's Lowfat Frozen Yogurt, Peach (3 oz)	80	1.0	(0.7)	7	40
Yarnell's Lowfat Frozen Yogurt, Raspberry (3 oz)	80	1.0	(0.7)	7	40
Yarnell's Lowfat Frozen Yogurt, Strawberry (3 oz)	80	1.0	(0.7)	7	40
Yarnell's Lowfat Frozen Yogurt, Strawberry/Banana (3 oz)	80	1.0	(0.7)	7	40
Yarnell's Lowfat Frozen Yogurt, Vanilla (3 oz)	80	1.0	(0.7)	7	45
Yarnell's Nonfat Frozen Yogurt, Black Cherry (3 oz)	80	0.0	0.0	0	40

Frozen Yogurts (continued)	Calories	Fat g	Saturated Fat g	Choles- terol mg	Sodium mg
Yarnell's Nonfat Frozen Yogurt, Lemon (3 oz)	70	0.0	0.0	0	40
Yarnell's Nonfat Frozen Yogurt, Pineapple (3 oz)	70	0.0	0.0	0	45
Yarnell's Nonfat Frozen Yogurt, Raspberry (3 oz)	80	0.0	0.0	0	40
Yoplait Soft Frozen Yogurt (3 fl oz)	90	2.0	(1.3)	5	40
ICE CREAM CONES					
Cup-O-Joy Honey & Bran Cones (1 cone)	20	0.0	(0.0)	0	0
Food Club Color Cake Cones (1 cone)	18	0.0	(0.0)	0	15
Food Club Sugar Cones (1 cone)	45	0.0	(0.0)	0	5
Nabisco Comet Cups (1 cup)	18	< 1.0	(0.0)	0	5
Nabisco Comet Sugar Cones (1 cone)	50	< 1.0	(0.0)	0	40
Sunshine Cake Cones (1 cone)	20	< 1.0	(0.0)	0	20
Sunshine Sugar Cones (1 cone)	50	1.0	(0.3)	0	10
ICE MILK AND FROZEN DAIRY DESSERTS					
Blue Bell Extra Light, Cherry Vanilla (1/2 cup)	90	0.0	0.0	0	50
Blue Bell Extra Light, Peach (1/2 cup)	90	0.0	0.0	0	40
Blue Bell Extra Light, Strawberry (1/2 cup)	90	0.0	0.0	0	40
Blue Bell Extra Light, Vanilla (1/2 cup)	90	0.0	0.0	0	60
Blue Bell Free, Chocolate (1/2 cup)	80	0.0	0.0	0	55
Blue Bell Free, Strawberry (1/2 cup)	80	0.0	0.0	0	65
Blue Bell Free, Vanilla (1/2 cup)	80	0.0	0.0	0	65
Blue Bell Light, Cookies 'N Cream (1/2 cup)	100	2.0	(1.3)	9	95
Blue Bell Light, Neapolitan (1/2 cup)	100	2.0	(1.3)	9	60
Blue Bell Light, Vanilla (1/2 cup)	100	2.0	1.0	10	65

Ice Milk and Frozen Dairy Desserts (continued)	Calories	Fat g	Saturated Fat g	Cholesterol mg	Sodium mg
Blue Bell Light, Vanilla Fudge (1/2 cup)	110	2.0	(1.3)	9	70
Borden Ice Milk, Chocolate (1/2 cup)	100	2.0	(1.2)	(9)	80
Borden Ice Milk, Strawberry (1/2 cup)	90	2.0	(1.2)	(9)	65
Borden Ice Milk, Vanilla Flavored (1/2 cup)	90	2.0	(1.2)	(9)	65
Carnation Smooth 'N Lite Ice Milk, Cherry Vanilla (1/2 cup)	100	2.0	2.0	10	55
Carnation Smooth 'N Lite Ice Milk, Chocolate (1/2 cup)	90	2.0	2.0	10	90
Dreyer's American Dream, Chocolate (3 fl oz)	90	1.0	(0.6)	0	45
Dreyer's American Dream, Chocolate Chip (3 fl oz)	100	1.0	(0.6)	0	45
Dreyer's American Dream, Cookies 'N Cream (3 fl oz)	100	1.0	(0.6)	0	45
Dreyer's American Dream, Mocha Almond Fudge (3 fl oz)	110	1.0	(0.6)	0	45
Dreyer's American Dream, Rocky Road (3 fl oz)	110	1.0	(0.6)	0	45
Dreyer's American Dream, Strawberry (3 fl oz)	70	<1.0	0.0	0	40
Dreyer's American Dream, Toasted Almond (3 fl oz)	110	1.0	(0.6)	0	45
Dreyer's American Dream, Vanilla (3 fl oz)	80	<1.0	0.0	0	45
Dreyer's American Dream, Vanilla/Chocolate/Strawberry (3 fl oz)	80	1.0	(0.6)	0	45
Dreyer's Frozen Dietary Dairy Dessert, Chocolate (3 fl oz)	110	3.0	(1.9)	10	45
Dreyer's Frozen Dietary Dairy Dessert, Marble Fudge (3 fl oz)	120	3.0	(1.9)	10	45
Dreyer's Frozen Dietary Dairy Dessert, Strawberry (3 fl oz)	90	3.0	(1.9)	10	40
Dreyer's Frozen Dietary Dairy Dessert, Vanilla (3 fl oz)	100	3.0	(1.9)	10	45
Edy's American Dream, Chocolate (3 fl oz)	90	1.0	(0.6)	0	45
Edy's American Dream, Chocolate Chip (3 fl oz)	100	1.0	(0.6)	0	45

Ice Milk and Frozen Dairy Desserts (continued)	Calories	Fat g	Saturated Fat g	Choles-terol mg	Sodium mg
Edy's American Dream, Cookies 'N Cream (3 fl oz)	100	1.0	(0.6)	0	45
Edy's American Dream, Mocha Almond Fudge (3 fl oz)	110	1.0	(0.6)	0	45
Edy's American Dream, Rocky Road (3 fl oz)	110	1.0	(0.6)	0	45
Edy's American Dream, Strawberry (3 fl oz)	70	<1.0	0.0	0	40
Edy's American Dream, Toasted Almond (3 fl oz)	110	1.0	(0.6)	0	45
Edy's American Dream, Vanilla (3 fl oz)	80	<1.0	0.0	0	45
Edy's American Dream, Vanilla/Chocolate/Strawberry (3 fl oz)	80	1.0	(0.6)	0	45
Edy's Frozen Dietary Dairy Dessert, Chocolate (3 fl oz)	110	3.0	(1.9)	10	45
Edy's Frozen Dietary Dairy Dessert, Marble Fudge (3 fl oz)	120	3.0	(1.9)	10	45
Edy's Frozen Dietary Dairy Dessert, Strawberry (3 fl oz)	90	3.0	(1.9)	10	40
Edy's Frozen Dietary Dairy Dessert, Vanilla (3 fl oz)	100	3.0	(1.9)	10	45
Giant Ice Milk, Butter Almond (1/2 cup)	100	2.0	2.0	10	85
Giant Ice Milk, Cherry Vanilla (1/2 cup)	100	2.0	2.0	10	80
Giant Ice Milk, Chocolate Chip (1/2 cup)	110	3.0	2.0	10	80
Giant Ice Milk, Vanilla (1/2 cup)	100	2.0	2.0	10	85
Giant Ice Milk, Vanilla Chocolate (1/2 cup)	100	2.0	2.0	10	80
Giant Dreamy Tofu, Apple Caramel Swirl (1/2 cup)	110	2.0	<1.0	0	20
Giant Dreamy Tofu, Chocolate (1/2 cup)	110	2.0	<1.0	0	15
Giant Dreamy Tofu, Wildberry Swirl (1/2 cup)	100	2.0	<1.0	0	15
Gise Creme Glace, Chocolate (3.5 fl oz)	34	0.1	(0.0)	(0)	0
Gise Creme Glace, all flavors except chocolate (3.5 fl oz)	33	0.0	0.0	0	0

Ice Milk and Frozen Dairy Desserts (continued)	Calories	Fat g	Saturated Fat g	Choles- terol mg	Sodium mg
Grant Dreamy Tofu, Mint Chocolate Swirl (1/2 cup)	100	3.0	< 1.0	0	15
Grant Light, Chocolate (1/2 cup)	100	3.0	(1.9)	(9)	80
Grant Light, Vanilla (1/2 cup)	100	3.0	(1.9)	(9)	80
Healthy Choice Frozen Dairy Dessert, Bordeaux Cherry (4 fl oz)	120	2.0	1.0	5	50
Healthy Choice Frozen Dairy Dessert, Chocolate (4 fl oz)	130	2.0	1.0	5	70
Healthy Choice Frozen Dairy Dessert, Cookies N' Cream (4 fl oz)	130	2.0	1.0	5	80
Healthy Choice Frozen Dairy Dessert, Neapolitan (4 fl oz)	120	2.0	1.0	5	60
Healthy Choice Frozen Dairy Dessert, Old Fashioned Vanilla (4 fl oz)	120	2.0	1.0	5	60
Healthy Choice Frozen Dairy Dessert, Praline & Caramel (4 fl oz)	130	2.0	1.0	5	70
Healthy Choice Frozen Dairy Dessert, Rocky Road (4 fl oz)	160	2.0	1.0	5	70
Healthy Choice Frozen Dairy Dessert, Strawberry (4 fl oz)	120	2.0	1.0	5	50
Healthy Choice Frozen Dairy Dessert, Vanilla (4 fl oz)	120	2.0	1.0	5	60
Healthy Choice Frozen Dairy Dessert, Wild Berry Swirl (4 fl oz)	120	2.0	1.0	5	60
Jerseymaid Lightly Maid Ice Milk, Chocolate Chip (1/2 cup)	100	2.0	(1.2)	(9)	60
Jerseymaid Lightly Maid Ice Milk, Neapolitan (1/2 cup)	90	2.0	(1.2)	(9)	65
Jerseymaid Lightly Maid Ice Milk, Rocky Road (1/2 cup)	100	2.0	(1.2)	(9)	65
Jerseymaid Lightly Maid Ice Milk, Vanilla (1/2 cup)	90	2.0	(1.2)	(9)	65
Kemp's Lite Ice Milk, Vanilla (4 oz)	100	2.0	(1.2)	10	60
King Sooper's Deluxe Fat Free Frozen Dessert, Chocolate/ Vanilla (1/2 cup)	90	0.0	0.0	0	55
Land O'Lakes Ice Milk, Vanilla (4 fl oz)	110	3.0	2.0	10	55

Ice Milk and Frozen Dairy Desserts (continued)	Calories	Fat g	Saturated Fat g	Choles-terol mg	Sodium mg
Light N' Lively Ice Milk, Coffee (1/2 cup)	100	3.0	1.0	10	40
Light N' Lively Ice Milk, Cookies N' Cream (1/2 cup)	110	3.0	2.0	10	65
Light N' Lively Ice Milk, Vanilla Flavored (1/2 cup)	100	3.0	2.0	10	40
Light N' Lively Ice Milk, Vanilla Flavored Chocolate-Strawberry (1/2 cup)	100	3.0	2.0	10	35
Light N' Lively Ice Milk, Vanilla Flavored with Red Raspberry Swirl (1/2 cup)	110	3.0	1.0	10	35
Light N' Lively Ice Milk, Vanilla Fudge Twirl (1/2 cup)	110	3.0	2.0	10	45
Lucerne Ice Milk, Caramel Nut (1/2 cup)	105	2.0	(1.2)	5	45
Lucerne Ice Milk, Cherry Vanilla (1/2 cup)	100	2.0	(1.2)	5	45
Lucerne Ice Milk, Chocolate (1/2 cup)	110	2.0	(1.2)	5	45
Lucerne Ice Milk, Chocolate Chip (1/2 cup)	100	2.0	(1.2)	5	45
Lucerne Ice Milk, Chocolate Marble (1/2 cup)	110	2.0	(1.2)	5	45
Lucerne Ice Milk, Light Chocolate (1/2 cup)	120	3.0	(1.9)	(9)	60
Lucerne Ice Milk, Light Strawberry & Cream (1/2 cup)	105	2.0	(1.2)	(5)	55
Lucerne Ice Milk, Light Toasted Almond (1/2 cup)	125	3.0	(1.9)	(9)	65
Lucerne Ice Milk, Light Vanilla (1/2 cup)	110	3.0	(1.9)	(9)	65
Lucerne Ice Milk, Pecan Crunch (1/2 cup)	100	2.0	(1.2)	5	45
Lucerne Ice Milk, Rocky Road (1/2 cup)	110	2.0	(1.2)	5	45
Lucerne Ice Milk, Strawberry (1/2 cup)	95	2.0	(1.2)	5	45
Lucerne Ice Milk, Triple Treat (1/2 cup)	100	2.0	(1.2)	5	45
Lucerne Light Ice Milk, Mocha Almond Fudge (1/2 cup)	125	3.0	(1.9)	(9)	68
Lucerne Kreme Koolers (4 oz)	50	1.0	(0.6)	3	10

Ice Milk and Frozen Dairy Desserts (continued)	Calories	Fat g	Saturated Fat g	Choles- terol mg	Sodium mg
Meadow Gold Light Premium Ice Milk, Vanilla (1/2 cup)	110	3.0	(1.9)	(9)	55
Ralph's Nonfat Ice Cream, Chocolate (1/2 cup)	100	<1.0	(0.0)	0	50
Ralph's Nonfat Ice Cream, Double Strawberry (1/2 cup)	100	<1.0	(0.0)	0	65
Ralph's Nonfat Ice Cream, Fudge Marble (1/2 cup)	100	<1.0	(0.0)	0	65
Ralph's Nonfat Ice Cream, Vanilla (1/2 cup)	100	<1.0	(0.0)	0	55
Ralph's Lite 'n Lean Ice Milk, Chocolate (1/2 cup)	100	2.0	(1.2)	(9)	60
Ralph's Lite 'n Lean Ice Milk, Chocolate Chip (1/2 cup)	120	2.0	(1.2)	(9)	75
Ralph's Lite 'n Lean Ice Milk, Fudge Marble (1/2 cup)	130	2.0	(1.2)	(9)	70
Ralph's Lite 'n Lean Ice Milk, Neapolitan (1/2 cup)	100	2.0	(1.2)	(9)	60
Ralph's Lite 'n Lean Ice Milk, Raspberry Swirl (1/2 cup)	130	2.0	(1.2)	(9)	60
Sealtest Free Nonfat Frozen Dessert, Black Cherry (1/2 cup)	100	0.0	0.0	0	45
Sealtest Free Nonfat Frozen Dessert, Chocolate (1/2 cup)	100	0.0	0.0	0	50
Sealtest Free Nonfat Frozen Dessert, Peach (1/2 cup)	100	0.0	0.0	0	45
Sealtest Free Nonfat Frozen Dessert, Strawberry (1/2 cup)	100	0.0	0.0	0	40
Sealtest Free Nonfat Frozen Dessert, Vanilla-Chocolate-Strawberry (1/2 cup)	100	0.0	0.0	0	40
Sealtest Free Nonfat Frozen Dessert, Vanilla Flavored (1/2 cup)	100	0.0	0.0	0	45
Sealtest Free Nonfat Frozen Dessert, Vanilla Fudge Royale (1/2 cup)	100	0.0	0.0	0	50
Sealtest Free Nonfat Frozen Dessert, Vanilla Strawberry Royale (1/2 cup)	100	0.0	0.0	0	35
Simple Pleasures Frozen Dairy Dessert, Chocolate (4 fl oz)	134	0.9	0.5	5	73

Ice Milk and Frozen Dairy Desserts (continued)	Calories	Fat g	Saturated Fat g	Choles- terol mg	Sodium mg
Simple Pleasures Frozen Dairy Dessert, Chocolate Chip (4 fl oz)	144	2.3	0.9	13	54
Simple Pleasures Frozen Dairy Dessert, Coffee (4 fl oz)	116	0.4	0.2	13	69
Simple Pleasures Frozen Dairy Dessert, Cookies 'N Cream (4 fl oz)	145	2.2	0.7	11	85
Simple Pleasures Frozen Dairy Dessert, Mint Chocolate Chocolate Chip (4 fl oz)	138	1.6	1.1	4	51
Simple Pleasures Frozen Dairy Dessert, Peach (4 fl oz)	118	0.4	0.4	5	59
Simple Pleasures Frozen Dairy Dessert, Pecan Praline (4 fl oz)	127	1.5	0.3	4	63
Simple Pleasures Frozen Dairy Dessert, Rum Raisin (4 fl oz)	128	0.5	0.2	13	65
Simple Pleasures Frozen Dairy Dessert, Strawberry (4 fl oz)	111	0.3	0.3	5	57
Simple Pleasures Frozen Dairy Dessert, Toffee Crunch (4 fl oz)	131	0.6	0.3	6	105
Simple Pleasures Frozen Dairy Dessert, Vanilla (4 fl oz)	116	0.7	0.2	12	50
Simple Pleasures Light Frozen Dairy Dessert, Chocolate (4 fl oz)	74	0.5	0.3	10	74
Simple Pleasures Light Frozen Dairy Dessert, Chocolate Caramel Sundae (4 fl oz)	86	0.5	0.2	9	82
Simple Pleasures Light Frozen Dairy Dessert, Vanilla (4 fl oz)	72	0.4	0.2	9	68
Simple Pleasures Light Frozen Dairy Dessert, Vanilla Fudge Swirl (4 fl oz)	90	0.2	0.1	10	81
Ultra Slim-Fast Frozen Delight Lowfat Frozen Dessert, Chocolate (4 fl oz)	100	<1.0	(<1.0)	0	45
Ultra Slim-Fast Frozen Delight Lowfat Frozen Dessert, Chocolate Fudge (4 fl oz)	120	<1.0	(<1.0)	0	65
Ultra Slim-Fast Frozen Delight Lowfat Frozen Dessert, Peach (4 fl oz)	100	<1.0	(<1.0)	0	55

Ice Milk and Frozen Dairy Desserts (continued)	Calories	Fat g	Saturated Fat g	Choles-terol mg	Sodium mg
Ultra Slim-Fast Frozen Delight Lowfat Frozen Dessert, Pralines and Caramel (4 fl oz)	120	< 1.0	(< 1.0)	0	95
Ultra Slim-Fast Frozen Delight Lowfat Frozen Dessert, Vanilla (4 fl oz)	90	< 1.0	(< 1.0)	0	55
Weight Watchers Grand Collection Fat Free, Chocolate (1/2 cup)	80	0.0	0.0	5	75
Weight Watchers Grand Collection Fat Free, Chocolate Swirl (1/2 cup)	90	0.0	0.0	5	75
Weight Watchers Grand Collection Fat Free, Neapolitan (1/2 cup)	80	0.0	0.0	5	75
Weight Watchers Grand Collection Fat Free, Vanilla (1/2 cup)	80	0.0	0.0	5	75
Weight Watchers Premium Ice Milk, Chocolate (1/2 cup)	110	3.0	2.0	10	75
Weight Watchers Premium Ice Milk, Chocolate Swirl (1/2 cup)	120	3.0	2.0	5	75
Weight Watchers Premium Ice Milk, Heavenly Hash (4 fl oz)	120	3.0	1.9	10	90
Weight Watchers Premium Ice Milk, Neapolitan (1/2 cup)	110	3.0	1.0	10	75
Weight Watchers Premium Ice Milk, Vanilla (1/2 cup)	100	3.0	1.0	10	75
Well's Blue Bunny Nonfat Frozen Dessert, Chocolate (3 fl oz)	50	0.0	0.0	0	60
Well's Blue Bunny Nonfat Frozen Dessert, Raspberry (3 fl oz)	50	0.0	0.0	0	50
Well's Blue Bunny Nonfat Frozen Dessert, Strawberry (3 fl oz)	50	0.0	0.0	0	50
Well's Blue Bunny Nonfat Frozen Dessert, Vanilla (3 fl oz)	50	0.0	0.0	0	50
Wells Blue Bunny Hi Lite Ice Milk, Cherry Nut (3 fl oz)	90	2.0	(1.2)	(7)	50
Wells Blue Bunny Hi Lite Ice Milk, Dutch Chocolate (3 fl oz)	90	2.0	(1.2)	(7)	50

Ice Milk and Frozen Dairy Desserts (continued)	Calories	Fat g	Saturated Fat g	Choles- terol mg	Sodium mg
Wells Blue Bunny Hi Lite Ice Milk, English Toffee (3 fl oz)	90	2.0	(1.2)	(7)	60
Wells Blue Bunny Hi Lite Ice Milk, Fresh Peach (3 fl oz)	90	2.0	(1.2)	(7)	50
Wells Blue Bunny Hi Lite Ice Milk, Neapolitan (3 fl oz)	90	2.0	(1.2)	(7)	50
Wells Blue Bunny Hi Lite Ice Milk, Strawberry Cheesecake (3 fl oz)	90	2.0	(1.2)	(7)	50
Yarnell's Guilt Free Frozen Dietary Dairy Dessert, Chocolate (4 fl oz)	90	0.0	0.0	0	80
Yarnell's Guilt Free Frozen Dietary Dairy Dessert, Strawberry (4 fl oz)	90	0.0	0.0	0	65
Yarnell's Guilt Free Frozen Dietary Dairy Dessert, Vanilla (4 fl oz)	90	0.0	0.0	0	70
Yarnell's Premium Lite, Cafe Au Lait (Coffee) (1/2 cup)	100	3.0	(1.9)	(9)	50
Yarnell's Premium Lite, Peaches N' Cream (1/2 cup)	100	3.0	(1.9)	(9)	40
Yarnell's Premium Lite, Real Vanilla (1/2 cup)	100	3.0	(1.9)	(9)	50
Yarnell's Premium Lite, Strawberries N' Cream (1/2 cup)	90	3.0	(1.9)	(9)	40
Yarnell's Premium Lite, Swiss Milk Chocolate (1/2 cup)	100	3.0	(1.9)	(9)	60

POPS AND BARS

A&P Fudge Bars (2.5 fl oz = 1 bar)	110	1.0	(0.5)	(1)	80
A&P Twin Pops (3 fl oz = 1/2 of a double bar)	70	0.0	0.0	0	10
Blue Bell Fruit 'N Cream Light Bars, Strawberry (1 bar)	60	1.0	0.5	4	35
Blue Bell Sugar Free Bullet Bar (1 bar)	15	0.0	0.0	(0)	5
Blue Bell Twin Pop (1 pop)	70	0.0	0.0	0	5
Crystal Light Bars, all flavors (1 bar)	14	0.0	0.0	0	10

Pops and Bars (continued)	Calories	Fat g	Saturated Fat g	Choles- terol mg	Sodium mg
Dole Fresh Lites 25 Calorie Fruit and Juice Bars, Variety Pack, Lemon and Cherry (1 bar)	25	<1.0	(0.0)	(0)	12–30
Dole Fresh Lites 25 Calorie Fruit and Juice Bars, Variety Pack, Raspberry and Pineapple-Orange (1 bar)	25	<1.0	(0.0)	(0)	6–11
Dole Fruit'N Juice Bars, Dark Sweet Cherry (1 bar)	70	<1.0	(0.0)	(0)	6
Dole Fruit'N Juice Bars, Peach Passion Fruit (1 bar)	70	<1.0	(0.0)	(0)	<1
Dole Fruit'N Juice Bars, Pineapple (1 bar)	70	<1.0	(0.0)	(0)	5
Dole Fruit'N Juice Bars, Pine-Orange Banana (1 bar)	60	<1.0	(0.0)	(0)	5
Dole Fruit'N Juice Bars, Raspberry (1 bar)	60	<1.0	(0.0)	(0)	13
Dole Fruit'N Juice Bars, Strawberry (1 bar)	60	<1.0	(0.0)	(0)	9
Dole Fruit'N Yogurt Bars, Cherry (1 bar)	80	<1.0	(<1.0)	(2)	22
Dole Fruit'N Yogurt Bars, Mixed Berry (1 bar)	70	<1.0	(<1.0)	(2)	18
Dole Fruit'N Yogurt Bars, Strawberry (1 bar)	70	<1.0	(<1.0)	(2)	16
Dole Fruit'N Yogurt Bars, Strawberry Banana (1 bar)	60	<1.0	(<1.0)	(2)	15
Dole SunTops Real Fruit Juice Bars, Variety Pack, Fruit Punch/Lemonade (1 bar)	40	<1.0	(0.0)	(0)	5
Dole SunTops Real Fruit Juice Bars, Variety Pack, Grape/Tropical Orange (1 bar)	40	<1.0	(0.0)	(0)	5
Dole Yogurt Bars, Chocolate (1 bar)	70	<1.0	(<1.0)	(3)	50
Fat Freedom Eskimo Pie Sandwiches (1 sandwich)	130	0.0	0.0	0	150
Flintstone Push-Up, Cherry (1 push-up)	90	1.0	0.5	4	20
Flintstone Push-Up, Grape (4 fl oz)	90	1.0	0.5	4	20
Flintstone Push-Up, Orange (4 fl oz)	90	1.0	0.5	4	20

Pops and Bars (continued)	Calories	Fat g	Saturated Fat g	Choles- terol mg	Sodium mg
FrozFruit Bars, Chunky Strawberry (4 fl oz)	70	0.0	0.0	0	(10)
Fudgsicle Sugar Free Fudge Pops (3/4 fl oz = 1 pop)	35	1.0	(0.6)	(1)	50
Giant Assorted Pops, Creme (1 bar)	40	0.0	0.0	(0)	15
Giant Assorted Pops, Ice (1 bar)	35	0.0	0.0	0	10
Giant Assorted Pops, Twin (1 bar)	60	0.0	0.0	0	10
Giant Bars, Chocolate Fudge (1 bar)	100	1.0	(0.5)	(1)	85
Jackson's Fudge Jrs Sugar Free Frozen Dairy Confections (1.75 fl oz = 1 pop)	32	0.0	0.0	(0)	78
Jell-O Gelatin Pops Bars, all flavors (1 bar)	35	0.0	0.0	0	25
Jell-O Snowburst Bars, Lemon (1 bar)	45	0.0	0.0	0	10
Jell-O Snowburst Bars, Orange (1 bar)	45	0.0	0.0	0	10
Kemp's Lite Fudge Jr's (1 bar)	45	<1.0	(<1.0)	(1)	50
Kemp's Lite Pops (1 pop)	12	0.0	0.0	0	0
Klondike Lite Sandwich (1 sandwich)	90	2.0	1.0	5	110
Knudsen Push Ups Lowfat Frozen Yogurt, Orange (3 fl oz)	90	1.0	(0.6)	(3)	25
Knudsen Push Ups Lowfat Frozen Yogurt, Strawberry (3 fl oz)	90	1.0	(0.6)	(3)	25
Kool-Aid Kool Pops, all flavors (1 bar)	40	0.0	0.0	0	10
Lifesavers Flavor Pops (1-3/4 oz = 1 bar)	40	0.0	0.0	(0)	5
Lucerne Mini Pops (1 pop)	40	0.0	0.0	0	3
Lucerne Natural Fruit Juice Bar (1 bar)	85	0.0	0.0	0	5
Lucerne Twin Pops, assorted (1 pop)	60	0.0	0.0	0	5
Party Pride Twin Pops, all flavors (1 pop)	60	0.0	0.0	0	5
Popsicle Big Stick Ice Pops, Orange (3-1/4 fl oz = 1 pop)	80	0.0	0.0	(0)	20

Pops and Bars (continued)	Calories	Fat g	Saturated Fat g	Choles- terol mg	Sodium mg
Popsicle Ice Pops, Lime, Banana, Root Beer, Strawberry, Wild Berry, or Raspberry (1-3/4 fl oz = 1 pop)	50	0.0	0.0	(0)	10
Popsicle Sugar Free Ice Pops (1-3/4 fl oz = 1 pop)	18	0.0	0.0	(0)	10
Sealtest Free Nonfat Frozen Dessert Bars, Chocolate with Fudge Swirl (1 bar)	90	0.0	0.0	0	30
Sealtest Free Nonfat Frozen Dessert Bars, Vanilla with Fudge Swirl (1 bar)	80	0.0	0.0	0	30
Sealtest Free Nonfat Frozen Dessert Bars, Vanilla with Strawberry Swirl (1 bar)	80	0.0	0.0	0	40
Weight Watchers Bars, Fruit Juice (1 bar)	35	0.0	0.0	0	10
Weight Watchers Bars, Peanut Butter Fudge (1.75 oz = 1 bar)	60	< 1.0	(0.0)	(1)	120
Weight Watchers Sugar Free 98% Fat Free Chocolate Mousse Bar (1.75 oz = 1 bar)	35	< 1.0	(0.0)	5	30
Weight Watchers Sugar Free 99% Fat Free Orange Vanilla Treat Bar (1.75 oz = 1 bar)	30	< 1.0	(0.0)	5	40
Weight Watchers 98% Fat Free Double Fudge Bar (1.75 fl oz = 1 bar)	60	1.0	(0.5)	5	50
Welch's Fruit Juice Bars, all flavors (1.75 oz = 1 bar)	45	0.0	0.0	0	0
Welch's Fruit Juice Bars, all flavors (3 fl oz = 1 bar)	80	0.0	0.0	0	0
Welch's Fruit Juice Bars, No Sugar Added, all flavors (3 fl oz = 1 bar)	25	0.0	0.0	0	0
Well's Blue Bunny Nutrasweet Bar, Citrus (1.75 fl oz = 1 bar)	16	0.0	0.0	0	10
Well's Blue Bunny Nutrasweet Bar, Fudge (1.75 fl oz = 1 bar)	35	0.0	0.0	0	45
Well's Blue Bunny Nutrasweet Sugar Free Pops, Cherry, Orange, Blue Raspberry, and Root Beer (1.75 fl oz = 1 bar)	8	0.0	0.0	0	10
Yarnell's Nonfat Bars, Fudge (2-1/2 fl oz = 1 bar)	60	0.0	0.0	0	105

Sherbets and Sorbets	Calories	Fat g	Saturated Fat g	Choles-terol mg	Sodium mg
SHERBETS AND SORBETS					
A&P Sherbet, Orange (1/2 cup)	110	1.0	(0.6)	(<5)	45
Blue Bell Sherbet, Lime (1/2 cup)	130	1.0	0.5	0	30
Blue Bell Sherbet, Orange (1/2 cup)	130	1.0	0.5	4	30
Blue Bell Sherbet, Pineapple (1/2 cup)	130	1.0	0.5	0	30
Blue Bell Sherbet, Rainbow (1/2 cup)	130	1.0	0.5	0	30
Borden Sherbet, Orange (1/2 cup)	110	1.0	(0.6)	(<5)	40
Carnation Sherbet, Lime (1/2 cup)	106	1.0	<1.0	3	30
Carnation Sherbet, Orange (1/2 cup)	110	0.8	<1.0	3	40
Carnation Sherbet, Raspberry (1/2 cup)	110	1.0	<1.0	<5	35
Carnation Sherbet, White Lemon (1/2 cup)	110	1.0	<1.0	<5	40
Dole Fruit Sorbet, Peach (4 fl oz)	110	<1.0	(0.0)	0	10
Dole Fruit Sorbet, Pineapple (4 fl oz)	120	<1.0	(0.0)	0	10
Dole Fruit Sorbet, Raspberry (4 fl oz)	110	<1.0	(0.0)	0	10
Dole Fruit Sorbet, Strawberry (4 fl oz)	110	<1.0	(0.0)	0	10
Frusen Gladje, Raspberry Sorbet (1/2 cup)	140	0.0	0.0	0	10
Giant Sherbet, Lemon (1/2 cup)	110	2.0	1.0	5	40
Giant Sherbet, Lime (1/2 cup)	110	2.0	1.0	5	30
Giant Sherbet, Orange (1/2 cup)	110	2.0	1.0	5	40
Giant Sherbet, Pineapple (1/2 cup)	110	2.0	1.0	5	30
Giant Sherbet, Raspberry (1/2 cup)	110	2.0	1.0	5	30
Giant Sherbet, Triple Treat, Orange Pineapple Raspberry (1/2 cup)	110	2.0	1.0	5	40

Sherbets and Sorbets (continued)	Calories	Fat g	Saturated Fat g	Choles- terol mg	Sodium mg
Land O'Lakes Sherbet, Fruit Flavors (4 fl oz)	130	2.0	1.0	5	25
Lucerne Sherbet, Lime (1/2 cup)	120	2.0	(1.2)	5	15
Lucerne Sherbet, Orange (1/2 cup)	120	2.0	(1.2)	5	15
Lucerne Sherbet, Pineapple (1/2 cup)	120	2.0	(1.2)	5	15
Lucerne Sherbet, Raspberry (1/2 cup)	120	2.0	(1.2)	5	15
Lucerne Sherbet, Triple Treat (1/2 cup)	120	2.0	(1.2)	5	15
Mama Tish's Gourmet Italian Ices (4 fl oz)	90	0.0	0.0	0	0
Mama Tish's Sorbetto (4 fl oz)	100	0.0	0.0	0	0
Mazzone's Sorbetto Molle, Lemon (4 fl oz)	113	<1.0	(0.0)	<1	20
Mazzone's Sorbetto Molle, Kiwi (4 fl oz)	116	<1.0	(0.0)	<1	10
Mazzone's Sorbetto Molle, Orange (4 fl oz)	120	<1.0	(0.0)	<1	14
Mazzone's Sorbetto Molle, Passion Fruit (4 fl oz)	112	<1.0	(0.0)	<1	11
Mazzone's Sorbetto Molle, Peach (4 fl oz)	106	<1.0	(0.0)	<1	7
Mazzone's Sorbetto Molle, Raspberry (4 fl oz)	112	<1.0	(0.0)	<1	10
Mazzone's Sorbetto Molle, Strawberry (4 fl oz)	116	<1.0	(0.0)	<1	15
Neilson Orange Sherbet Sundae Cup (3-1/3 fl oz = 1 cup)	116	0.8	0.5	2	(54)
Neilson Sherbet, Lime (1/2 cup)	116	1.0	0.6	2	(65)
Neilson Sherbet, Orange (1/2 cup)	116	1.0	0.6	2	(65)
Sealtest Sherbet, Lime (1/2 cup)	130	1.0	0.0	5	30
Sealtest Sherbet, Red Raspberry (4 fl oz)	130	1.0	0.0	5	30
Wyler's Fruit Slush, Grape (4 fl oz)	157	0.0	0.0	0	10

Sherbets and Sorbets (continued)	Calories	Fat g	Saturated Fat g	Choles- terol mg	Sodium mg
Wyler's Fruit Slush, Strawberry (4 fl oz)	157	0.0	0.0	0	10
Wyler's Fruit Slush, Tropical Punch (4 fl oz)	157	0.0	0.0	0	10

FRUITS

Fruits naturally contain no cholesterol, are low in sodium, and provide little or no fat. Avocado and olives are exceptions, since they do contain fat. Avocado and olives are listed in the Fats and Oils section, beginning on page 210. Fruit snacks are found in the Snack Foods section, beginning on page 340. Values for the fresh fruit in this section are based on information from USDA handbooks.

CUTOFF POINTS FOR FRUITS

Fat (grams)	Saturated Fat (grams)	Cholesterol (milligrams)
3	1	10

SERVINGS

Food	Serving Sizes
Canned	5 ounces
Pickled	1 ounce
Sauce or Relish	3 ounces
Dried	½ ounce
Candied	1 ounce
Dehydrated and freeze-dried	½ ounce
Fresh, all types except watermelon	5 ounces
Watermelon	12 ounces
Frozen	5 ounces

The following abbreviations are used in the Food Sections: oz = ounce; fl oz = fluid ounce; pkg = package; pkt = packet; env = envelope; g = gram; prep (w/ . . .) = prepared with; < = less than; and tr = trace.

Canned Fruits	Calories	Fat g	Saturated Fat g	Choles-terol mg	Sodium mg
CANNED FRUITS					
Applesauce, Giant Applesauce, Chunky, Sweetened (1/2 cup)	80	0.0	0.0	0	5
Applesauce, Giant Applesauce, Cinnamon, Sweetened (1/2 cup)	100	0.0	0.0	0	5
Applesauce, IGA Applesauce, Chunky (4 oz)	80	0.0	0.0	0	(5)
Applesauce, sweetened—Most Brands (1/2 cup)	97	0.2	0.0	0	4
Applesauce, unsweetened—Most Brands (1/2 cup)	53	0.1	0.0	0	2
Apricots in heavy syrup—Most Brands (3 halves)	70	0.7	0.0	0	3
Apricots in juice—Most Brands (3 halves)	40	0.0	0.0	0	3
Apricots in light syrup—Most Brands (3 halves)	54	0.0	0.0	0	3
Apricots in water—Most Brands (3 halves)	22	0.1	0.0	0	2
Blackberries in heavy syrup—Most Brands (1/2 cup)	118	0.1	0.0	0	3
Blueberries in heavy syrup—Most Brands (1/2 cup)	112	0.4	0.0	0	4
Boysenberries in heavy syrup—Most Brands (1/2 cup)	113	0.2	0.0	0	4
Cherries, Giant Maraschino Cherries, Syrup Pack (1/2 cup)	120	< 1.0	< 1.0	0	10
Cherries, Sweet in heavy syrup—Most Brands (1/2 cup)	107	0.2	0.0	0	3
Cherries, Sweet in juice—Most Brands (1/2 cup)	68	0.0	0.0	0	3
Cherries, Sweet in light syrup—Most Brands (1/2 cup)	85	0.2	0.0	0	3
Cherries, Sweet in water—Most Brands (1/2 cup)	57	0.2	0.0	0	2
Cranberry Sauce, sweetened—Most Brands (1/2 cup)	209	0.2	0.0	0	40
Cranberry-Orange Relish—Most Brands (1/2 cup)	246	0.1	0.0	0	44
Figs in heavy syrup—Most Brands (3)	75	0.1	0.0	0	1

Canned Fruits (continued)	Calories	Fat g	Saturated Fat g	Choles-terol mg	Sodium mg
Figs in light syrup—Most Brands (3)	58	0.1	0.0	0	1
Figs in water—Most Brands (3)	42	0.1	0.0	0	1
Fruit Cocktail in heavy syrup—Most Brands (1/2 cup)	93	0.1	0.0	0	7
Fruit Cocktail in juice—Most Brands (1/2 cup)	56	0.0	0.0	0	4
Fruit Cocktail in light syrup—Most Brands (1/2 cup)	72	0.1	0.0	0	7
Fruit Cocktail in water—Most Brands (1/2 cup)	40	0.1	0.0	0	5
Fruit Salad, Dole Tropical Fruit Salad in Light Syrup and Passion Fruit Juice (1/2 cup with juice)	70	0.0	0.0	0	10
Fruit Salad, Kraft Pure Chilled Fruit Salad (1/2 cup)	80	0.0	0.0	0	10
Grapefruit in juice—Most Brands (1/2 cup)	46	0.1	0.0	0	9
Grapefruit in light syrup—Most Brands (1/2 cup)	76	0.1	0.0	0	2
Grapefruit in water—Most Brands (1/2 cup)	44	0.1	0.0	0	2
Grapefruit, Kraft Pure Chilled Unsweetened Grapefruit Sections (1/2 cup)	50	0.0	0.0	0	0
Peaches in heavy syrup—Most Brands (1/2 cup)	95	0.1	0.0	0	8
Peaches in juice—Most Brands (1/2 cup)	55	0.0	0.0	0	6
Peaches in light syrup—Most Brands (1/2 cup)	68	0.0	0.0	0	7
Peaches in water—Most Brands (1/2 cup)	29	0.1	0.0	0	4
Peaches, Spiced in heavy syrup—Most Brands (1/2 cup)	90	0.1	0.0	0	5
Pears in heavy syrup—Most Brands (1 half)	58	0.1	0.0	0	4
Pears in juice—Most Brands (1 half)	38	0.1	0.0	0	3
Pears in light syrup—Most Brands (1 half)	45	0.0	0.0	0	4

Canned Fruits (continued)	Calories	Fat g	Saturated Fat g	Choles- terol mg	Sodium mg
Pears in water—Most Brands (1 half)	22	0.0	0.0	0	2
Pineapple Tidbits in heavy syrup—Most Brands (1/2 cup)	100	0.1	0.0	0	2
Pineapple Tidbits in juice—Most Brands (1/2 cup)	75	0.1	0.0	0	2
Pineapple Tidbits in light syrup—Most Brands (1/2 cup)	66	0.1	0.0	0	2
Pineapple Tidbits in water—Most Brands (1/2 cup)	40	0.1	0.0	0	2
Pineapple, Dole Pineapple and Mandarin Orange Segments in Light Syrup (1/2 cup with syrup)	75	0.0	0.0	0	6
Plums in heavy syrup—Most Brands (3)	119	0.1	0.0	0	26
Plums in juice—Most Brands (3)	55	0.0	0.0	0	1
Plums in light syrup—Most Brands (3)	83	0.1	0.0	0	26
Plums in water—Most Brands (3)	39	0.0	0.0	0	1
Prunes in heavy syrup—Most Brands (5)	90	0.2	0.0	0	2
Pumpkin, Libby's Solid Pack Pumpkin (1/2 cup)	42	0.4	(0.0)	(0)	6
Rasperries in heavy syrup—Most Brands (1/2 cup)	117	0.2	0.0	0	4
Strawberries in heavy syrup—Most Brands (1/2 cup)	117	0.3	0.0	0	5
Tangerines in juice—Most Brands (1/2 cup)	46	0.0	0.0	0	7
Tangerines in light syrup—Most Brands (1/2 cup)	76	0.1	0.0	0	8
DRIED FRUITS					
Apples, Dried—Most Brands (10 rings)	155	0.2	0.0	0	56
Apricots, Dried—Most Brands (10 halves)	83	0.2	0.0	0	3
Currants—Most Brands (1/2 cup)	204	0.2	0.0	0	6
Dates—Most Brands (10)	228	0.4	0.0	0	2
Figs, Dried—Most Brands (2)	95	0.4	0.1	0	4

Dried Fruits (continued)	Calories	Fat g	Saturated Fat g	Choles-terol mg	Sodium mg
Peaches, Dried, cooked without sugar—Most Brands (1/2 cup)	99	0.3	0.0	0	3
Peaches, Dried—Most Brands (10 halves)	311	1.0	0.1	0	9
Pears, Dried, cooked without sugar—Most Brands (1/2 cup)	163	0.4	0.0	0	4
Pears, Dried, uncooked—Most Brands (5 halves)	230	0.6	0.0	0	5
Prunes, cooked without sugar—Most Brands (1/2 cup)	113	0.3	0.0	0	2
Prunes—Most Brands (10)	201	0.4	0.0	0	3
Raisins—Most Brands (1/4 cup)	127	0.2	0.1	0	5
FRESH FRUITS					
Apple (2-3/4" diam)	81	0.5	0.1	0	1
Apricot (3)	51	0.4	0.0	0	1
Banana (8-3/4" long)	105	0.6	0.2	0	1
Blackberries (1/2 cup)	37	0.3	0.0	0	0
Blueberries (1/2 cup)	41	0.6	0.0	0	5
Breadfruit (1/2 cup)	114	0.6	0.0	0	2
Cherries (10)	49	0.7	0.1	0	0
Crabapple, sliced (1/2 cup)	42	0.2	0.1	0	1
Cranberries, chopped (1/2 cup)	27	0.1	0.0	0	1
Currants, red or white (1/2 cup)	31	0.1	0.0	0	1
Fig (1 medium)	37	0.2	0.0	0	1
Gooseberries (1/2 cup)	34	0.9	0.1	0	1
Grapefruit (1/2 of a 3-3/4" diam grapefruit)	38	0.1	0.0	0	0
Grapes (10)	15	0.1	0.0	0	0
Guava (1)	45	0.5	0.2	0	2
Kiwifruit (1 medium)	46	0.3	0.0	0	4
Kumquat (1)	12	0.0	0.0	0	1
Lemon (1 medium)	17	0.2	0.0	0	1
Lime (1)	20	0.1	0.0	0	1
Loquat (1)	5	0.0	0.0	0	0
Lychee (1)	6	0.0	0.0	0	0
Mango (1)	135	0.6	0.1	0	4

Fresh Fruits (continued)	Calories	Fat g	Saturated Fat g	Choles-terol mg	Sodium mg
Melon, Cantaloupe (1/2 of a 5″ diam)	94	0.7	0.0	0	23
Melon, Casaba, cubed (1/2 cup)	23	0.1	0.0	0	10
Melon, Honeydew, cubed (1/2 cup)	30	0.1	0.0	0	9
Mulberries (1/2 cup)	31	0.6	0.0	0	7
Nectarine (2-1/2″ diam)	67	0.6	0.0	0	0
Orange (2-5/8″ diam)	62	0.2	0.0	0	0
Papaya, cubes (1/2 cup)	27	0.1	0.1	0	2
Passion Fruit (1)	18	0.1	0.0	0	5
Peach (2-1/2″ diam)	37	0.1	0.0	0	0
Pear (2-1/2″ × 3-1/2″ diam)	98	0.7	0.0	0	1
Pear, Asian, 2-1/4″ × 2-1/2″ diam (1)	51	0.3	0.0	0	0
Persimmon, Japanese (2-1/2″ × 3-1/2″ diam)	118	0.3	0.0	0	3
Persimmon, native (1)	32	0.1	0.0	0	0
Pineapple, diced (1/2 cup)	39	0.3	0.1	0	1
Plaintain, raw (1)	218	0.7	0.0	0	7
Plum (2-1/8″ diam)	36	0.4	0.0	0	0
Pomegranate (3-3/8″ x 3-3/4″ diam)	104	0.5	0.0	0	5
Prickly Pear (1)	42	0.5	0.0	0	6
Pummelo (5-1/2″ diam)	228	0.2	0.0	0	7
Quince (1)	53	0.1	0.0	0	4
Raspberries (1/2 cup)	31	0.3	0.0	0	0
Rhubarb, diced (1/2 cup)	13	0.1	0.0	0	3
Strawberries (1/2 cup)	23	0.3	0.0	0	1
Tamarind (3″ long × 1″ wide)	5	0.0	0.0	0	1
Tangerine (2-3/8″ diam)	37	0.2	0.0	0	1
Watermelon, diced (1/2 cup)	25	0.3	0.0	0	2

FROZEN FRUITS

	Calories	Fat g	Saturated Fat g	Choles-terol mg	Sodium mg
Blackberries, unsweetened—Most Brands (1/2 cup)	49	0.3	0.0	0	1
Blueberries, unsweetened—Most Brands (1/2 cup)	39	0.5	0.0	0	1

Frozen Fruits (continued)	Calories	Fat g	Saturated Fat g	Choles- terol mg	Sodium mg
Boysenberries, unsweetened—Most Brands (1/2 cup)	33	0.2	0.0	0	1
Loganberries—Most Brands (1/2 cup)	40	0.2	0.0	0	1
Melon balls—Most Brands (1/2 cup)	28	0.2	0.0	0	27
Peaches, sliced, sweetened—Most Brands (1/2 cup)	118	0.1	0.0	0	8
Pineapple, chunks, sweetened—Most Brands (1/2 cup)	104	0.1	0.0	0	2
Raspberries, sweetened—Most Brands (1/2 cup)	128	0.2	0.0	0	1
Rhubarb, uncooked—Most Brands (1/2 cup)	14	0.0	0.0	0	1
Strawberries, sweetened—Most Brands (1/2 cup)	100	0.0	0.0	0	2
Strawberries, unsweetened—Most Brands (1/2 cup)	26	0.0	0.0	0	2

GRAVIES AND SAUCES

Gravies and sauces can be a source of fat, saturated fat, and sodium in the diet. All of the gravies and sauces in this Guide are low in fat and saturated fat *as purchased* or when *prepared as indicated* in the Guide. One serving of the foods included in this section of the Guide does not exceed the cutoff points shown below.

The values given in the Guide are only for the gravy or sauce and do not include any food with which it may be combined. For example, if ground beef is added to a spaghetti sauce found in this section of the Guide, values for the meat must be added to the values listed for the sauce.

CUTOFF POINTS FOR GRAVIES AND SAUCES

Fat (grams)	Saturated Fat (grams)	Cholesterol (milligrams)
3	1	10

SERVINGS

Food	Serving Sizes
Gravies, all types	¼ cup
Sauces:	
Barbecue	2 tablespoons
Pizza	¼ cup
Spaghetti	½ cup
Sweet and Sour	½ cup
Teriyaki	1 tablespoon
Tomato	3 ounces
Worcestershire	1 tablespoon

The following abbreviations are used in the Food Sections: oz = ounce; fl oz = fluid ounce; pkg = package; pkt = packet; env = envelope; g = gram; prep (w/ . . .) = prepared with; < = less than; and tr = trace.

Gravies	Calories	Fat g	Saturated Fat g	Choles- terol mg	Sodium mg
GRAVIES					
AU JUS					
Knorr Sauce Mix, Au Jus, prep (w/water) (2 fl oz = 1/4 cup)	8	<1.0	(0.0)	(tr)	160
McCormick Gravy Mix, Au Jus, prep (as directed) (1/4 cup)	20	0.3	(0.1)	(tr)	786
BEEF/BROWN GRAVY					
Franco-American Gravy, Beef, canned (2 oz)	25	1.0	(0.5)	(2)	340
Hain Seasoning and Gravy Mix, Brown Gravy (1/4 pkg)	16	0.0	0.0	0	600
Heinz Home Style Gravy, Brown (2 oz)	25	1.0	<1.0	(tr)	320
Knorr Sauce Mix, Classic Brown Gravy, prep (w/water) (2 fl oz)	25	1.0	(0.5)	(tr)	300
McCormick Gravy Mix, Brown, prep (as directed) (1/4 cup)	23	0.8	(0.4)	(tr)	313
McCormick Gravy Mix, Lite Brown, prep (as directed) (1/4 cup)	10	1.0	(0.5)	(tr)	450
Pillsbury Gravy Mix, Brown, prep (w/water) (1/4 cup)	16	0.0	0.0	0	180
CHICKEN GRAVY					
Heinz Home Style Gravy, Chicken (2 oz)	35	2.0	(0.6)	(tr)	350
McCormick Gravy Mix, Chicken, prep (as directed (1/4 cup)	22	0.4	(0.1)	(1)	300
McCormick Gravy Mix, Lite Chicken, prep (as directed) (1/4 cup)	12	1.0	(0.3)	(1)	450
Pillsbury Gravy, Chicken, prep (w/water and 2% milk) (1/4 cup)	18	0.0	0.0	0	170
MUSHROOM GRAVY					
Franco-American Gravy, Mushroom, canned (2 oz)	25	1.0	(0.1)	(0)	290
Heinz Home Style Gravy, Mushroom (2 oz)	25	1.0	<1.0	(0)	340

Gravies (continued)	Calories	Fat g	Saturated Fat g	Choles- terol mg	Sodium mg
McCormick Gravy Mix, Mushroom, prep (as directed) (1/4 cup)	19	0.5	(0.3)	(tr)	270
PORK GRAVY					
McCormick Gravy Mix, Pork, prep (as directed) (1/4 cup)	20	0.6	(0.2)	(1)	297
TURKEY GRAVY					
Heinz Home Style Gravy, Turkey (2 oz)	25	1.0	<1.0	(tr)	370
McCormick Gravy Mix, Turkey, prep (as directed) (1/4 cup)	22	0.5	(0.1)	(1)	353
OTHER GRAVIES					
McCormick Gravy Mix, Herb, prep (as directed) (1/4 cup)	20	0.5	(0.2)	(tr)	312
McCormick Gravy Mix, Homestyle, prep (as directed) (1/4 cup)	24	0.8	(0.4)	(tr)	295
McCormick Gravy Mix, Onion, prep (as directed) (1/4 cup)	22	0.6	(0.4)	(tr)	337
Pillsbury Gravy Mix, Homestyle, prep (w/water) (1/4 cup)	16	0.0	0.0	0	240
SAUCES					
BARBECUE SAUCE					
Bovril Sauce Mix, B.B.Q., prep (as directed) (1/2 cup)	57	0.6	(0.1)	(0)	n/a
Featherweight Barbecue Sauce (1 tbsp)	14	0.0	0.0	0	90
Giant Barbecue Sauce, Hickory (1 tbsp)	25	0.0	0.0	0	240
Giant Barbecue Sauce, Original (1 tbsp)	25	0.0	0.0	0	240
Hain Bar-B-Que Sauce, Honey (1 tbsp)	14	1.0	(0.1)	0	120
Hunt's Barbecue Sauce, Country Style (1/2 oz)	20	<1.0	(0.0)	0	140
Hunt's Barbecue Sauce, Hickory (1/2 oz)	20	<1.0	(0.0)	0	160
Hunt's Barbecue Sauce, Homestyle (1/2 oz)	20	<1.0	(0.0)	0	170

Sauces (continued)	Calories	Fat g	Saturated Fat g	Choles-terol mg	Sodium mg
Hunt's Barbecue Sauce, Kansas City (1/2 oz)	20	<1.0	(0.0)	0	85
Hunt's Barbecue Sauce, New Orleans (1/2 oz)	20	<1.0	(0.0)	0	150
Hunt's Barbecue Sauce, Original (1/2 oz)	20	<1.0	(0.0)	0	160
Hunt's Barbecue Sauce, Southern Style (1/2 oz)	20	<1.0	(0.0)	0	170
Hunt's Barbecue Sauce, Texas (1/2 oz)	25	<1.0	(0.0)	0	150
Hunt's Barbecue Sauce, Western (1/2 oz)	20	<1.0	(0.0)	0	170
IGA Barbeque Sauce (1 tbsp)	20	0.0	0.0	0	(125)
IGA Barbeque Sauce, Hickory (1 tbsp)	20	0.0	0.0	0	(125)
Kraft Barbecue Sauce (2 tbsp)	45	1.0	0.0	0	460
Kraft Barbecue Sauce, Garlic (2 tbsp)	40	0.0	0.0	0	420
Kraft Barbecue Sauce, Hickory Smoke (2 tbsp)	45	1.0	0.0	0	440
Kraft Barbecue Sauce, Hickory Smoke Onion Bits (2 tbsp)	50	1.0	0.0	0	340
Kraft Barbecue Sauce, Hot (2 tbsp)	45	1.0	0.0	0	520
Kraft Barbecue Sauce, Hot Hickory Smoke (2 tbsp)	45	1.0	0.0	0	360
Kraft Barbecue Sauce, Italian Seasonings (2 tbsp)	50	1.0	0.0	0	280
Kraft Barbecue Sauce, Kansas City Style (2 tbsp)	50	1.0	0.0	0	270
Kraft Barbecue Sauce, Mesquite Smoke (2 tbsp)	45	1.0	0.0	0	410
Kraft Barbecue Sauce, Onion Bits (2 tbsp)	50	1.0	0.0	0	340
Kraft Thick'n Spicy Barbecue Sauce, Chunky (2 tbsp)	60	1.0	0.0	0	120
Kraft Thick'n Spicy Barbecue Sauce, Hickory Smoke (2 tbsp)	50	1.0	0.0	0	430
Kraft Thick'n Spicy Barbecue Sauce, Kansas City Style (2 tbsp)	60	1.0	0.0	0	270

Sauces (continued)	Calories	Fat g	Saturated Fat g	Choles- terol mg	Sodium mg
Kraft Thick'n Spicy Barbecue Sauce, Mesquite Smoke (2 tbsp)	50	1.0	0.0	0	430
Kraft Thick'n Spicy Barbecue Sauce, Original (2 tbsp)	50	1.0	0.0	0	430
Kraft Thick'n Spicy Barbecue Sauce, With Honey (2 tbsp)	60	1.0	0.0	0	340
Ralph's Barbecue Sauce, Hickory (1 tbsp)	15	0.0	0.0	(0)	240
Western Ham Glaze (1 tbsp)	25	0.0	0.0	0	20
CHILI SAUCE (see Condiments, page 139)					
COCKTAIL SAUCE (see Condiments, page 139)					
ENCHILADA SAUCE (see Condiments, page 139)					
HORSERADISH SAUCE (see Condiments, page 139)					
HOT SAUCE (see Condiments, page 140)					
PASTA, SPAGHETTI, AND MARINARA SAUCE					
A&P All Natural Premium Italian Style Spaghetti Sauce, Meatless (1/2 cup)	70	1.0	(0.1)	(0)	490
A&P All Natural Traditional Italian Style Spaghetti Sauce, Meatless (1/2 cup)	80	3.0	(0.4)	(0)	740
A&P Garden Style Spaghetti Sauce, Extra Tomatoes, Garlic and Onions (1/2 cup)	60	2.0	(0.3)	(4)	420
A&P Garden Style Spaghetti Sauce, Green Peppers and Mushrooms (1/2 cup)	60	2.0	(0.3)	(4)	380
A&P Garden Style Spaghetti Sauce, Mushrooms and Onions (1/2 cup)	60	2.0	(0.3)	(4)	350
Aunt Millie's Family Style Spaghetti Sauce, Chunky Tomato Flavored with Ground Beef (4 oz)	80	2.0	< 1.0	5	520

Sauces (continued)	Calories	Fat g	Saturated Fat g	Choles- terol mg	Sodium mg
Aunt Millie's Family Style Spaghetti Sauce, Chunky Tomato and Italian Spices (4 oz)	80	< 1.0	0.0	0	600
Aunt Millie's Family Style Spaghetti Sauce, Chunky Tomato and Sliced Mushrooms (4 oz)	80	< 1.0	0.0	0	480
Aunt Millie's Old Fashioned Italian Style Marinara Cooking Sauce (4 oz)	60	2.0	0.0	0	320
Aunt Millie's Old Fashioned Italian Style Spaghetti Sauce, Flavored with Meat (4 oz)	60	2.0	< 1.0	5	270
Aunt Millie's Old Fashioned Italian Style Spaghetti Sauce, Mushroom (4 oz)	60	2.0	0.0	< 5	250
Aunt Millie's Old Fashioned Italian Style Spaghetti Sauce, Sweet Peppers and Italian Sausage (4 oz)	60	2.0	0.0	5	320
Aunt Millie's Old Fashioned Italian Style Spaghetti Sauce, Traditional Meatless (4 oz)	60	2.0	0.0	0	290
Buitoni Marinara Sauce (4 fl oz)	70	3.0	< 1.0	0	570
Buitoni Spaghetti Sauce, Marinara (4 oz)	70	3.0	0.4	0	630
Buitoni Spaghetti Sauce, Meatless (4 oz)	60	2.0	0.3	0	680
Buitoni Spaghetti Sauce, Mushroom (4 oz)	60	2.0	0.3	0	660
Chef Boyardee Spaghetti Sauce with Meat (3.75 oz)	90	3.0	(1.1)	(9)	(430)
Classico Pasta Sauce, Di Napoli Tomato and Basil (4 oz)	60	3.0	< 1.0	0	340
Classico Pasta Sauce, Di Roma Arrabbiata Spicy Red Pepper (4 oz)	50	2.0	0.0	0	250
Classico Pasta Sauce, Di Sicilia Ripe Olives and Mushrooms (4 oz)	50	2.0	0.0	0	470
Classico Pasta Sauce, Di Veneto Shrimp and Crab (4 oz)	60	2.0	0.0	15	390

Sauces (continued)	Calories	Fat g	Saturated Fat g	Choles-terol mg	Sodium mg
Contadina Fresh, Marinara Sauce (7-1/2 oz)	100	4.0*	(0.6)	0	700
Contadina Original Recipe Spaghetti Sauce, Meat-Flavored (1/2 cup)	100	3.2	1.1	2	430
Contadina Original Recipe Spaghetti Sauce, Mushroom (1/2 cup)	90	2.3	0.4	0	430
Contadina Original Recipe Spaghetti Sauce, Traditional (1/2 cup)	90	2.3	0.4	0	440
Eden Organic Spaghetti Sauce, No Salt Added (4 oz)	80	2.0	(0.3)	(0)	0
Enrico's All Natural Spaghetti Sauce (4 oz)	60	1.0	(0.1)	(0)	(770)
Enrico's All Natural Spaghetti Sauce (4 oz)	60	1.0	(0.0)	(0)	345
Enrico's All Natural Spaghetti Sauce, Mushrooms and Green Peppers (4 oz)	60	1.0	(0.1)	(0)	(770)
Enrico's All Natural Spaghetti Sauce, No Salt Added (4 oz)	60	1.0	(0.1)	(0)	30
Featherweight Spaghetti Sauce (4 oz)	60	1.0	(0.1)	0	310
Featherweight Spaghetti Sauce with Mushrooms (4 oz)	60	1.0	(0.1)	0	310
Giant Marinara Sauce (1/2 cup)	70	1.0	(0.1)	0	660
Giant Spaghetti Sauce, Meatless (1/2 cup)	60	0.0	0.0	0	660
Giant Spaghetti Sauce, Mushroom (1/2 cup)	60	1.0	(0.3)	0	810
Hunt's Classic Italian Spaghetti Sauce with Garlic and Herbs (4 oz)	50	2.0	(0.6)	0	550
Hunt's Classic Italian Spaghetti Sauce with Parmesan (4 oz)	60	2.0	(0.2)	0	550
Hunt's Classic Italian Spaghetti Sauce with Tomato and Basil (4 oz)	50	2.0	(0.6)	0	550
Hunt's Spaghetti Sauce, Chunky (4 oz)	50	< 1.0	(0.0)	0	470
Hunt's Spaghetti Sauce, Homestyle (4 oz)	60	2.0	0.3	0	530

*The value printed for fat is higher than the cutoff point because the manufacturer's serving size is larger than the standard serving size used in evaluating the food.

Sauces (continued)	Calories	Fat g	Saturated Fat g	Choles- terol mg	Sodium mg
Hunt's Spaghetti Sauce, Homestyle with Meat (4 oz)	60	2.0	0.2	2	570
Hunt's Spaghetti Sauce, Homestyle with Mushrooms (4 oz)	50	1.0	0.2	0	530
Hunt's Spaghetti Sauce, Meat (4 oz)	70	2.0	0.3	2	570
Hunt's Spaghetti Sauce, Mushrooms (4 oz)	70	2.0	0.3	0	560
Hunt's Spaghetti Sauce, Traditional (4 oz)	70	2.0	0.3	0	530
IGA Italian Style Spaghetti Sauce, Meat Flavored (4 oz)	80	2.0	(0.3)	2	(815)
IGA Italian Style Spaghetti Sauce, Meatless (4 oz)	80	3.0	(0.4)	0	(815)
Newman's Own Sauce, Bandito Diavalo Spicy Sauce (4 oz)	70	2.0	(0.6)	0	530
Newman's Own Spaghetti Sauce, Sockarooni (Spaghetti Sauce with Mushrooms) (4 oz)	70	2.0	(0.3)	0	630
Prego Extra Chunky Spaghetti Sauce, Garden Combination (4 oz)	80	2.0	(0.3)	(0)	420
Prego Extra Chunky Spaghetti Sauce, Mushroom with Extra Spice (4 oz)	100	3.0	(0.4)	(0)	450
Prego Spaghetti Sauce, Three Cheese (4 oz)	100	2.0	(0.3)	(0)	410
Prego Spaghetti Sauce, Tomato and Basil (4 oz)	100	2.0	(0.3)	(0)	370
Prince All Natural Spaghetti Sauce with Mushrooms (4 oz)	70	3.0	<1.0	<5	580
Prince Chunky Homestyle Spaghetti Sauce, Meat Flavored (4 oz)	80	2.0	<1.0	<5	620
Prince Chunky Homestyle Spaghetti Sauce, Meatless (4 oz)	70	1.0	0.0	0	590
Pritikin Spaghetti Sauce (4 oz = 1/2 cup)	60	0.6	0.1	0	35
Pritikin Spaghetti Sauce, Chunky Garden Style (4 oz = 1/2 cup)	50	0.4	0.1	0	30

Sauces (continued)	Calories	Fat g	Saturated Fat g	Choles- terol mg	Sodium mg
Ragu Chunky Gardenstyle Spaghetti Sauce, all flavors (4 oz)	70	3.0	(0.4)	0	440
Ragu Fresh Italian Spaghetti Sauce, Garlic & Basil Garden Medley (4 oz)	80	3.0	(0.4)	0	490
Ragu Fresh Italian Spaghetti Sauce, Mushroom (4 oz)	80	3.0	(0.4)	0	490
Ragu Fresh Italian Spaghetti Sauce, Parmesan (4 oz)	90	3.0	(0.4)	2	540
Ragu Fresh Italian Spaghetti Sauce, Tomato and Herbs (4 oz)	90	3.0	(0.4)	0	490
Ragu Fresh Italian Spaghetti Sauce, Zesty Tomato (4 oz)	70	3.0	(0.4)	0	490
Ragu Thick and Hearty Spaghetti Sauce, Plain or Mushroom (4 oz)	100	3.0	(0.4)	0	460
Town House Spaghetti Sauce (4 oz)	80	3.0	(0.4)	0	710
Town House Spaghetti Sauce, Chunk Style (4 oz)	80	2.0	(0.3)	0	400
Town House Spaghetti Sauce, Meat (4 oz)	80	3.0	(1.1)	2	710
Town House Spaghetti Sauce, Plain (4 oz)	80	3.0	(0.4)	0	710
Tree of Life Pasta Sauce (4 oz)	66	3.0	(0.4)	(0)	290
Tree of Life Pasta Sauce, Calabrese (4 oz)	70	3.0	(0.4)	(0)	190
Tree of Life Pasta Sauce, No Salt Added (4 oz)	65	3.0	(0.4)	(0)	10
Weight Watchers Spaghetti Sauce Flavored with Meat (1/3 cup)	50	1.0	(0.4)	(2)	440
Weight Watchers Spaghetti Sauce Flavored with Mushrooms (1/3 cup)	40	0.0	0.0	0	430
PICANTE SAUCE (see Condiments, page 141)					
PIZZA SAUCE					
Contadina Pizza Sauce, Italian Cheeses (1/4 cup)	30	1.0	(0.4)	(10)	380

Sauces (continued)	Calories	Fat g	Saturated Fat g	Choles-terol mg	Sodium mg
Contadina Pizza Sauce, Original Quick and Easy (1/4 cup)	30	1.0	(0.1)	(0)	330
Contadina Pizza Sauce, Pepperoni (1/4 cup)	40	2.0	(0.7)	(6)	390
Contadina Pizza Sauce, Pizza Squeeze (1/4 cup)	30	1.0	(0.1)	(0)	330
Prince All Natural Pizza Sauce (3 tbsp)	18	0.0	0.0	0	120
Ragu Pizza Quick Sauce, Cheese (1.7 oz = 3 tbsp)	35	2.0	(0.3)	0	200
Ragu Pizza Quick Sauce, Garlic and Basil (1.7 oz = 3 tbsp)	35	2.0	(0.3)	0	200
Ragu Pizza Quick Sauce, Mushroom (1.7 oz = 3 tbsp)	35	2.0	(0.3)	0	200
Ragu Pizza Quick Sauce, Pepperoni (1.7 oz = 3 tbsp)	35	2.0	(0.7)	1	330
Ragu Pizza Quick Sauce, Sausage (1.7 oz = 3 tbsp)	35	2.0	(0.7)	1	330
Ragu Pizza Quick Sauce, Traditional (1.7 oz = 3 tbsp)	35	2.0	(0.3)	0	330
Ragu Pizza Sauce (4 oz)	25	1.0	(0.1)	0	200
SALSA (see Condiments, page 141)					
SOY SAUCE (see Condiments, page 146)					
STIR-FRY SAUCE					
Maggie Gin's Stir-Fry Sauce, Mandarin (1 tbsp)	22	tr	0.0	0	59
Maggie Gin's Stir-Fry Sauce, Traditional (1 tbsp)	27	0.2	(0.1)	tr	304
SWEET AND SOUR SAUCE					
Contadina International Sauces, Sweet 'n Sour (4 oz)	150	3.0	(<1.0)	(0)	430
Kraft Sauceworks, Sweet'N Sour Sauce (1 tbsp)	25	0.0	0.0	0	50
La Choy Sauce, Sweet & Sour Duck Sauce (1 tbsp)	25	<1.0	(0.0)	0	40
La Choy Sweet and Sour Sauce (1 tbsp)	25	<1.0	(0.0)	0	190
Maggie Gin's Sweet and Sour Sauce (1 tbsp)	27	0.0	0.0	0	58

Sauces (continued)	Calories	Fat g	Saturated Fat g	Choles- terol mg	Sodium mg
Western Sweet & Sour (1 tbsp)	20	0.0	0.0	0	120
TACO SAUCE (see Condiments, page 141)					
TERIYAKI SAUCE					
La Choy Thick & Rich Teriyaki Sauce (1 tbsp)	25	<1.0	(0.0)	0	300
Maggie Gin's Lite and Low Teriyaki and Stir-Fry (1 tbsp)	20	0.0	0.0	0	245
TOMATO PASTE (see Vegetables, page 387)					
TOMATO PUREE (see Vegetables, page 387)					
TOMATO SAUCE					
Contadina Fresh Sauces, Plum Tomato with Basil (7-1/2 oz)	100	4.0*	(0.5)	5	700
Contadina Tomato Sauce, Italian Style (1/2 cup)	30	<1.0	(0.0)	(0)	670
Contadina Tomato Sauce, Thick & Zesty (1/2 cup)	40	<1.0	(0.0)	(0)	650
Giant Tomato Sauce, No Salt Added (1/2 cup)	45	0.0	0.0	0	25
Giant Tomato Sauce, Regular (1/2 cup)	40	0.0	0.0	0	625
Hunt's Tomato Sauce, Garlic (4 oz)	70	2.0	0.3	0	480
Hunt's Tomato Sauce, Herb Flavored (4 oz)	70	2.0	0.6	<1	470
Hunt's Tomato Sauce, Italian (4 oz)	60	2.0	0.5	<1	460
Hunt's Tomato Sauce, Meatloaf Fixings (2 oz)	20	<1.0	(0.0)	0	580
Hunt's Tomato Sauce, Mushrooms (4 oz)	25	<1.0	(0.0)	0	710
Hunt's Tomato Sauce, No Salt Added (4 oz)	35	<1.0	(0.0)	0	20
Hunt's Tomato Sauce, Onions (4 oz)	40	<1.0	(0.0)	0	650
Hunt's Tomato Sauce, Special (4 oz)	35	<1.0	(0.0)	0	280
Hunt's Tomato Sauce, Tomato Bits (4 oz)	30	<1.0	(0.0)	0	620

*The value printed for fat is higher than the cutoff point because the manufacturer's serving size is larger than the standard serving size used in evaluating the food.

Sauces (continued)	Calories	Fat g	Saturated Fat g	Choles- terol mg	Sodium mg
IGA Tomato Sauce (1/2 cup)	45	0.0	0.0	(0)	(740)
IGA Tomato Sauce, Fancy (1/2 cup)	45	0.0	0.0	0	(740)
Rokeach Tomato Sauce, Italian Style (3 oz)	60	2.0	(0.3)	0	243
Rokeach Tomato Sauce, Low Sodium (3 oz)	60	2.0	(0.3)	0	124
Rokeach Tomato Sauce, Marinara Style (3 oz)	60	2.0	(0.3)	0	257
OTHER SAUCES					
Bovril Sauce Mix, 3 Pepper, prep (as directed) (1/2 cup)	56	0.8	(0.3)	(0)	n/a
Bovril Sauce Mix, Beef, prep (as directed) (1/2 cup)	51	0.7	(0.4)	(tr)	n/a
Bovril Sauce Mix, Chicken, prep (as directed) (1/2 cup)	46	0.8	(0.3)	(1)	n/a
Gebhardt Chili Hot Dog Sauce (2 tbsp)	30	1.0	0.4	3	180
Hunt's Manwich Sauce, Chili Fixins (sauce only) (5.3 oz)	110	<1.0	(0.0)	0	900
Hunt's Manwich Sauce, Extra Thick and Chunky (sauce only) (2.5 oz)	60	<1.0	(0.0)	0	640
Hunt's Manwich Sauce, Mexican (sauce only) (2.5 oz)	35	1.0	(<1.0)	0	460
Hunt's Manwich Sauce, Sloppy Joe (sauce only) (2.5 oz)	40	<1.0	(0.0)	0	390
Just Rite Hot Dog Sauce (2 oz)	60	3.0	1.1	7	220
Knorr Grilling and Broiling Sauce, Chardonnay (1.6 oz)	50	4.0*	(1.2)	(<1)	630
Knorr Grilling and Broiling Sauce, Spicy Plum (1.7 oz)	60	2.0	(0.6)	(0)	790
Knorr Grilling and Broiling Sauce, Tequila Lime (1.6 oz)	50	3.0	(0.9)	(<1)	690
Knorr Grilling and Broiling Sauce, Tuscan Herb (1.6 oz)	50	4.0*	(1.2)	(0)	600
Knorr Microwave Sauce, Vera Cruz (3.3 oz)	70	3.0	(0.4)	(0)	580
Knorr Sauce Mix, Demi- Glace, prep (w/water) (2 fl oz = 1/4 cup)	30	1.0	(0.2)	(<1)	310

*The value printed for fat is higher than the cutoff point because the manufacturer's serving size is larger than the standard serving size used in evaluating the food.

Sauces (continued)	Calories	Fat g	Saturated Fat g	Choles- terol mg	Sodium mg
Knorr Sauce Mix, Hunter, prep (w/water) (2 fl oz = 1/4 cup)	25	<1.0	(0.0)	(0)	340
Knorr Sauce Mix, Lyonnaise, prep (w/water) (2 fl oz = 1/4 cup)	20	<1.0	(0.0)	(0)	360
Knorr Sauce Mix, Napoli, prep (w/tomato puree and oil) (4 fl oz = 1/2 cup)	100	3.0	(0.4)	(2)	960
Knorr Sauce Mix, Pepper, prep (w/water) (2 fl oz = 1/4 cup)	20	1.0	(<1.0)	(0)	380
Maggie Gin's Canton Noodle Sauce (1 tbsp)	18	0.0	0.0	0	305
Progresso Sauce, Sicilian (1/2 cup)	30	2.5	<1.0	0	660
Ragu Italian Cooking Sauce (4 oz)	70	2.0	(0.3)	0	540
Ragu Joe (3.5 oz)	50	0.0	0.0	0	650
Wolf Brand Chili Hot Dog Sauce (1/6 cup)	40	2.0	(0.9)	(0)	200

INGREDIENTS

Cookïing ingredients usually provide little or no fat and saturated fat and contain no cholesterol. Values for many of the foods in this section are given for "most brands."

Many cooking ingredients are high in sodium; however, several low-sodium seasonings, which can be used to bring out the flavor of food, are listed in the Guide.

CUTOFF POINTS FOR COOKING INGREDIENTS, SPICES, AND SEASONINGS

Fat (grams)	Saturated Fat (grams)	Cholesterol (milligrams)
3	1	10

SERVINGS

Food	Serving Sizes
Cooking Ingredients:	
Baking Candies, Chips, etc.	½ ounce (about ⅔ tablespoons)
Cornmeal	1 ounce (about ¼ cup)
Cornstarch	1 tablespoon
Flours	1 ounce (about ¼ cup)
Spices and Seasonings:	
Salt, Seasoned Salt	1 gram (about ⅕ teaspoon)
Salt Substitutes	1 serving as listed by manufacturer
Seasoning Mixes	1 serving as listed by manufacturer
Spices	1 serving as listed by manufacturer
Sugar	
Granulated	2 teaspoons
Confectioner's	½ ounce (about 5⅔ teaspoons)

The following abbreviations are used in the Food Sections: oz = ounce; fl oz = fluid ounce; pkg = package; pkt = packet; env = envelope; g = gram; prep (w/ . . .) = prepared with; < = less than; and tr = trace.

Cooking Ingredients	Calories	Fat g	Saturated Fat g	Choles-terol mg	Sodium mg
COOKING INGREDIENTS					
Apollo Fillo Dough (1 oz = 1-1/3 leaves)	80	0.0	0.0	0	100
Athens Fillo Dough (1 oz = 1-1/3 leaves)	80	0.0	0.0	0	100
Baking Powder, Featherweight Baking Powder, low sodium (1 tsp)	8	0.0	0.0	0	2
Baking Powder—Most Brands (1 tsp)	4	0.0	0.0	0	329
Baking Soda—Most Brands (1 tsp)	0	0.0	0.0	0	821
Barley, Medium or Quick, Pearled, dry—Most Brands (1/4 cup)	176	0.6	0.1	0	5
Buttermilk, Dried, Saco Cultured Buttermilk Blend (.8 oz dry = 3–4 tbsp = 1 cup reconstituted)	79	0.7	(0.4)	<5	168
Cocoa Powder, Hershey's European Cocoa (1 oz)	90	3.0	(1.8)	0	15
Cocoa Powder, unsweetened—Most Brands (1 tbsp)	21	1.7	1.0	0	0
Corn Syrup, Karo Dark Corn Syrup (1 tbsp)	60	0.0	0.0	(0)	40
Corn Syrup, Karo Light Corn Syrup (1 tbsp)	60	0.0	0.0	(0)	30
Cornmeal, White, Self-rising—Most Brands (1/4 cup)	100	1.0	0.1	0	374
Cornmeal, Whole Grain—Most Brands (1/4 cup)	109	1.1	0.2	0	11
Cornmeal, Degermed—Most Brands (1.2 oz = 1/4 cup)	125	0.6	0.1	0	1
Cornstarch, not packed—Most Brands (1 tbsp)	29	0.0	0.0	0	0
Cornstarch, packed—Most Brands (1 tbsp)	31	0.0	0.0	0	1
Cracker Meal, Lance Cracker Meal (1 oz)	100	1.0	(0.2)	0	1
Cream of Tartar—Most Brands (1 tsp)	2	0.0	0.0	0	219
Flour, All-Purpose—Most Brands (1/2 cup)	226	0.6	0.1	0	1

Cooking Ingredients (continued)	Calories	Fat g	Saturated Fat g	Choles- terol mg	Sodium mg
Flour, Buckwheat—Most Brands (1/2 cup)	201	1.9	0.4	0	5
Flour, Corn, Masa, Quaker Masa Harina De Maiz (2 6″ tortillas)	137	1.5	0.0	(0)	5
Flour, Corn, Masa—Most Brands (1/2 cup)	208	2.2	0.1	0	3
Flour, Corn, Whole Grain—Most Brands (1/2 cup)	209	2.2	0.3	0	3
Flour, Graham, Ceresota Whole Wheat Graham Flour (1/2 cup)	200	1.0	(<1.0)	0	0
Flour, Graham, Heckers Whole Wheat Graham Flour (1/2 cup)	200	1.0	(<1.0)	0	0
Flour, Rice, Brown—Most Brands (1/2 cup)	287	2.2	0.4	0	6
Flour, Rice, Featherweight Rice Flour (1/2 cup)	250	0.5	(0.0)	0	4
Flour, Rice, White—Most Brands (1/2 cup)	289	1.0	0.3	0	0
Flour, Rye, Dark—Most Brands (1/2 cup)	207	1.7	0.2	0	1
Flour, Rye, Light—Most Brands (1/2 cup)	187	0.7	0.1	0	1
Flour, Rye, Medium—Most Brands (1/2 cup)	181	0.9	0.1	0	2
Flour, Rye, Pillsbury's Best Bohemian Style Rye and Wheat (1/2 cup)	200	0.5	(0.0)	(0)	0
Flour, Soy, Elam's Soy Flour, Roasted, Defatted (1/4 cup)	116	<1.0	(0.0)	(0)	5
Flour, Wheat, White, Bread—Most Brands (1/2 cup)	249	1.1	0.2	0	1
Flour, Wheat, White, Cake—Most Brands (1/2 cup)	195	0.5	0.1	0	1
Flour, Wheat, White, Self-rising—Most Brands (1/2 cup)	219	0.6	0.1	0	787
Flour, White, All Purpose—Most Brands (1/2 cup)	219	0.6	0.1	0	0
Flour, Whole Grain, Triticale—Most Brands (1/2 cup)	220	1.2	0.2	0	1

Cooking Ingredients (continued)	Calories	Fat g	Saturated Fat g	Choles- terol mg	Sodium mg
Flour, Whole Grain, Wheat—Most Brands (1/2 cup)	203	1.1	0.2	0	3
Graham Cracker Crumbs, Sunshine Graham Cracker Crumbs (2-1/2 tbsp)	70	2.0	<1.0	<2	130
Graham Cracker Crumbs—Most Brands (1/3 cup=1 oz)	109	2.7	0.8	0	190
Matzo, Manischewitz Matzo Farfel (Daily) (1 cup)	180	0.8	0.0	0	2
Matzo, Manischewitz Matzo Meal (Daily) (1 cup)	514	1.4	0.0	0	3
Natural Ovens of Manitowac Oat Bran, dry (1 oz=1/3 cup)	109	2.0	(0.4)	(0)	0
Potato Starch, Featherweight Potato Starch (1 cup)	620	1.0	(0.0)	0	51
Rennet Tablet—Most Brands (1 tablet)	1	0.0	0.0	0	201
Sugar Substitute, Equal, powder (1 pkt)	4	0.0	0.0	0	0
Sugar Substitute, Featherweight Fructose Sweetener (1 tsp)	12	0.0	0.0	0	0
Sugar Substitute, Saccharin— Most Brands (1 pkt)	4	0.0	0.0	0	2
Sugar Substitute, Sugar Twin Sweetener (1 tsp)	<2	0.0	(0.0)	0	0
Sugar Substitute, Sweet Magic Sweetener (1 pkt)	(0)	(0.0)	(0.0)	(0)	57
Sugar Substitute, Sweet One Sweetener (1 pkt)	(4)	0.0	0.0	(0)	0
Sugar, Brown, packed—Most Brands (1 tsp)	17	0.0	0.0	0	1
Sugar, Powdered Confectioner's—Most Brands (1 tsp)	10	0.0	0.0	0	0
Sugar, White—Most Brands (1 tsp)	15	0.0	0.0	0	(0)
Tapioca, Pearl or Granulated Quick Cooking—Most Brands (1 tbsp)	30	0.0	0.0	0	0
Tapioca, Pearl—Most Brands (1/3 cup)	174	0.1	0.0	0	0

Cooking Ingredients (continued)	Calories	Fat g	Saturated Fat g	Choles- terol mg	Sodium mg
Vanilla Extract—Most Brands (1 tsp)	6	0.0	0.0	0	0
Vinegar, all flavors—Most Brands (1 tbsp)	2	0.0	0.0	0	0
Yeast, Brewer's—Most Brands (1 tbsp)	25	0.0	0.0	0	9

SPICES AND SEASONINGS

	Calories	Fat g	Saturated Fat g	Choles- terol mg	Sodium mg
Ac'cent Flavor Enhancer (1/2 tsp)	5	0.0	0.0	0	300
Ac'cent Herbal All Purpose Seasoning (1/2 tsp)	(5)	0.0	0.0	0	0
Ac'cent Lemon Pepper (1/2 tsp)	(5)	0.0	0.0	0	0
Ac'cent Seasoned Pepper (1/2 tsp)	(5)	0.0	0.0	0	0
Best O'Butter, Cheddar Cheese Flavor (1/2 tsp)	6	<1.0	(0.0)	(0)	75
Best O'Butter, Original (1/2 tsp)	4	<1.0	(0.0)	(0)	65
Best O'Butter, Sour Cream Flavor (1/2 tsp)	4	<1.0	(0.0)	(0)	65
Garlic Powder—Most Brands (1/2 tsp)	9	0.0	0.0	0	1
Gebhardt Chili Quick Seasoning Mix (1 tsp)	10	<1.0	(0.0)	0	165
Gebhardt Menudo Mix (1 tsp)	5	<1.0	(0.0)	0	310
Giant Seasoning Mix, Taco (1/12 pkg)	8	<1.0	0.0	0	300
Hain Seasoning Mix, Chili Seasoning, Hot (1/4 pkg)	30	1.0	<1.0	0	370
Hain Seasoning Mix, Chili Seasoning, Medium (1/4 pkg)	30	1.0	(<1.0)	(0)	300
Hain Seasoning Mix, Chili Seasoning, Mild (1/4 pkg)	30	1.0	<1.0	0	330
Hain Seasoning Mix, Taco Seasoning (1/10 pkg)	10	0.0	0.0	0	200
Lawry's Garlic Powder with Parsley (1 tsp)	12	0.1	(0.0)	(0)	5
Lawry's Minced Onion with Green Onion Flakes (1 tsp)	7	0.2	(0.0)	(0)	1
Manwich Dry Mix (1/4 oz)	20	<1.0	(0.0)	0	350
McCormick Bac'N Chips (1/4 tsp)	7	0.1	(0.0)	(0)	51

Spices and Seasonings (continued)	Calories	Fat g	Saturated Fat g	Choles- terol mg	Sodium mg
McCormick Garlic Bread Sprinkle (1/4 tsp)	5	0.4	(0.0)	(0)	25
Molly McButter Sprinkles, Bacon Flavor (1/2 tsp)	4	0.0	0.0	0	65
Molly McButter Sprinkles, Butter Flavor (1/2 tsp)	4	0.0	0.0	0	90
Molly McButter Sprinkles, Cheese Flavor (1/2 tsp)	4	0.0	0.0	0	60
Molly McButter Sprinkles, Sour Cream and Butter Flavor (1/2 tsp)	4	0.0	0.0	0	65
Morton Lite Salt Mixture (1 tsp)	<1	0.0	0.0	(0)	1110
Mrs. Dash, Extra Spicy (1 tsp)	12	0.1	(0.0)	0	4
Mrs. Dash, Garlic and Herb (1 tsp)	12	0.0	0.0	0	2
Mrs. Dash, Lemon and Herb (1 tsp)	12	0.1	(0.0)	0	4
Mrs. Dash, Low Pepper Blend (1 tsp)	12	0.1	(0.0)	0	4
Mrs. Dash, Original (1 tsp)	12	0.0	0.0	0	4
Mrs. Dash, Table Blend (1 tsp)	12	0.0	0.0	0	4
Old El Paso Fajita Marinade (1/8 jar)	14	0.0	0.0	0	450
Papa Dash Lite Lite Lite Salt (1/4 tsp)	1	0.0	0.0	0	87
Papa Dash Salt Lover's Blend (1/4 tsp)	0	0.0	0.0	0	240
Parsley Patch Garlic Bread Sprinkle (1/4 tsp)	5	0.4	(0.0)	(0)	25
Parsley Patch, All Purpose Seasoning (1/2 tsp)	3	0.0	0.0	(0)	2
Parsley Patch, Garlic Seasoning, Saltless (1/2 tsp)	5	0.0	0.0	(0)	1
Parsley Patch, It's A Dilly (1/2 tsp)	4	0.0	0.0	(0)	2
Parsley Patch, Lemon Pepper (1/2 tsp)	5	<1.0	(0.0)	0	4
Parsley Patch, Popcorn Blend (1/2 tsp)	5	0.0	0.0	(0)	2
Parsley Patch, Sesame All Purpose Seasoning (1/2 tsp)	8	1.0	(0.0)	0	1
Pepper—Most Brands (1/2 tsp)	3	0.0	0.0	0	1

Spices and Seasonings (continued)	Calories	Fat g	Saturated Fat g	Cholesterol mg	Sodium mg
Salt—Most Brands (1/2 tsp)	0	0.0	0.0	0	1066
Spices, all varieties without salt—Most Brands (1 tsp)	0	0.0	0.0	0	0

JUICES

Fruit and vegetable juices contain no cholesterol and little or no fat and saturated fat. Values for many of the foods in this section are given for "most brands."

Vegetable juices may be high in sodium from salt added during processing. Individuals needing to limit their intake of salt or sodium may wish to try low-sodium vegetable juices.

CUTOFF POINTS FOR JUICES

Fat (grams)	Saturated Fat (grams)	Cholesterol (milligrams)
3	1	10

SERVINGS

Food	Serving Sizes
Clam Juice	6 fluid ounces
Fruit Juice	6 fluid ounces
Fruit Nectar	6 fluid ounces
Lemon and Lime Juice	1 tablespoon
Vegetable Juice	6 fluid ounces

The following abbreviations are used in the Food Sections: oz = ounce; fl oz = fluid ounce; pkg = package; pkt = packet; env = envelope; g = gram; prep (w/ . . .) = prepared with; < = less than; and tr = trace.

Juices	Calories	Fat g	Saturated Fat g	Cholesterol mg	Sodium mg
JUICES					
Apple Cider, Giant Sweet Apple Cider (6 fl oz)	90	0.0	0.0	0	5
Apple Cider, IGA Apple Cider (6 fl oz)	90	0.0	0.0	0	(5)
Apple Juice, Libby's Juicy Juice, Apple-Grape (6 fl oz)	90	0.0	0.0	(0)	10
Apple Juice, Smucker's Fruit Juice, Apple/Cranberry (8 fl oz)	120	0.0	0.0	(0)	10
Apple Juice, Welch's Sparkling Juice, Sparkling Apple (6 fl oz)	100	0.0	0.0	(0)	5
Apple Juice—Most Brands (6 fl oz)	90	<1.0	0.0	0	6
Apple Nectar, Kern's Nectar, Apple (6 fl oz)	110	0.0	0.0	(0)	5
Apple Nectar, Kern's Nectar, Cinnamon Apple (6 fl oz)	110	0.0	0.0	(0)	10
Apple Nectar, Libby's Nectar, Apple (6 fl oz)	100	0.0	0.0	(0)	25
Apricot Nectar, Kern's Nectar, Apricot-Orange (6 fl oz)	112	0.0	0.0	(0)	<10
Apricot Nectar, Kern's Nectar, Apricot-Pineapple (6 fl oz)	110	0.0	0.0	(0)	10
Apricot Nectar—Most Brands (6 fl oz)	108	<1.0	0.0	0	6
Banana Nectar, Kern's Nectar, Banana Pineapple (6 fl oz)	120	0.0	0.0	(0)	10
Banana Nectar, Libby's Nectar, Banana (6 fl oz)	110	0.0	0.0	(0)	15
Berry Juice, Libby's Juicy Juice, Berry (6 fl oz)	90	0.0	0.0	(0)	10
Boysenberry Juice, Smucker's 100% Fruit Juice Sparklers, Boysenberry (10 fl oz)	130	<1.0	0.0	(0)	5
Boysenberry Juice, Smucker's Fruit Juice, Boysenberry (8 fl oz)	120	0.0	0.0	(0)	10
Carrot Juice, Hain Carrot Juice (6 fl oz)	80	0.0	0.0	0	170
Cherry Juice, Dole Pure & Light, Mountain Cherry (6 fl oz)	90	0.0	0.0	(0)	10

Juices (continued)	Calories	Fat g	Saturated Fat g	Choles- terol mg	Sodium mg
Cherry Juice, Libby's Juicy Juice, Cherry (6 fl oz)	90	0.0	0.0	0	10
Cherry Juice, Smucker's 100% Fruit Juice Sparklers, Black Cherry (10 fl oz)	120	< 1.0	0.0	(0)	5
Cherry Juice, Smucker's Fruit Juice, Black Cherry (8 fl oz)	130	0.0	0.0	(0)	10
Clam Juice, Doxsee Clam Juice (3 fl oz)	4	0.0	0.0	(0)	110
Cranberry Juice, Smucker's 100% Fruit Juice Sparklers, Cranberry (10 fl oz)	140	< 1.0	0.0	(0)	5
Grape Juice, Welch's Juice, White Grape, sweetened, prep (from frozen) (6 fl oz)	100	0.0	0.0	(0)	5
Grape Juice, Welch's Sparkling Juice, Red Grape (6 fl oz)	128	0.0	0.0	(0)	30
Grape Juice, Welch's Sparkling Juice, White Grape (6 fl oz)	120	0.0	0.0	(0)	30
Grape Juice—Most Brands (6 fl oz)	114	< 1.0	0.0	0	6
Grape Nectar, McCain Nectar, Grape (8 fl oz = 1 box)	155	0.2	0.1	0	8
Grapefruit Juice, sweetened—Most Brands (6 fl oz)	87	< 1.0	0.0	0	3
Grapefruit Juice, unsweetened—Most Brands (6 fl oz)	72	< 1.0	0.0	0	2
Guava Juice, Welch's Juices, Guava, prep (from frozen) (6 fl oz)	100	0.0	0.0	(0)	20
Guava Nectar, Kern's Nectar, Guava (6 fl oz)	110	0.0	0.0	(0)	10
Guava Nectar, Libby's Nectar, Guava (6 fl oz)	110	0.0	0.0	(0)	15
Guava Nectar, Libby's Nectar, Ripe Guava (8 fl oz)	140	0.0	0.0	(0)	20
Lemon Juice—Most Brands (2 tbsp)	3	0.0	0.0	0	3
Lime Juice—Most Brands (2 tbsp)	3	0.0	0.0	0	2
Mango Nectar, Kern's Nectar, Mango (6 fl oz)	110	0.0	0.0	(0)	10

Juices (continued)	Calories	Fat g	Saturated Fat g	Choles- terol mg	Sodium mg
Mango Nectar, Libby's Nectar, Mango (6 fl oz)	110	0.0	0.0	(0)	0
Mixed Juice, Kern's Nectar, Tropical (6 fl oz)	112	0.0	0.0	(0)	10
Mixed Juice, Libby's Juicy Juice, Punch (6 fl oz)	100	0.0	0.0	(0)	10
Mixed Juice, Libby's Juicy Juice, Tropical (6 fl oz)	110	0.0	0.0	(0)	10
Orange Juice, Land O'Lakes Fruit Juices, Orange Pineapple Banana (6 fl oz)	100	0.0	0.0	0	0
Orange Juice, Welch's Juices, Orange Blend (6 fl oz)	90	0.0	0.0	(0)	20
Orange Juice, frozen, diluted—Most Brands (6 fl oz)	84	< 1.0	0.0	0	2
Orange Juice—Most Brands (6 fl oz)	78	< 1.0	0.0	0	5
Orange and Banana Juice, Smucker's Fruit Juice (8 fl oz)	120	0.0	0.0	(0)	10
Orange and Grapefruit Juice—Most Brands (6 fl oz)	78	< 1.0	0.0	0	6
Orange and Pineapple Juice, Kraft Pure 100% Unsweetened Orange-Pineapple Juice (6 fl oz)	80	0.0	0.0	(0)	0
Orange and Pineapple Juice, Land O'Lakes Fruit Juices, Orange Pineapple (6 fl oz)	90	0.0	0.0	0	0
Papaya Nectar, Kern's Nectar, Papaya-Pineapple (6 fl oz)	110	0.0	0.0	(0)	< 1
Papaya Nectar—Most Brands (6 fl oz)	108	< 1.0	0.0	0	12
Passion Fruit Juice, Purple, unsweetened—Most Brands (6 fl oz)	96	< 1.0	0.0	0	12
Passion Fruit Juice, Yellow, unsweetened—Most Brands (6 fl oz)	114	< 1.0	0.0	0	12
Passion Fruit Nectar, Kern's Nectar, Passionfruit-Orange (6 fl oz)	120	0.0	0.0	(0)	10
Passion Fruit Nectar, Libby's Nectar, Ripe Passion Fruit–Orange (8 fl oz)	150	0.0	0.0	(0)	10

Juices (continued)	Calories	Fat g	Saturated Fat g	Choles-terol mg	Sodium mg
Passion Fruit Nectar, IGA Passion Fruit Nectar (6 fl oz)	90	0.0	0.0	0	(10)
Peach Juice, Dole Pure & Light, Orchard Peach (6 fl oz)	90	0.0	0.0	(0)	10
Peach Juice, Smucker's Fruit Juice, Peach (8 fl oz)	120	0.0	0.0	(0)	10
Peach Nectar—Most Brands (6 fl oz)	102	0.0	0.0	0	12
Pear Nectar, Kern's Nectar, Pear-Pineapple (6 fl oz)	112	2.0	(<1.0)	(0)	<10
Pear Nectar—Most Brands (6 fl oz)	114	0.0	0.0	0	6
Pineapple Juice, Dole Pine-Orange-Banana Juice (6 fl oz)	90	0.0	0.0	(0)	5
Pineapple Juice, Dole Pine-Orange-Guava Juice (6 fl oz)	100	<1.0	(0.0)	(0)	10
Pineapple Juice, Dole Pine-Passion-Banana Juice (6 fl oz)	100	<1.0	(0.0)	(0)	10
Pineapple Juice, Dole Pineapple Grapefruit Juice (6 fl oz)	90	0.0	0.0	(0)	10
Pineapple Juice, Dole Pineapple Orange Juice (6 fl oz)	90	0.0	0.0	(0)	20
Pineapple Juice, Dole Pineapple Orange Juice, prep (from frozen) (6 fl oz)	90	0.0	0.0	(0)	10
Pineapple Juice, Dole Pineapple Pink Grapefruit Juice-Drink (6 fl oz)	100	0.0	0.0	(0)	20
Pineapple Juice, Minute Maid Pineapple Orange Juice, prep (from frozen) (6 fl oz)	98	0.1	(0.0)	(0)	19
Pineapple Juice—Most Brands (6 fl oz)	102	<1.0	0.0	0	0
Pineapple Nectar, Libby's Nectar, Pineapple (6 fl oz)	110	0.0	0.0	(0)	30
Pineapple and Grapefruit Juice, IGA Pineapple Grapefruit Juice Reconstituted (6 fl oz)	90	<1.0	(0.0)	0	(10)

Juices (continued)	Calories	Fat g	Saturated Fat g	Choles- terol mg	Sodium mg
Pineapple and Orange Juice, IGA Pineapple Orange Juice Reconstituted (6 fl oz)	90	0.0	0.0	0	(20)
Plum Nectar, Kern's Nectar, Plum (6 fl oz)	110	0.0	0.0	(0)	10
Prune Juice—Most Brands (6 fl oz)	138	<1.0	0.0	0	6
Raspberry Juice, Dole Pure & Light, Country Raspberry (6 fl oz)	90	0.0	0.0	(0)	10
Raspberry Juice, Smucker's 100% Fruit Juice Sparklers, Red Raspberry (10 fl oz)	130	<1.0	0.0	(0)	5
Red Raspberry Juice, Smucker's Fruit Juice (8 fl oz)	120	0.0	0.0	(0)	10
Strawberry Juice, Smucker's Fruit Juice (8 fl oz)	130	0.0	0.0	(0)	10
Strawberry Nectar, Kern's Nectar, Strawberry (6 fl oz)	110	0.0	0.0	(0)	0
Strawberry Nectar, Kern's Nectar, Strawberry-Banana (6 fl oz)	100	0.0	0.0	(0)	10
Strawberry Nectar, Libby's Nectar, Ripe Strawberry (8 fl oz)	150	0.0	0.0	(0)	5
Strawberry Nectar, Libby's Nectar, Ripe Strawberry-Banana (8 fl oz)	150	0.0	0.0	(0)	5
Strawberry Nectar, Libby's Nectar, Strawberry (6 fl oz)	110	0.0	0.0	(0)	0
Tangerine Juice, Dole Pure & Light, Mandarin Tangerine (6 fl oz)	100	0.0	0.0	(0)	10
Tangerine Juice, sweetened, canned—Most Brands (6 fl oz)	96	<1.0	0.0	0	2
Tomato Juice, no salt added— Most Brands (6 fl oz)	32	<1.0	0.0	0	18
Tomato Juice—Most Brands (6 fl oz)	32	<1.0	0.0	0	658
Tropical Juice, IGA Tropical Juice (6 fl oz)	100	0.0	0.0	0	(10)
Vegetable Juice, Smucker's Hearty Vegetable Juice (8 fl oz)	58	0.0	0.0	(0)	714

Juices (continued)	Calories	Fat g	Saturated Fat g	Choles- terol mg	Sodium mg
Vegetable Juice, Smucker's Hearty Vegetable Juice, Hot & Spicy (8 fl oz)	58	0.0	0.0	(0)	650
Vegetable Juice Cocktail, V-8 Vegetable Juice Cocktail (6 oz)	35	0.0	0.0	(0)	560
Vegetable Juice Cocktail, V-8 Vegetable Juice Cocktail, No Salt Added (6 oz)	35	0.0	0.0	(0)	45
Vegetable Juice Cocktail, V-8 Vegetable Juice Cocktail, Spicy Hot (6 oz)	35	0.0	0.0	(0)	650
Vegetable Juice Cocktail—Most Brands (6 fl oz)	34	< 1.0	0.0	0	664

MEAT, POULTRY, AND FISH

It is important to choose lean cuts of meat and poultry, since the meat group is a source of fat, saturated fat, and cholesterol in the American diet; most fish is low in fat. The goal is to select meat, poultry, and fish that contains no more than 10% fat (90% fat free). This is approximately the same as 9 grams of fat in a 3-ounce cooked serving or 3 grams of fat in 1 ounce. In this Guide, 3 ounces of cooked meat, poultry, and fish; 1 ounce of processed/luncheon meat; and 3 ounces of meat substitutes are used for evaluation purposes. The Guide includes those meats that do not contain more fat, saturated fat, and cholesterol than the cutoff points listed below.

Since most fresh cut beef, pork, lamb, and chicken do not have brand names, the values for many of the foods in this section are based on information from USDA handbooks.

CUTOFF POINTS FOR MEAT, POULTRY, AND FISH AND MEAT SUBSTITUTES

	Fat (grams)	Saturated Fat (grams)	Cholesterol (milligrams)
Meat, Poultry, Fish, Shellfish (3 ounces)	9	3	80
Meat Substitutes (3 ounces)	9	3	10
Processed/Luncheon Meat (1 ounce)	3	1	27

SERVINGS

Food	Serving Sizes
Meat, Poultry, and Fish (cooked):	
Beef	3 ounces
Chicken	3 ounces
Fish (Finfish and Shellfish):	
Anchovies	1 ounce
Canned	3 ounces
Fresh, Refrigerated, and Frozen	3 ounces
Smoked and Pickled	3 ounces
Surimi	3 ounces
Game	3 ounces
Lamb	3 ounces
Pork	3 ounces
Turkey	3 ounces
Meat Substitutes:	
Tofu (soybean curd)	4 ounces
Other Soybean Products:	
Bacon Substitutes	1 ounce
Imitation Bacon Bits	¼ ounce

Food	Serving Sizes
Luncheon Meat, Sandwich Spread, Canadian Bacon, Sausage, and Hot Dog	2 ounces
Processed Luncheon Meat:	
Beef	1 ounce
Jerky	1 ounce
Chicken	1 ounce
Pork	1 ounce
Turkey	1 ounce

Beef. The amount of fat in beef is a major factor in determining its grade. As a result, of the grades of beef available to the consumer, Prime is highest in fat, followed by Choice and then Select, which has the least fat. Most beef sold in the United States is Choice; however, the amount of Select beef available in supermarkets is increasing. Although some cuts of Select grade beef contain 3 grams of fat or less per ounce when external fat is left at ¼ inch, we still recommend that lean beef be trimmed of all visible external fat before cooking. When beef is cooked without removing the external fat, a small amount of fat migrates into the lean meat. When ¼ inch of external fat is left on beef during cooking, the meat contains about 1 gram of fat more per 3½-ounce serving than the same cut cooked without the external fat.

Almost half of the beef sold in the United States is in the form of ground beef. On the average, ground beef contains about 20% fat. In the past, the only way to get ground beef much leaner than this was to ask the butcher to trim all the fat off a steak or roast and grind it. However, a new type of very lean ground beef, containing less than 10% fat, is becoming increasingly available. These products are made by combining very lean ground beef with water and carrageenan, oat bran, or dairy solids. Salt and hydrolyzed vegetable protein also may be added. Combining these ingredients with lean beef helps it retain moisture, resulting in juicier cooked beef.

Chicken. Most light meat of chicken, when eaten without skin, contains less than 3 grams of fat in a 3-ounce serving. The amount of fat in cooked chicken depends on the method of preparation. Since light meat that is stewed is so low in fat, it qualifies for the Guide even with the skin. Most dark meat exceeds the cutoff point for inclusion in the Guide; however, dark meat of chicken without skin that is stewed does not exceed the cutoff point for fat.

Finfish. Most finfish is low in fat. Warm water varieties (flounder and snapper) are lower in fat than cold water fish, such as salmon and mackerel.

Game. Several types of game are listed on the following pages. Often game is low in fat because the animals are more physically active than domestic animals.

Lamb. All cuts should be well trimmed before cooking.

Meat Substitutes. Tofu (soybean curd) is often used as a meat substitute. Most meat substitutes, in fact, are based on soybeans, a source of good-quality vegetable protein. Some of these products are processed and seasoned to resemble meat or meat-mixture dishes.

Pork. An increasing number of lean fresh and cured pork products are becoming available. To reduce the fat in cooked pork, trim all external fat before cooking the meat. There are a number of very lean hams on the market, but it is important to remember that the curing process makes ham high in sodium.

Processed/Luncheon Meats. Traditionally, processed luncheon meat is made of beef, pork, or a combination of the two and is high in fat and saturated fat. However, the following pages include many types of beef, pork, turkey, and chicken processed luncheon meats that are low enough in fat, saturated fat, and cholesterol to qualify for the Guide.

Shellfish. With a few exceptions (clams, crab, and lobster), most shellfish have more than 80 mg of cholesterol per 3-ounce cooked serving. However, all shellfish are very low in fat and saturated fat.

Surimi. Surimi is cooked finfish (often pollack) that is processed and then shaped and colored to resemble shrimp, lobster, or other seafood. It may be high in salt, which is usually added during processing. Since surimi products are actually made of finfish, they are lower in cholesterol than real shellfish.

Turkey. Turkey can be cooked without removing the skin to preserve moisture in the meat; however, the skin should be removed before the meat is eaten. Turkey can be flavored to taste like ham, sausage, or various types of processed luncheon meat. Much, but not all, ground turkey is low in fat; some brands have skin and fat added.

Veal. There are no cuts of veal included in the Guide. Although most cuts are low in fat and saturated fat, veal exceeds the cutoff point of 80 mg of cholesterol per 3-ounce cooked serving. Veal is higher in cholesterol than beef because it comes from a young animal, in which cholesterol is concentrated in the tissues.

The following abbreviations are used in the Food Sections: oz = ounce; fl oz = fluid ounce; pkg = package; pkt = packet; env = envelope; g = gram; prep (w/ . . .) = prepared with; < = less than; and tr = trace.

Beef	Calories	Fat g	Saturated Fat g	Choles- terol mg	Sodium mg
BEEF					
CANNED					
Underwood Light Meat Spreads, Roast Beef (2-1/8 oz)	90	6.0	2.0	30	210
FRESH AND FROZEN					
Beef Bottom Round, Choice, lean only, trimmed to 0″ fat, braised—USDA Data (3 oz)	181	7.4	2.5	82	43
Beef Bottom Round, Choice, lean only, trimmed to 0″ fat, roasted—USDA Data (3 oz)	164	6.6	2.2	66	56
Beef Bottom Round, Choice, lean only, trimmed to 1/4″ fat, braised—USDA Data (3 oz)	187	8.0	2.7	82	43
Beef Bottom Round, Choice, lean only, trimmed to 1/4″ fat, roasted—USDA Data (3 oz)	168	7.1	2.4	66	56
Beef Bottom Round, Select, lean only, trimmed to 0″ fat, braised—USDA Data (3 oz)	163	5.4	1.8	82	43
Beef Bottom Round, Select, lean only, trimmed to 0″ fat, roasted—USDA Data (3 oz)	146	4.6	1.5	66	56
Beef Bottom Round, Select, lean only, trimmed to 1/4″ fat, braised—USDA Data (3 oz)	167	5.8	2.0	82	43
Beef Bottom Round, Select, lean only, trimmed to 1/4″ fat, roasted—USDA Data (3 oz)	152	5.3	1.8	66	56
Beef Brisket, Flat Half, All Grades, lean only, trimmed to 0″ fat, braised—USDA Data (3 oz)	162	5.3	1.7	81	54
Beef Eye of Round, Choice, lean only, trimmed to 0″ fat, roasted—USDA Data (3 oz)	149	4.8	1.8	59	53
Beef Eye of Round, Choice, lean only, trimmed to 1/4″ fat, roasted—USDA Data (3 oz)	149	4.8	1.8	59	53

Beef (continued)	Calories	Fat g	Saturated Fat g	Choles-terol mg	Sodium mg
Beef Eye of Round, Select, lean only, trimmed to 0″ fat, roasted—USDA Data (3 oz)	132	3.0	1.1	59	53
Beef Eye of Round, Select, lean only, trimmed to 1/4″ fat, roasted—USDA Data (3 oz)	136	3.4	1.2	59	53
Beef Rib, Small End, Select, lean only, trimmed to 0″ fat, broiled—USDA Data (3 oz)	168	7.4	3.0	68	59
Beef Rib, Small End, Select, lean only, trimmed to 1/4″ fat, broiled—USDA Data (3 oz)	176	8.2	3.3	68	59
Beef Ribs, Small End, Select, lean only, trimmed to 1/4″ fat, roasted—USDA Data (3 oz)	172	8.3	3.3	67	61
Beef Shank, Crosscuts, Choice, lean only, trimmed to 1/4″ fat, simmered—USDA Data (3 oz)	171	5.4	1.9	54	66
Beef Tenderloin, Select, lean only, trimmed to 0″ fat, broiled—USDA Data (3 oz)	170	7.5	2.8	71	54
Beef Tenderloin, Select, lean only, trimmed to 1/4″ fat, broiled—USDA Data (3 oz)	169	7.4	2.8	71	54
Beef Tip Round, Choice, lean only, trimmed to 0″ fat, roasted—USDA Data (3 oz)	153	5.4	1.9	69	55
Beef Tip Round, Choice, lean only, trimmed to 1/4″ fat, roasted—USDA Data (3 oz)	160	6.2	2.2	69	55
Beef Tip Round, Select, lean only, trimmed to 0″ fat, roasted—USDA Data (3 oz)	145	4.5	1.6	69	55
Beef Tip Round, Select, lean only, trimmed to 1/4″ fat, roasted—USDA Data (3 oz)	153	5.4	1.9	69	55
Beef Top Loin, Choice, lean only, trimmed to 0″ fat, broiled—USDA Data (3 oz)	177	8.2	3.1	65	58
Beef Top Loin, Select, lean only, trimmed to 0″ fat, broiled—USDA Data (3 oz)	157	5.9	2.2	65	58

Beef (continued)	Calories	Fat g	Saturated Fat g	Choles- terol mg	Sodium mg
Beef Top Loin, Select, lean only, trimmed to 1/4" fat, broiled—USDA Data (3 oz)	164	6.6	2.5	65	58
Beef Top Round, Choice, lean only, trimmed to 0" fat, braised—USDA Data (3 oz)	176	4.9	1.7	76	38
Beef Top Round, Choice, lean only, trimmed to 1/4" fat, braised—USDA Data (3 oz)	181	5.5	1.9	76	38
Beef Top Round, Choice, lean only, trimmed to 1/4" fat, broiled—USDA Data (3 oz)	160	5.0	1.7	71	52
Beef Top Round, Choice, lean only, trimmed to 1/4" fat, pan fried—USDA Data (3 oz)	193	7.3	2.1	82	60
Beef Top Round, Select, lean only, trimmed to 0" fat, braised—USDA Data (3 oz)	162	3.4	1.2	76	38
Beef Top Round, Select, lean only, trimmed to 1/4" fat, braised—USDA Data (3 oz)	166	3.9	1.3	76	38
Beef Top Round, Select, lean only, trimmed to 1/4" fat, broiled—USDA Data (3 oz)	143	3.1	1.1	71	52
Beef Top Sirloin, Choice, lean only, trimmed to 0" fat, broiled—USDA Data (3 oz)	170	6.6	2.6	76	56
Beef Top Sirloin, Choice, lean only, trimmed to 1/4" fat, broiled—USDA Data (3 oz)	172	6.8	2.7	76	56
Beef Top Sirloin, Select, lean only, trimmed to 0" fat, broiled—USDA Data (3 oz)	153	4.8	1.9	76	56
Beef Top Sirloin, Select, lean only, trimmed to 1/4" fat, broiled—USDA Data (3 oz)	158	5.3	2.1	76	56
Beef Tripe, raw—USDA Data (3 oz)	84	3.4	1.7	80	39
Ground Beef, 7% fat, with carrageenan or oat bran, no added salt, cooked (3 oz)	149	7.0	(2.5)	64	(53)

Beef (continued)	Calories	Fat g	Saturated Fat g	Choles- terol mg	Sodium mg
Ground Beef, 7% fat, with carrageenan or oat bran, salt added, cooked (3 oz)	149	7.0	(2.5)	64	(238)
Ground Beef, Fairbank Farms Tender-Lite Low-Fat Ground Beef, cooked (4 oz)	160	8.0	4.0	53	77
Ground Beef, Healthy Choice Extra-Lean Ground Beef, cooked (4 oz)	150	4.0	1.0	55	240

CHICKEN AND TURKEY

CANNED CHICKEN

Featherweight Chunk Chicken (3 oz)	90	3.0	(0.8)	65	60
Swanson Premium Chunk Poultry, White Chicken (2-1/2 oz)	100	4.0	(1.1)	(54)	235
Swanson Premium Chunk Poultry, White and Dark Chicken (2-1/2 oz)	100	4.0	(1.1)	(58)	240
Underwood Light Meat Spreads, Chunky Chicken (2-1/8 oz)	80	3.0	1.0	30	330

FRESH AND FROZEN CHICKEN

Banquet Boneless Chicken Hot Bites, Breast Tenders (2-1/4 oz)	150	6.0	(1.2)	(29)	280
Chicken Breast, meat and skin, roasted—USDA Data (3 oz)	167	6.6	1.9	72	60
Chicken Breast, meat and skin, stewed—USDA Data (3 oz)	156	6.3	1.8	64	53
Chicken Breast, without skin, roasted—USDA Data (3 oz)	142	3.1	0.9	73	63
Chicken Breast, without skin, stewed—USDA Data (3 oz)	129	2.6	0.7	65	52
Chicken Dark Meat, without skin, cooked, roasted—USDA Data (3 oz)	174	8.3	2.3	79	79
Chicken Dark Meat, without skin, stewed—USDA Data (3 oz)	163	7.6	2.1	75	63

Chicken and Turkey (continued)	Calories	Fat g	Saturated Fat g	Choles- terol mg	Sodium mg
Chicken Drumstick, without skin, roasted—USDA Data (1.6 oz)	76	2.5	0.7	41	42
Chicken Drumstick, without skin, stewed—USDA Data (1.6 oz)	78	2.6	0.7	40	37
Chicken Light Meat, with skin, stewed—USDA Data (3 oz)	171	8.4	2.4	63	54
Chicken Light Meat, without skin, cooked, roasted—USDA Data (3 oz)	147	3.8	1.1	72	66
Chicken Light Meat, without skin, stewed—USDA Data (3 oz)	135	3.4	1.0	65	55
Chicken Thigh, without skin, stewed—USDA Data (2 oz)	110	5.6	1.5	50	42
Chicken Wing, without skin, roasted—USDA Data (3/4 oz)	43	1.7	0.5	18	19
Chicken Wing, without skin, stewed—USDA Data (1 oz)	50	2.0	0.6	21	21
Tyson Frozen Boneless Chicken, Diced Meat (3 oz)	150	5.0	(1.4)	70	50
Tyson Fully Cooked Roasted Chicken, Roasted Breast Fillet (1 oz)	50	2.0	(0.6)	15	160
PRE-SEASONED CHICKEN					
Banquet Healthy Balance Baked Boneless Chicken, Breast Nuggets (2.25 oz)	120	4.0	(2.0)	30	310
Banquet Healthy Balance Baked Boneless Chicken, Breast Patties (2.25 oz)	120	4.0	(2.0)	30	310
Banquet Healthy Balance Baked Boneless Chicken, Breast Tenders (2.25 oz)	120	4.0	2.0	30	310
Chicken By George, Cajun Style (5 oz)	200	9.0	(2.5)	80	450
Chicken By George, Caribbean Grill (5 oz)	180	4.0	(1.1)	(75)	n/a
Chicken By George, Italian Style Beau Cheese (5 oz)	190	8.0	(2.3)	80	650
Chicken By George, Lemon Herb (5 oz)	150	4.0	(1.1)	70	480

Chicken and Turkey (continued)	Calories	Fat g	Saturated Fat g	Choles-terol mg	Sodium mg
Chicken By George, Mesquite Barbecue (5 oz)	170	4.0	(1.1)	70	680
Chicken By George, Mexican Style (5 oz)	200	9.0	(2.5)	(75)	n/a
Chicken By George, Mustard and Dill (5 oz)	180	7.0	(2.0)	80	530
Chicken By George, Teriyaki (5 oz)	180	4.0	(1.1)	65	340
Chicken By George, Tomato Herb with Basil (5 oz)	190	7.0	(2.0)	90	430
Tyson Marinated Chicken Breast Fillets, Barbecue (3.75 oz)	120	3.0	(0.9)	(90)	400
Tyson Marinated Chicken Breast Fillets, Italian (3.75 oz)	130	2.0	(0.6)	(90)	430
Tyson Marinated Chicken Breast Fillets, Lemon Pepper (3.75 oz)	120	2.0	(0.6)	(90)	210
Tyson Marinated Chicken Breast Fillets, Teriyaki (3.75 oz)	130	2.0	(0.6)	(90)	290
CANNED TURKEY					
Swanson Premium Chunk Poultry, White Turkey (2-1/2 oz)	80	1.0	(0.3)	(61)	260
Underwood Light Meat Spreads, Chunky Turkey (2-1/8 oz)	75	2.0	< 1.0	25	330
FRESH AND FROZEN TURKEY					
Louis Rich Breast of Turkey, Barbecued (1 oz)	33	0.9	0.3	12	315
Louis Rich Breast of Turkey, Hickory Smoked (1 oz)	33	1.0	0.3	13	346
Louis Rich Breast of Turkey, Honey Roasted (1 oz)	33	0.8	0.3	12	318
Louis Rich Breast of Turkey, Oven Roasted (1 oz)	31	0.9	0.2	13	296
Louis Rich Hen Turkey Breast with No Wing Portion (1 oz)	50	2.0	0.4	19	19
Louis Rich Lean Ground Turkey (1 oz)	52	2.1	0.7	25	32

Chicken and Turkey (continued)	Calories	Fat g	Saturated Fat g	Choles- terol mg	Sodium mg
Louis Rich Lean Ground Turkey with Natural Flavorings (1 oz)	50	2.2	0.7	24	33
Louis Rich Turkey Breast (1 oz)	47	1.5	0.6	21	21
Louis Rich Turkey Breast Steaks (1 oz)	39	0.5	0.1	17	24
Louis Rich Turkey Breast Tenderloins (1 oz)	39	0.5	0.2	18	24
Louis Rich Turkey Breast, Roast (1 oz)	42	0.8	0.3	19	20
Louis Rich Turkey Breast, Slices (1 oz)	39	0.5	0.1	17	24
Louis Rich Turkey Breast, Smoked (1 oz)	33	1.0	0.4	11	268
Louis Rich Whole Turkey, excluding giblets (1 oz)	52	2.3	0.7	22	23
Manor House Smoked Turkey (1 oz)	52	2.0	(0.4)	(11)	220
Turkey Dark Meat, without skin, roasted—USDA Data (3 oz)	159	6.1	2.1	72	67
Turkey Ham, Cured, thigh meat—Most Brands (3 oz)	110	4.3	1.5	(16)	848
Turkey Light Meat, meat only, roasted—USDA Data (3 oz)	133	2.7	0.9	59	54
Turkey Young Toms, light meat only, roasted—USDA Data (3 oz)	129	2.5	0.8	59	58
Turkey Young Toms, meat only, roasted—USDA Data (3 oz)	143	4.0	1.3	66	63
Turkey, Young Toms, dark meat without skin, roasted—USDA Data (3 oz)	158	5.9	2.0	75	70
Turkey, Young Toms, light meat with skin, roasted—USDA Data (3 oz)	163	6.5	1.8	64	57

FISH

FINFISH, CANNED

Featherweight Light Chunk Tuna (2 oz)	60	1.0	(0.3)	30	30
Featherweight Pink Salmon (2 oz)	70	3.0	(0.8)	20	45

Fish (continued)	Calories	Fat g	Saturated Fat g	Choles- terol mg	Sodium mg
Giant Tuna in Water, Light Chunk (3 oz)	90	2.0	<1.0	40	375
Giant Tuna in Water, Solid White (3 oz)	110	2.0	<1.0	40	375
Libby's Salmon, Keta or Pink (3.7 oz)	130	6.0	2.0	40	450
Libby's Salmon, Skinless and Boneless (3.25 oz)	120	4.0	1.0	50	420
Libby's Salmon, Sockeye Red (3.7 oz)	150	7.0	2.0	40	340
Mackerel, drained solids—Most Brands (3 oz)	132	5.4	1.5	67	322
Salmon, Chum, drained solids with bone—Most Brands (3 oz)	120	4.7	1.3	33	414
Salmon, Pink, solids with bone and liquid—Most Brands (3 oz)	118	5.1	1.3	(37)	471
Salmon, Sockeye, drained, solids with bone—Most Brands (3 oz)	130	6.2	1.4	37	458
Sea Trader Chunk Light Tuna in Water (3-1/4 oz)	110	2.0	(0.6)	(16)	(328)
Sea Trader White Albacore Tuna in Water (2 oz)	100	5.0	(1.6)	(17)	310
Tuna, Light, in oil, drained solids—Most Brands (3 oz)	169	7.0	1.3	15	301
Tuna, Light, in water, drained solids—Most Brands (3 oz)	111	0.4	0.1	(20)	303
Tuna, White, in oil, drained solids—Most Brands (3 oz)	158	6.9	1.3	26	336
Tuna, White, in water, drained solids—Most Brands (3 oz)	116	2.1	0.6	35	333
Underwood Herring Steaks in Picante Sauce (3.5 oz)	130	6.0	(1.3)	(76)	510
FINFISH, FRESH AND FROZEN					
Bass, Freshwater, cooked, dry heat—USDA Data (3 oz)	124	4.0	0.9	74	87
Captain's Choice Fillets, Cod (3 oz)	89	1.0	(0.2)	47	66
Captain's Choice Fillets, Flounder (3 oz)	99	1.0	(0.2)	58	89

Fish (continued)	Calories	Fat g	Saturated Fat g	Choles-terol mg	Sodium mg
Captain's Choice Fillets, Haddock (3 oz)	95	1.0	(0.2)	63	74
Captain's Choice Fillets, Mahi Mahi (3 oz)	73	1.0	(0.2)	62	74
Captain's Choice Fillets, Perch (3 oz)	103	2.0	(0.3)	46	82
Captain's Choice Fillets, Sole (3 oz)	99	1.0	(0.2)	58	89
Captain's Choice Steaks, Halibut (3 oz)	119	2.0	(0.3)	35	59
Captain's Choice Steaks, Swordfish (3 oz)	132	4.0	(1.1)	43	98
Cod, Atlantic, cooked, dry heat—USDA Data (3 oz)	89	0.7	0.1	47	66
Cod, Pacific, cooked, dry heat—USDA Data (3 oz)	89	0.7	0.1	40	77
Flounder, cooked, dry heat—USDA Data (3 oz)	99	1.3	0.3	58	89
Giant Fillets, Mackerel (3 oz)	150	8.0	2.0	60	310
Grouper, cooked, dry heat—USDA Data (3 oz)	100	1.1	0.3	40	45
Haddock, cooked, dry heat—USDA Data (3 oz)	95	0.8	0.1	63	74
Halibut, cooked, dry heat—USDA Data (3 oz)	119	2.5	0.4	35	59
Newfoundland Imperial Fillets, Cod (4 oz)	90	0.0	0.0	(49)	80
Ocean Perch, cooked, dry heat—USDA Data (3 oz)	103	1.8	0.3	46	82
Orange Roughy, cooked, dry heat—USDA Data (3 oz)	75	0.8	0.0	22	69
Perch, cooked, dry heat—USDA Data (3 oz)	99	1.0	0.2	98	67
Pike, Northern, cooked, dry heat—USDA Data (3 oz)	96	0.8	0.1	43	42
Pollack, Walleye, cooked, dry heat—USDA Data (3 oz)	96	1.0	0.2	82	98
Redfish (see Ocean Perch)					
Rockfish, cooked, dry heat—USDA Data (3 oz)	103	1.7	0.4	38	65
Salmon, Atlantic, cooked, dry heat—USDA Data (3 oz)	155	6.9	1.1	60	48
Salmon, Chinook, smoked—USDA Data (3 oz)	99	3.7	0.8	20	666

Fish (continued)	Calories	Fat g	Saturated Fat g	Choles-terol mg	Sodium mg
Salmon, Chum, cooked, dry heat—USDA Data (3 oz)	131	4.1	0.9	81	54
Salmon, Coho, cooked, moist heat—USDA Data (3 oz)	157	6.4	1.2	42	50
Salmon, Pink, cooked, dry heat—USDA Data (3 oz)	127	3.8	0.6	57	73
Scrod (see Cod, Atlantic)					
Sea Bass, cooked, dry heat—USDA Data (3 oz)	105	2.2	0.6	45	74
Snapper, cooked, dry heat—USDA Data (3 oz)	109	1.5	0.3	40	48
Sole (see Flounder)					
Swordfish, cooked, dry heat—USDA Data (3 oz)	132	4.4	1.2	43	98
Trout, Rainbow, cooked, dry heat—USDA Data (3 oz)	129	3.7	0.7	62	29
Tuna, Bluefish, fresh, cooked, dry heat—USDA Data (3 oz)	157	5.3	1.4	42	43
Tuna, Yellowfin, fresh, cooked, dry heat—USDA Data (3 oz)	118	1.0	0.3	49	40
Van de Kamp's Natural Fillets, Cod (4 oz)	90	1.0	0.0	25	90
Van de Kamp's Natural Fillets, Flounder (4 oz)	100	2.0	0.0	35	100
Van de Kamp's Natural Fillets, Haddock (4 oz)	90	1.0	0.0	20	125
Van de Kamp's Natural Fillets, Ocean Perch (4 oz)	130	5.0	2.0	40	65
Van de Kamp's Natural Fillets, Sole (4 oz)	100	2.0	1.0	35	105
Whitefish, Smoked—USDA Data (3 oz)	92	0.8	0.2	28	866
Whiting, cooked, dry heat—USDA Data (3 oz)	98	1.4	0.3	71	113
SHELLFISH, CANNED					
Clams, drained solids—Most Brands (3 oz)	126	1.7	0.2	57	95
Crab, Blue—Most Brands (3 oz)	84	1.0	0.2	76	283
Giant Clams, chopped (3 oz)	70	<1.0	<1.0	15	290
Oyster, Eastern—Most Brands (3 oz)	58	2.1	0.5	46	95

Fish (continued)	Calories	Fat g	Saturated Fat g	Choles- terol mg	Sodium mg
SHELLFISH, FRESH AND FROZEN					
Captain Jac Imitation Crab (3 oz)	70	<1.0	0.0	15	700
Captain Jac Imitation Lobster (4 oz)	100	<1.0	0.0	16	670
Captain Jac Imitation Shrimp (1 oz)	30	<1.0	0.0	5	230
Clam, Cooked, moist heat—USDA Data (3 oz)	126	1.8	0.3	57	96
Crab, Alaska King, Imitation, made from surimi—USDA Data (3 oz)	87	1.1	(0.2)	17	715
Crab, Alaska King, cooked, moist heat—USDA Data (3 oz)	82	1.3	0.1	45	911
CrabTasties Choice with Crab Meat (2 oz)	50	0.0	0.0	10	400
CrabTasties Premium with Crab Meat and Crab Extract (2 oz)	50	0.0	0.0	10	400
CrabTasties Select with Natural Crab Flavor (2 oz)	50	0.0	0.0	2	400
Lobster, Northern, cooked, moist heat—USDA Data (3 oz)	83	0.5	0.1	61	323
Mrs. Paul's Prepared Seafood, Fried Scallops (3 oz)	160	7.0	(1.4)	10	320
Octopus, Common, cooked, moist heat—USDA Data (3 oz)	140	1.8	0.4	82	(50)
Scallops, Imitation, made from surimi—USDA Data (3 oz)	84	0.4	0.1	18	676
Shrimp, Imitation, made from surimi—USDA Data (3 oz)	86	1.3	0.3	31	599
GAME, FRESH					
Beefalo, cooked, roasted— USDA Data (3 oz)	160	5.4	2.3	49	70
Deer, cooked, roasted— USDA Data (3 oz)	134	2.7	1.1	95	46
Elk, cooked, roasted—USDA Data (3 oz)	124	1.6	0.6	62	52

Game (continued)	Calories	Fat g	Saturated Fat g	Choles- terol mg	Sodium mg
Goat, cooked, roasted— USDA Data (3 oz)	122	2.6	0.8	64	73
Horse, cooked, roasted— USDA Data (3 oz)	149	5.1	1.6	58	47
Moose, cooked, roasted— USDA Data (3 oz)	114	0.8	0.3	66	58
Rabbit, Domesticated, cooked, stewed—USDA Data (3 oz)	175	7.2	2.1	73	31
Squirrel, cooked, roasted— USDA Data (3 oz)	116	3.1	0.4	80	80
Waterbuffalo, cooked, roasted—USDA Data (3 oz)	111	1.5	0.5	52	48
LAMB, FRESH					
Lamb, average, all grades, lean only, cooked—USDA Data (3 oz)	175	8.1	2.9	78	64
Lamb Loin Chops, lean only, broiled—USDA Data (3 oz)	183	8.3	3.0	80	71
Lamb, Cubed for Stew or Kabob (leg and shoulder), lean only, cooked, broiled—USDA Data (3 oz)	158	6.2	2.2	77	65
Lamb, Leg, Shank Half, lean only, choice, cooked, roasted—USDA Data (3 oz)	153	5.7	2.0	74	56
Lamb, Loin, lean only, choice, cooked, broiled—USDA Data (3 oz)	183	8.3	3.0	80	71
Lamb, Loin, lean only, choice, cooked, roasted—USDA Data (3 oz)	171	8.3	3.2	74	56
Lamb, Shoulder, Arm, lean only, choice, cooked, broiled—USDA Data (3 oz)	170	7.7	2.9	78	70
Lamb, Shoulder, Arm, lean only, choice, cooked, roasted—USDA Data (3 oz)	163	7.9	3.1	73	57
PORK, FRESH AND CURED					
Canadian Bacon, grilled—USDA Data (3 oz)	157	7.2	2.4	49	1316
Fresh Pork, Boneless Loin Chops, lean only, broiled—USDA Data (3 oz)	165	6.6	2.3	68	n/a

Pork (continued)	Calories	Fat g	Saturated Fat g	Choles-terol mg	Sodium mg
Fresh Pork, Boneless Loin Roasts, lean only, roasted—USDA Data (3 oz)	160	6.4	2.4	66	n/a
Fresh Pork, Boneless Sirloin Chops, lean and fat, roasted—USDA Data (3 oz)	171	7.5	2.6	79	n/a
Fresh Pork, Boneless Sirloin Chops, lean only, roasted—USDA Data (3 oz)	156	5.7	1.9	78	n/a
Fresh Pork, Loin Chops, lean only, broiled—USDA Data (3 oz)	165	6.9	2.5	70	n/a
Ham, Boneless, extra lean, canned, roasted—USDA Data (3 oz)	116	4.1	1.4	25	966
Ham, Boneless, extra lean, roasted—USDA Data (3 oz)	123	4.7	1.5	45	1023
Jones Canadian Bacon (1/2 oz = 1 slice)	30	1.0	(0.3)	7	160
Jones Family Ham (1 oz = 1 slice)	40	1.5	(0.5)	14	290
Jones Ham Slices (.8 oz = 1 slice)	30	1.0	(0.3)	21	200
Oscar Mayer Boneless Jubilee Ham (1 oz)	43	2.4	0.8	15	365
Oscar Mayer Breakfast Ham (1.5 oz = 1 slice)	47	1.5	0.6	21	582
Oscar Mayer Canadian Style Bacon (.8 oz = 1 slice)	28	1.0	0.3	11	305
Oscar Mayer Jubilee Canned Ham (1 oz)	29	0.9	0.4	14	287
Oscar Mayer Jubilee Ham Slice (1 oz)	29	1.1	0.4	14	335
Oscar Mayer Jubilee Ham Steaks (2 oz = 1 slice)	57	1.9	0.7	31	754

PROCESSED/ LUNCHEON MEAT

BEEF

Carl Buddig Beef (1 oz)	40	2.0	1.0	20	430
Carl Buddig Corned Beef (1 oz)	40	2.0	1.0	20	380
Carl Buddig Pastrami (1 oz)	40	2.0	1.0	20	320

Processed/Luncheon Meat (continued)	Calories	Fat g	Saturated Fat g	Choles- terol mg	Sodium mg
Eckrich Lean Slender Sliced, Beef, chopped, formed, and cured (1 oz)	50	3.0	(1.2)	(12)	300
Eckrich Lean Slender Sliced, Corned Beef, chopped, formed, and smoked (1 oz)	40	1.0	(0.4)	(12)	290
Food Club Lean Beef (1 oz)	40	2.0	(0.8)	(12)	390
Food Club Lean Corned Beef (1 oz)	40	2.0	(0.8)	(12)	350
Food Club Lean Pastrami (1 oz)	40	2.0	(0.8)	(12)	350
Hillshire Farm Deli Select, Roasted Cured Beef (1/3 oz = 1 slice)	10	<1.0	(tr)	5	100
IGA Beef, Sliced (1 oz)	40	2.0	(0.8)	(12)	(470)
IGA Corned Beef, Sliced (1 oz)	40	2.0	(0.8)	(20)	(375)
IGA Pastrami, Sliced (1 oz)	40	2.0	(0.8)	(20)	(360)
Klement's Deli Lean Cooked Beef (1 oz)	40	0.9	(0.5)	20	370
Klement's Deli Lean Cooked Corned Beef (1 oz)	40	0.9	(0.4)	20	370
Klement's Deli Lean Italian Beef (1 oz)	40	0.9	(0.4)	20	370
Klement's Deli Lean Jellied Beef (1 oz)	29	0.6	(0.2)	20	370
Klement's Deli Lean Pastrami (1 oz)	40	0.9	(0.4)	20	370
Land O' Frost Beef, thin sliced, chopped, pressed (1 oz)	40	2.0	(0.8)	(12)	(450)
Oscar Mayer Corned Beef (.6 oz = 1 slice)	17	0.3	0.2	8	204
Oscar Mayer Pastrami (.6 oz = 1 slice)	16	0.3	0.2	7	217
Oscar Mayer Roast Beef, thin sliced (.4 oz = 1 slice)	14	0.4	0.2	5	55
Oscar Mayer Smoked Beef (1/2 oz = 1 slice)	14	0.3	0.1	7	173
Peter Eckrich Deli Lite Roast Beef, Extra Lean, 97% Fat Free (1 oz)	25	1.0	(0.4)	(12)	370

Processed/Luncheon Meat (continued)	Calories	Fat g	Saturated Fat g	Choles-terol mg	Sodium mg
Peter Eckrich Deli Lite Roast Beef, Lean, 94% Fat Free (1 oz)	40	2.0	(0.8)	(12)	220
Ralph's Sliced Beef, chopped and pressed (1 oz)	40	2.0	(0.8)	(12)	430
Weight Watchers 98% Fat Free Oven Roasted Cured Beef (1/3 oz = 1 slice)	10	< 1.0	(0.0)	5	85
World's Fare Lite n' Low Meats, Roast Beef (1 oz)	30	1.0	(0.4)	5	220
BEEF AND PORK					
IGA New England Brand Loaf (1 oz)	46	1.9	(0.6)	14	(350)
Klement's Deli Lean Honey Loaf (1 oz)	39	1.7	(0.5)	17	370
Klement's Deli Lean Yachtwurst (1 oz)	38	2.3	(0.7)	17	370
Oscar Mayer Bar-B-Q Loaf (1 oz = 1 slice)	46	2.3	1.0	14	333
Oscar Mayer Honey Loaf (1 oz = 1 slice)	34	1.0	0.4	16	378
Oscar Mayer New England Brand Sausage (.8 oz = 1 slice)	29	1.3	0.6	14	291
Oscar Mayer Peppered Loaf (1 oz = 1 slice)	39	1.5	0.8	14	367
CHICKEN					
Butterball Chicken Breast (1 oz)	30	1.0	(0.3)	(16)	210
Butterball Fresh from the Deli, Smoked Chicken Breast (.3 oz = 1 slice)	10	< 1.0	(0.0)	(5)	70
Chicken Roll, light—USDA Data (3 oz)	135	6.3*	1.7	42	497
Eckrich Lean Slender Sliced, Chicken, smoked (1 oz)	40	2.0	(0.6)	(15)	290
Eckrich Lite Smoked Chicken Breast (1 oz = 1 slice)	30	1.0	(0.4)	(14)	230
Hillshire Farm Deli Select, Oven Roasted Chicken Breast (1/3 oz = 1 slice)	10	< 1.0	(tr)	5	100
Hillshire Farm Deli Select, Smoked Chicken Breast (1/3 oz = 1 slice)	10	< 1.0	(tr)	5	100

*The value printed for fat is higher than the cutoff point because the manufacturer's serving size is larger than the standard serving size used in evaluating the food.

Processed/Luncheon Meat (continued)	Calories	Fat g	Saturated Fat g	Choles-terol mg	Sodium mg
Klement's Deli Lean Chicken Breast (1 oz)	42	2.3	(0.6)	18	200
Land O Frost Chicken Breast (1 oz)	30	<1.0	(0.0)	(14)	(300)
Louis Rich Chicken Breast, Deluxe Oven Roasted (1 oz)	30	0.8	0.3	14	332
Louis Rich Chicken Breast, Hickory Smoked (1 oz)	30	0.8	0.3	14	356
Louis Rich Chicken Breast, Oven Roasted, Thin Sliced (.4 oz = 1 slice)	12	0.3	0.1	6	130
Louis Rich White Chicken, Oven Roasted (1 oz = 1 slice)	35	1.7	0.5	16	301
Oscar Mayer Chicken Breast, Oven Roasted (1 oz = 1 slice)	29	0.7	0.2	15	414
Oscar Mayer Chicken Breast, Roast, Thin Sliced (.4 oz = 1 slice)	13	0.4	0.1	5	151
Oscar Mayer Chicken Breast, Smoked (1 oz = 1 slice)	25	0.2	0.1	15	397
Weight Watchers 97% Fat Free Roasted & Smoked Chicken Breast (3/4 oz = 1 slice)	25	1.0	(0.3)	15	220
PORK					
Bryan Cooked Ham, Lower Salt (1 oz = 1 slice)	30	1.0	(0.3)	(13)	300
Bryan Honey Ham (1 oz = 1 slice)	35	1.0	(0.3)	(13)	(350)
Bryan Smoked Ham, Mesquite (1 oz = 1 slice)	30	1.0	(0.3)	(13)	(350)
Carl Buddig Ham (1 oz)	50	3.0	1.0	20	400
Danola Ham, Lower Salt (.8 oz = 1 slice)	25	<1.0	(0.0)	15	330
Eckrich Chopped Ham (1 oz = 1 slice)	35	2.0	(0.6)	(13)	350
Eckrich Cooked Ham (1 oz = 1 slice)	25	1.0	(0.3)	(13)	380
Eckrich Lean 'N Fresh, Cooked Ham (.3 oz = 1 slice)	10	<1.0	(0.0)	5	100
Eckrich Lean 'N Fresh, Smoked Ham (.3 oz = 1 slice)	10	<1.0	(0.0)	5	100

Processed/Luncheon Meat (continued)	Calories	Fat g	Saturated Fat g	Choles- terol mg	Sodium mg
Eckrich Lean Slender Sliced, Smoked Ham, chopped and formed (1 oz)	40	2.0	(0.7)	(13)	400
Farmland Deli Cooked Ham (3/4 oz = 1 slice)	20	1.0	(0.3)	(13)	200
Food Club Lean Ham (1 oz)	50	3.0	(1.0)	(13)	400
Giant Ham, Imported, sliced (1 oz)	25	1.0	(0.3)	15	370
Giant Ham, Smoked, sliced (1 oz)	30	2.0	(0.6)	15	250
Hafnia Cooked Ham (1 oz)	30	1.0	(0.3)	15	380
Hafnia Cooked Ham, Lower Salt (1 oz)	25	1.0	(0.3)	15	240
Hillshire Farm Deli Select, Baked Ham (1/3 oz = 1 slice)	10	< 1.0	(tr)	5	110
Hillshire Farm Deli Select, Cajun Style Ham (1/3 oz = 1 slice)	10	< 1.0	(tr)	5	110
Hillshire Farm Deli Select, Honey Ham (1/3 oz = 1 slice)	10	< 1.0	(tr)	5	90
Hillshire Farm Deli Select, Smoked Ham (1/3 oz = 1 slice)	10	< 1.0	(tr)	5	110
IGA Ham, Sliced (1 oz)	50	3.0	(1.0)	(20)	(400)
Jesse Jones Cooked Ham (1 oz = 1 slice)	30	1.0	(0.3)	(15)	120
Klement's Deli Lean Canadian Bacon (1 oz)	42	0.9	(0.3)	19	370
Klement's Deli Lean Cooked Ham (1 oz)	38	1.4	(0.6)	19	370
Klement's Deli Lean Honey Cured Ham (1 oz)	38	1.4	(0.5)	19	370
Klement's Deli Lean New England Ham (1 oz)	38	2.3	(0.8)	17	370
Klement's Deli Lean Roast Pork (1 oz)	38	1.4	(0.5)	19	370
Oscar Mayer Baked Cooked Ham (3/4 oz = 1 slice)	21	0.5	0.1	11	238
Oscar Mayer Boiled Ham (3/4 oz = 1 slice)	23	0.7	0.1	12	275
Oscar Mayer Boiled Ham, Thin Sliced (.4 oz = 1 slice)	13	0.4	0.1	7	157
Oscar Mayer Chopped Ham (1 oz = 1 slice)	41	2.3	0.7	14	303

Processed/Luncheon Meat (continued)	Calories	Fat g	Saturated Fat g	Choles- terol mg	Sodium mg
Oscar Mayer Cooked Ham, Smoked (3/4 oz = 1 slice)	22	0.7	0.3	12	266
Oscar Mayer Cracked Black Pepper Ham (3/4 oz = 1 slice)	22	0.7	0.3	11	284
Oscar Mayer Ham, Lower Salt (3/4 oz = 1 slice)	23	0.7	0.3	10	174
Oscar Mayer Honey Ham (3/4 oz = 1 slice)	23	0.6	0.3	12	268
Oscar Mayer Honey Ham, Thin Sliced (.4 oz = 1 slice)	13	0.4	0.2	7	153
Peter Eckrich Deli Lite Ham, 25% Lower Cholesterol and Sodium (1 oz)	30	1.0	(0.3)	12	240
Peter Eckrich Deli Lite Ham, Extra Lean, 96% Fat Free and 25% Less Sodium (1 oz)	31	1.0	(0.3)	(13)	240
Ralph's Imported Cooked Ham (1 oz)	30	1.0	(0.3)	(13)	360
Ralph's Sliced Ham, chopped and pressed (1 oz)	50	3.0	(0.9)	(13)	430
Smok-A-Roma Cooked Ham, 97% Fat Free (1 oz = 1 slice)	30	1.0	(0.3)	(13)	340
Smok-A-Roma Honey Ham, 97% Fat Free (1 oz = 1 slice)	30	1.0	(0.3)	(13)	340
Swift Premium Deli Lite Ham, Extra Lean, 96% Fat Free and 25% Less Sodium (1 oz)	31	1.0	(0.3)	(13)	240
Vons Chopped Ham (1 oz)	40	2.0	(0.7)	(18)	300
Vons Cooked Ham (1 oz)	30	1.0	(0.3)	(13)	300
Weight Watchers 97% Fat Free Oven Roasted Ham (3/4 oz = 1 slice)	12	<1.0	(0.0)	5	95
Weight Watchers 97% Fat Free Oven Roasted Honey Ham (1/3 oz = 1 slice)	12	<1.0	(0.0)	5	95
Weight Watchers 97% Fat Free Premium Cooked Ham (1/3 oz = 1 slice)	25	<1.0	(0.0)	15	220
Wilson Extra Lean Ham (1 oz)	30	1.0	(0.3)	(13)	(400)
World's Fare Lite n' Low Meats, Cooked Ham (1 oz)	35	1.0	(0.3)	20	250
World's Fare Lite n' Low Meats, Honey Cooked Ham (1 oz)	35	1.0	(0.3)	10	260

Processed/Luncheon Meat (continued)	Calories	Fat g	Saturated Fat g	Choles- terol mg	Sodium mg
TURKEY					
Bel Mar Turkey (1 oz = 1 slice)	35	1.0	(0.3)	(12)	240
Bel Mar Turkey Breast (1 oz = 1 slice)	35	1.0	(0.3)	(12)	300
Bel Mar Turkey Ham (1 oz = 1 slice)	30	1.0	(0.3)	(16)	290
Butterball Fresh from the Deli, Honey Roasted Turkey Breast (.3 oz = 1 slice)	10	< 1.0	(0.0)	(4)	70
Butterball Fresh from the Deli, Oven Roasted Turkey Breast (.3 oz = 1 slice)	10	< 1.0	(0.0)	(4)	80
Butterball Fresh from the Deli, Smoked Turkey Breast (.3 oz = 1 slice)	10	< 1.0	(0.0)	(4)	70
Butterball Honey Roasted Turkey Breast (1 slice)	10	< 1.0	(0.0)	(4)	70
Butterball Lite Deli Turkey Breast, Extra Lean, 96% Fat Free and 25% Less Sodium (1 oz)	30	1.0	(0.3)	(12)	150
Butterball Lite Turkey Ham, Extra Lean, 97% Fat Free (1 oz)	30	1.0	(0.3)	(16)	390
Butterball Lite Turkey Pastrami, Extra Lean, 97% Fat Free (1 oz)	35	1.0	(0.3)	(15)	320
Butterball Oven Roasted Turkey Breast (1 slice)	10	< 1.0	(0.0)	(4)	80
Butterball Smoked Turkey Breast (1 slice)	10	< 1.0	(0.0)	(4)	70
Butterball Turkey Breast (1 oz)	30	1.0	(0.3)	(12)	280
Butterball Turkey Breast, Honey Roasted (1 oz = 1 slice)	35	1.0	(0.3)	(12)	230
Butterball Turkey Breast, Oven Roasted (1 oz = 1 slice)	30	1.0	(0.3)	(12)	280
Butterball Turkey Breast, Smoked (1 oz = 1 slice)	30	1.0	(0.3)	(12)	220
Butterball Turkey Ham (1 oz = 1 slice)	35	1.0	(0.3)	(12)	390
Butterball Turkey Ham (1 slice)	10	< 1.0	(0.0)	(4)	120
Carl Buddig Turkey (1 oz)	50	3.0	1.0	15	400

Processed/Luncheon Meat (continued)	Calories	Fat g	Saturated Fat g	Choles-terol mg	Sodium mg
Carl Buddig Turkey Ham (1 oz)	40	2.0	1.0	15	430
Eckrich Lean 'N Fresh, Oven Roasted Turkey Breast (.3 oz = 1 slice)	10	<1.0	(0.0)	(4)	80
Eckrich Lean 'N Fresh, Smoked Turkey Breast (.3 oz = 1 slice)	10	<1.0	(0.0)	(4)	70
Eckrich Lean Slender Sliced, White Turkey, smoked (1 oz)	45	2.0	(0.6)	(12)	300
Eckrich Lite Oven Roasted Turkey Breast (1 oz = 1 slice)	30	1.0	(0.3)	(12)	(300)
Eckrich Lite Smoked Turkey Breast (1 oz = 1 slice)	30	1.0	(0.3)	(12)	(300)
Food Club Turkey (1 oz)	50	3.0	(0.9)	(12)	430
Hillshire Farm Deli Select, Honey Roasted Turkey Breast (1/3 oz = 1 slice)	10	<1.0	(tr)	5	100
Hillshire Farm Deli Select, Oven Roasted Turkey Breast (1/3 oz = 1 slice)	10	<1.0	(tr)	5	100
Hillshire Farm Deli Select, Smoked Turkey Breast (.33 oz = 1 slice)	10	<1.0	(<1.0)	5	100
Hillshire Farm Deli Select, Turkey Ham (1/3 oz = 1 slice)	10	<1.0	(tr)	5	100
IGA Turkey, Sliced (1 oz)	50	3.0	(1.0)	20	(420)
Klement's Deli Lean Turkey Breast (1 oz)	29	0.6	(0.2)	22	261
Land O Frost Turkey Breast (1 oz)	30	<1.0	(0.0)	(12)	(400)
Land O' Frost Turkey Ham, thin sliced, chopped, pressed (1 oz)	50	3.0	(1.0)	(16)	(280)
Louis Rich Deli-Thin, Hickory Smoked Turkey Breast (11 g = 1 slice)	10	<1.0	(tr)	5	120
Louis Rich Deli-Thin, Oven Roasted Turkey Breast (11 g = 1 slice)	12	<1.0	(tr)	5	130
Louis Rich Deli-Thin, Smoked Turkey Ham (11 g = 1 slice)	12	<1.0	(tr)	10	130
Louis Rich Smoked Turkey (1 oz = 1 slice)	32	1.0	0.4	14	284

Processed/Luncheon Meat (continued)	Calories	Fat g	Saturated Fat g	Choles- terol mg	Sodium mg
Louis Rich Turkey Breast, Honey Roasted (1 oz = 1 slice)	32	0.8	0.3	11	315
Louis Rich Turkey Breast, Oven Roasted (1 oz)	31	0.8	0.3	11	323
Louis Rich Turkey Breast, Oven Roasted, Thin Sliced (.4 oz = 1 slice)	12	0.3	0.1	4	127
Louis Rich Turkey Breast, Smoked (3/4 oz = 1 slice)	21	0.3	0.1	9	211
Louis Rich Turkey Breast, Smoked, Thin Sliced (.4 oz = 1 slice)	11	0.1	tr	5	111
Louis Rich Turkey Ham (1 oz)	33	1.4	0.4	19	294
Louis Rich Turkey Ham (round) (1 oz = 1 slice)	34	1.2	0.5	19	300
Louis Rich Turkey Ham (square) (3/4 oz = 1 slice)	24	0.7	0.3	14	213
Louis Rich Turkey Ham, Chopped (1 oz = 1 slice)	46	2.8	0.7	19	289
Louis Rich Turkey Ham, Honey Cured (1 oz)	25	0.7	0.2	14	217
Louis Rich Turkey Ham, Thin Sliced (.4 oz = 1 slice)	12	0.4	0.1	7	111
Louis Rich Turkey Luncheon Loaf (1 oz = 1 slice)	45	2.8	0.8	16	270
Louis Rich Turkey Pastrami (1 oz = 1 slice)	32	1.1	0.4	18	288
Louis Rich Turkey Pastrami (square) (.8 oz = 1 slice)	24	0.7	0.1	14	262
Louis Rich Turkey Pastrami, Thin Sliced (.4 oz = 1 slice)	11	0.4	0.2	7	125
Oscar Mayer Turkey Breast, Oven Roasted (3/4 oz = 1 slice)	23	0.5	0.1	9	290
Oscar Mayer Turkey Breast, Roast, Thin Sliced (.4 oz = 1 slice)	12	0.2	0.1	5	151
Oscar Mayer Turkey Breast, Smoked (3/4 oz = 1 slice)	20	0.2	0.1	9	300
Ralph's Sliced Turkey, chopped and pressed (1 oz)	50	3.0	(0.9)	(12)	430
Smok-A-Roma Turkey Breast (1 oz = 1 slice)	30	1.0	(0.3)	(12)	280

Processed/Luncheon Meat (continued)	Calories	Fat g	Saturated Fat g	Choles-terol mg	Sodium mg
Thorn Apple Valley Turkey Breast, sliced (1 slice)	25	1.0	(0.3)	(12)	270
Turkey Pastrami—Most Brands (1 oz)	40	1.8	0.5	15	297
Turkey, Roll, light and dark meat—Most Brands (3 oz)	126	5.9*	1.7	47	498
Vons Turkey Breast (1 oz)	30	1.0	(0.3)	(12)	300
World's Fare Lite n' Low Meats, Turkey Breast (1 oz)	25	1.0	(0.3)	10	230

SAUSAGE AND HOT DOGS

	Calories	Fat g	Saturated Fat g	Choles-terol mg	Sodium mg
Armour 90% Fat Free Hot Dogs, 33% Less Salt (1.6 oz)	80	5.0*	(2.0)	30	410
Fairbank Farms Tender-Lite Low Fat Breakfast Sausage (2 oz)	70	4.0	2.0	33	300
Fairbank Farms Tender-Lite Low Fat Italian Sausage (4 oz)	157	8.0	4.0	65	830
Hormel Light & Lean 97% Fat Free Franks (1.6 oz = 1 frank)	45	1.0	(< 1.0)	10	350
Hormel Light and Lean 90% Fat Free Franks (1.6 oz = 1 frank)	70	5.0*	(2.0)	20	510
Hormel Light and Lean Turkey Franks (1.6 oz = 1 frank)	70	4.0*	(1.3)	30	660
Louis Rich Turkey Polska Kielbasa (1 oz)	40	2.2	0.7	19	247
Louis Rich Turkey Smoked Sausage (1 oz)	43	2.4	0.6	19	249
Louis Rich Turkey Smoked Sausage with Cheese (1 oz)	47	2.8	0.8	18	269

MEAT SUBSTITUTES

	Calories	Fat g	Saturated Fat g	Choles-terol mg	Sodium mg
Heartline Meatless Meats, Beef Fillet Style, prep (as directed) (4 oz = 1/4 pkg)	176	7.0	(1.0)	0	480
Heartline Meatless Meats, Chicken Fillet Style, prep (as directed) (4 oz = 1/4 pkg)	176	7.0	(1.0)	0	260
Heartline Meatless Meats, Ground Beef Style, prep (as directed) (4 oz = 1/4 pkg)	176	7.0	(1.0)	0	480

*The value printed for fat is higher than the cutoff point because the manufacturer's serving size is larger than the standard serving size used in evaluating the food.

Meat Substitutes (continued)	Calories	Fat g	Saturated Fat g	Choles- terol mg	Sodium mg
Heartline Meatless Meats, Imitation Canadian Bacon, prep (as directed) (4 oz = 1/4 pkg)	176	7.0	(1.0)	0	260
Heartline Meatless Meats, Italian Sausage Style, prep (as directed) (4 oz = 1/4 pkg)	176	7.0	(1.0)	0	680
Heartline Meatless Meats, Teriyaki Beef Style, prep (as directed) (4 oz = 1/4 pkg)	176	7.0	(1.0)	0	450
Tree of Life Tofu (4 oz)	120	7.0	(0.6)	(0)	15
Worthington Bolono (1-1/3 oz = 2 slices)	60	2.0	0.0	0	390
Worthington Chic-Ketts, baked (3 oz = 1/2 cup)	160	7.0	1.0	0	640
Worthington Choplets (3-1/4 oz = 2 slices)	100	2.0	(0.3)	0	350
Worthington Harvest Bake Lentil Rice Loaf (4 oz = 2-1/2 slices)	190	9.0*	1.0	0	620
Worthington Meatless Beef Style (2.5 oz = 4 slices)	130	6.0	(0.9)	0	750
Worthington Multigrain Cutlets (3-1/4 oz = 2 slices)	90	2.0	(0.3)	0	550
Worthington Tofu Garden Patties (2.5 oz = 1 patty)	90	4.0	1.0	0	260
Worthington Vegetable Skallops, No Salt Added (3 oz = 1/2 cup)	80	1.0	(<1.0)	0	80
Worthington Vegetable Skallops, baked (3 oz = 1/2 cup)	90	2.0	(0.3)	0	430
Worthington Vegetable Steaks (3.2 oz = 2-1/2 pieces)	110	2.0	(0.3)	0	400
Worthington Vegetarian Burger (4 oz = 1/2 cup)	150	4.0	1.0	0	780
Worthington Vegetarian Burger, No Salt Added (4 oz = 1/2 cup)	160	6.0	(0.9)	0	500
Worthington Vegetarian Cutlets (3-1/4 oz = 2 slices)	100	2.0	(0.3)	0	270

*The value printed for fat is higher than the cutoff point because the manufacturer's serving size is larger than the standard serving size used in evaluating the food.

PASTA, RICE, AND OTHER GRAIN PRODUCTS

When cooked without added ingredients, pasta, rice, and other grain products provide very little or no fat, saturated fat, or cholesterol. However, when pasta, rice, or grain dishes have oil, butter, margarine, bacon, bacon fat, cheese, and/or meat fat added, the levels of fat, saturated fat, and cholesterol in them increase.

Servings of the foods included in this section of the Guide do not exceed the cutoff points for fat, saturated fat, and cholesterol shown below. Some packaged products not listed may qualify for the Guide when ingredients containing less fat are substituted for ingredients that are higher in fat (see page 401). Values for many of the foods in this section are given for "most brands."

CUTOFF POINTS FOR PASTA, RICE,
AND OTHER GRAIN PRODUCTS

Fat (grams)	Saturated Fat (grams)	Cholesterol (milligrams)
3	1	10

SERVINGS

Food	Serving Sizes
Pasta:	
Cooked	5 ounces
Dry	2 ounces
Dry, ready-to-eat	1 ounce
Salad (without meat)	5 ounces
Rice:	
Cooked	1 cup
Dry	2 ounces
Other Grain Products, cooked or prepared	1 cup

Refer to pages 402 and 403 for cooked yields of rice and pasta.

The following abbreviations are used in the Food Sections: oz = ounce; fl oz = fluid ounce; pkg = package; pkt = packet; env = envelope; g = gram; prep (w/ . . .) = prepared with; < = less than; and tr = trace.

Pasta	Calories	Fat g	Saturated Fat g	Choles-terol mg	Sodium mg
PASTA					
Acine de Pepe, P&R Acine de Pepe, dry (2 oz)	210	1.0	(0.1)	(0)	0
Acini de Pepe, San Giorgio Acini de Pepe, dry (2 oz)	210	1.0	(0.1)	(0)	0
Alphabets, Giant Pasta, Alphabets, dry (1 oz)	110	< 1.0	< 1.0	0	0
Alphabets, P&R Alphabets, dry (2 oz)	210	1.0	(0.1)	(0)	0
Alphabets, San Giorgio Alphabets, dry (2 oz)	210	1.0	(0.1)	(0)	0
Alphabets, Skinner Alphabets, dry (2 oz)	210	1.0	(0.1)	(0)	0
Buitoni High Protein Pasta, Spinach Linguini or Spinach Shells, dry (2 oz)	210	1.0	0.2	0	20
Buitoni High Protein Pasta, Thin Spaghetti, Spaghetti, Twists, Linguine, Vermicelli, Mostaccioli, Rigatoni, Wagon Wheels or Ziti, dry (2 oz)	210	1.0	0.2	0	10
Buitoni High Protein Pasta, Tricolor Rotelle, dry (2 oz)	210	1.0	0.2	0	5
Capellini, Giant Pasta, Capellini, dry (1 oz)	110	< 1.0	< 1.0	0	0
Capellini, P&R Capellini, dry (2 oz)	210	1.0	(0.1)	(0)	0
Capellini, San Giorgio Capellini, dry (2 oz)	210	1.0	(0.1)	(0)	0
Cappellini, Delmonico Capellini, dry (2 oz)	210	1.0	(0.1)	(0)	0
Chef Boyardee Sharks (pasta shapes in tomato and cheese flavored sauce) (7.5 oz)	160	1.0	(0.4)	(5)	770
Chef Boyardee Tic Tac Toe (pasta shapes in spaghetti sauce with cheese flavor) (7.5 oz)	170	1.0	(0.4)	(5)	950
Ditali, P&R Ditali, dry (2 oz)	210	1.0	(0.1)	(0)	0
Ditalini, P&R Ditalini, dry (2 oz)	210	1.0	(0.1)	(0)	0
Ditalini, San Giorgio Ditalini, dry (2 oz)	210	1.0	(0.1)	(0)	0
Dumplings, Skinner Dumplings, dry (2 oz)	220	1.0	(0.1)	(0)	0

Pasta (continued)	Calories	Fat g	Saturated Fat g	Choles- terol mg	Sodium mg
Elbows, P&R Elbows, Large, dry (2 oz)	210	1.0	(0.1)	(0)	0
Fettuccini, P&R Fettuccini, dry (2 oz)	210	1.0	(0.1)	(0)	0
Fettucini, Skinner Fettucini, dry (2 oz)	220	1.0	(0.1)	(0)	0
Fideo Enrollaclo, Skinner Fideo Enrollaclo, dry (2 oz)	210	1.0	(0.1)	(0)	0
Flakes, San Giorgio Flakes, dry (2 oz)	210	1.0	(0.1)	(0)	0
Food Club Pasta Salad Bowtie, frozen (4 oz)	80	0.0	0.0	(0)	25
Food Club Pasta Salad Rotini, frozen (4 oz)	80	0.0	0.0	(0)	25
Franco-American CircusO's Pasta in Tomato and Cheese Sauce (7-3/8 oz)	170	2.0	(0.7)	(5)	860
Franco-American Spaghetti in Tomato Sauce with Cheese (7-3/8 oz)	180	2.0	(0.7)	(5)	840
Franco-American SpaghettiO's in Tomato and Cheese Sauce (7-1/2 oz)	170	2.0	(0.7)	(5)	860
Franco-American SportyO's in Tomato and Cheese Sauce (7-1/2 oz)	170	2.0	(1.2)	(5)	860
Franco-American TeddyO's in Tomato and Cheese Sauce (7-1/2 oz)	170	2.0	(0.7)	(5)	900
Fusili, San Giorgio Fusili, Cut, dry (2 oz)	210	1.0	(0.1)	(0)	0
Fusilli, P&R Fusilli, Cut, dry (2 oz)	210	1.0	(0.1)	(0)	0
Lasagna, Delmonico Lasagna, dry (2 oz)	210	1.0	(0.1)	(0)	0
Lasagna, IGA Lasagna, dry (2 oz)	210	1.0	(0.1)	0	(5)
Lasagna, P&R Lasagna, Jumbo, dry (2 oz)	210	1.0	(0.1)	(0)	0
Lasagna, San Giorgio Lasagna, Rippled, dry (2 oz)	210	1.0	(0.1)	(0)	0
Lasagna, Skinner Lasagna, dry (2 oz)	220	1.0	(0.1)	(0)	0
Lasagne, Giant Pasta, Lasagna, dry (1 oz)	110	< 1.0	< 1.0	0	0

Pasta (continued)	Calories	Fat g	Saturated Fat g	Choles- terol mg	Sodium mg
Linguini, Giant Pasta, Linguini, fresh (3 oz)	260	1.0	(0.2)	(0)	45
Linguini, P&R Linguini, dry (2 oz)	210	1.0	(0.1)	(0)	0
Linguini, San Giorgio Linguini, dry (2 oz)	210	1.0	(0.1)	(0)	0
Linguini, Skinner Linguini, dry (2 oz)	210	1.0	(0.1)	(0)	0
Macaroni, Elbow, Delmonico Elbow Macaroni, dry (2 oz)	210	1.0	(0.1)	(0)	0
Macaroni, Elbow, Giant Pasta, Elbow Macaroni, dry (1 oz)	110	<1.0	<1.0	0	0
Macaroni, Elbow, P&R Elbow Macaroni, dry (2 oz)	210	1.0	(0.1)	(0)	0
Macaroni, Elbow, San Giorgio Elbow Macaroni, dry (2 oz)	210	1.0	(0.1)	(0)	0
Macaroni, Elbow, Skinner Elbow Macaroni, Jumbo, dry (2 oz)	210	1.0	(0.1)	(0)	0
Macaroni, Elbow, Skinner Elbow Macaroni, Large, dry (2 oz)	210	1.0	(0.1)	(0)	0
Macaroni, Elbow, Skinner Elbow Macaroni, Short, Cut, dry (2 oz)	210	1.0	(0.1)	(0)	0
Macaroni, Salad, Skinner Salad Macaroni, dry (2 oz)	210	1.0	(0.1)	(0)	0
Macaroni, Sea Shell, Skinner Sea Shell Macaroni, dry (2 oz)	210	1.0	(0.1)	(0)	0
Macaroni, Shell, Skinner Shell Macaroni, dry (2 oz)	210	1.0	(0.1)	(0)	0
Macaroni, Vegetable, cooked—Most Brands (1 cup)	171	<1.0	0.0	0	9
Macaroni, Whole-Wheat, cooked—Most Brands (1 cup)	174	1.0	<1.0	0	4
Macaroni, cooked—Most Brands (1 cup)	197	1.0	<1.0	0	1
Manicotti, P&R Manicotti, dry (2 oz)	210	1.0	(0.1)	(0)	0
Manicotti, San Giorgio Manicotti, dry (2 oz)	210	1.0	(0.1)	(0)	0
Manicotti, Skinner Manicotti, dry (2 oz)	220	1.0	(0.1)	(0)	0

Pasta (continued)	Calories	Fat g	Saturated Fat g	Choles- terol mg	Sodium mg
Mostaccioli, Delmonico Mostaccioli, dry (2 oz)	210	1.0	(0.1)	(0)	0
Mostaccioli, Skinner Mostaccioli, dry (2 oz)	210	1.0	(0.1)	(0)	0
Mueller's Lasagna, dry (2 oz)	210	1.3	(0.2)	0	4
Mueller's Spaghetti, Macaroni, and Other Pasta Products (except egg noodles, tricolor twists, and lasagna), dry (2 oz)	210	1.1	(0.2)	0	3
Mueller's Super Shapes, dry (2 oz)	210	1.1	(0.2)	0	3
Mueller's Tri Color Twists, dry (2 oz)	210	1.2	(0.2)	0	10
Noodles, Japanese Soba, cooked—Most Brands (1 cup)	113	<1.0	0.0	0	68
Noodles, Japanese Somen, cooked—Most Brands (1 cup)	230	<1.0	0.0	0	284
Orzo, San Giorgio Orzo, dry (2 oz)	210	1.0	(0.1)	(0)	0
Pasta, Eden Homestyle Organic Pasta, Extra Fine, dry (2 oz)	228	<1.0	(0.0)	0	0
Pasta, Golden Grain Pasta, dry (2 oz)	200	1.0	0.1	0	25
Pastina, Baby, San Giorgio Baby Pastina, dry (2 oz)	210	1.0	(0.1)	(0)	0
Pastina, P&R Pastina, dry (2 oz)	210	1.0	(0.1)	0	0
Perciatelli, P&R Perciatelli, dry (2 oz)	210	1.0	(0.1)	(0)	0
Perciatelli, San Giorgio Perciatelli, dry (2 oz)	210	1.0	(0.1)	(0)	0
Racing Wheels, San Giorgio Racing Wheels, dry (2 oz)	210	1.0	(0.1)	(0)	0
Rainbow Twirls, Giant Pasta, Rainbow Twirls, dry (1 oz)	110	<1.0	<1.0	0	15
Ribbed Angle Cuts, P&R Ribbed Angle Cuts, dry (2 oz)	210	1.0	(0.1)	(0)	0
Ribbons, Eden Homestyle Organic Pasta, Provencal Ribbons, dry (2 oz)	228	<1.0	0.0	0	0
Rigati, San Giorgio Mostaccioli Rigati, dry (2 oz)	210	1.0	(0.1)	(0)	0

Pasta (continued)	Calories	Fat g	Saturated Fat g	Choles- terol mg	Sodium mg
Rigatoni, Delmonico Rigatoni, dry (2 oz)	210	1.0	(0.1)	(0)	0
Rigatoni, Giant Pasta, Rigatoni, dry (1 oz)	110	<1.0	<1.0	0	0
Rigatoni, P&R Rigatoni, Small, dry (2 oz)	210	1.0	(0.1)	(0)	0
Rigatoni, P&R Rigatoni, dry (2 oz)	210	1.0	(0.1)	(0)	0
Rigatoni, San Giorgio Rigatoni, dry (2 oz)	210	1.0	(0.1)	(0)	0
Rigatoni, Skinner Rigatoni, dry (2 oz)	210	1.0	(0.1)	(0)	0
Rings, P&R Rings, dry (2 oz)	210	1.0	(0.1)	(0)	0
Ripplets, Skinner Ripplets, dry (2 oz)	220	1.0	(0.1)	(0)	0
Rosa Marini, P&R Rosa Marini, dry (2 oz)	210	1.0	(0.1)	(0)	0
Rotelle, P&R Rotelle, dry (2 oz)	210	1.0	(0.1)	(0)	0
Rotini, Delmonico Rotini, dry (2 oz)	210	1.0	(0.1)	(0)	0
Rotini, Giant Pasta, Rotini, dry (1 oz)	110	<1.0	<1.0	0	0
Rotini, San Giorgio Rotini, dry (2 oz)	210	1.0	(0.1)	(0)	0
Shells, Delmonico Shells, dry (2 oz)	210	1.0	(0.1)	(0)	0
Shells, Eden Homestyle Organic Pasta, Vegetable Shells, dry (2 oz)	228	<1.0	0.0	0	0
Shells, Jumbo, Delmonico Shells, Jumbo, dry (2 oz)	210	1.0	(0.1)	(0)	0
Shells, Jumbo, P&R Shells, Jumbo, dry (2 oz)	210	1.0	(0.1)	(0)	0
Shells, Jumbo, San Giorgio Shells, Jumbo, dry (2 oz)	210	1.0	(0.1)	(0)	0
Shells, Large, Giant Pasta, Large Shells, dry (1 oz)	110	<1.0	<1.0	0	0
Shells, Large, P&R Shells, Large, dry (2 oz)	210	1.0	(0.1)	(0)	0
Shells, Large, San Giorgio Shells, Large, dry (2 oz)	210	1.0	(0.1)	(0)	0
Shells, Medium, P&R Shells, Medium, dry (2 oz)	210	1.0	(0.1)	(0)	0

Pasta (continued)	Calories	Fat g	Saturated Fat g	Choles- terol mg	Sodium mg
Shells, Medium, San Giorgio Shells, Medium, dry (2 oz)	210	1.0	(0.1)	(0)	0
Shells, Small, P&R Shells, Small, dry (2 oz)	210	1.0	(0.1)	(0)	0
Shells, Small, San Giorgio Shells, Small, dry (2 oz)	210	1.0	(0.1)	(0)	0
Spaghetti, Delmonico Spaghetti, dry (2 oz)	220	1.0	(0.1)	(0)	0
Spaghetti, Elbow, Delmonico Spaghetti, Elbow, dry (2 oz)	210	1.0	(0.1)	(0)	0
Spaghetti, Giant Pasta, Spaghetti, dry (1 oz)	110	<1.0	<1.0	0	0
Spaghetti, Long, Skinner Spaghetti, Long, dry (2 oz)	210	1.0	(0.1)	(0)	0
Spaghetti, plain, cooked—Most Brands (5 oz = 1 cup)	197	0.9	0.1	0	1
Spaghetti, P&R Spaghetti, dry (2 oz)	210	1.0	(0.1)	(0)	0
Spaghetti, San Giorgio Spaghetti, dry (2 oz)	210	1.0	(0.1)	(0)	0
Spaghetti, Skinner Spaghetti, Ready Cut, dry (2 oz)	210	1.0	(0.1)	(0)	0
Spaghetti, Spinach, cooked—Most Brands (1 cup)	183	1.0	0.0	0	20
Spaghetti, Thin P&R Spaghetti, Thin, dry (2 oz)	210	1.0	(0.1)	(0)	0
Spaghetti, Thin, Skinner Spaghetti, Thin Italian Style, dry (2 oz)	210	1.0	(0.1)	(0)	0
Spaghetti, Thin, Skinner Spaghetti, Thin, dry (2 oz)	210	1.0	(0.1)	(0)	0
Spaghetti, Whole-Wheat, cooked—Most Brands (1 cup)	174	1.0	0.0	0	4
Spaghettini, Delmonico Spaghettini, dry (2 oz)	220	1.0	(0.1)	(0)	0
Spaghettini, Giant Pasta, Spaghettini, dry (1 oz)	110	<1.0	<1.0	0	0
Spaghettini, San Giorgio Spaghettini, dry (2 oz)	210	1.0	(0.1)	(0)	0
Spirals, Eden Homestyle Organic Pasta, Vegetable Spirals, dry (2 oz)	212	1.0	0.2	0	0
Spirals, P&R Spirals, dry (2 oz)	210	1.0	(0.1)	(0)	0

Pasta (continued)	Calories	Fat g	Saturated Fat g	Choles- terol mg	Sodium mg
Tree of Life Pasta, all varieties, dry (2 oz)	200	1.0	(0.2)	(0)	50
Tubettini, P&R Tubettini, dry (2 oz)	210	1.0	(0.1)	(0)	0
Tubettini, San Giorgio Tubettini, dry (2 oz)	210	1.0	(0.1)	(0)	0
Twirls, Skinner Twirls, dry (2 oz)	210	1.0	(0.1)	(0)	0
Vermicelli, Delmonico Vermicelli, dry (2 oz)	210	1.0	(0.1)	(0)	0
Vermicelli, IGA Vermicelli, dry (2 oz)	210	1.0	(0.1)	0	(5)
Vermicelli, P&R Vermicelli, dry (2 oz)	210	1.0	(0.1)	(0)	0
Vermicelli, San Giorgio Vermicelli, dry (2 oz)	210	1.0	(0.1)	(0)	0
Vermicelli, Skinner Vermicelli, Twisted, dry (2 oz)	220	1.0	(0.1)	(0)	0
Vermicelli, Skinner Vermicelli, dry (2 oz)	210	1.0	(0.1)	(0)	0
Ziti, Delmonico Ziti, Cut, dry (2 oz)	210	1.0	(0.1)	(0)	0
Ziti, P&R Ziti, Cut, dry (2 oz)	210	1.0	(0.1)	(0)	0
Ziti, San Giorgio Ziti, Cut, dry (2 oz)	210	1.0	(0.1)	(0)	0
RICE AND OTHER GRAIN PRODUCTS					
A&P Rice Mix with Vermicelli, Beef Flavored, prep (according to package) (1/2 cup)	130	1.0	(0.4)	(0)	500
A&P Rice Mix with Vermicelli, Chicken Flavored, prep (according to package) (1/2 cup)	130	1.0	(0.4)	(0)	550
Couscous, cooked—Most Brands (1 cup)	201	<1.0	0.0	0	9
Eden Quinoa, dry (2 oz)	200	4.0	(0.4)	0	<30
Giant Ricelli, Beef, prep (without fat or salt) (1/2 cup)	130	0.0	0.0	0	640
Giant Ricelli, Chicken, prep (without fat or salt) (1/2 cup)	130	0.0	0.0	0	680
Green Giant Rice Originals, Rice Pilaf (1/2 cup)	110	1.0	(<1.0)	2	530

Rice and Other Grain Products (continued)	Calories	Fat g	Saturated Fat g	Choles- terol mg	Sodium mg
Hain 3-Grain Side Dish, Chicken Meatless Style Side Dish (1/2 cup)	100	1.0	(<1.0)	0	390
Hain 3-Grain Side Dish, Herb (1/2 cup)	80	1.0	(<1.0)	0	470
Kashi Breakfast Pilaf, prep (w/water) (2 oz dry = 1/2 cup cooked)	177	1.2	(0.1)	(<1)	5
La Choy Chinese Fried Rice (3/4 cup)	190	1.0	0.1	0	820
Lipton Long Grain and Wild Rice, Mushrooms and Herbs (1/2 cup)	125	0.5	(0.1)	0	325
Lipton Rice and Sauce Mix, Chicken Flavor (1/2 cup)	124	1.1	(0.3)	(0)	469
Minute Boil-in-Bag Rice, prep (without salt or butter) (1/2 cup)	90	0.0	0.0	0	0
Minute Rice, prep (without salt or butter) (2/3 cup)	120	0.0	0.0	0	0
Old El Paso Spanish Rice (1/2 cup)	70	1.0	0.0	0	400
Pritikin Cajun Dinner Mix, prep (w/water only) (1 cup)	170	1.3	0.1	0	14
Pritikin Mexican Dinner Mix, prep (w/water only) (1 cup)	170	1.2	0.1	0	87
Pritikin Oriental Dinner Mix, prep (w/water only) (1 cup)	170	1.2	0.0	0	189
Pritikin Pilaf Brown Rice, prep (w/water) (1/2 cup)	90	0.7	0.0	0	40
Pritikin Spanish Brown Rice, prep (w/water) (1/2 cup)	90	0.7	0.0	0	11
Rice, Brown, Long-Grain, prep (without salt)—Most Brands (1 cup)	216	2.0	0.0	0	9
Rice, White, Long-Grain, prep (without salt)—Most Brands (1 cup)	264	1.0	0.0	0	4
Rice, Wild, prep (without salt)—Most Brands (1 cup)	166	1.0	0.0	0	6

SALAD DRESSINGS AND SANDWICH SPREADS

The foods included in this section of the Guide are low in saturated fat and cholesterol *as purchased* or when *prepared according to package directions.* Regular salad dressings containing unsaturated oil are included in this section of the Guide if they are low in saturated fat and cholesterol. They can be used in limited amounts in the eating patterns on page 45. Other foods that are sources of unsaturated fat are found in the Fats and Oils section of the Guide. A serving of salad dressing and sandwich spread does not exceed the cutoff points for saturated fat and cholesterol listed below.

CUTOFF POINTS FOR SALAD
DRESSINGS AND SANDWICH SPREADS

Fat (grams)	Saturated Fat (grams)	Cholesterol (milligrams)
*	2	10

No cutoff point; since salad dressings are naturally high in fat, the level of saturated fat is used as the cutoff point.

SERVINGS

Food	Serving Sizes
Mayonnaise and Mayonnaise-Type Salad Dressing	1 tablespoon
Salad Dressing	2 tablespoons
Sandwich Spread	1 tablespoon

Mayonnaise and Mayonnaise-Type Dressings. Products labeled "mayonnaise" contain more fat than those labeled "salad dressing." The cholesterol found in mayonnaise is from egg yolk.

Salad Dressing. Salad dressings can be regular (high in fat), low-calorie (usually lower in fat), or oil- or fat-free (containing no fat). Regular dressing is often the primary source of unsaturated fat in a cholesterol-lowering diet; however, the amount needs to be monitored, since it adds to the intake of fat and calories. The following food list includes the amount of fat and saturated fat in various name-brand diet or low-calorie salad dressings.

Salad Dressing Mix. Dry salad dressing mixes should be prepared with an unsaturated oil, such as safflower, corn, olive, canola, or sunflower oil.

The following abbreviations are used in the Food Sections: oz = ounce; fl oz = fluid ounce; pkg = package; pkt = packet; env = envelope; g = gram; prep (w/ . . .) = prepared with; < = less than; and tr = trace.

Salad Dressings	Calories	Fat g	Saturated Fat g	Choles- terol mg	Sodium mg
SALAD DRESSINGS					
BACON					
Henri's Salad Dressing, Bacon 'n Tomato (1 tbsp)	70	6.0	(1.0)	(4)	140
Kraft Salad Dressing, Bacon and Tomato (1 tbsp)	70	7.0	1.0	0	130
BLUE CHEESE					
Barondorf Lite Dressing, Bleu Cheese (1 tbsp)	7	0.0	0.0	(0)	130
Hain No Oil Dry Dressing Mix, Bleu Cheese, prep (as directed) (1 tbsp)	14	1.0	(0.2)	<5	190
Henri's Salad Dressing, Blue Cheese (1 tbsp)	60	5.0	(0.8)	(4)	220
Hidden Valley Ranch Take Heart Salad Dressing, Blue Cheese (1 tbsp)	12	0.0	0.0	0	140
Kraft Free Nonfat Pourable Dressing, Blue Cheese (1 tbsp)	16	0.0	0.0	0	120
Kraft Reduced Calorie Salad Dressing, Roka Blue Cheese (1 tbsp)	16	1.0	1.0	5	280
Kraft Salad Dressing, Chunky Blue Cheese (1 tbsp)	60	6.0	1.0	<5	230
Slim-ette Low Calorie Dressing, Bleu Cheese (1 tbsp)	6	<1.0	(0.0)	(2)	130
Wish-Bone Lite Salad Dressing, Chunky Blue Cheese (1 tbsp)	40	3.7	0.8	1	197
BUTTERMILK					
Hain No Oil Dry Dressing Mix, Buttermilk, prep (as directed) (1 tbsp)	11	<1.0	(0.0)	0	150
Hain Salad Dressing, Old Fashioned Buttermilk (1 tbsp)	70	7.0	(1.0)	0	100
Hollywood Salad Dressing, Old Fashion Buttermilk (1 tbsp)	75	8.0	1.0	0	40
Kraft Salad Dressing, Creamy Buttermilk (1 tbsp)	80	8.0	1.0	<5	120
Nu Made Salad Dressing, Creamy Buttermilk (1 tbsp)	50	5.0	(1.0)	0	135
Seven Seas Salad Dressing, Buttermilk Recipe (1 tbsp)	80	8.0	1.0	5	130

Salad Dressings (continued)	Calories	Fat g	Saturated Fat g	Choles- terol mg	Sodium mg
CAESAR					
Barondorf Lite Dressing, Caesar (1 tbsp)	12	0.0	(0.0)	(1)	130
Hain No Oil Dry Dressing Mix, Caesar, prep (as directed) (1 tbsp)	6	< 1.0	(0.0)	0	200
Hollywood Salad Dressing, Caesar (1 tbsp)	70	7.0	1.0	0	65
Kraft Salad Dressing, Golden Caesar (1 tbsp)	70	7.0	1.0	0	180
Slim-ette Low Calorie Dressing, Caesar (1 tbsp)	6	< 1.0	0.0	(1)	130
Weight Watchers Single Serve Salad Dressing, Caesar (1 pouch)	6	0.0	0.0	(0)	270
CATALINA					
Kraft Free Nonfat Salad Dressing, Catalina (1 tbsp)	16	0.0	0.0	0	120
Kraft Reduced Calorie Salad Dressing, Catalina (1 tbsp)	18	1.0	0.0	0	120
CUCUMBER					
Featherweight Salad Dressing, Creamy Cucumber (1 tbsp)	4	0.0	0.0	0	80
Giant Light Salad Dressing, Cucumber (1 tbsp)	35	3.0	1.0	0	160
Herb Magic Reduced Calorie Dressing, Creamy Cucumber (1 tbsp)	8	0.0	0.0	0	100
Kraft Salad Dressing, Creamy Cucumber (1 tbsp)	70	8.0	1.0	0	190
Slim-ette Low Calorie Dressing, Creamy Cucumber (1 tbsp)	6	1.0	(0.2)	(3)	130
FRENCH					
Barondorf Lite Dressing, French Style (1 tbsp)	6	< 1.0	(0.0)	(0)	130
Featherweight Salad Dressing, French (1 tbsp)	14	0.0	0.0	0	15
Giant Light Salad Dressing, French (1 tbsp)	20	1.0	0.0	0	150
Giant Reduced Calorie Dressing, French (1 tbsp)	10	0.0	0.0	0	140

Salad Dressings (continued)	Calories	Fat g	Saturated Fat g	Choles- terol mg	Sodium mg
Giant Salad Dressing, Country French (1 tbsp)	70	7.0	1.0	5	100
Giant Salad Dressing, Saucy French (1 tbsp)	60	5.0	1.0	0	180
Hain No Oil Dry Dressing Mix, French, prep (as directed) (1 tbsp)	12	0.0	0.0	0	340
Henri's Salad Dressing, Frontier French (1 tbsp)	70	6.0	(1.0)	(4)	95
Henri's Salad Dressing, Hearty French (1 tbsp)	70	6.0	(1.0)	(4)	95
Henri's Salad Dressing, Original French (1 tbsp)	60	6.0	(1.0)	(4)	110
Hidden Valley Ranch Take Heart Salad Dressing, French (1 tbsp)	20	0.0	0.0	0	115
Hollywood Salad Dressing, Creamy French (1 tbsp)	70	7.0	1.0	0	45
IGA Traditional Salad Dressing, French (1 tbsp)	60	5.0	(1.2)	0	(215)
IGA Traditional Salad Dressing, Spicy & Sweet French (1 tbsp)	60	5.0	(1.2)	0	(215)
Kraft Free Nonfat Salad Dressing, French (1 tbsp)	20	0.0	0.0	0	120
Kraft Miracle Salad Dressing, French (1 tbsp)	70	6.0	1.0	0	240
Kraft Reduced Calorie Salad Dressing, French (1 tbsp)	20	1.0	0.0	0	120
Kraft Salad Dressing, Catalina French (1 tbsp)	60	5.0	1.0	0	180
Kraft Salad Dressing, French (1 tbsp)	60	6.0	1.0	0	125
Pritikin Salad Dressing, Sweet & Spicy French Style (1 tbsp)	18	0.1	0.0	0	2
Richard Simmons Salad Spray, French-Style (1 tbsp = 16 spritzes)	14	<1.0	(0.0)	0	130
Seven Seas Light Reduced Calorie Dressing, French! (1 tbsp)	35	3.0	0.0	0	210
Seven Seas Salad Dressing, Creamy French (1 tbsp)	60	6.0	1.0	0	240
Slim-ette Low Calorie Dressing, French Style (1 tbsp)	6	0.0	0.0	0	130

Salad Dressings (continued)	Calories	Fat g	Saturated Fat g	Choles- terol mg	Sodium mg
Walden Farms Reduced Calorie Salad Dressing, French (1 tbsp)	33	2.4	(0.3)	2	132
Western Dressing, French (1 tbsp)	70	5.0	(1.2)	0	105
Western Dressing, Lite French (1 tbsp)	35	1.0	(0.2)	0	125
Wish-Bone Lite Salad Dressing, Red French (1/2 fl oz = 1 tbsp)	17	0.4	(0.0)	0	155
Wish-Bone Lite Salad Dressing, Sweet 'N Spicy French Style (1/2 oz = 1 tbsp)	18	0.5	(0.1)	0	110
Wish-Bone Salad Dressing, Deluxe French Dressing (1 tbsp)	57	5.4	0.8	0	83
Wish-Bone Salad Dressing, Red French (1 tbsp)	64	5.6	0.8	0	170
Wish-Bone Salad Dressing, Sweet 'n Spicy French Dressing (1 tbsp)	61	5.7	0.8	0	156
HERB					
Barondorf Lite Dressing, Bunch Of Herbs (1 tbsp)	6	0.0	0.0	(0)	95
Barondorf Lite Dressing, Dill (1 tbsp)	6	0.0	0.0	(0)	130
Barondorf Lite Dressing, Onion Chive (1 tbsp)	6	0.0	0.0	(0)	130
Hain No Oil Dry Dressing Mix, Herb, prep (as directed) (1 tbsp)	2	0.0	0.0	0	140
Herb Magic Reduced Calorie Dressing, Herb Basket (1 tbsp)	6	0.0	0.0	0	170
Seven Seas Light Reduced Calorie Dressing, Viva Herbs and Spices! (1 tbsp)	30	3.0	0.0	0	200
Seven Seas Salad Dressing, Viva Herb & Spice (1 tbsp)	60	6.0	1.0	0	170
ITALIAN					
Barondorf Lite Dressing, Creamy Italian (1 tbsp)	6	<1.0	(0.0)	0	130
Barondorf Lite Dressing, Italian (1 tbsp)	4	<1.0	(0.0)	0	130

Salad Dressings (continued)	Calories	Fat g	Saturated Fat g	Choles-terol mg	Sodium mg
Bernstein's Light Fantastic Dressing, Cheese and Garlic Italian (1 tbsp)	50	5.0	0.0	0	170
Bernstein's Light Fantastic Dressing, Herb and Garlic Italian (1 tbsp)	60	6.0	0.0	5	140
Bernstein's Light Fantastic Dressing, Italian (1 tbsp)	18	<1.0	0.0	0	150
Bernstein's Light Fantastic Dressing, Restaurant Recipe Italian (1 tbsp)	70	7.0	1.0	0	170
Featherweight Salad Dressing, Italian Cheese (1 tbsp)	20	2.0	(0.3)	0	70
Giant Light Salad Dressing, Italian (1 tbsp)	35	3.0	0.0	0	290
Giant Reduced Calorie Dressing, Italian (1 tbsp)	6	0.0	0.0	0	280
Giant Salad Dressing, Italian with Olive Oil (1 tbsp)	60	7.0	1.0	0	240
Good Seasons Salad Dressing Mix, Lite Cheese Italian, prep (w/vinegar, water, and salad oil) (1 tbsp)	25	3.0	(0.4)	0	135
Good Seasons Salad Dressing Mix, Lite Italian, prep (w/vinegar, water, and salad oil) (1 tbsp)	25	3.0	(0.4)	0	180
Good Seasons Salad Dressing Mix, Lite Zesty Italian, prep (w/vinegar, water, and salad oil) (1 tbsp)	25	3.0	(0.4)	0	135
Good Seasons Salad Dressing Mix, No Oil Italian, prep (w/vinegar and water) (1 tbsp)	6	0.0	0.0	0	30
Hain Canola Oil Salad Dressing, Italian (1 tbsp)	50	5.0	(0.3)	0	150
Hain No Oil Dry Dressing Mix, Italian, prep (as directed) (1 tbsp)	2	0.0	0.0	0	170
Hain Salad Dressing, Traditional Italian Dressing, No Salt Added (1 tbsp)	60	6.0	(0.9)	0	20
Henri's Salad Dressing, Creamy Garlic Italian (1 tbsp)	50	5.0	(0.8)	(4)	150

Salad Dressings (continued)	Calories	Fat g	Saturated Fat g	Choles- terol mg	Sodium mg
Herb Magic Reduced Calorie Dressing, Italian (1 tbsp)	4	0.0	0.0	0	125
Hidden Valley Ranch Take Heart Salad Dressing, Italian (1 tbsp)	16	0.0	0.0	0	140
Hollywood Salad Dressing, Creamy Italian (1 tbsp)	90	9.0	1.0	0	140
Hollywood Salad Dressing, Italian (1 tbsp)	90	9.0	1.0	0	300
Hollywood Salad Dressing, Italian Cheese (1 tbsp)	80	8.0	1.0	0	60
IGA Reduced Calorie Salad Dressing, Italian (1 tbsp)	6	0.0	0.0	0	(120)
IGA Traditional Salad Dressing, Italian (1 tbsp)	45	4.0	(0.6)	0	(115)
Kraft Free Nonfat Salad Dressing, Italian (1 tbsp)	6	0.0	0.0	0	210
Kraft Salad Dressing, Creamy Italian with Real Sour Cream (1 tbsp)	50	5.0	1.0	0	120
Kraft Salad Dressing, House Italian (1 tbsp)	60	6.0	1.0	0	115
Kraft Salad Dressing, Oil-Free Italian (1 tbsp)	4	0.0	0.0	0	220
Kraft Salad Dressing, Presto Italian (1 tbsp)	70	7.0	1.0	0	150
Kraft Salad Dressing, Zesty Italian (1 tbsp)	50	5.0	1.0	0	260
Newman's Own Reduced Calorie Light Salad Dressing, Italian (1 tbsp)	40	4.0	< 1.0	0	150
Newman's Own Salad Dressing, Olive Oil and Vinegar (1 tbsp)	80	9.0	1.0	0	80
Richard Simmons Salad Spray, Italian (1 tbsp = 16 spritzes)	14	< 1.0	(0.0)	0	190
Seven Seas Free Nonfat Dressing, Viva Italian (1 tbsp)	4	0.0	0.0	0	220
Seven Seas Light Reduced Calorie Dressing, Viva Creamy Italian! (1 tbsp)	45	4.0	1.0	0	230
Seven Seas Light Reduced Calorie Dressing, Viva Italian! (1 tbsp)	30	3.0	0.0	0	230

Salad Dressings (continued)	Calories	Fat g	Saturated Fat g	Choles- terol mg	Sodium mg
Seven Seas Salad Dressing, Creamy Italian (1 tbsp)	70	7.0	1.0	0	240
Seven Seas Salad Dressing, Viva Italian (1 tbsp)	50	5.0	1.0	0	240
Slim-ette Low Calorie Dressing, Creamy Italian (1 tbsp)	6	0.0	0.0	(0)	130
Slim-ette Low Calorie Dressing, Italian (1 tbsp)	6	<1.0	0.0	0	130
Walden Farms Reduced Calorie Salad Dressing, Italian (1 tbsp)	9	0.0	0.0	0	300
Walden Farms Reduced Calorie Salad Dressing, No Sugar Added, Italian (1 tbsp)	6	0.0	0.0	0	180
Walden Farms Reduced Calorie Salad Dressing, Sodium Free Italian (1 tbsp)	9	0.0	0.0	0	5
Weight Watchers Salad Dressing, Creamy Italian (1 tbsp)	50	5.0	1.0	5	80
Weight Watchers Single Serve Salad Dressing, Italian Style (1 pouch)	9	0.0	0.0	(0)	430
Western Dressing, Creamy Italian (1 tbsp)	60	5.0	(0.7)	0	135
Western Dressing, Italian (1 tbsp)	60	6.0	(0.9)	0	150
Wish-Bone Lite Salad Dressing, Italian (1/2 oz = 1 tbsp)	7	0.3	(0.0)	0	212
Wish-Bone Salad Dressing, Blended Italian (1 tbsp)	36	3.6	0.5	0	199
Wish-Bone Salad Dressing, Classic Olive Oil Italian (1 tbsp)	33	3.0	0.4	0	190
Wish-Bone Salad Dressing, Creamy Italian (1 tbsp)	54	5.5	0.9	0	149
Wish-Bone Salad Dressing, Italian (1 tbsp)	45	4.5	0.7	0	281
Wish-Bone Salad Dressing, Robusto Italian (1 tbsp)	46	4.5	0.6	0	288
RANCH					
Barondorf Lite Dressing, Ranch (1 tbsp)	12	<1.0	(0.0)	0	130

Salad Dressings (continued)	Calories	Fat g	Saturated Fat g	Choles- terol mg	Sodium mg
Bernstein's Light Fantastic Dressing, Parmesan Garlic Ranch (1 tbsp)	30	2.0	0.0	<5	140
Bernstein's Light Fantastic Dressing, Restaurant Ranch (1 tbsp)	25	2.0	0.0	0	140
Giant Salad Dressing, Garden Ranch (1 tbsp)	90	10.0	1.0	0	130
Giant Salad Dressing, Ranch Style (1 tbsp)	70	6.0	1.0	0	110
Henri's Salad Dressing, Chef's Recipe Ranch (1 tbsp)	70	7.0	(1.0)	(3)	125
Henri's Salad Dressing, Parmesan Ranch (1 tbsp)	70	7.0	(1.0)	(3)	110
Herb Magic Reduced Calorie Dressing, Ranch (1 tbsp)	6	0.0	0.0	0	110
Hidden Valley Ranch Salad Dressing, Original Buttermilk, prep (w/buttermilk and mayonnaise (1 tbsp)	58	3.0	(1.1)	4	110
Hidden Valley Ranch Take Heart Salad Dressing, Original Ranch (1 tbsp)	20	1.0	(<1.0)	0	140
Hollywood Salad Dressing, Poppy Seed Rancher's (1 tbsp)	75	8.0	1.0	0	35
IGA Reduced Calorie Salad Dressing, Creamy Ranch (1 tbsp)	40	4.0	(0.6)	5	(150)
Kraft Free Nonfat Salad Dressing, Ranch (1 tbsp)	16	0.0	0.0	0	150
Kraft Salad Dressing, Creamy Rancher's Choice (1 tbsp)	90	10.0	1.0	5	140
Richard Simmons Salad Spray, Ranch (1 tbsp = 16 spritzes)	17	<1.0	(0.0)	1	190
Seven Seas Free Nonfat Salad Dressing, Ranch (1 tbsp)	16	0.0	0.0	0	12
Seven Seas Light Reduced Calorie Dressing, Buttermilk Recipe Ranch! (1 tbsp)	50	5.0	1.0	0	135
Seven Seas Light Reduced Calorie Dressing, Viva Ranch! (1 tbsp)	50	5.0	1.0	5	125
Seven Seas Salad Dressing, Viva Ranch (1 tbsp)	80	8.0	1.0	5	135

Salad Dressings (continued)	Calories	Fat g	Saturated Fat g	Choles- terol mg	Sodium mg
Weight Watchers Single Serve Salad Dressing, Creamy Ranch (1 pouch)	35	0.0	0.0	(0)	140
Wish-Bone Lite Salad Dressing, Ranch (1 tbsp)	46	4.1	0.6	3	145
RED WINE VINEGAR					
Featherweight Salad Dressing, Red Wine Vinegar (1 tbsp)	6	0.0	0.0	0	100
Kraft Salad Dressing, Red Wine Vinegar and Oil (1 tbsp)	60	4.0	1.0	0	200
Seven Seas Free Nonfat Dressing, Red Wine Vinegar (1 tbsp)	6	0.0	0.0	0	190
Seven Seas Light Reduced Calorie Dressing, Viva Red Wine! Vinegar and Oil (1 tbsp)	45	4.0	1.0	0	190
Seven Seas Salad Dressing, Viva Red Wine Vinegar & Oil (1 tbsp)	70	7.0	1.0	0	290
Wish-Bone Lite Salad Dressing, Red Wine Vinaigrette Olive Oil (1/2 fl oz)	20	1.6	0.2	0	151
RUSSIAN					
Featherweight Salad Dressing, Russian (1 tbsp)	6	0.0	0.0	0	125
Henri's Salad Dressing, Russian (1 tbsp)	60	5.0	(0.8)	(4)	95
Kraft Reduced Calorie Salad Dressing, Russian (1 tbsp)	30	1.0	0.0	0	130
Kraft Salad Dressing, Creamy Russian (1 tbsp)	60	5.0	1.0	5	150
Kraft Salad Dressing, Russian with Pure Honey (1 tbsp)	60	5.0	1.0	0	130
Weight Watchers Salad Dressing, Russian (1 tbsp)	50	5.0	1.0	5	80
Wish-Bone Salad Dressing, Russian (1/2 fl oz = 1 tbsp)	46	2.5	0.4	0	147
THOUSAND ISLAND					
Barondorf Lite Dressing, Thousand Island (1 tbsp)	9	0.0	0.0	(0)	95
Featherweight Salad Dressing, Thousand Island (1 tbsp)	18	0.0	0.0	0	70

Salad Dressings (continued)	Calories	Fat g	Saturated Fat g	Choles- terol mg	Sodium mg
Giant Reduced Calorie Dressing, Thousand Island (1 tbsp)	20	0.0	0.0	0	160
Giant Salad Dressing, Thousand Island (1 tbsp)	70	7.0	1.0	5	120
Hain No Oil Dry Dressing Mix, 1000 Island, prep (as directed) (1 tbsp)	12	0	0.0	<1	150
Hain Salad Dressing, Thousand Island (1 tbsp)	50	5.0	(0.8)	0	85
Henri's Salad Dressing, 1000 Island (1 tbsp)	50	4.0	(0.7)	(4)	120
Herb Magic Reduced Calorie Dressing, Thousand Island (1 tbsp)	8	0.0	0.0	0	45
Hidden Valley Ranch Take Heart Salad Dressing, Thousand Island (1 tbsp)	20	0.0	0.0	0	140
Hollywood Salad Dressing, Thousand Island (1 tbsp)	60	6.0	1.0	5	15
IGA Reduced Calorie Salad Dressing, 1000 Island (1 tbsp)	30	2.0	(0.3)	5	(153)
IGA Salad Dressing, Thick & Rich 1000 Island (1 tbsp)	60	5.0	(0.7)	0	(115)
Kraft Free Nonfat Salad Dressing, Thousand Island (1 tbsp)	20	0.0	0.0	0	135
Kraft Salad Dressing, Thousand Island (1 tbsp)	60	5.0	1.0	5	150
Kraft Salad Dressing, Thousand Island and Bacon (1 tbsp)	60	6.0	1.0	0	100
Nu Made Salad Dressing, Thousand Island (1 tbsp)	60	5.0	(1.0)	5	120
Seven Seas Reduced Calorie Dressing, Thousand Island! (1 tbsp)	30	2.0	0.0	5	160
Seven Seas Salad Dressing, Creamy Thousand Island (1 tbsp)	50	5.0	1.0	5	150
Slim-ette Low Calorie Dressing, Thousand Island (1 tbsp)	6	<1.0	0.0	(2)	130

Salad Dressings (continued)	Calories	Fat g	Saturated Fat g	Choles-terol mg	Sodium mg
Walden Farms Reduced Calorie Salad Dressing, Thousand Island (1 tbsp)	24	1.7	(0.2)	8	132
Weight Watchers Salad Dressing, Thousand Island (1 tbsp)	50	5.0	1.0	5	80
Western Dressing, 1000 Island (1 tbsp)	60	5.0	(0.8)	5	140
VINAIGRETTE					
Barondorf Lite Dressing, Vinaigrette (1 tbsp)	5	<1.0	0.0	(0)	130
Hain Canola Oil Salad Dressing, Garden Tomato Vinaigrette (1 tbsp)	60	6.0	(0.3)	0	150
Hain Salad Dressing, Dijon Vinaigrette (1 tbsp)	50	5.0	(0.8)	<5	180
Hain Salad Dressing, Italian Cheese Vinaigrette (1 tbsp)	55	6.0	(0.9)	<5	130
Hain Salad Dressing, Swiss Cheese Vinaigrette (1 tbsp)	60	7.0	(1.0)	<5	160
Henri's Reduced Calorie Dressings, Light Vinaigrette (1 tbsp)	16	1.0	(0.1)	(2)	70
Herb Magic Reduced Calorie Dressing, Vinaigrette (1 tbsp)	6	0.0	0.0	0	170
Hollywood Salad Dressing, Dijon Vinaigrette (1 tbsp)	60	6.0	1.0	0	40
Kraft Salad Dressing, Oil and Vinegar (1 tbsp)	70	8.0	1.0	0	210
Pritikin Salad Dressing, Herb Vinaigrette (1 tbsp)	8	0.0	0.0	0	1
Richard Simmons Salad Spray, Dijon Vinaigrette (1 tbsp = 16 spritzes)	14	1.0	(0.1)	(0)	160
Wish-Bone Lite Salad Dressing, Classic Dijon Vinaigrette (1 tbsp)	30	2.8	(0.4)	0	176
Wish-Bone Salad Dressing, Classic Dijon Vinaigrette (1 tbsp)	57	5.7	0.8	0	159
Wish-Bone Salad Dressing, Red Wine Olive Oil Vinaigrette (1 tbsp)	34	3.2	0.5	0	191

Salad Dressings (continued)	Calories	Fat g	Saturated Fat g	Choles- terol mg	Sodium mg
OTHER					
Bernstein's Light Fantastic Dressing, Cheese Fantastico (1 tbsp)	14	<1.0	0.0	<5	160
Bernstein's Light Fantastic Dressing, Creamy Dijon (1 tbsp)	20	<1.0	0.0	0	130
Giant Salad Dressing, Celery Seed and Onion (1 tbsp)	70	6.0	1.0	0	95
Giant Salad Dressing, Romano Caesar (1 tbsp)	80	9.0	1.0	0	200
Giant Salad Dressing, Sweet 'n Saucy (1 tbsp)	60	5.0	1.0	0	190
Giant Salad Dressing, Sweet 'n Sour (1 tbsp)	70	7.0	1.0	0	130
Hain Canola Oil Salad Dressing, Spicy French Mustard (1 tbsp)	50	5.0	(0.3)	5	190
Hain Canola Oil Salad Dressing, Tangy Citrus (1 tbsp)	50	5.0	(0.3)	0	75
Hain No Oil Dry Dressing Mix, Garlic and Cheese, prep (as directed) (1 tbsp)	6	<1.0	(0.0)	0	180
Hain Salad Dressing, Honey & Sesame (1 tbsp)	60	5.0	(0.7)	0	210
Henri's Salad Dressing, Tas-Tee (1 tbsp)	60	5.0	(0.7)	(0)	105
Herb Magic Reduced Calorie Dressing, Sweet & Sour (1 tbsp)	18	0.0	0.0	0	80
Herb Magic Reduced Calorie Dressing, Zesty Tomato (1 tbsp)	14	0.0	0.0	0	70
Kraft Salad Dressing, Creamy Garlic (1 tbsp)	50	5.0	1.0	0	170
Maggie Gin's Salad Dressing, Chili and Garlic (1 tbsp)	55	5.6	(0.8)	0	204
Maggie Gin's Salad Dressing, Chinese Chicken (1 tbsp)	66	6.4	(0.9)	0	226
Maggie Gin's Salad Dressing, Peanut and Sesame (1 tbsp)	63	6.7	(1.0)	0	44
Maggie Gin's Salad Dressing, Tofu and Chives (1 tbsp)	70	7.5	(1.1)	0	81

Salad Dressings (continued)	Calories	Fat g	Saturated Fat g	Cholesterol mg	Sodium mg
Richard Simmons Salad Spray, Honey Mustard (1 tbsp = 16 spritzes)	16	<1.0	(0.0)	0	165
Richard Simmons Salad Spray, Oriental (1 tbsp = 16 spritzes)	14	1.0	(0.1)	(0)	130
Richard Simmons Salad Spray, Roma Cheese (1 tbsp = 16 spritzes)	14	<1.0	(0.0)	0	190
Western Dressing, Poppy Seed (1 tbsp)	50	4.0	(0.6)	0	120

SANDWICH SPREADS, MAYONNAISE, AND MAYONNAISE-TYPE DRESSINGS

	Calories	Fat g	Saturated Fat g	Cholesterol mg	Sodium mg
Bama Mayonnaise (1 tbsp)	100	11.0	(1.6)	8	65
Bennett's Real Mayonnaise (1 tbsp)	110	12.0	(1.8)	8	65
Best Food Real Mayonnaise (1 tbsp)	100	11.0	1.7	5	80
Bright Day Cholesterol Free Dressing (1 tbsp)	60	6.0	1.0	0	75
Bright Day Light Cholesterol Free Dressing (1 tbsp)	45	5.0	(1.0)	0	140
Featherweight Mayonnaise, Reduced Calorie (1 tbsp)	30	2.0	(0.3)	0	40
Featherweight Salad Dressing, Low Sodium Soyannaise (1 tbsp)	100	11.0	(1.2)	5	3
Food Club Lite Reduced Calorie Mayonnaise (1 tbsp)	50	5.0	1.0	5	60
Giant Reduced Calorie Mayonnaise (1 tbsp)	50	5.0	1.0	10	110
Giant Regular Mayonnaise (1 tbsp)	110	12.0	2.0	5	110
Giant Salad Dressing (1 tbsp)	70	7.0	1.0	10	90
Hain Mayonnaise, Canola (1 tbsp)	100	11.0	1.0	5	100
Hain Mayonnaise, Canola, Reduced Calorie (1 tbsp)	60	5.0	0.0	0	160
Hain Mayonnaise, Cold-Processed (1 tbsp)	110	12.0	2.0	5	70
Hain Mayonnaise, Eggless, No Salt Added (1 tbsp)	110	12.0	2.0	0	<5

Sandwich Spreads, Mayonnaise, and Mayonnaise-Type Dressings (continued)	Calories	Fat g	Saturated Fat g	Choles- terol mg	Sodium mg
Hain Mayonnaise, Light, Low Sodium (1 tbsp)	60	6.0	1.0	10	95
Hain Mayonnaise, Real, No Salt Added (1 tbsp)	110	12.0	2.0	5	0
Hain Mayonnaise, Safflower (1 tbsp)	110	12.0	1.0	5	70
Hellmann's Real Mayonnaise (1 tbsp)	100	11.0	1.7	5	80
Hellmann's Sandwich Spred (1 tbsp)	55	5.2	0.8	5	170
Hollywood Mayonnaise, Canola (1 tbsp)	100	11.0	1.0	5	100
Hollywood Mayonnaise, Regular (1 tbsp)	110	12.0	1.0	5	80
Hollywood Mayonnaise, Safflower (1 tbsp)	100	12.0	1.0	5	75
IGA Mayonnaise (1 tbsp)	100	11.0	(1.6)	5	(80)
IGA Salad Dressing (1 tbsp)	70	7.0	(1.1)	5	(85)
IGA Sandwich Spread (1 tbsp)	50	5.0	(1.0)	5	(95)
Kraft Free Nonfat Mayonnaise Dressing (1 tbsp)	12	0.0	0.0	0	190
Kraft Miracle Whip Coleslaw Dressing (1 tbsp)	70	6.0	1.0	5	105
Kraft Miracle Whip Free Nonfat Dressing (1 tbsp)	20	0.0	0.0	0	210
Kraft Miracle Whip Salad Dressing (1 tbsp)	70	7.0	1.0	5	85
Kraft Real Mayonnaise (1 tbsp)	100	12.0	2.0	5	70
Nu Made Mayonnaise (1 tbsp)	100	11.0	2.0	10	80
Nucoa Heart Beat Reduced Calorie Cholesterol Free Mayonnaise (1 tbsp)	40	4.0	<1.0	0	110
Piedmont Salad Dressing (1 tbsp)	100	11.0	2.0	10	80
Weight Watchers Fat-Free Mayonnaise Style Dressing (1 tbsp)	12	0.0	0.0	0	125
Weight Watchers Light Reduced Calorie Mayonnaise Alternative (1 tbsp)	50	5.0	1.0	5	100

SINGLE-SERVING ENTRÉES
AND DINNERS

In this Guide, single-serving entrées and dinners are defined as products containing meat, fish, poultry, or cheese that represent either the entrée for a meal or provide the entire meal. Single-serving entrées and dinners included in this section of the Guide are low in fat, saturated fat, and cholesterol *as purchased* or when *prepared according to package directions*. To be included in this Guide, a single-serving entrée or dinner must provide no more fat, saturated fat, and cholesterol than the cutoff points indicated below.

CUTOFF POINTS FOR SINGLE-SERVING
ENTRÉES AND DINNERS

Fat (grams)	Saturated Fat (grams)	Cholesterol (milligrams)
9	3	80

SERVINGS

Food	Serving Sizes
Canned and Shelf-Stable	1 serving as listed by manufacturer
Frozen	1 serving as listed by manufacturer

The following abbreviations are used in the Food Sections: oz = ounce; fl oz = fluid ounce; pkg = package; pkt = packet; env = envelope; g = gram; prep (w/ . . .) = prepared with; < = less than; and tr = trace.

Canned and Shelf-Stable	Calories	Fat g	Saturated Fat g	Choles- terol mg	Sodium mg
CANNED AND SHELF-STABLE					
Chef Boyardee Beef Ravioli (7.5 oz)	210	5.0	(2.5)	(18)	(955)
Chef Boyardee Beefaroni (7.5 oz)	200	6.0	(2.0)	(14)	(950)
Chef Boyardee Mini Ravioli (7.5 oz)	190	4.0	(2.0)	(18)	(955)
Chef Boyardee Sharks (Pasta shapes with mini meatballs and tomato sauce) (7.5 oz)	230	8.0	(2.7)	(19)	(950)
Chef Boyardee Spaghetti and Meat Balls (7.5 oz)	210	8.0	(2.7)	(19)	(950)
Featherweight Entrees, Beef Ravioli (8 oz)	220	4.0	(1.9)	(20)	75
Featherweight Entrees, Beef Stew (7-1/2 oz)	160	3.0	(1.3)	35	400
Featherweight Entrees, Chicken Stew with Wild Rice (7-1/2 oz)	140	1.0	(0.3)	20	400
Featherweight Entrees, Spaghetti and Meatballs (7-1/2 oz)	160	3.0	(0.9)	20	400
Franco-American Beef RavioliO's in Meat Sauce (7-1/2 oz)	250	8.0	(2.7)	(19)	920
Franco-American CircusO's Pasta with Meatballs in Tomato Sauce (7-3/8 oz)	210	8.0	(2.7)	(19)	950
Franco-American Spaghetti with Meatballs in Tomato Sauce (7-3/8 oz)	220	8.0	(2.7)	(19)	870
Franco-American SportyO's Pasta with Meatballs in Tomato Sauce (7-3/8 oz)	210	8.0	(2.7)	(19)	950
Franco-American TeddyO's Pasta with Meatballs (7-3/8 oz)	210	8.0	(2.7)	(19)	950
Giant Spaghetti Twists in Sauce (1 cup)	160	4.0	(0.6)	0	650
Hain Spicy Chili with Chicken (7-1/2 oz)	130	2.0	(0.5)	40	1030
Kraft Spaghetti Dinner, Mild American (1 cup)	300	7.0	2.0	0	630
Kraft Spaghetti Dinner, Tangy Italian Syle (1 cup)	310	8.0	2.0	5	670
La Choy Bi-Pack, Beef Chow Mein (3/4 cup)	70	1.0	0.3	20	840

Canned and Shelf-Stable (continued)	Calories	Fat g	Saturated Fat g	Choles- terol mg	Sodium mg
La Choy Bi-Pack, Beef Pepper (3/4 cup)	80	2.0	0.6	17	950
La Choy Bi-Pack, Chicken Chow Mein (3/4 cup)	80	3.0	0.8	18	970
La Choy Bi-Pack, Chicken Teriyaki (3/4 cup)	85	2.0	0.5	20	850
La Choy Bi-Pack, Pork Chow Mein (3/4 cup)	80	4.0	1.3	14	950
La Choy Bi-Pack, Shrimp Chow Mein (3/4 cup)	70	1.0	0.2	19	860
La Choy Bi-Pack, Sweet and Sour Chicken (3/4 cup)	120	2.0	0.4	13	440
La Choy Dinner Classics, Sweet and Sour, prep (w/skinned chicken breast and oil) (3/4 cup)	310	6.0	1.1	50	860
La Choy Entree, Beef Chow Mein (3/4 cup)	60	1.0	0.4	16	890
La Choy Entree, Chicken Chow Mein (3/4 cup)	70	2.0	0.5	16	800
La Choy Entree, Meatless Chow Mein (3/4 cup)	25	1.0	(0.0)	0	860
La Choy Entree, Sweet and Sour Chicken (3/4 cup)	240	2.0	0.5	19	1420
La Choy Entree, Sweet and Sour Pork (3/4 cup)	250	4.0	1.4	18	1540
La Choy Entrees, Beef Pepper Oriental (3/4 cup)	100	4.0	1.6	9	1340
La Choy Entrees, Shrimp Chow Mein (3/4 cup)	35	1.0	0.3	50	940
Libby's Entree, Beef Stew (7-1/2 oz)	160	5.0	(2.0)	(16)	870
Light Balance, Beef 'n Pasta Bordeaux (8.25 oz)	180	1.0	< 1.0	25	660
Light Balance, Beef Americana (8.25 oz)	170	3.0	1.0	15	700
Light Balance, Chicken Cacciatore (8.25 oz)	200	1.0	< 1.0	25	730
Light Balance, Chicken Fiesta (8.25 oz)	210	3.0	1.0	15	640
Light Balance, Mushroom Stroganoff (8.25 oz)	180	5.0	2.0	15	620
Light Balance, Pasta and Garden Vegetables (8.25 oz)	190	1.0	< 1.0	0	650

Canned and Shelf-Stable (continued)	Calories	Fat g	Saturated Fat g	Choles- terol mg	Sodium mg
Mountain House Main Course Entrees, Chicken Polynesian (1 cup)	210	4.0	(1.1)	(30)	810
Mountain House Main Course Entrees, Chicken Stew (1 cup)	230	8.0	(2.3)	(65)	1200
Mountain House Main Course Entrees, Chili Mac with Beef (1 cup)	220	6.0	(3.0)	(22)	540
Mountain House Main Course Entrees, Green Pepper and Onion Sauce with Beef and Rice (1 cup)	230	7.0	(2.6)	(25)	1200
Mountain House Main Course Entrees, Noodles and Chicken (1 cup)	200	4.0	(1.2)	(68)	970
Mountain House Main Course Entrees, Spaghetti with Meat and Sauce (1 cup)	220	8.0	(2.7)	(21)	940
Mountain House Main Course Entrees, Sweet and Sour Pork with Rice (1 cup)	270	6.0	(1.7)	(12)	730
Mountain House Main Course Entrees, Turkey Tetrazzini (1 cup)	210	8.0	(2.3)	(67)	1150
Mountain House Main Course Entrees, Vegetable Stew with Beef (1 cup)	230	7.0	(2.7)	(23)	580
Old El Paso Chili Con Carne (1 cup)	162	7.0	(2.8)	47	510
Swanson Entrees, Chicken Stew (7-5/8 oz)	160	7.0	(2.0)	(46)	990
Van Camp's Noodlee Weenee (1 cup)	240	8.0	(2.8)	(26)	1250
Van Camp's Spaghettee Weenee (1 cup)	240	7.0	(2.5)	(26)	1130
Worthington Natural Touch Stroganoff Mix, prep (w/water) (4 oz)	90	3.0	(1.9)	(12)	n/a
FROZEN ENTRÉES AND DINNERS					
Armour Classics Lite, Beef Pepper Steak (11.25 oz)	220	4.0	(1.5)	35	970
Armour Classics Lite, Beef Stroganoff (11.25 oz)	250	6.0	(2.3)	55	510
Armour Classics Lite, Chicken Ala King (11.25 oz)	290	7.0	(2.3)	55	630

Frozen Entrées and Dinners (continued)	Calories	Fat g	Saturated Fat g	Choles- terol mg	Sodium mg
Armour Classics Lite, Chicken Burgundy (10 oz)	210	2.0	(0.6)	45	780
Armour Classics Lite, Chicken Marsala (10.5 oz)	250	7.0	(3.2)	80	930
Armour Classics Lite, Chicken Oriental (10 oz)	180	1.0	(0.3)	35	660
Armour Classics Lite, Seafood with Natural Herbs (10 oz)	190	2.0	(0.4)	35	1020
Armour Classics Lite, Shrimp Creole (11.25 oz)	260	2.0	(0.4)	45	900
Armour Classics Lite, Sweet and Sour Chicken (11 oz)	240	2.0	(0.6)	35	820
Armour Classics, Chicken and Noodles (11 oz)	230	7.0	(2.7)	50	660
Armour Classics, Ham Steak (10.75 oz)	270	7.0	(2.4)	50	1320
Armour Classics, Sirloin Roast (10.45 oz)	190	4.0	(2.7)	55	970
Armour Classics, Sirloin Tips (10.25 oz)	230	7.0	(2.7)	70	820
Banquet Cookin' Bags, Barbecue Sauce and Sliced Beef (4 oz)	100	2.0	(0.8)	(6)	260
Banquet Cookin' Bags, Chicken Ala King (4 oz)	110	5.0	(1.4)	(18)	499
Banquet Cookin' Bags, Chicken and Vegetables Primavera (4 oz)	100	2.0	(0.5)	(23)	221
Banquet Cookin' Bags, Creamed Chipped Beef (4 oz)	100	4.0	(2.4)	(21)	624
Banquet Cookin' Bags, Gravy and Sliced Beef (4 oz)	100	5.0	(2.0)	(14)	375
Banquet Family Entrees, Beef Stew (7 oz)	140	5.0	(1.9)	(15)	(930)
Banquet Family Entrees, Chicken and Vegetables Primavera (7 oz)	140	3.0	(0.8)	(39)	(385)
Banquet Family Entrees, Gravy and Sliced Beef (8 oz)	160	5.0	(1.9)	(15)	(900)
Banquet Family Entrees, Mostaccioli and Meat Sauce (7 oz)	170	3.0	(1.1)	(32)	(695)
Banquet Healthy Balance, Chicken Enchilada (10.6 oz)	280	4.0	(1.2)	15	600
Banquet Healthy Balance, Chicken Mesquite (10 oz)	260	5.0	(2.2)	55	770

Frozen Entrées and Dinners (continued)	Calories	Fat g	Saturated Fat g	Choles- terol mg	Sodium mg
Banquet Healthy Balance, Chicken Parmesan (10 oz)	240	6.0	(1.5)	55	770
Banquet Healthy Balance, Homestyle Barbecue (9.8 oz)	270	8.0	(2.3)	35	720
Banquet Healthy Balance, Meat Loaf (10 oz)	240	6.0	(2.4)	30	780
Banquet Healthy Balance, Salisbury Steak (10 oz)	260	8.0	(3.4)	35	730
Banquet Healthy Balance, Sweet & Sour Chicken (10 oz)	260	6.0	(1.6)	45	720
Banquet Healthy Balance, Turkey & Gravy with Dressing (10 oz)	240	6.0	(2.6)	45	710
Banquet Supreme Entrees, Beef Stew (8 oz)	180	5.0	(1.9)	40	1010
Banquet Supreme Entrees, Lasagna with Meat Sauce (8 oz)	190	5.0	(2.4)	30	890
Banquet Supreme Entrees, Macaroni and Beef (8 oz)	210	6.0	(2.0)	25	500
Banquet Supreme Entrees, Mini Ravioli (8 oz)	200	3.0	(1.2)	30	640
Banquet Supreme Entrees, Spaghetti with Meat Sauce (8 oz)	210	6.0	(2.0)	30	950
Budget Gourmet Entrees, Sweet and Sour Chicken (11 oz)	340	5.0	(1.5)	40	630
Budget Gourmet Hearty and Healthy Dinners, Shrimp and Scallops Mariner (13 oz)	320	8.0	2.0	65	730
Budget Gourmet Hearty and Healthy Dinners, Sweet and Sour Chicken (13 oz)	350	5.0	1.0	50	800
Budget Gourmet Light Dinners, Breast of Chicken in Wine Sauce (1 dinner)	250	5.0	(1.3)	40	830
Budget Gourmet Light Dinners, Sliced Turkey Breast with Herb Gravy (1 dinner)	290	8.0	(2.9)	45	1050
Budget Gourmet Light Entrees, Glazed Turkey (9 oz)	270	5.0	(1.8)	40	760
Budget Gourmet Light Entrees, Mandarin Chicken (10 oz)	300	7.0	(1.9)	40	670
Budget Gourmet Light Entrees, Orange Glazed Chicken (9 oz)	250	3.0	(1.1)	10	350
Budget Gourmet Light and Healthy Dinners, Beef Pot Roast (10.5 oz)	230	7.0	(2.8)	60	510

Frozen Entrées and Dinners (continued)	Calories	Fat g	Saturated Fat g	Choles-terol mg	Sodium mg
Budget Gourmet Light and Healthy Dinners, Chicken Breast Parmigiana (11 oz)	260	8.0	(2.2)	50	420
Budget Gourmet Light and Healthy Dinners, Herbed Chicken Breast with Fettucini (11 oz)	240	6.0	(1.7)	45	430
Budget Gourmet Light and Healthy Dinners, Mesquite Chicken Breast (11 oz)	280	5.0	2.0	35	520
Budget Gourmet Light and Healthy Dinners, Sirloin of Beef in Wine Sauce (11 oz)	280	8.0	(3.2)	25	560
Budget Gourmet Light and Healthy Dinners, Stuffed Turkey Breast (11 oz)	250	6.0	(2.2)	35	570
Budget Gourmet Light and Healthy Dinners, Teriyaki Beef (10.75 oz)	270	6.0	1.0	35	520
Budget Gourmet Light and Healthy Entrees, Glazed Turkey (10 oz)	260	5.0	2.0	35	740
Budget Gourmet Light and Healthy Entrees, Mandarin Chicken (10 oz)	300	7.0	2.0	40	670
Budget Gourmet Light and Healthy Entrees, Oriental Beef (10 oz)	290	8.0	3.0	45	840
Chun King Entrees, Beef Pepper Oriental (13 oz)	310	3.0	(1.2)	(10)	1300
Chun King Entrees, Beef Teriyaki (13 oz)	380	2.0	(1.2)	(10)	2200
Chun King Entrees, Chicken Chow Mein (13 oz)	370	6.0	(1.6)	(25)	1560
Chun King Entrees, Crunchy Walnut Chicken (13 oz)	310	5.0	(1.4)	(25)	1700
Chun King Entrees, Imperial Chicken (13 oz)	300	1.0	(0.3)	(25)	1540
Chun King Entrees, Sweet and Sour Pork (13 oz)	400	5.0	(1.4)	(10)	1460
Chun King Entrees, Szechuan Beef (13 oz)	340	3.0	(1.2)	(10)	1810
Dining Light from Armour Classics, Chicken Chow Mein with Rice (9 oz)	180	2.0	(0.6)	30	650

Frozen Entrées and Dinners (continued)	Calories	Fat g	Saturated Fat g	Choles- terol mg	Sodium mg
Dining Light from Armour Classics, Chicken Ala King with Rice (9 oz)	240	7.0	(1.9)	40	780
Dining Light from Armour Classics, Chicken with Noodles (9 oz)	240	7.0	(1.9)	50	570
Dining Light from Armour Classics, Lasagna with Meat Sauce (9 oz)	240	5.0	(2.1)	25	800
Dining Light from Armour Classics, Salisbury Steak and Vegetables (9 oz)	200	8.0	(3.3)	55	1000
Dining Light from Armour Classics, Spaghetti with Beef and Mushroom Sauce (9 oz)	220	8.0	(3.3)	20	440
Dining Lite Dinners, Beef Teriyaki (9 oz)	270	5.0	(2.0)	45	850
Dining Lite Dinners, Cheese Lasagna (9 oz)	260	6.0	(3.0)	30	800
Dining Lite Dinners, Chicken Ala King (9 oz)	240	7.0	(2.3)	40	780
Dining Lite Dinners, Chicken Chow Mein (9 oz)	180	2.0	(0.6)	30	650
Dining Lite Dinners, Chicken with Noodles (9 oz)	240	7.0	(1.8)	50	570
Dining Lite Dinners, Glazed Chicken (9 oz)	220	4.0	(0.8)	45	680
Dining Lite Dinners, Lasagna with Meat Sauce (9 oz)	240	5.0	(2.5)	25	800
Dining Lite Dinners, Oriental Pepper Steak (9 oz)	260	6.0	(1.5)	40	1050
Dining Lite Dinners, Salisbury Steak (9 oz)	200	8.0	(3.1)	55	1000
Dining Lite Dinners, Spaghetti with Beef (9 oz)	220	8.0	(2.3)	20	440
Healthy Choice Breakfast, English Muffin Sandwich (4.25 oz)	200	3.0	1.0	20	510
Healthy Choice Breakfast, Turkey Sausage Omelet on English Muffin (4.75 oz)	210	4.0	2.0	20	470
Healthy Choice Breakfast, Western Style Omelet on English Muffin (4.75 oz)	200	3.0	2.0	15	480

Frozen Entrées and Dinners (continued)	Calories	Fat g	Saturated Fat g	Choles- terol mg	Sodium mg
Healthy Choice Dinner, Lemon Pepper Fish (10.7 oz)	300	5.0	1.0	40	370
Healthy Choice Dinner, Pasta Primavera (11 oz)	280	3.0	2.0	15	360
Healthy Choice Dinner, Turkey Tetrazzini (12.6 oz)	340	6.0	3.0	40	490
Healthy Choice Dinners, Beef Enchilada (12.75 oz)	350	5.0	2.0	30	430
Healthy Choice Dinners, Beef Pepper Steak (11 oz)	290	6.0	3.0	65	530
Healthy Choice Dinners, Beef Sirloin Tips (11.75 oz)	280	8.0	3.0	65	370
Healthy Choice Dinners, Breast of Turkey (10.5 oz)	290	5.0	2.0	45	420
Healthy Choice Dinners, Chicken Dijon (11 oz)	260	3.0	1.0	45	420
Healthy Choice Dinners, Chicken Enchilada (12.75 oz)	330	5.0	3.0	30	440
Healthy Choice Dinners, Chicken Oriental (11.25 oz)	230	1.0	<1.0	35	460
Healthy Choice Dinners, Chicken Parmigiana (11.5 oz)	270	3.0	2.0	50	310
Healthy Choice Dinners, Chicken and Pasta Divan (11.5 oz)	310	4.0	2.0	60	510
Healthy Choice Dinners, Herb Roasted Chicken (12.3 oz)	290	4.0	2.0	50	430
Healthy Choice Dinners, Mesquite Chicken (10.5 oz)	340	1.0	<1.0	45	290
Healthy Choice Dinners, Pasta Primavera (11 oz)	280	3.0	2.0	15	360
Healthy Choice Dinners, Salisbury Steak (11.5 oz)	300	7.0	3.0	50	480
Healthy Choice Dinners, Salsa Chicken (11.25 oz)	240	2.0	1.0	50	450
Healthy Choice Dinners, Shrimp Creole (11.25 oz)	230	2.0	<1.0	60	430
Healthy Choice Dinners, Shrimp Marinara (10.5 oz)	260	1.0	<1.0	60	320
Healthy Choice Dinners, Sirloin Beef with Barbecue Sauce (11 oz)	300	6.0	3.0	50	320
Healthy Choice Dinners, Sole Au Gratin (11 oz)	270	5.0	3.0	55	470

Frozen Entrées and Dinners (continued)	Calories	Fat g	Saturated Fat g	Choles- terol mg	Sodium mg
Healthy Choice Dinners, Sweet and Sour Chicken (11.5 oz)	280	2.0	<1.0	50	260
Healthy Choice Dinners, Yankee Pot Roast (11 oz)	260	4.0	2.0	55	310
Healthy Choice Entree, Broccoli & Cheese Sauce with Baked Potato Wedges (9.5 oz)	240	5.0	2.0	15	510
Healthy Choice Entree, Chicken Enchiladas (9.5 oz)	280	6.0	2.0	30	510
Healthy Choice Entree, Macaroni and Cheese (9 oz)	280	6.0	3.0	20	520
Healthy Choice Entrees, Baked Cheese Ravioli (9 oz)	240	2.0	1.0	30	460
Healthy Choice Entrees, Beef Fajitas (7 oz)	210	4.0	2.0	35	250
Healthy Choice Entrees, Beef Pepper Steak (9.5 oz)	250	4.0	2.0	40	340
Healthy Choice Entrees, Cheese Manicotti (9.25 oz)	230	4.0	2.0	20	450
Healthy Choice Entrees, Chicken A L'Orange (9 oz)	240	2.0	<1.0	45	220
Healthy Choice Entrees, Chicken Chow Mein (8.5 oz)	220	3.0	1.0	45	440
Healthy Choice Entrees, Chicken Fajitas (7 oz)	200	3.0	1.0	35	310
Healthy Choice Entrees, Chicken Fettucini (8.5 oz)	240	4.0	2.0	45	370
Healthy Choice Entrees, Chicken and Vegetables (11.5 oz)	210	1.0	<1.0	35	490
Healthy Choice Entrees, Fettucini Alfredo (8 oz)	240	7.0	2.0	45	370
Healthy Choice Entrees, Glazed Chicken (8.5 oz)	220	3.0	1.0	50	390
Healthy Choice Entrees, Lasagna with Meat Sauce (9 oz)	260	5.0	2.0	20	420
Healthy Choice Entrees, Linguini with Shrimp (9.5 oz)	230	2.0	1.0	60	420
Healthy Choice Entrees, Mandarin Chicken (11 oz)	260	2.0	<1.0	50	400
Healthy Choice Entrees, Rigatoni in Meat Sauce (9.5 oz)	240	4.0	2.0	20	470
Healthy Choice Entrees, Seafood Newburg (8 oz)	200	3.0	1.0	55	440

Frozen Entrées and Dinners (continued)	Calories	Fat g	Saturated Fat g	Choles- terol mg	Sodium mg
Healthy Choice Entrees, Sole with Lemon Butter Sauce (8.25 oz)	230	4.0	2.0	45	390
Healthy Choice Entrees, Spaghetti with Meat Sauce (10 oz)	280	6.0	2.0	20	480
Healthy Choice Entrees, Zucchini Lasagna (11.5 oz)	240	3.0	2.0	15	390
Healthy Choice French Bread Pizza, Cheese (6.25 oz)	270	2.0	1.0	20	420
Healthy Choice French Bread Pizza, Deluxe (6.25 oz)	330	8.0	3.0	35	490
Healthy Choice French Bread Pizza, Italian Turkey Sausage (6.45 oz)	320	7.0	3.0	30	440
Healthy Choice French Bread Pizza, Pepperoni (6.25 oz)	320	8.0	3.0	30	490
Healthy Choice Homestyle Classics, Barbecue Beef Ribs (11 oz)	330	6.0	2.0	70	530
Healthy Choice Homestyle Classics, Salisbury Steak with Mushroom Gravy (11 oz)	280	6.0	3.0	55	500
Healthy Choice Homestyle Classics, Sliced Turkey with Gravy and Dressing (10 oz)	270	4.0	2.0	50	530
Healthy Choice Pasta Classics, Cacciatore Chicken (12.5 oz)	310	3.0	< 1.0	35	430
Healthy Choice Pasta Classics, Fettucini with Turkey and Vegetables (12.5 oz)	350	6.0	3.0	60	480
Healthy Choice Pasta Classics, Pasta with Italian Turkey Sausage (12 oz)	310	5.0	1.0	15	440
Healthy Choice Pasta Classics, Pasta with Shrimp (12.5 oz)	270	4.0	2.0	50	490
Healthy Choice Pasta Classics, Rigatoni with Chicken (12.5 oz)	360	4.0	2.0	60	430
Healthy Choice Pasta Classics, Stuffed Pasta Shells in Tomato Sauce (12 oz)	330	3.0	2.0	35	470
Healthy Choice Pasta Classics, Teriyaki Pasta with Chicken (12.6 oz)	350	3.0	1.0	45	370

Frozen Entrées and Dinners (continued)	Calories	Fat g	Saturated Fat g	Choles- terol mg	Sodium mg
Kraft Eating Right Entree, Beef Sirloin Salisbury Steak (9.5 oz)	230	8.0	3.0	50	510
Kraft Eating Right Entree, Fettucini Alfredo (10 oz)	220	7.0	3.0	20	410
Kraft Eating Right Entree, Glazed Chicken Breast (10 oz)	240	4.0	1.0	35	560
Kraft Eating Right Entree, Lasagna with Meat Sauce (10 oz)	270	7.0	3.0	30	440
Kraft Eating Right Entree, Macaroni and Cheese (9 oz)	270	8.0	3.0	15	590
Kraft Eating Right Entree, Sliced Turkey Breast (10 oz)	250	7.0	2.0	50	560
Kraft Eating Right Entree, Swedish Meatballs (10 oz)	290	7.0	2.0	55	470
La Choy Frozen Products, Beef Pepper Oriental (1/3 cup)	72	1.5	(0.5)	11	160
Le Menu Frozen Dinner, Chicken in Wine Sauce (10 oz)	280	7.0	(1.6)	(80)	680
Le Menu Frozen Dinner, Sliced Breast of Turkey with Mushroom Gravy (10-1/2 oz)	300	7.0	(2.2)	(63)	1020
Le Menu LightStyle Healthy Dinners, 3-Cheese Stuffed Shells (10 oz)	280	8.0	(3.2)	25	690
Le Menu LightStyle Healthy Dinners, Cheese Tortellini (10 oz)	230	6.0	(2.4)	15	460
Le Menu LightStyle Healthy Dinners, Glazed Chicken Breast (10 oz)	230	3.0	(0.6)	55	480
Le Menu LightStyle Healthy Dinners, Herb Roasted Chicken (10 oz)	240	7.0	(1.1)	70	400
Le Menu LightStyle Healthy Dinners, Sliced Turkey (10 oz)	210	5.0	(1.5)	30	540
Le Menu LightStyle Healthy Dinners, Sweet and Sour Chicken (10 oz)	250	7.0	(1.4)	2	530
Le Menu LightStyle Healthy Dinners, Turkey Divan (10 oz)	260	7.0	(2.3)	60	420
Le Menu LightStyle Healthy Dinners, Veal Marsala (10 oz)	230	3.0	(1.0)	75	700
Le Menu LightStyle Healthy Entrees, Chicken Dijon (8 oz)	240	7.0	(1.6)	40	500

Frozen Entrées and Dinners (continued)	Calories	Fat g	Saturated Fat g	Choles- terol mg	Sodium mg
Le Menu LightStyle Healthy Entrees, Chicken Enchiladas (8 oz)	280	8.0	(2.5)	35	530
Le Menu LightStyle Healthy Entrees, Chicken a la King (8-1/4 oz)	240	5.0	(2.0)	30	670
Le Menu LightStyle Healthy Entrees, Empress Chicken (8-1/4 oz)	210	5.0	(1.1)	30	690
Le Menu LightStyle Healthy Entrees, Glazed Turkey (8-1/4 oz)	260	6.0	(1.9)	35	720
Le Menu LightStyle Healthy Entrees, Herb Roasted Chicken (7-3/4 oz)	260	6.0	(0.9)	45	500
Le Menu LightStyle Healthy Entrees, Spaghetti with Beef Sauce and Mushrooms (9 oz)	280	6.0	(2.5)	15	450
Le Menu LightStyle Healthy Entrees, Swedish Meatballs (8 oz)	260	8.0	(3.3)	40	700
Le Menu LightStyle Healthy Entrees, Traditional Turkey (8 oz)	200	5.0	(1.5)	25	610
Lean Cuisine Entrees, Baked Cheese Ravioli (8-1/2 oz)	240	8.0	3.0	55	590
Lean Cuisine Entrees, Breast of Chicken Marsala with Vegetables (8-1/8 oz)	190	5.0	1.0	80	850
Lean Cuisine Entrees, Breast of Chicken Parmesan (10 oz)	260	8.0	2.0	80	870
Lean Cuisine Entrees, Chicken Cacciatore with Vermicelli (10-7/8 oz)	250	7.0	1.0	45	860
Lean Cuisine Entrees, Chicken Chow Mein with Rice (11-1/4 oz)	250	5.0	1.0	40	980
Lean Cuisine Entrees, Chicken a l'Orange with Almond Rice (8 oz)	260	5.0	1.0	55	430
Lean Cuisine Entrees, Chicken and Vegetables with Vermicelli (11-3/4 oz)	260	8.0	2.0	45	980
Lean Cuisine Entrees, Chicken Italiano (9 oz)	290	8.0	2.0	45	490
Lean Cuisine Entrees, Chicken Tenderloins in Peanut Sauce with Linguini and Vegetables (9 oz)	290	7.0	2.0	45	530

Frozen Entrées and Dinners (continued)	Calories	Fat g	Saturated Fat g	Choles- terol mg	Sodium mg
Lean Cuisine Entrees, Fiesta Chicken with Rice and Vegetables (8-1/2 oz)	240	5.0	2.0	40	560
Lean Cuisine Entrees, Glazed Chicken with Vegetable Rice (8-1/2 oz)	260	8.0	2.0	55	570
Lean Cuisine Entrees, Homestyle Turkey with Vegetables and Rice (9-3/8 oz)	230	5.0	2.0	50	550
Lean Cuisine Entrees, Lasagna with Meat and Sauce (10-1/4 oz)	260	5.0	2.0	25	590
Lean Cuisine Entrees, Linguini with Clam Sauce (9-5/8 oz)	270	7.0	1.0	30	890
Lean Cuisine Entrees, Macaroni and Beef in Tomato Sauce (10 oz)	240	6.0	1.0	40	590
Lean Cuisine Entrees, Oriental Beef with Vegetables and Rice (8-5/8 oz)	250	7.0	2.0	45	900
Lean Cuisine Entrees, Sliced Turkey Breast in Mushroom Sauce (8 oz)	240	7.0	2.0	50	790
Lean Cuisine Entrees, Sliced Turkey Breast with Gravy and Cornbread Dressing (7-7/8 oz)	240	6.0	1.0	45	720
Lean Cuisine Entrees, Spaghetti with Beef and Mushroom Sauce (11-1/2 oz)	270	6.0	2.0	30	940
Lean Cuisine Entrees, Swedish Meatballs (9-1/8 oz)	290	8.0	3.0	50	590
Lean Cuisine Entrees, Zucchini Lasagna (11 oz)	260	5.0	2.0	20	550
Lean Line Entree, Seafood Fettucini Alfredo (8 oz)	260	4.0	(1.3)	(18)	760
Lean Line Entree, Vegetable Chow Mein (10 oz)	70	1.0	(0.3)	(0)	597
Legume Entree, Manicotti Florentine with Tofu and Sauce (11 oz)	260	7.0	(1.1)	0	650
Legume Entree, Vegetable Lasagna (12 oz)	240	8.0	(1.2)	0	520
Looney Tunes Meals, Elmer Fudd Turkey and Dressing (6.45 oz)	240	7.0	(3.3)	(32)	610
Looney Tunes Meals, Tweety Macaroni and Cheese (9.75 oz)	280	8.0	(3.1)	(14)	630

Frozen Entrées and Dinners (continued)	Calories	Fat g	Saturated Fat g	Choles- terol mg	Sodium mg
McCain Lite Delite Dinners, Beef Teriyaki (9.9 oz)	253	6.2	3.0	27	535
McCain Lite Delite Dinners, Chicken A L'Orange (10 oz)	209	7.9	2.4	14	1067
McCain Lite Delite Dinners, Chicken Italian (9.7 oz)	224	4.5	2.3	23	648
McCain Lite Delite Dinners, Chicken Oriental (10 oz)	236	3.7	1.4	23	1614
McCain Lite Delite Dinners, Chicken Supreme (10-1/4 oz)	278	4.9	2.3	16	828
McCain Lite Delite Dinners, Chicken in BBQ Sauce (9.3 oz)	305	4.4	1.7	23	403
McCain Lite Delite Dinners, Roast Turkey (10 oz)	229	4.1	2.2	15	731
Morton Dinners, Ham (10 oz)	290	4.0	(1.4)	45	1400
Morton Dinners, Sliced Beef (10 oz)	220	5.0	(1.9)	65	950
Morton Dinners, Spaghetti & Meatball (10 oz)	200	3.0	(1.0)	10	1090
Morton Dinners, Turkey (10 oz)	230	6.0	(2.8)	45	1300
Swanson 4-Compartment Dinner, Beef (11-1/4 oz)	310	6.0	(2.5)	(60)	770
Swanson Entree, Sirloin Beef Tips (7 oz)	160	5.0	(1.8)	(43)	550
Swanson Homestyle Recipe Frozen Entrees, Sirloin Tips in Burgundy Sauce (7 oz)	160	5.0	(1.9)	(67)	550
Tombstone Light Pizza, Chicken Deluxe (8.95 oz)	240	8.0	3.0	25	450
Tombstone Light Pizza, Vegetable (8.8 oz)	250	8.0	3.0	10	500
Tyson Dinner, Chicken Marsala (9 oz)	200	4.0	(1.1)	50	670
Tyson Dinner, Chicken with Gravy (9 oz)	230	6.0	(2.3)	50	480
Tyson Dinner, Glazed Chicken with Sauce (9.25 oz)	240	4.0	(1.6)	45	930
Tyson Gourmet Selection Dinners, A L'Orange (9.5 oz)	300	8.0	(3.3)	(56)	670
Ultra Slim-Fast Entrees, Chicken Chow Mein (12 oz)	320	6.0	(1.7)	60	580
Ultra Slim-Fast Entrees, Glazed Turkey with Dressing (10.5 oz)	340	5.0	(2.2)	50	570

Frozen Entrées and Dinners (continued)	Calories	Fat g	Saturated Fat g	Choles- terol mg	Sodium mg
Ultra Slim-Fast Entrees, Mushroom Gravy over Salisbury Steak (10.5 oz)	290	5.0	(1.7)	35	830
Ultra Slim-Fast Entrees, Vegetable Lasagna (12 oz)	240	4.0	(2.1)	15	730
Ultra Slim-Fast Frozen Entrees, Beef Pepper Steak and Parsleyed Rice (12 oz)	270	4.0	2.0	45	690
Ultra Slim-Fast Frozen Entrees, Cheese Ravioli (9.5 oz)	300	6.0	(2.2)	6	920
Ultra Slim-Fast Frozen Entrees, Chicken and Vegetables (12 oz)	290	3.0	<1.0	30	850
Ultra Slim-Fast Frozen Entrees, Country Style Vegetables and Beef Tips (12 oz)	230	5.0	2.0	45	960
Ultra Slim-Fast Frozen Entrees, Mesquite Chicken (12 oz)	360	1.0	<1.0	65	300
Ultra Slim-Fast Frozen Entrees, Roasted Chicken In Mushroom Sauce (12 oz)	280	6.0	2.0	55	830
Ultra Slim-Fast Frozen Entrees, Rotini Primavera (10.5 oz)	250	5.0	(0.7)	8	600
Ultra Slim-Fast Frozen Entrees, Shrimp Creole (12 oz)	240	4.0	1.0	80	730
Ultra Slim-Fast Frozen Entrees, Shrimp Marinara (12 oz)	290	3.0	1.0	70	880
Ultra Slim-Fast Frozen Entrees, Sweet and Sour Chicken (12 oz)	330	2.0	<1.0	45	340
Ultra Slim-Fast Frozen Entrees, Turkey Medallions in Herb Sauce (12 oz)	280	6.0	2.0	40	950
Weight Watchers Frozen Entrees, Fettucini Alfredo (9 oz)	210	8.0	3.0	35	600
Weight Watchers Frozen Entrees, Spaghetti with Meat Sauce (10.5 oz)	280	7.0	3.0	25	610
Weight Watchers, Angel Hair Pasta (10 oz)	210	5.0	1.0	20	420
Weight Watchers, Baked Potato, Broccoli & Cheese (10.5 oz)	290	8.0	2.0	25	600
Weight Watchers, Baked Potato, Chicken Divan (11 oz)	280	4.0	2.0	40	730
Weight Watchers, Baked Potato, Ham Lorraine (11 oz)	250	4.0	2.0	15	670

Frozen Entrées and Dinners (continued)	Calories	Fat g	Saturated Fat g	Choles- terol mg	Sodium mg
Weight Watchers, Baked Potato, Homestyle Turkey (12 oz)	300	6.0	3.0	60	670
Weight Watchers, Beef Fajitas (6.75 oz)	250	7.0	2.0	20	630
Weight Watchers, Beef Salisbury Steak Romano (8.75 oz)	190	7.0	2.0	40	470
Weight Watchers, Beef Sirloin Tips and Mushrooms in Wine Sauce (7.5 oz)	220	7.0	3.0	50	540
Weight Watchers, Cheese Tortellini (9 oz)	310	6.0	1.0	15	570
Weight Watchers, Chicken Fajitas (6.75 oz)	230	5.0	2.0	30	590
Weight Watchers, Chicken ala King (9 oz)	240	6.0	3.0	20	490
Weight Watchers, Filet of Fish Au Gratin (9.25 oz)	200	6.0	1.0	60	700
Weight Watchers, Garden Lasagna (11 oz)	290	7.0	2.0	20	670
Weight Watchers, Homestyle Chicken and Noodles (9 oz)	240	7.0	2.0	30	450
Weight Watchers, Imperial Chicken (9.25 oz)	240	3.0	1.0	35	640
Weight Watchers, London Broil in Mushroom Sauce (7.37 oz)	140	3.0	1.0	40	510
Weight Watchers, Oven Fried Fish (7.08 oz)	240	7.0	<1.0	15	380
Weight Watchers, Sweet 'N Sour Chicken Tenders (10.19 oz)	240	1.0	<1.0	40	600
Weight Watchers, Veal Patty Parmigiana (8.44 oz)	190	6.0	3.0	55	650

SNACK FOODS

Foods included in this section of the Guide are low in fat, saturated fat, and cholesterol *as purchased* or when *prepared as indicated* in the Guide. One serving of these products, as defined below, does not exceed the following cutoff points.

Other foods that are good as snacks include choices from the dairy, fruit, vegetable, bread, cracker, and cereal sections of the Guide.

CUTOFF POINTS FOR SNACK FOODS

Fat (grams)	Saturated Fat (grams)	Cholesterol (milligrams)
3	1	10

SERVINGS

Food	Serving Sizes
Snacks:	
Caramel Corn	1 ounce
Chips	1 ounce
Granola Bars	2 ounces
Popcorn, plain or flavored	1 ounce
Pretzels	1 ounce
Dips:	
Dry Mix, prepared as directed	2 tablespoons
Ready-to-Eat	2 tablespoons

Dip Mix. Most dry dip mixes do not contain fat. However, package directions usually specify combining the mix with sour cream or cream cheese. Prepared products containing these ingredients—both of which are high in fat and saturated fat—do not qualify for the Guide. However, if a dry dip mix is added to pureed low-fat or nonfat cottage cheese or low-fat or nonfat yogurt, the prepared dip will be lower in fat and saturated fat.

The following abbreviations are used in the Food Sections: oz = ounce; fl oz = fluid ounce; pkg = package; pkt = packet; env = envelope; g = gram; prep (w/ . . .) = prepared with; < = less than; and tr = trace.

Chips	Calories	Fat g	Saturated Fat g	Choles- terol mg	Sodium mg
CHIPS					
Arrowhead Mills Blue Corn Curls, Salted (1 oz)	120	3.0	(0.3)	(0)	53
Arrowhead Mills Blue Corn Curls, Unsalted (1 oz)	120	2.0	(0.3)	(0)	1
Arrowhead Mills Yellow Corn Chips (3/4 oz)	90	1.0	(0.1)	(0)	41
Arrowhead Mills Yellow Corn Chips with Cheese (3/4 oz)	90	2.0	(0.3)	(0)	39
Crackle Rice, Cheese & Tomato (1/2 oz)	60	1.7	(0.4)	(0)	92
Guiltless Gourmet Baked Tortilla Chips (1 oz = 12 chips)	110	1.4	(0.2)	0	46
Guiltless Gourmet Baked Tortilla Chips, No Salt (1 oz = 12 chips)	110	1.4	(0.2)	0	0
Happy Heart No Oil Corn Chips, Barbeque (3/8 oz)	40	<1.0	(0.0)	0	50
Happy Heart No Oil Corn Chips, Cheddar Cheese (3/8 oz)	40	<1.0	(0.0)	0	50
Happy Heart No Oil Corn Chips, Nacho Cheese (3/8 oz)	40	<1.0	(0.0)	0	50
Happy Heart No Oil Corn Chips, Original (3/8 oz)	40	<1.0	(0.0)	0	50
Happy Heart No Oil Corn Chips, Sour Cream & Onion (3/8 oz)	40	<1.0	(0.0)	0	50
Heart Lovers No Oil Corn Chips, Barbeque (3/8 oz)	40	<1.0	(0.0)	0	50
Heart Lovers No Oil Corn Chips, Cheddar Cheese (3/8 oz)	40	<1.0	(0.0)	0	50
Heart Lovers No Oil Corn Chips, Nacho Cheese (3/8 oz)	40	<1.0	(0.0)	0	50
Heart Lovers No Oil Corn Chips, Sour Cream and Onion (3/8 oz)	40	<1.0	(0.0)	(0)	50
Rice & Bean Tortilla Bites, Jalapeno & Jack (1/2 oz)	60	0.0	0.0	(0)	84
Ultra Slim-Fast Lite 'N Tasty Cheese Curls (1 oz bag)	110	3.0	(0.5)	0	360

Dips	Calories	Fat g	Saturated Fat g	Choles-terol mg	Sodium mg
DIPS, READY-TO-EAT					
Eagle Brand Dip, Bean (1 oz = 1.9 tbsp)	35	2.0	(0.8)	0	140
Frito-Lay's Dip, Jalapeno Bean (1 oz)	30	1.0	(0.4)	0	180
Frito-Lay's Dip, Picante (1 oz)	10	0.0	0.0	0	160
Guiltless Gourmet Black Bean Dip, Mild (1 oz = 2 tbsp)	25	0.0	0.0	0	80
Guiltless Gourmet Black Bean Dip, Spicy (1 oz = 2 tbsp)	25	0.0	0.0	0	80
Guiltless Gourmet Pinto Bean Dip, Mild (1 oz = 2 tbsp)	25	0.0	0.0	0	80
Guiltless Gourmet Pinto Bean Dip, Spicy (1 oz = 2 tbsp)	25	0.0	0.0	0	80
Hain Canned Dips, Hot Bean (4 tbsp)	70	1.0	(0.4)	5	250
Hain Canned Dips, Mexican Bean (4 tbsp)	60	1.0	(0.4)	5	260
Hain Canned Dips, Onion Bean (4 tbsp)	70	1.0	(0.4)	5	270
Hain Canned Dips, Taco Dip and Sauce (4 tbsp)	25	1.0	(0.3)	5	350
La Victoria Chili Dip (1 tbsp)	6	<1.0	(0.0)	(0)	90
Old El Paso Chili Bean Dip (2 tbsp)	16	<1.0	(0.0)	(0)	100
Old El Paso Taco Dip (2 tbsp)	14	<1.0	(0.0)	(0)	74
Wise Jalapeno Flavored Bean Dip (2 tbsp)	25	0.0	0.0	(0)	100
Wise Taco Dip (2 tbsp)	12	0.0	0.0	(0)	115
FRUIT SNACKS					
A&P Dinosaurs Fruit Snacks (1 pouch)	100	1.0	(0.0)	(0)	14
A&P Fruit Snacks, all flavors (1 pouch)	100	1.0	(0.0)	(0)	10
Barbara's Bakery Real Fruit, Apple (.5 oz)	50	1.0	(0.1)	(0)	(10)
Barbara's Bakery Real Fruit, Apricot (.5 oz)	50	1.0	(0.1)	(0)	(10)
Barbara's Bakery Real Fruit, Cherry (.5 oz)	50	1.0	(0.1)	(0)	(10)
Barbara's Bakery Real Fruit, Grape (.5 oz)	50	1.0	(0.1)	(0)	(10)

Fruit Snacks (continued)	Calories	Fat g	Saturated Fat g	Choles- terol mg	Sodium mg
Barbara's Bakery Real Fruit, Raspberry (.5 oz)	50	1.0	(0.1)	(0)	(10)
Berry Bears, all varieties (1 pouch)	100	<1.0	0.0	0	20
Del Monte Fruit Snacks, Orchard Fruit Mix (.9 oz = 1 pouch)	70	0.0	0.0	(0)	10
Flavor Tree Fruit Snacks: Assorted Fruit Nibbles, Fruit Packets, Fruit Bears, Fruit Dinosaurs, Fruit Circus (1.05 oz)	120	2.0	(0.4)	(0)	10
Fruit Corners Thunder Jets, all varieties (1 pouch)	100	1.0	(0.1)	0	30
Fruit Corners, Fruit Roll-Ups and Peel-Outs, all flavors (1/2 oz roll)	50	<1.0	(0.0)	0	40
Garfield and Friends, 1-2 Punch (1 pouch)	100	2.0	(0.3)	(0)	70
Garfield and Friends, Fruit Party (1/2 oz roll)	50	<1.0	(0.0)	(0)	40
Garfield and Friends, Very Strawberry (1 pouch)	90	1.0	(0.1)	(0)	60
Garfield and Friends, Wild Blue (1/2 oz roll)	50	<1.0	(0.0)	(0)	20
Giant Fruit Snacks, Dinosaurs (.9 oz = 1 pouch)	100	1.0	(0.0)	0	15
Giant Fruit Snacks, Sharks (.9 oz = 1 pouch)	100	1.0	(0.0)	0	15
Giant Fruit Snacks, Strawberry (.9 oz = 1 pouch)	100	1.0	(0.0)	0	10
Giant Fruit Snacks, Variety (.9 oz = 1 pouch)	100	1.0	(0.0)	0	10
Mountain House Fruit Crisps, Mixed Fruit (.55 oz = 1-1/8 cups)	60	0.0	0.0	(0)	5
Mountain House Fruit Crisps, Peaches (.55 oz = 1-1/8 cups)	60	0.0	0.0	(0)	5
Mountain House Fruit Crisps, Pears (.55 oz = 1-1/8 cups)	60	0.0	0.0	(0)	0
Mountain House Fruit Crisps, Strawberries (.55 oz = 1-1/8 cups)	60	1.0	<1.0	(0)	0
Shark Bites, all varieties (1 pouch)	100	<1.0	(0.0)	(0)	20

Fruit Snacks (continued)	Calories	Fat g	Saturated Fat g	Choles- terol mg	Sodium mg
Sunkist Fruit Roll, Apple (3/4 oz = 1 roll)	75	0.0	(0.0)	0	17
Sunkist Fruit Roll, Apricot (3/4 oz = 1 roll)	76	0.5	(0.0)	0	17
Sunkist Fruit Roll, Cherry (3/4 oz = 1 roll)	75	0.1	(0.0)	0	18
Sunkist Fruit Roll, Fruit Punch (3/4 oz = 1 roll)	74	0.0	(0.0)	0	12
Sunkist Fruit Roll, Grape (3/4 oz = 1 roll)	76	0.1	(0.0)	0	13
Sunkist Fruit Roll, Raspberry (3/4 oz = 1 roll)	75	0.1	(0.0)	0	20
Sunkist Fruit Roll, Strawberry (3/4 oz = 1 roll)	74	0.1	(0.0)	0	11
Sunkist Fun Fruit, Funny Feet, Link Nintendo, Mario Nintendo, Rock and Roll Shapes, Wild Safari, or Wacky Players (.9 oz)	100	1.4	(0.1)	(0)	10
Sunkist Fun Fruits, Alphabets, Animals, Dinosaurs, Numbers, Space Shapes, Spooky Fruit, or Strawberry (.9 oz)	100	1.4	(0.1)	0	10
Weight Watchers Apple Chips (1 bag)	70	0.0	0.0	0	200
Weight Watchers Fruit Snacks, Apple (1 pouch)	50	<1.0	(<1.0)	(0)	75
Weight Watchers Fruit Snacks, Cinnamon (1 pouch)	50	<1.0	(<1.0)	(0)	75
Weight Watchers Fruit Snacks, Peach (1 pouch)	50	<1.0	(<1.0)	(0)	75
Weight Watchers Fruit Snacks, Strawberry (1 pouch)	50	<1.0	(<1.0)	(0)	75
GRANOLA BARS					
Fi-Bar A.M., Apple-Oatmeal Spice (1.5 oz = 1 bar)	150	3.0	(0.5)	0	25
POPCORN					
Arrowhead Mills Pop Corn, Yellow (2 oz)	210	3.0	(0.3)	(0)	2
Featherweight Microwave Popcorn, Natural Flavor (3 cups popped)	80	1.0	(<1.0)	0	0

Popcorn (continued)	Calories	Fat g	Saturated Fat g	Choles-terol mg	Sodium mg
Jiffy Pop Light Microwave Popcorn, Butter Flavor (3 cups popped)	80	2.0	(0.3)	0	70
Jolly Time Light Microwave Pop Corn, Natural Butter Flavored (3 cups popped)	70	2.0	(0.3)	0	90
Jolly Time Pop Corn, White, Air Popped (3 cups popped)	56	1.0	(0.1)	0	tr
Jolly Time Pop Corn, Yellow, Air Popped (3 cups popped)	66	1.0	(0.1)	0	tr
Nature's Choice Caramel Corn (1.67 oz)	180	1.0	(0.6)	(0)	(230)
Nature's Choice Caramel Corn with Peanuts (1.67 oz)	190	2.0	(1.1)	(0)	(230)
Newman's Own Oldstyle Picture Show Microwave Popcorn, Light Butter Flavor (3 cups popped)	90	3.0	1.0	0	100
Newman's Own Oldstyle Picture Show Microwave Popcorn, Light Natural Flavor (3 cups popped)	90	3.0	1.0	0	100
Newman's Own Oldstyle Picture Show Popcorn (3 cups popped)	80	1.0	(0.0)	0	0
Orville Redenbacher's Gourmet Hot Air Popping Corn (3 cups popped)	40	<1.0	(0.0)	0	0
Orville Redenbacher's Light Gourmet Microwave Popping Corn, Butter (3 cups popped)	50	1.0	0.2	0	70
Orville Redenbacher's Light Gourmet Microwave Popping Corn, Natural (3 cups popped)	50	1.0	0.2	0	85
Pop*Secret Light, Butter Flavor (3 cups popped)	70	3.0	<1.0	0	115
Pop*Secret Light, Natural Flavor (3 cups popped)	70	3.0	<1.0	0	160
Popcorn, prep (without fat or salt)—Most Brands (3-1/2 cups popped)	109	1.4	0.2	0	1
Pops-Rite Light Microwave Popcorn, Butter Flavor (3 cups popped)	60	2.0	0.0	0	70

Popcorn (continued)	Calories	Fat g	Saturated Fat g	Choles-terol mg	Sodium mg
Pops-Rite Light Microwave Popcorn, Natural Flavor (3 cups popped)	60	2.0	0.0	0	70
TV Time Merry Poppin "Light" Microwave Popping Corn, Butter Flavor (4 cups popped)	120	3.0	(2.2)	0	225
TV Time Merry Poppin "Light" Microwave Popping Corn, Natural Flavor (4 cups popped)	120	3.0	(2.2)	0	225
Tom's Caramel Corn (1.6 oz = 1 pkg)	190	3.0	(1.7)	0	130
Weight Watchers Microwave Popcorn (1 oz)	100	1.0	(0.1)	(0)	5
PRETZELS					
Andy Capp's Pub Pretzels (1 oz)	110	1.0	(0.5)	0	500
Barbara's Bakery Pretzels, 9 Grain (1 oz = 2 pretzels)	112	2.0	(0.4)	0	(475)
Barbara's Bakery Pretzels, Honeysweet (1 oz = 2 pretzels)	127	3.0	(0.5)	0	(475)
Barbara's Bakery Pretzels, Whole Wheat (1 oz = 2 pretzels)	120	3.0	(0.5)	0	(475)
Bell Brand Mini-Pretzels (1 oz)	110	1.0	(0.5)	0	570
Eagle Brand Pretzels (1 oz)	110	2.0	(1.0)	0	570
Eagle Brand Pretzels, Beer (1 oz)	110	2.0	(1.0)	0	610
Giant Pretzels, Logs (1 oz)	110	2.0	(1.0)	0	470
Giant Pretzels, Nibs (1 oz)	110	2.0	(1.0)	0	470
Giant Pretzels, Old Fashioned Hard Salted (1 oz)	100	0.0	0.0	0	590
Giant Pretzels, Old Fashioned Twist (1 oz)	110	2.0	(1.0)	0	410
Giant Pretzels, Petite (1 oz)	110	2.0	(1.0)	0	410
Giant Pretzels, Petite, Unsalted (1 oz)	110	2.0	(1.0)	0	0
Giant Pretzels, Rings (1 oz)	110	2.0	(1.0)	0	410
Giant Pretzels, Rods (1 oz)	110	2.0	(1.0)	0	240
Giant Pretzels, Stix (1 oz)	100	1.0	(0.5)	0	1070
Giant Pretzels, Thin (1 oz)	110	2.0	(1.0)	0	410
Jays Pretzel Rods (1 oz)	110	1.0	(0.5)	0	410

Pretzels (continued)	Calories	Fat g	Saturated Fat g	Choles-terol mg	Sodium mg
Jays Pretzel Stix (1 oz)	110	1.0	(0.5)	0	620
Jays Pretzel Twists (1 oz)	110	1.0	(0.5)	0	770
Lance Pretzel Twist (1-1/2 oz = 1 pkg)	150	1.0	0.0	0	700
Lance Pretzels (1 oz)	100	1.0	0.0	0	470
Mr. Salty Fat Free Pretzels, Twists (1 oz)	100	0.0	0.0	0	380
Old Dutch Pretzels (1 oz)	114	1.0	(0.5)	(0)	411
Pretzels—Most Brands (1 oz)	117	1.4	(0.3)	(0)	504
Quinlan Beers Pretzels (1 oz)	110	2.0	<1.0	0	420
Quinlan Minis (Tiny Thins) Pretzels (1 oz)	110	2.0	<1.0	0	600
Quinlan Oat Bran Pretzels (1 oz)	120	2.0	<1.0	0	190
Quinlan Pretzel Nuggets (1 oz)	120	2.0	<1.0	0	210
Quinlan Pretzel Rods (1 oz)	100	<1.0	0.0	0	480
Quinlan Pretzel Sticks (1 oz)	110	1.0	<1.0	0	390
Quinlan Pretzels, Unsalted (1 oz)	120	2.0	<1.0	0	5
Quinlan Thins Pretzels (1 oz)	110	1.0	<1.0	0	670
Quinlan Tiny Thins Pretzels, Unsalted (1 oz)	120	2.0	<1.0	0	5
Quinlan Ultra Thins Pretzels (1 oz)	110	1.0	<1.0	0	780
Ralph's Pretzels, Bavarian (1 oz)	110	1.0	(0.2)	(0)	475
Ralph's Pretzels, Bavarian, Low Sodium (1 oz)	110	1.0	(0.2)	(0)	20
Ralph's Pretzels, Mini Twist (1 oz)	110	1.0	(0.2)	(0)	570
Ralph's Pretzels, Sticks (1 oz)	110	1.0	(0.2)	(0)	570
Ralph's Pretzels, Twist (1 oz)	110	1.0	(0.2)	(0)	570
Rold Gold Pretzels, Bavarian (1 oz = 3 pretzels)	120	2.0	(1.0)	0	430
Rold Gold Pretzels, Pretzel Twist (1 oz = 10 twist)	110	1.0	(0.5)	0	510
Rold Gold Pretzels, Rods (1 oz = 3 rods)	110	2.0	(1.0)	0	410
Rold Gold Pretzels, Sticks (1 oz = 50 sticks)	110	2.0	(1.0)	0	490
Rold Gold Pretzels, Tiny Twists (1 oz = 15 pretzels)	110	1.0	(0.5)	0	420

Pretzels (continued)	Calories	Fat g	Saturated Fat g	Choles- terol mg	Sodium mg
Rold Gold Pretzels, Unsalted (1 oz)	110	1.0	(0.2)	0	115
Seyfert's Butter Pretzels, Rods (1 oz)	110	1.0	(0.5)	(0)	530
Soft Pretzel Bites (1-1/2 oz = 5 bites)	110	0.0	0.0	0	95
Soft Pretzels (2-1/4 oz)	170	0.0	0.0	0	140
Sunshine Butter Pretzels (1 oz)	110	1.0	<1.0	0	220
Ultra Slim-Fast Pretzel Twists (1 oz bag)	100	1.0	(0.2)	0	460
Wise Hard Pretzels, Original Sourdough Recipe (1 oz)	110	1.0	<1.0	0	660
OTHER SNACKS					
Cheerios-to-Go, Apple Cinnamon (1 oz = 1 pouch)	110	2.0	(0.4)	0	180
Cheerios-to-Go, Cheerios (3/4 oz = 1 pouch)	80	2.0	(0.4)	0	220
Cheerios-to-Go, Honey Nut (1 oz = 1 pouch)	110	1.0	(0.2)	0	250
Pepperidge Farm Snack Sticks, Pretzel (8 crackers)	120	3.0	0.0	0	430

SOUPS

The foods included in this section of the Guide are low in fat, saturated fat, and cholesterol *as purchased* or when *prepared as indicated* in the Guide. One serving of these foods does not exceed the cutoff points listed below. Some cream soups not listed in the Guide do not exceed the cutoff points when water, skim milk, ½%, or 1% low-fat milk is substituted for the whole milk listed in package directions.

CUTOFF POINTS FOR SOUPS

Fat (grams)	Saturated Fat (grams)	Cholesterol (milligrams)
3	1	10

SERVINGS

Food	Serving Size
Soups, all types	1 cup

The following abbreviations are used in the Food Sections: oz = ounce; fl oz = fluid ounce; pkg = package; pkt = packet; env = envelope; g = gram; prep (/w . . .) = prepared with; < = less than; and tr = trace.

Bean and Lentil Soups	Calories	Fat g	Saturated Fat g	Choles- terol mg	Sodium mg
BEAN AND LENTIL SOUPS					
Campbell's Home Cookin' Soup, Bean and Ham (10-3/4 oz individual size)	210	4.0*	(1.0)	(3)	1000
Campbell's Home Cookin' Soup, Bean and Ham (9-1/2 oz)	180	4.0	(1.6)	(10)	890
Campbell's Home Cookin' Soup, Hearty Lentil (10-3/4 oz individual size)	170	2.0	(0.8)	(9)	930
Campbell's Home Cookin' Soup, Hearty Lentil (9-1/2 oz)	140	1.0	(0.4)	(8)	820
Campbell's Soup, Homestyle Bean, prep (w/water) (8 fl oz)	130	1.0	(0.4)	(0)	700
Hain Savory Soup Mix, Lentil, prep (w/water) (3/4 cup)	130	2.0	(0.5)	(0)	810
Hain Soups, Vegetarian Lentil (9-1/2 oz)	160	3.0	(1.4)	5	690
Hain Soups, Vegetarian Lentil, No Salt Added (9-1/2 oz)	160	3.0	(1.4)	5	65
Health Valley Fat-Free Soup, 5 Bean Vegetable (7-1/2 oz)	70	< 1.0	(0.0)	0	290
IGA Bean with Bacon Soup, prep (w/water) (8 oz)	130	3.0	(0.8)	0	(840)
Pritikin Soup, Lentil (8.31 oz)	90	0.8	0.2	0	180
Progresso Soup, Ham & Bean (9-1/2 oz=1/2 of a 19 oz can)	140	2.0	(0.8)	10	950
Progresso Soup, Lentil (9.25 oz)	140	4.0*	(1.6)	0	1000
Progresso Soup, Macaroni and Bean (10.5 oz)	180	4.0*	(1.2)	0	1120
BEEF SOUPS					
Campbell's Chunky Soup, Pepper Steak (10-3/4 oz individual size)	180	3.0	(1.5)	(11)	1050
Campbell's Chunky Soup, Pepper Steak (9-1/2 oz)	160	3.0	(1.5)	(10)	920
Campbell's Home Cookin' Soup, Beef with Vegetables and Pasta (10-3/4 oz individual size)	140	2.0	(1.1)	(7)	1060

*The value printed for fat is higher than the cutoff point because the manufacturer's serving size is larger than the standard serving size used in evaluating the food.

Beef Soups (continued)	Calories	Fat g	Saturated Fat g	Choles-terol mg	Sodium mg
Campbell's Home Cookin' Soup, Beef with Vegetables and Pasta (9-1/2 oz)	120	2.0	(0.7)	(6)	940
Campbell's Home Cookin' Soup, Vegetable Beef (10-3/4 oz individual size)	140	3.0	(1.3)	(7)	1160
Campbell's Home Cookin' Soup, Vegetable Beef (9-1/2 oz)	120	2.0	(0.9)	(6)	1020
Campbell's Microwave Soup, Vegetable Beef (7-1/2 oz)	100	2.0	(0.9)	(5)	830
Campbell's Soup, Beef Noodle, prep (w/water) (8 fl oz)	70	3.0	(1.1)	(5)	830
Campbell's Soup, Beef, prep (w/water) (8 fl oz)	80	2.0	(1.0)	(7)	830
Campbell's Soup, Vegetable Beef, prep (w/water) (8 fl oz)	70	2.0	(0.9)	(5)	780
Campbell's Special Request Soup, 1/3 Less Salt, Vegetable Beef, prep (w/water) (8 fl oz)	70	2.0	(0.9)	10	470
IGA Beef Noodle Soup, prep (w/water) (8 fl oz)	70	3.0	(1.1)	(5)	(830)
Knorr Soupmix, Oxtail Hearty Beef, prep (w/water) (8 fl oz)	70	2.0	(1.0)	(3)	1120
Lipton Hearty Ones, Beef Vegetable, prep (w/water) (11 oz)	229	3.0	(1.5)	(0)	921
Town House Soup, Vegetable Beef, prep (w/water) (8 fl oz)	70	2.0	(1.0)	(5)	890
Ultra Slim-Fast Instant Soup, Beef Noodle, prep (w/water) (6 fl oz)	45	< 1.0	(0.0)	5	700
BROTHS AND CONSOMMÉS					
Campbell's Consomme, prep (w/water) (8 fl oz)	25	0.0	(0.0)	(0)	750
Campbell's Low Sodium Broth, Chicken (10-1/2 oz)	30	1.0	(0.3)	(1)	85
Campbell's Soup, Beef Broth (Bouillon), prep (w/water) (8 fl oz)	16	0.0	0.0	(tr)	820
Campbell's Soup, Chicken Broth, prep (w/water) (8 fl oz)	30	2.0	(0.6)	(1)	710

Broths and Consommés (continued)	Calories	Fat g	Saturated Fat g	Cholesterol mg	Sodium mg
College Inn Broth, Beef (7 fl oz)	16	0.0	0.0	0	960
College Inn Broth, Chicken (7 fl oz)	35	3.0	1.0	5	990
College Inn Broth, Chicken, Lower Salt (7 fl oz)	20	2.0	1.0	5	550
Featherweight Instant Bouillon, Beef (1 tsp)	12	1.0	(0.5)	5	5
Featherweight Instant Bouillon, Chicken (1 tsp)	12	1.0	(0.2)	5	25
Hain Soups, Vegetable Broth (9-1/2 oz)	45	0.0	0.0	0	1180
Hain Soups, Vegetable Broth Low Sodium (9-1/2 oz)	40	<1.0	(0.0)	0	85
Herb-Ox Instant Broth and Seasoning (1 pkt)	11	<1.0	0.0	(1)	10
IGA Beef Broth, condensed (7.25 oz)	25	2.0	(1.0)	tr	(745)
IGA Chicken Broth, condensed (7.25 oz)	20	1.0	(0.3)	5	(643)
Knorr Bouillon, Beef Flavor, prep (w/water) (8 fl oz)	15	1.0	(0.5)	(1)	1220
Knorr Bouillon, Chicken Flavor, prep (w/water) (8 fl oz)	16	1.0	(0.2)	(1)	1200
Knorr Bouillon, Fish Flavor, prep (w/water) (8 fl oz)	10	<1.0	0.0	(1)	1130
Knorr Bouillon, Vegetarian Vegetable, prep (w/water) (8 fl oz)	16	2.0	(0.8)	(4)	990
Lipton Cup-A-Soup, Chicken Flavored Broth, prep (w/water) (6 fl oz)	20	0.6	(0.1)	1	605
Lite-Line Low Sodium Instant Bouillon, Beef Flavor (1 tsp)	12	<1.0	(0.0)	(tr)	5
Lite-Line Low Sodium Instant Bouillon, Chicken Flavor (1 tsp)	12	<1.0	(0.0)	(tr)	5
Pritikin Broth, Chicken (7.7 oz)	18	0.3	0.2	1	163
Progresso Broth, Chicken (4 oz)	8	0.0	(0.0)	<5	360
Progresso Seasoned Broth, Beef (4 oz)	10	<1.0	(0.0)	0	380

Broths and Consommés (continued)	Calories	Fat g	Saturated Fat g	Choles- terol mg	Sodium mg
Swanson Broth, Beef (7-1/4 oz)	18	1.0	(0.5)	(tr)	750
Swanson Broth, Chicken (7-1/4 oz)	30	2.0	(0.6)	(1)	900
Swanson Natural Goodness Clear Broth, Chicken (7-1/4 oz)	20	1.0	(0.3)	(1)	580
Weight Watchers Instant Broth Mix, Beef (1 pkg)	8	0.0	0.0	(0)	930
Weight Watchers Instant Broth Mix, Chicken (1 pkg)	8	0.0	0.0	(0)	990
Wyler's Instant Bouillon, Beef Flavor (1 tsp or 1 cube)	6	< 1.0	(0.0)	(tr)	930
Wyler's Instant Bouillon, Chicken Flavor (1 tsp or 1 cube)	8	< 1.0	(0.0)	(tr)	900
Wyler's Instant Bouillon, Onion Flavor (1 tsp)	10	< 1.0	(0.0)	(tr)	670
Wyler's Instant Bouillon, Vegetable Flavor (1 tsp)	6	< 1.0	(0.0)	(tr)	910

CHICKEN SOUPS

	Calories	Fat g	Saturated Fat g	Choles- terol mg	Sodium mg
Campbell's Chunky Soup, Chicken with Rice (9-1/2 oz)	140	4.0*	(1.2)	(14)	1060
Campbell's Chunky Soup, Old Fashioned Chicken (9-1/2 oz)	150	4.0*	(0.9)	(13)	1070
Campbell's Cup 2 Minute Soup Mix, Chicken Noodle with White Meat, prep (w/water) (6 fl oz)	90	2.0	(0.4)	(2)	770
Campbell's Cup 2 Minute Soup Mix, Noodle with Chicken Broth, prep (w/water) (6 fl oz)	90	2.0	(0.4)	(2)	910
Campbell's Home Cookin' Soup, Chicken Gumbo with Sausage (10-3/4 oz individual size)	140	4.0*	(0.9)	(7)	1090
Campbell's Home Cookin' Soup, Chicken Gumbo with Sausage (9-1/2 oz)	120	3.0	(0.7)	(6)	960
Campbell's Home Cookin' Soup, Chicken with Noodles (10-3/4 oz individual size)	140	4.0*	(1.1)	(9)	1150

*The value printed for fat is higher than the cutoff point because the manufacturer's serving size is larger than the standard serving size used in evaluating the food.

Chicken Soups (continued)	Calories	Fat g	Saturated Fat g	Choles- terol mg	Sodium mg
Campbell's Home Cookin' Soup, Chicken with Noodles (9-1/2 oz)	110	3.0	(0.8)	(8)	1020
Campbell's Quality Soup and Recipe Mix, Chicken Noodle, prep (w/water) (8 fl oz)	100	2.0	(0.4)	(3)	710
Campbell's Soup, Chicken Alphabet, prep (w/water) (8 fl oz)	80	3.0	(0.8)	(7)	800
Campbell's Soup, Chicken Barley, prep (w/water) (8 fl oz)	70	2.0	(0.8)	(5)	850
Campbell's Soup, Chicken Broth and Noodles, prep (w/water) (8 fl oz)	45	1.0	(0.3)	(7)	860
Campbell's Soup, Chicken Gumbo, prep (w/water) (8 fl oz)	60	2.0	(0.5)	(5)	900
Campbell's Soup, Chicken Noodle, prep (w/water) (8 fl oz)	60	2.0	(0.5)	(7)	900
Campbell's Soup, Chicken Noodle-O's, prep (w/water) (8 fl oz)	70	2.0	(0.5)	(7)	820
Campbell's Soup, Chicken Vegetable, prep (w/water) (8 fl oz)	70	3.0	(0.9)	(10)	850
Campbell's Soup, Chicken and Stars, prep (w/water) (8 fl oz)	60	2.0	(0.5)	(7)	870
Campbell's Soup, Chicken with Rice, prep (w/water) (8 fl oz)	60	3.0	(0.7)	(7)	790
Campbell's Soup, Curly Noodle with Chicken, prep (w/water) (8 fl oz)	80	3.0	(0.8)	(7)	800
Campbell's Soup, Homestyle Chicken Noodle, prep (w/water) (8 fl oz)	70	3.0	(0.8)	(7)	880
Campbell's Special Request Soup, 1/3 Less Salt, Chicken Noodle, prep (w/water) (8 fl oz)	60	2.0	(0.5)	15	440

Chicken Soups (continued)	Calories	Fat g	Saturated Fat g	Choles- terol mg	Sodium mg
Campbell's Special Request Soup, 1/3 Less Salt, Chicken with Rice, prep (w/water) (8 fl oz)	60	3.0	(0.7)	10	480
IGA Chicken Noodle Homestyle Soup, prep (w/water) (8 oz)	70	2.0	(0.5)	15	(880)
IGA Chicken O'Noodle Soup, prep (w/water) (8 oz)	70	3.0	(0.8)	15	(820)
IGA Chicken Vegetable Soup, prep (w/water) (8 oz)	70	2.0	0.6	(10)	(850)
IGA Chicken and Stars Soup, prep (w/water) (8 oz)	50	2.0	(0.4)	(7)	(870)
IGA Chicken with Rice Soup, prep (w/water) (8 oz)	50	2.0	(0.5)	0	(790)
IGA Noodle Soup with Real Chicken Broth, prep (w/water) (8 oz)	50	2.0	(0.6)	(7)	(860)
Knorr Soupmix, Chick 'N Pasta, prep (w/water) (8 fl oz)	90	2.0	(0.4)	(3)	850
Knorr Soupmix, Chicken Flavored Noodle, prep (w/water) (8 fl oz)	100	2.0	(0.4)	(3)	710
Kohl's Soup, Chicken Noodle, prep (w/water) (8 fl oz)	70	2.0	(0.5)	(7)	890
Lipton Cup-A-Soup, Chicken Noodle with Chicken Meat, prep (w/water) (6 fl oz)	46	1.0	(0.2)	(2)	660
Lipton Cup-A-Soup, Chicken Vegetable, prep (w/water) (6 fl oz)	47	0.6	(0.1)	8	566
Lipton Cup-A-Soup, Chicken'N Rice, prep (w/water) (6 fl oz)	47	0.8	(0.2)	(2)	667
Lipton Cup-A-Soup, Country Style Hearty Chicken, prep (w/water) (6 fl oz)	69	1.1	(0.2)	(2)	688
Lipton Cup-A-Soup, Hearty Chicken Flavor and Noodles, prep (w/water) (6 fl oz)	110	1.6	(0.4)	(3)	587
Lipton Hearty Noodle Soup Mix, Chicken, prep (w/water) (8 fl oz)	83	1.3	(0.3)	(3)	753

Chicken Soups (continued)	Calories	Fat g	Saturated Fat g	Choles- terol mg	Sodium mg
Lipton Hearty Ones, Homestyle Chicken Flavor Noodle, prep (w/water) (11 oz)	227	4.0*	(0.9)	37	989
Lipton Instant Oriental Noodle Soup, Chicken Flavor, prep (w/water) (8 fl oz)	180	1.7	(0.4)	(3)	785
Lipton Lite Cup-A-Soup, Chicken Florentine, prep (w/water) (6 fl oz)	42	0.5	(0.1)	6	481
Lipton Lite Cup-A-Soup, Lemon Chicken, prep (w/water) (6 fl oz)	48	0.4	(0.1)	4	419
Lipton Noodle Soup Mix with Real Chicken Broth, prep (w/water) (8 fl oz)	62	1.5	(0.3)	(3)	708
Lipton Noodle Soup Mix, Chicken with Diced White Chicken Meat, prep (w/water) (8 fl oz)	81	1.8	(0.4)	(3)	795
Lipton Noodle Soup Mix, Giggle Noodle with Real Chicken Broth, prep (w/water) (8 fl oz)	72	1.6	(0.4)	(3)	708
Lipton Ring-O-Noodle Soup Mix with Real Chicken Broth, prep (w/water) (8 fl oz)	67	1.5	(0.3)	(3)	708
Pritikin Soup, Chicken Vegetable (8 oz)	60	0.9	0.1	4	144
Pritikin Soup, Chicken with Ribbon Pasta (8 oz)	80	1.1	0.2	6	173
Progresso Soup, Chicken Barley (9-1/4 oz = 1/2 of an 18-1/2 oz can)	100	2.0	(0.7)	20	710
Progresso Soup, Escarole in Chicken Broth (9.25 oz)	30	1.0	(<1.0)	<5	1100
Progresso Soup, Homestyle Chicken (9-1/2 oz = 1/2 of a 19 oz can)	110	3.0	(0.9)	20	740
Town House Soup, Chicken Noodle, prep (w/water) (8 fl oz)	70	2.0	(0.5)	(7)	890
Town House Soup, Chicken with Rice, prep (w/water) (8 fl oz)	40	2.0	(0.5)	(7)	870

*The value printed for fat is higher than the cutoff point because the manufacturer's serving size is larger than the standard serving size used in evaluating the food.

Chicken Soups (continued)	Calories	Fat g	Saturated Fat g	Choles- terol mg	Sodium mg
Ultra Slim-Fast Instant Soup, Chicken Leek, prep (w/water) (6 fl oz)	50	<1.0	(0.0)	<2	1070
Ultra Slim-Fast Instant Soup, Chicken Noodle, prep (w/water) (6 fl oz)	45	<1.0	(0.0)	5	970
Weight Watchers Soup, Chicken Noodle (10.5 oz)	80	2.0	(0.4)	(4)	1230

CLAM CHOWDER

	Calories	Fat g	Saturated Fat g	Choles- terol mg	Sodium mg
Campbell's Chunky Soup, Manhattan Style Clam Chowder (10-3/4 oz individual size)	160	4.0*	(0.8)	(3)	1110
Campbell's Chunky Soup, Manhattan Style Clam Chowder (9-1/2 oz)	150	4.0*	(0.8)	(2)	980
Campbell's Soup, Manhattan Style Clam Chowder, prep (w/water) (8 fl oz)	70	2.0	(1.2)	(12)	820
Campbell's Soup, New England Clam Chowder, prep (w/water) (8 fl oz)	80	3.0	(0.4)	(5)	870
Lipton Kettle Ready Frozen Soup, Manhattan Clam Chowder (6 fl oz)	69	2.6	0.5	(2)	549
Progresso Soup, Manhattan Clam Chowder (9.5 oz)	120	2.0	(0.4)	(2)	1050
Snow's Soups, New England Clam Chowder, prep (w/skim milk) (8 fl oz)	108	2.2	(0.5)	(6)	675

CREAM SOUPS

	Calories	Fat g	Saturated Fat g	Choles- terol mg	Sodium mg
Campbell's Healthy Request Soups, Cream of Mushroom, prep (w/water) (8 oz)	60	2.0	(0.5)	<5	460
Campbell's Soup, Homestyle Cream of Tomato, prep (w/water) (8 fl oz)	110	3.0	(0.0)	(0)	810
Lipton Cup-A-Soup, Creamy Broccoli, prep (w/water) (6 fl oz)	62	2.4	(0.4)	(0)	610
Lipton Lite Cup-A-Soup, Creamy Tomato and Herb, prep (w/water) (6 fl oz)	66	0.3	(0.1)	2	305

*The value printed for fat is higher than the cutoff point because the manufacturer's serving size is larger than the standard serving size used in evaluating the food.

Cream Soups (continued)	Calories	Fat g	Saturated Fat g	Choles- terol mg	Sodium mg
Weight Watchers Soup, Cream Of Mushroom (10.5 oz)	90	2.0	(0.5)	(1)	1250

MINESTRONE

	Calories	Fat g	Saturated Fat g	Choles- terol mg	Sodium mg
Campbell's Healthy Request Soups, Hearty Minestrone, ready to serve (8 fl oz)	90	3.0	(0.6)	<2	430
Campbell's Home Cookin' Soup, Minestrone (10-3/4 oz individual size)	140	3.0	(0.6)	(3)	1220
Campbell's Home Cookin' Soup, Minestrone (9-1/2 oz)	120	3.0	(0.6)	(2)	1080
Campbell's Soup, Minestrone, prep (w/water) (8 fl oz)	80	2.0	(0.4)	(2)	900
Hain Savory Soup Mix, Minestrone, prep (w/water) (3/4 cup)	110	1.0	(0.2)	(2)	870
Hain Soups, Minestrone (9-1/2 oz)	170	2.0	(0.4)	0	1060
Hain Soups, Minestrone, No Salt Added (9-1/2 oz)	160	4.0*	(0.9)	0	35
Health Valley Fat-Free Soup, Real Italian Minestrone (7-1/2 oz)	70	<1.0	(0.0)	0	290
Healthy Choice Soups, Minestrone (7.5 oz)	160	2.0	<1.0	0	520
Knorr Soupmix, Hearty Minestrone, prep (w/water) (10 fl oz)	130	2.0	(1.0)	(11)	940
Lipton Hearty Ones, Minestrone, prep (w/water) (11 oz)	189	3.2	(1.5)	6	821
Pritikin Soup, Minestroni (8.2 oz)	80	0.9	0.2	0	135
Progresso Soup, Hearty Minestrone (9.25 oz)	110	2.0	(1.1)	<5	740
Progresso Soup, Minestrone (10.5 oz)	120	3.0	(0.6)	0	930
Town House Soup, Minestrone, prep (w/water) (8 fl oz)	80	3.0	(0.6)	(2)	900

*The value printed for fat is higher than the cutoff point because the manufacturer's serving size is larger than the standard serving size used in evaluating the food.

Mushroom Soups	Calories	Fat g	Saturated Fat g	Choles- terol mg	Sodium mg
MUSHROOM SOUPS **(see also Cream Soups)**					
Campbell's Soup, Golden Mushroom, prep (w/water) (8 fl oz)	70	3.0	(1.2)	(7)	870
Featherweight Soup, Mushroom (3.75 oz)	60	1.0	(0.3)	5	320
Hain Soups, Mushroom Barley (9-1/2 oz)	100	2.0	(0.4)	10	600
Lipton Recipe and Soup Mix, Beef Flavor Mushroom, prep (w/water) (8 fl oz)	38	0.5	(0.1)	(1)	763
ONION SOUPS					
Campbell's Quality Soup and Recipe Mix, Onion, prep (w/water) (8 fl oz)	30	0.0	0.0	(0)	700
Campbell's Soup, French Onion, prep (w/water) (8 fl oz)	60	2.0	(0.3)	(0)	900
Hain Savory Soup, Dip and Recipe Mix, Onion, prep (w/water) (3/4 cup)	50	2.0	(0.6)	(0)	900
Hain Savory Soup, Dip and Recipe Mix-No Sodium Added, Onion, prep (w/water) (3/4 cup)	50	1.0	(0.3)	(0)	470
Knorr Soupmix, French Onion, prep (w/water) (8 fl oz)	50	1.0	(0.2)	(0)	970
Lipton Cup-A-Soup, Onion, prep (w/water) (6 fl oz)	27	0.5	(1.0)	0	665
Lipton Kettle Ready Frozen Soup, French Onion (6 fl oz)	42	2.2	0.4	(0)	562
Lipton Recipe and Soup Mix, Beefy Onion, prep (w/water) (8 fl oz)	29	1.0	(0.3)	(2)	803
Lipton Recipe and Soup Mix, Onion, prep (w/water) (8 fl oz)	20	0.2	(0.0)	(0)	632
Lipton Recipe and Soup Mix, Onion Mushroom, prep (w/water) (8 fl oz)	41	0.9	(0.2)	0	684
Lipton Soup Mix, Golden Onion with Real Chicken Broth, prep (w/water) (8 fl oz)	62	1.5	(0.3)	(3)	716

Onion Soups (continued)	Calories	Fat g	Saturated Fat g	Choles-terol mg	Sodium mg
Ultra Slim-Fast Instant Soup, Onion, prep (w/water) (6 fl oz)	45	< 1.0	(0.0)	0	930

PEA SOUPS

	Calories	Fat g	Saturated Fat g	Choles-terol mg	Sodium mg
Campbell's Home Cookin' Soup, Split Pea with Ham (10-3/4 oz individual size)	230	1.0	(0.4)	(10)	1310
Campbell's Home Cookin' Soup, Split Pea with Ham (9-1/2 oz)	200	1.0	(0.4)	(9)	1150
Campbell's Low Sodium Soup, Split Pea (10-3/4 oz)	230	4.0*	(1.6)	(11)	30
Campbell's Soup, Green Pea, prep (w/water) (8 fl oz)	160	3.0	(1.4)	(0)	820
Hain Soups, Split Pea (9-1/2 oz)	170	1.0	(0.5)	0	970
Hain Soups, Split Pea, No Salt Added (9-1/2 oz)	170	1.0	(0.5)	0	40
Healthy Choice Soups, Split Pea and Ham (7.5 oz)	170	3.0	1.0	10	460
IGA Split Pea with Ham and Bacon, prep (w/water) (8 oz)	140	2.0	(0.8)	(8)	(780)
Pritikin Soup, Split Pea (8.84 oz)	140	0.4	0.1	0	160
Progresso Soup, Green Split Pea (10.5 oz)	201	3.0	(1.4)	(0)	920

TOMATO SOUPS
(see also Cream Soups)

	Calories	Fat g	Saturated Fat g	Choles-terol mg	Sodium mg
Campbell's Healthy Request Soups, Tomato, prep (w/skim milk) (8 oz)	130	2.0	(0.4)	< 5	490
Campbell's Healthy Request Soups, Tomato, prep (w/water) (8 oz)	90	2.0	(0.4)	0	430
Campbell's Home Cookin' Soup, Tomato Garden (10-3/4 oz individual size)	150	3.0	(0.6)	(4)	930
Campbell's Home Cookin' Soup, Tomato Garden (9-1/2 oz)	130	2.0	(0.4)	(2)	820
Campbell's Soup, Old Fashioned Tomato Rice, prep (w/water) (8 fl oz)	110	2.0	(0.4)	(2)	730

*The value printed for fat is higher than the cutoff point because the manufacturer's serving size is larger than the standard serving size used in evaluating the food.

Tomato Soups (continued)	Calories	Fat g	Saturated Fat g	Choles- terol mg	Sodium mg
Campbell's Soup, Tomato Bisque, prep (w/water) (8 fl oz)	120	3.0	(0.6)	(4)	820
Campbell's Soup, Tomato, prep (w/water) (8 fl oz)	90	2.0	(0.4)	(0)	680
Campbell's Soup, Zesty Tomato, prep (w/water) (8 fl oz)	100	2.0	(0.0)	(4)	760
Campbell's Special Request Soup, 1/3 Less Salt, Tomato, prep (w/water) (8 fl oz)	90	2.0	(0.4)	0	430
Featherweight Soup, Tomato (3.75 oz)	80	1.0	(0.2)	5	240
Healthy Choice Soups, Tomato Garden (7.5 oz)	130	3.0	1.0	5	510
IGA Tomato Soup, prep (w/water) (8 oz)	100	1.0	(0.2)	0	(680)
Knorr Soupmix, Tomato Basil, prep (w/water) (8 fl oz)	90	3.0	(1.4)	(1)	940
Kohl's Soup, Tomato, prep (w/water) (8 fl oz)	80	0.0	0.0	(0)	700
Lipton Cup-A-Soup, Tomato, prep (w/water) (6 fl oz)	103	0.9	(0.4)	(1)	524
Progresso Soup, Tomato (9.5 oz)	120	3.0	(0.6)	0	1100
Town House Soup, Tomato, prep (w/water) (1/2 of can)	100	1.0	(0.2)	(0)	(700)
Ultra Slim-Fast Instant Soup, Creamy Tomato, prep (w/water) (6 fl oz)	80	< 1.0	(0.0)	0	800
TURKEY SOUPS					
Campbell's Soup, Turkey Vegetable, prep (w/water) (8 fl oz)	70	3.0	(0.9)	(2)	710
IGA Turkey Noodle Soup, prep (w/water) (8 oz)	70	3.0	0.9	(5)	(880)
Weight Watchers Soup, Turkey Vegetable (10.5 oz)	70	2.0	(0.5)	(4)	1020
VEGETABLE SOUPS					
Campbell's Chunky Soup, Vegetable (10-3/4 oz individual size)	160	4.0	(0.6)	(0)	1100
Campbell's Chunky Soup, Vegetable (9-1/2 oz)	150	4.0	(0.6)	(0)	970

Vegetable Soups (continued)	Calories	Fat g	Saturated Fat g	Choles-terol mg	Sodium mg
Campbell's Healthy Request Soups, Hearty Vegetable, ready to serve (8 fl oz)	110	3.0	(0.5)	0	480
Campbell's Healthy Request Soups, Vegetable Beef, prep (w/water) (8 fl oz)	70	2.0	(0.9)	<5	490
Campbell's Healthy Request Soups, Vegetable, prep (w/water) (8 fl oz)	90	2.0	(0.3)	<5	500
Campbell's Home Cookin' Soup, Country Vegetable (10-3/4 oz individual size)	120	2.0	(0.3)	(0)	1070
Campbell's Home Cookin' Soup, Country Vegetable (9-1/2 oz)	100	2.0	(0.3)	(0)	940
Campbell's Quality Soup and Recipe Mix, Vegetable, prep (w/water) (8 fl oz)	40	0.0	0.0	(0)	710
Campbell's Soup, Homestyle Vegetable, prep (w/water) (8 fl oz)	60	2.0	(0.5)	(2)	880
Campbell's Soup, Old Fashioned Vegetable, prep (w/water) (8 fl oz)	60	2.0	(0.5)	(2)	880
Campbell's Soup, Vegetable, prep (w/water) (8 fl oz)	90	2.0	(0.0)	(0)	830
Campbell's Soup, Vegetarian Vegetable, prep (w/water) (8 fl oz)	80	2.0	(0.3)	(0)	790
Campbell's Special Request Soup, 1/3 Less Salt, Vegetable, prep (w/water) (8 fl oz)	90	2.0	(0.3)	<5	500
Hain Savory Soup Mix, Vegetable, prep (w/water) (3/4 cup)	80	1.0	(0.2)	(0)	730
Hain Savory Soup Mix, No Sodium Added, Vegetable, prep (w/water) (3/4 cup)	80	1.0	(0.2)	(0)	330
Health Valley Fat-Free Soup, 14 Garden Vegetables (7-1/2 oz)	60	<1.0	(0.0)	0	290
Health Valley Fat-Free Soup, Vegetable Barley (7-1/2 oz)	50	<1.0	(0.0)	0	290
Healthy Choice Soups, Country Vegetable (7.5 oz)	120	1.0	<1.0	0	540

Vegetable Soups (continued)	Calories	Fat g	Saturated Fat g	Choles- terol mg	Sodium mg
IGA Vegetable Beef Soup, prep (w/water) (8 oz)	80	3.0	(1.4)	5	(780)
IGA Vegetable with Beef Stock, prep (w/water) (8 oz)	80	1.0	(0.4)	0	(960)
IGA Vegetarian Vegetable Soup, prep (w/water) (8 oz)	80	2.0	(0.3)	0	(825)
Knorr Soupmix, Spring Vegetable With Herbs, prep (w/water) (8 fl oz)	30	< 1.0	0.0	0	710
Knorr Soupmix, Vegetable, prep (w/water) (8 fl oz)	35	1.0	(0.5)	(tr)	840
Lean Line Soup, Vegetable (7.5 oz)	97	1.0	(0.5)	(6)	700
Lipton Cup-A-Soup, Country Style Harvest Vegetable, prep (w/water) (6 fl oz)	91	1.2	(0.3)	(0)	459
Lipton Cup-A-Soup, Spring Vegetable, prep (w/water) (6 fl oz)	33	0.8	(0.4)	6	746
Lipton Hearty Noodle Soup with Vegetables, prep (w/water) (8 fl oz)	75	1.6	(0.7)	(0)	687
Lipton Instant Oriental Noodle Soup, Garden Vegetable, prep (w/water) (8 fl oz)	199	1.0	(0.4)	(0)	915
Lipton Lots-A-Noodles Cup-A-Soup, Garden Vegetable, prep (w/water) (7 fl oz)	123	1.5	(0.6)	(3)	720
Lipton Recipe and Soup Mix, Vegetable, prep (w/water) (8 fl oz)	39	0.5	(0.2)	(1)	640
Lipton Soup Mix, Country Vegetable, prep (w/water) (8 fl oz)	80	0.7	(0.3)	0	803
Pritikin Soup, Vegetable (8.31 oz)	90	1.3	0.2	0	161
Progresso Soup, Vegetable (10.5 oz)	90	2.0	(0.4)	< 5	1100
Town House Soup, Vegetable, prep (w/water) (1/2 of can)	100	1.0	(0.2)	(5)	860
Ultra Slim-Fast Instant Soup, Hearty Vegetable, prep (w/water) (6 fl oz)	50	< 1.0	(0.0)	0	750

Vegetable Soups (continued)	Calories	Fat g	Saturated Fat g	Choles- terol mg	Sodium mg
Weight Watchers Soup, Chunky Vegetarian (10.5 oz)	100	2.0	(0.7)	(5)	1250
Weight Watchers Soup, Vegetable with Beef Stock (10.5 oz)	90	2.0	(1.2)	(1)	1370

OTHER SOUPS

	Calories	Fat g	Saturated Fat g	Choles- terol mg	Sodium mg
Campbell's Low Fat Block Ramen Noodle Soup, Beef flavor, prep (w/water) (8 fl oz)	160	1.0	(0.2)	(0)	890
Campbell's Low Fat Block Ramen Noodle Soup, Chicken flavor, prep (w/water) (8 fl oz)	160	1.0	(0.2)	(0)	940
Campbell's Low Fat Block Ramen Noodle Soup, Oriental flavor, prep (w/water) (8 fl oz)	150	1.0	(0.2)	(0)	940
Campbell's Low Fat Block Ramen Noodle Soup, Pork flavor, prep (w/water) (8 fl oz)	150	1.0	(0.2)	(0)	1140
Campbell's Low Fat Cup-A-Ramen Soup, Beef flavor with Vegetables, prep (w/water) (8 oz)	220	2.0	(0.3)	(0)	1600
Campbell's Low Fat Cup-A-Ramen Soup, Chicken flavor with Vegetables, prep (w/water) (8 oz)	220	2.0	(0.3)	(0)	1500
Campbell's Low Fat Cup-A-Ramen Soup, Oriental flavor with Vegetables, prep (w/water) (8 oz)	220	2.0	(0.3)	(0)	1400
Campbell's Low Fat Cup-A-Ramen Soup, Shrimp flavor with Vegetables, prep (w/water) (8 fl oz)	230	2.0	(0.3)	(0)	1290
Campbell's Quality Soup and Recipe Mix, Hearty Noodle, prep (w/water) (8 fl oz)	90	1.0	(0.2)	(3)	840
Campbell's Quality Soup and Recipe Mix, Noodle, prep (w/water) (8 fl oz)	110	2.0	(0.4)	(3)	700
Campbell's Soup, Teddy Bear, prep (w/water) (8 fl oz)	70	2.0	(0.8)	(5)	790

Other Soups (continued)	Calories	Fat g	Saturated Fat g	Choles-terol mg	Sodium mg
Health Valley Fat-Free Soup, Country Corn and Vegetable (7-1/2 oz)	60	<1.0	(0.0)	0	290
Health Valley Fat-Free Soup, Tomato Vegetable (7-1/2 oz)	40	<1.0	(0.0)	0	290
Knorr Soupmix, Asparagus, prep (w/water and milk) (8 fl oz)	80	3.0	(0.9)	(4)	770
Knorr Soupmix, Cauliflower, prep (w/water and milk) (8 fl oz)	100	3.0	(0.9)	(4)	750
Knorr Soupmix, Country Barley, prep (w/water) (10 fl oz)	120	2.0	(0.4)	(tr)	940
Knorr Soupmix, Tortellini in Brodo, prep (w/water) (8 fl oz)	60	1.0	(0.5)	(3)	820
Lipton Cup-A-Soup, Hearty Beef Flavor and Noodles, prep (w/water) (7 fl oz)	107	1.4	(0.7)	(3)	698
Lipton Cup-A-Soup, Ring Noodle, prep (w/water) (6 fl oz)	47	0.7	(0.3)	(3)	650
Lipton Hearty Ones, Italiano, prep (w/water) (11 oz)	328	1.9	(0.9)	0	1241
Lipton Hearty Ones, Pasta Garden Medley, prep (w/water) (11 oz)	323	3.8*	(1.9)	6	914
Lipton Instant Oriental Noodle Soup, Beef Flavor, prep (w/water) (8 fl oz)	177	0.8	(0.3)	(2)	912
Lipton Instant Oriental Noodle Soup, Oriental, prep (w/water) (8 fl oz)	198	1.3	(0.2)	(0)	781
Lipton Lite Cup-A-Soup, Golden Broccoli, prep (w/water) (6 fl oz)	42	1.2	(0.2)	1	427
Lipton Lite Cup-A-Soup, Oriental, prep (w/water) (6 fl oz)	45	1.7	(0.6)	3	457
Progresso Soup, Tortellini (9.5 oz)	90	3.0	(0.6)	10	840
Snow's Soups, New England Corn Chowder, prep (w/skim milk) (7-1/2 oz)	118	2.2	(0.5)	(8)	645

*The value printed for fat is higher than the cutoff point because the manufacturer's serving size is larger than the standard serving size used in evaluating the food.

Other Soups (continued)	Calories	Fat g	Saturated Fat g	Choles-terol mg	Sodium mg
Ultra Slim-Fast Instant Soup, Creamy Broccoli, prep (w/water) (6 fl oz)	75	< 1.0	(0.0)	0	800
Ultra Slim-Fast Instant Soup, Potato Leek, prep (w/water) (6 fl oz)	80	< 1.0	(0.0)	0	780

SWEETS

Many products in this section of the Guide, such as jelly, syrup, and low-fat candy, are made primarily of sugar. Candy that contains chocolate, nuts, peanut butter, and/or caramel is high in fat. When sweets are eaten, it should be in addition to well-balanced meals and not as a replacement for foods needed for good health. One serving of the foods included in this section of the Guide provides no more fat, saturated fat, and cholesterol than the cutoff points shown below.

CUTOFF POINTS FOR SWEETS

Fat (grams)	Saturated Fat (grams)	Cholesterol (milligrams)
3	1	10

SERVINGS

Food	Serving Sizes
Candy	1½ ounces
Marshmallows	1 ounce
Jams, Jellies, Preserves, Marmalades, and Honey	1 tablespoon
Molasses	2 tablespoons
Syrups	¼ cup
Toppings:	
Fruit Toppings and Syrups	2 tablespoons
Sprinkles	1 tablespoon

The following abbreviations are used in the Food Sections: oz = ounce; fl oz = fluid ounce; pkg = package; pkt = packet; env = envelope; g = gram; prep (w/ . . .) = prepared with; < = less than; and tr = trace.

Candy and Marshmallows	Calories	Fat g	Saturated Fat g	Choles- terol mg	Sodium mg
CANDY AND MARSHMALLOWS					
Beich's Laffy Taffy Candy Chews, Banana (1 oz = 2 pieces)	120	1.0	(0.3)	(0)	55
Beich's Laffy Taffy Candy Chews, Grape (1 oz = 2 pieces)	110	1.0	(0.3)	(0)	60
Beich's Laffy Taffy Candy Chews, Passion Punch (1 oz = 2 pieces)	120	1.0	(0.3)	(0)	50
Beich's Laffy Taffy Candy Chews, Apple, Strawberry, Sweet and Sour Cherry, or Watermelon (1 oz = 2 pieces)	110	1.0	(0.3)	(0)	55
Brach's Butterscotch Disks (1 oz)	110	0.0	0.0	(0)	110
Brach's Chocolate Covered Mint Patties (1 oz)	110	2.0	(0.9)	(<1)	10
Brach's Cinnamon Disks (1 oz)	110	0.0	0.0	(0)	15
Brach's Cinnamon Imperials (1 oz)	110	0.0	0.0	(0)	5
Brach's Circus Peanuts (1 oz)	100	0.0	0.0	(0)	10
Brach's Dessert Mints (1 oz)	110	0.0	0.0	(0)	0
Brach's Gummi Bears (1 oz)	100	0.0	0.0	(0)	15
Brach's Jelly Beans (1 oz)	100	0.0	0.0	(0)	5
Brach's Kentucky Mints (1 oz)	110	0.0	0.0	(0)	0
Brach's Lemon Drops (1 oz)	110	0.0	0.0	(0)	5
Brach's Licorice Twists (1 oz)	100	0.0	0.0	(0)	50
Brach's Lolly Drops (1 oz)	110	0.0	0.0	(0)	35
Brach's Sour Balls (1 oz)	110	0.0	0.0	(0)	15
Brach's Spicettes (1 oz)	100	0.0	0.0	(0)	15
Brach's Starlight Mints, Peppermint and Spearmint (1 oz)	110	0.0	0.0	(0)	15
Campfire Marshmallows (2 large or 24 mini)	40	0.0	0.0	0	10
Candy Corn—Most Brands (30 pieces)	155	0.9	0.2	(0)	90
Featherweight Candy, Apple Fruit Drops (1/3 oz)	30	0.0	0.0	0	15
Featherweight Candy, Berry Patch Blend (1 piece)	12	0.0	0.0	0	0

Candy and Marshmallows (continued)	Calories	Fat g	Saturated Fat g	Choles- terol mg	Sodium mg
Featherweight Candy, Butterscotch Candy (1 piece)	25	0.0	0.0	0	25
Featherweight Candy, Cool Blue Mints (1 piece)	25	0.0	0.0	0	0
Featherweight Candy, Grape Fruit Drops (1/3 oz)	30	0.0	0.0	0	15
Featherweight Candy, Orange Fruit Drops (1/3 oz)	30	0.0	0.0	0	15
Featherweight Candy, Orchard Blend (1 piece)	12	0.0	0.0	0	0
Featherweight Candy, Peppermint Swirls (1 piece)	20	0.0	0.0	0	0
Featherweight Candy, Raspberry Fruit Drops (1/3 oz)	30	0.0	0.0	0	15
Featherweight Candy, Strawberry Fruit Drops (1/3 oz)	30	0.0	0.0	0	15
Featherweight Candy, Tropical Blend (1 piece)	12	0.0	0.0	0	0
Giant Buttons, Butter Rum (2 pieces)	45	0.0	0.0	0	(4)
Giant Buttons, Butterscotch (2 pieces)	45	0.0	0.0	0	(4)
Giant Buttons, Sour Cherry (2 pieces)	45	0.0	0.0	0	(4)
Giant Buttons, Sour Lemon (2 pieces)	45	0.0	0.0	0	(4)
Giant Buttons, Spearmint (2 pieces)	45	0.0	0.0	0	(4)
Giant Hostess Mix (2 pieces)	45	0.0	0.0	0	(4)
Giant Iceland Mints (2 pieces)	45	0.0	0.0	0	(4)
Giant Sour Balls (3 pieces)	60	0.0	0.0	0	(5)
Giant Starlight Mints (3 pieces)	60	0.0	0.0	0	(5)
Gumdrops—Most Brands (1-1/2 oz)	147	0.3	0.0	0	15
Hard Candy—Most Brands (1-1/2 oz)	164	0.5	0.0	0	14
Heide Candy Corn (1.5 oz)	164	0.0	0.0	0	60
Heide Drops (1.5 oz)	159	0.0	0.0	0	22
Heide JujyFruits (1 oz)	100	<1.0	(0.0)	(0)	<10
IGA Marshmallows (1 oz)	90	0.0	0.0	<1	(11)
Jujubes (1.5 oz)	159	0.9	(<1.0)	<4	5
Kraft Butter Mints (1 piece)	8	0.0	0.0	0	0

Candy and Marshmallows (continued)	Calories	Fat g	Saturated Fat g	Choles- terol mg	Sodium mg
Kraft Funmallows Marshmallows (1 piece)	30	0.0	0.0	0	15
Kraft Funmallows Miniature Marshmallows (10 pieces)	18	0.0	0.0	0	5
Kraft Jet-Puffed Marshmallows (1 piece)	25	0.0	0.0	0	5
Kraft Miniature Marshmallows (10 pieces)	18	0.0	0.0	0	5
Kraft Party Mints (1 piece)	8	0.0	0.0	0	0
Lance Breath Mints (.65 oz = 1 pkg)	90	0.0	0.0	0	0
Lance Candy Rolls (.8 oz = 1 pkg)	100	0.0	0.0	0	0
Lance Chews (1 pkg)	120	1.0	1.0	0	0
Lance Michigan Cherries (1-7/8 oz = 1 pkg)	220	0.0	0.0	0	0
Lance Spice Drops (1-7/8 oz = 1 pkg)	220	0.0	0.0	0	0
Marshmallows—Most Brands (1-1/2 oz)	135	0.0	0.0	0	17
Mints, uncoated—Most Brands (1-1/2 oz)	155	0.9	0.2	0	90
Mrs. Wright's Fluf Puft Marshmallows (1 oz)	100	0.0	0.0	0	10
Mrs. Wright's Fluf Puft Miniature Marshmallows (1 oz)	100	0.0	0.0	0	10
Neilson Pep (1.7 oz = 1 bar)	181	3.8	(1.0)	(0)	n/a
Richardson Jellies (1 oz)	106	0.0	0.0	0	8
Richardson Mints, Anise (1 oz)	109	0.0	0.0	0	1
Richardson Mints, Butter (1 oz)	110	0.2	(0.0)	(0)	9
Richardson Mints, Green Jelly (1 oz)	106	0.0	0.0	0	9
Richardson Mints, Pastel (1 oz)	109	0.0	0.0	0	1
Shari Candies, Assorted Sugar Free (1 candy)	12	0.0	0.0	(0)	0
Skittles Bite Size Candies (2.3 oz)	265	3.0	(0.5)	0	35
Sugar Daddy Milk Caramel Pop (1-3/8 oz = 1 pop)	150	1.0	(0.8)	(1)	85
Sunkist Fruit Gems (.37 oz = 1 piece)	35	0.1	0.0	0	9
Velamints, Cocoamint (1 piece)	8	0.0	0.0	0	0

Candy and Marshmallows (continued)	Calories	Fat g	Saturated Fat g	Choles-terol mg	Sodium mg
Velamints, all flavors except Cocoamint (1 piece)	9	0.0	0.0	0	0
Willy Wonka Fruit Runts, Sour Hearts, Dinasour Eggs, Freckled Eggs, Gobstopper, Heart Breakers, or Merry Mix (1 oz)	104	0.0	0.0	0	0
Willy Wonka Nerds (1 oz)	108	0.0	0.0	0	0
Willy Wonka Tart 'N Tinys, Bottle Caps, Fruit Flurries, Sweet & Sour Hearts, Tangy Bunnys or Wacky Wafers (1 oz)	104	0.0	0.0	0	0
Y & S Bites Cherry Candy (1 oz)	100	1.0	(0.1)	0	85
Y & S Nibs Cherry Candy (1 oz)	100	1.0	(0.1)	0	80
Y & S Twizzlers Strawberry Candy (1 oz)	100	1.0	(0.1)	0	95
JAMS, JELLIES, PRESERVES, AND HONEY					
Bama Apple Butter (2 tsp)	25	0.0	0.0	0	5
Featherweight Low Calorie Fruit Spread, Apple Jelly (1 tsp)	4	0.0	(0.0)	0	0
Featherweight Low Calorie Fruit Spread, Apricot Preserves (1 tsp)	4	0.0	(0.0)	0	0
Featherweight Low Calorie Fruit Spread, Blackberry Jelly (1 tsp)	4	0.0	(0.0)	0	0
Featherweight Low Calorie Fruit Spread, Blackberry Preserves (1 tsp)	4	0.0	(0.0)	0	0
Featherweight Low Calorie Fruit Spread, Grape Jelly (1 tsp)	4	0.0	(0.0)	0	5
Featherweight Low Calorie Fruit Spread, Peach Preserves (1 tsp)	4	0.0	(0.0)	0	0
Featherweight Low Calorie Fruit Spread, Red Raspberry Preserves (1 tsp)	4	0.0	(0.0)	0	0

Jams, Jellies, Preserves, and Honey (continued)	Calories	Fat g	Saturated Fat g	Choles- terol mg	Sodium mg
Featherweight Low Calorie Fruit Spread, Strawberry Jelly (1 tsp)	4	0.0	(0.0)	0	0
Featherweight Low Calorie Fruit Spread, Strawberry Preserves (1 tsp)	4	0.0	(0.0)	0	0
Giant Seedless Preserves, Black Raspberry (2 tsp)	35	0.0	0.0	0	5
Giant Seedless Preserves, Blackberry (2 tsp)	35	0.0	0.0	0	5
Hickory Farms Light Choice Fruit Spread (1 tsp)	8	0.0	(0.0)	(0)	0
Honey—Most Brands (1 tbsp)	64	0.0	0.0	0	1
IGA Preserves, Blackberry Seedless (2 tsp)	35	0.0	0.0	0	(5)
Jellies, Marmalades, Preserves, or Jams, all flavors—Most Brands (2 tsp)	35	0.0	0.0	0	0
Kraft Reduced Calorie Jelly, Grape (1 tsp)	6	0.0	0.0	0	5
Kraft Reduced Calorie Preserves, Strawberry (1 tsp)	6	0.0	0.0	0	5
Smucker's Apple Butter, Autumn Harvest (1 tsp)	12	0.0	(0.0)	(0)	0
Smucker's Apple Butter, Cider (1 tsp)	12	0.0	(0.0)	(0)	0
Smucker's Apple Butter, Natural (1 tsp)	12	0.0	(0.0)	(0)	0
Smucker's Apple Butter, Simply Fruit (1 tsp)	12	0.0	(0.0)	(0)	0
Smucker's Low Sugar Spreads (1 tsp)	8	0.0	0.0	0	< 10
Smucker's Marmalade, Orange (1 tsp)	18	0.0	(0.0)	(0)	0
Smucker's Peach Butter (1 tsp)	15	0.0	(0.0)	(0)	0
Smucker's Pumpkin Butter, Autumn Harvest (1 tsp)	12	0.0	(0.0)	(0)	14
Smucker's Simply Fruit Spread (1 tsp)	16	0.0	0.0	0	0
Smucker's Slenderella Reduced Calorie Fruit Spreads (1 tsp)	7	0.0	(0.0)	(0)	0
Weight Watchers Fruit Spread, all flavors (2 tsp)	16	0.0	0.0	0	0

Jams, Jellies, Preserves, and Honey (continued)	Calories	Fat g	Saturated Fat g	Cholesterol mg	Sodium mg
Welch's All Fruit Spread, Grape (2 tsp)	28	0.0	0.0	0	5
Welch's Totally Fruit Spread, Apricot (1 tsp)	14	0.0	(0.0)	(0)	5
Welch's Totally Fruit Spread, Blackberry (1 tsp)	14	0.0	(0.0)	(0)	5
Welch's Totally Fruit Spread, Blueberry (1 tsp)	14	0.0	(0.0)	(0)	5
Welch's Totally Fruit Spread, Orange Marmalade (1 tsp)	14	0.0	(0.0)	(0)	5
Welch's Totally Fruit Spread, Red Raspberry (1 tsp)	14	0.0	(0.0)	(0)	5
Welch's Totally Fruit Spread, Strawberry (1 tsp)	14	0.0	(0.0)	(0)	5
SYRUPS					
Brer Rabbit Molasses, Dark (1 fl oz = 2 tbsp)	110	0.0	0.0	0	20
Brer Rabbit Syrup, Dark (1 fl oz = 2 tbsp)	120	0.0	0.0	0	0
Brer Rabbit Syrup, Light (1 fl oz = 2 tbsp)	120	0.0	0.0	0	0
IGA Light Corn Syrup (1 tbsp)	60	0.0	0.0	0	(14)
CHOCOLATE (see also Toppings, Chocolate and Fudge, page 375)					
Giant Chocolate Syrup (2 tbsp)	100	< 1.0	< 1.0	0	20
Hershey's Syrup, Chocolate Flavored (2 tbsp)	80	1.0	(0.6)	0	20
IGA Chocolate Syrup (1 tbsp)	100	0.0	0.0	0	(36)
Nestle Quik Syrup, Chocolate Flavor (1-3/4 tbsp)	100	1.0	(0.6)	(0)	45
Smucker's Syrup, Chocolate Flavored (2 tbsp)	130	0.0	0.0	(0)	35
FRUIT (see also Toppings, Fruit, page 375)					
Featherweight Syrup, Blueberry (1 tbsp)	16	0.0	0.0	0	35
Nestle Quik Syrup, Strawberry Flavor (1.2 oz)	130	0.0	(0.0)	0	0
Slim-ette Syrup, Blueberry Flavored (1 tbsp)	1	0.0	0.0	0	15
Smucker's Fruit Syrups (2 tbsp)	100	0.0	0.0	(0)	< 10

Syrups (continued)	Calories	Fat g	Saturated Fat g	Cholesterol mg	Sodium mg
PANCAKE					
Aunt Jemima Butter Lite Syrup (1 fl oz)	53	0.0	0.0	0	88
Aunt Jemima Lite Syrup (1 fl oz)	54	0.1	0.0	0	92
Aunt Jemima Syrup (1 fl oz)	109	0.0	0.0	0	32
Empress Syrup Lite (2 tbsp)	60	0.0	0.0	0	35
Empress Syrup, Butter Lite (2 tbsp)	60	0.0	(0.0)	(0)	35
Featherweight Syrup, Pancake (1 tbsp)	16	0.0	0.0	0	30
Giant Syrup, Cane & Maple (2 tbsp)	100	0.0	0.0	0	0
Giant Syrup, Lite Pancake (2 tbsp)	50	0.0	0.0	0	35
Giant Syrup, Pancake (2 tbsp)	120	0.0	0.0	0	0
Golden Griddle Syrup (1 tbsp)	55	0.0	0.0	(0)	15
Hungry Jack Syrup (2 tbsp)	100	0.0	0.0	0	25
Hungry Jack Syrup, Lite (2 tbsp)	50	0.0	0.0	0	115
IGA Pancake and Waffle Syrup (1 tbsp)	100	0.0	0.0	0	(28)
IGA Premium Blend Maple Syrup (2 tbsp)	100	0.0	0.0	0	(26)
Karo Pancake Syrup (1 tbsp)	60	0.0	0.0	(0)	35
Log Cabin Lite Reduced Calorie Syrup (1 fl oz)	50	0.0	0.0	0	90
Log Cabin Pancake Country Kitchen Syrup (1 fl oz)	100	0.0	0.0	0	20
Log Cabin Pancake and Waffle Syrup (1 fl oz)	100	0.0	0.0	0	35
Maple Syrup—Most Brands (1 tbsp)	50	0.0	0.0	0	2
Molasses, Blackstrap—Most Brands (1 tbsp)	43	0.0	0.0	0	39
Molasses, Light—Most Brands (1 tbsp)	50	0.0	0.0	0	3
Molasses, Medium—Most Brands (1 tbsp)	46	0.0	0.0	0	7
Piedmont Old Fashion Syrup (2 tbsp)	100	0.0	0.0	0	0
Piedmont Waffle & Pancake Syrup (2 tbsp)	90	0.0	0.0	0	35

Syrups (continued)	Calories	Fat g	Saturated Fat g	Choles- terol mg	Sodium mg
Scotch Buy Syrup (2 tbsp)	90	0.0	0.0	0	35
Slim-ette Syrup, Maple Flavored (1 tbsp)	1	<1.0	(0.0)	(0)	10
Weight Watchers Naturally Sweetened Syrup (1 tbsp)	25	0.0	0.0	(0)	25

TOPPINGS

BUTTERSCOTCH AND CARAMEL

	Calories	Fat g	Saturated Fat g	Choles- terol mg	Sodium mg
Knorr Sauce, Caramel (1 tbsp)	60	0.0	0.0	0	5
Kraft Topping, Artificially Flavored Butterscotch (1 tbsp)	60	1.0	0.0	0	70
Kraft Topping, Caramel (1 tbsp)	60	0.0	0.0	0	45
Smucker's Topping, Butterscotch Flavored (2 tbsp)	140	1.0	(<1.0)	(0)	75
Smucker's Topping, Caramel Flavored (2 tbsp)	140	1.0	(<1.0)	(0)	110

CHOCOLATE AND FUDGE

	Calories	Fat g	Saturated Fat g	Choles- terol mg	Sodium mg
Kraft Topping, Chocolate (1 tbsp)	50	0.0	0.0	0	15
Smucker's Topping, Chocolate Fudge (2 tbsp)	130	1.0	(0.6)	(4)	50
Smucker's Topping, Light Hot Fudge (2 tbsp)	70	<1.0	0.0	0	35
Smucker's Topping, Special Recipe Dark Chocolate Flavored (2 tbsp)	130	1.0	(0.6)	(4)	45
Smucker's Topping, Swiss Milk Chocolate Fudge (2 tbsp)	140	1.0	(0.6)	(0)	70

FRUIT

	Calories	Fat g	Saturated Fat g	Choles- terol mg	Sodium mg
Kraft Topping, Pineapple (1 tbsp)	50	0.0	0.0	0	0
Kraft Topping, Strawberry (1 tbsp)	50	0.0	0.0	0	5
Smucker's Topping, Pineapple (2 tbsp)	130	0.0	0.0	(0)	0
Smucker's Topping, Strawberry (2 tbsp)	120	0.0	0.0	(0)	0

MARSHMALLOW

	Calories	Fat g	Saturated Fat g	Choles- terol mg	Sodium mg
IGA Marshmallow Creme (1 oz)	90	0.0	0.0	<1	(6)

Toppings (continued)	Calories	Fat g	Saturated Fat g	Choles- terol mg	Sodium mg
Kraft Marshmallow Creme (1 oz)	90	0.0	0.0	0	20
Smucker's Topping, Marshmallow (2 tbsp)	120	0.0	0.0	(0)	0
OTHER TOPPINGS					
Smucker's Topping, Pecans in Syrup (2 tbsp)	130	1.0	(0.1)	(0)	0
Smucker's Topping, Walnuts in Syrup (2 tbsp)	130	1.0	(0.1)	(0)	0

VEGETABLES

Vegetables contain no cholesterol and little or no fat or saturated fat unless an ingredient containing fat is added in preparation. Frying vegetables or seasoning them with fat adds approximately 2 grams of fat per ½ cup; deep-fat frying potatoes or dipping vegetables in batter (breading) and frying them adds approximately 4 grams of fat per ½ cup serving. Butter, bacon, bacon fat, salt pork, cream sauce, and cheese are high in fat and saturated fat and should not be added to vegetables. One serving of the products included in this section of the Guide does not exceed the cutoff points listed below.

Fresh, frozen, canned, and dehydrated vegetables are listed separately in the Guide, since they are found in different sections of the supermarket. Values for most of the fresh vegetables in this section are based on information from the USDA handbooks, and many of the processed foods are listed as "most brands." Avocado and olives are listed in the Fats and Oils section, beginning on page 210.

The sodium values given for fresh vegetables are for foods that have not been salted. Although most plain frozen vegetables are unsalted, combination vegetables and vegetable mixes may be seasoned with salt. Many canned vegetables are high in sodium due to the salt and other sodium-containing compounds added in processing.

CUTOFF POINTS FOR VEGETABLES

Fat (grams)	Saturated Fat (grams)	Cholesterol (milligrams)
3	1	10

SERVINGS

Food	Serving Sizes
Beans and Legumes, dry	2½ ounces
Canned Vegetables:	
Beans and Legumes, plain or in sauce	6 ounces
Potatoes and Sweet Potatoes, plain	4 ounces
Other Vegetables:	
With sauce or canned in liquid	4½ ounces
Without sauce or vacuum-packed	3½ ounces
Dehydrated and Freeze-Dried Vegetables	½ ounce
Dried	1 ounce
Frozen Vegetables:	
With sauce	4½ ounces
Without sauce	3½ ounces
Combination and Specialty with sauce	4½ ounces
Combination and Specialty without sauce	3½ ounces
Potatoes and Sweet Potatoes, cooked	4 ounces

Food	Serving Sizes
Potatoes and Sweet Potatoes:	
French Fries, Hash Browns, Skins, Stuffed, or Pancake	3 ounces
Mashed, candied, or with sauce	6 ounces
Plain, cooked	4 ounces

Refer to page 403 for the cooked yield of some types of dried beans and for the number of tomatoes and potatoes in one pound.

The following abbreviations are used in the Food Sections: oz = ounce; fl oz = fluid ounce; pkg = package; pkt = packet; env = envelope; g = gram; prep (w/ . . .) = prepared with; < = less than; and tr = trace.

Beans, Cooked from Dry	Calories	Fat g	Saturated Fat g	Choles- terol mg	Sodium mg
BEANS, COOKED FROM DRY					
Beans, Kidney Beans, cooked, boiled—Most Brands (1/2 cup)	112	0.4	0.1	0	2
Beans, Navy, cooked, boiled—Most Brands (1/2 cup)	129	0.5	0.1	0	1
Beans, Pinto Beans, cooked, boiled—Most Brands (1/2 cup)	117	0.4	0.1	0	1
Beans, White Beans—Most Brands (1/2 cup)	153	0.4	0.1	0	7
Lentils, cooked, boiled—Most Brands (1/2 cup)	115	0.4	0.1	0	2
CANNED AND SHELF-STABLE VEGETABLES					
Artichoke Hearts, Giant Artichoke Hearts, Quartered (1/2 cup)	30	<1.0	<1.0	0	45
Asparagus, Spears, drained—Most Brands (1/2 cup)	24	0.8	0.2	0	(425)
Asparagus, no salt added, drained—Most Brands (1/2 cup)	24	0.8	0.2	0	(5)
Baked Beans (see Beans, Baked)					

Canned and Shelf-Stable Vegetables (continued)	Calories	Fat g	Saturated Fat g	Cholesterol mg	Sodium mg
Bamboo Shoots, sliced, drained—Most Brands (1/2 cup)	13	1.0	0.1	0	5
Bean Sprouts, La Choy Bean Sprouts (1 cup)	11	0.0	0.0	0	31
Bean Sprouts, La Choy Mung Bean Sprouts (2/3 cup)	8	<1.0	(0.0)	0	20
Beans, Adzuki, Eden Adzuki Beans with Kombu (1/2 cup)	80	<1.0	(0.0)	0	10
Beans, Adzuki, Eden Adzuki Beans with Tamari (1/2 cup)	100	<1.0	0.0	0	20
Beans, Baked, Allen Vegetarian Baked Beans (1/2 cup)	140	<1.0	<1.0	2	410
Beans, Baked, B & M Brick Oven Baked Beans, Barbecue (8 oz)	280	4.0*	(1.5)	5	850
Beans, Baked, B & M Brick Oven Baked Beans, Honey Baked (8 oz)	240	2.0	(0.5)	0	940
Beans, Baked, B & M Brick Oven Baked Beans, Hot N Spicy (8 oz)	240	3.0	1.0	3	990
Beans, Baked, B & M Brick Oven Baked Beans, Maple (8 oz)	240	2.0	1.0	<5	890
Beans, Baked, B & M Brick Oven Baked Beans, Red Kidney (8 oz)	240	4.0*	(1.0)	5	680
Beans, Baked, B & M Brick Oven Baked Beans, Tomato (8 oz)	230	3.0	1.0	1	1010
Beans, Baked, B & M Brick Oven Baked Beans, Vegetarian (8 oz)	280	2.0	(1.0)	0	750
Beans, Baked, B & M Brick Oven Baked Beans, Vegetarian, 50% Less Sodium (8 oz)	230	2.0	(1.0)	0	370
Beans, Baked, Bush's Best Baked Beans (4 oz)	110	1.0	(0.4)	(0)	550
Beans, Baked, Baked Beans with Pork and Tomato Sauce, canned—Most Brands (1/2 cup)	123	1.3	0.5	9	554

*The value printed for fat is higher than the cutoff point because the manufacturer's serving size is larger than the standard serving size used in evaluating the food.

Canned and Shelf-Stable Vegetables (continued)	Calories	Fat g	Saturated Fat g	Choles- terol mg	Sodium mg
Beans, Baked, Campbell's Canned Beans, Old Fashioned Beans in Molasses and Brown Sugar Sauce (8 oz)	230	3.0	(1.1)	(16)	730
Beans, Baked, Friends Baked Beans, Maple (8 oz)	240	2.0	1.0	<5	890
Beans, Baked, Green Giant Beans, Baked Style (solids and liquids) (1/2 cup)	150	2.0	(0.5)	0	670
Beans, Baked, Health Valley Fat-Free Boston Baked Beans with Honey (7.5 oz)	190	<1.0	(0.0)	0	290
Beans, Baked, Van Camp's Baked Beans (1 cup)	260	2.0	(0.8)	(0)	1020
Beans, Baked, Van Camp's Baked Beans, Deluxe (1 cup)	320	4.0*	(1.5)	(0)	970
Beans, Black, Eden Black Beans (1/2 cup)	70	<1.0	(0.0)	0	15
Beans, Broadbeans, canned—Most Brands (1/2 cup)	91	0.3	0.0	0	580
Beans, Butter, Baby, IGA Baby Butterbeans (4 oz)	70	<1.0	(0.0)	0	(420)
Beans, Butter, Large, IGA Large Butterbeans (4 oz)	110	<1.0	(0.0)	0	(420)
Beans, Butter, Van Camp's Butter Beans (1 cup)	162	0.5	(0.1)	(0)	710
Beans, Campbell's Canned Beans, Barbecue (7-7/8 oz)	210	4.0*	(1.5)	(16)	900
Beans, Campbell's Canned Beans, Home Style (8 oz)	220	4.0*	(1.5)	(16)	820
Beans, Chili, Campbell's Canned Beans, Hot Chili Beans (7-3/4 oz)	180	4.0*	(1.5)	(6)	870
Beans, Chili, Green Giant Caliente Style Chili Beans (1/2 cup)	100	1.0	(0.3)	0	700
Beans, Chili, Town House Chili Beans, Mexican Style (1/2 cup)	110	1.0	0.1	0	490
Beans, Chili, Van Camp's Chili Beans, Mexican Style (1 cup)	210	2.4	(0.9)	(0)	730
Beans, Chili Hot, Bush's Best Chili Hot Beans (4 oz)	70	<1.0	(0.0)	(0)	420

*The value printed for fat is higher than the cutoff point because the manufacturer's serving size is larger than the standard serving size used in evaluating the food.

Canned and Shelf-Stable Vegetables (continued)	Calories	Fat g	Saturated Fat g	Choles-terol mg	Sodium mg
Beans, Garbanzo, Bush's Best Garbanzo Beans (4 oz)	80	<1.0	(0.0)	(0)	350
Beans, Garbanzo, canned—Most Brands (1/2 cup)	143	1.4	0.1	0	359
Beans, Garbanzo, Eden Garbanzo Beans with Kombu (1/2 cup)	90	1.0	(0.1)	0	10
Beans, Garbanzo, Eden Garbanzo Beans with Tamari (1/2 cup)	110	2.0	(0.2)	0	15
Beans, Garbanzo, Green Giant Garbanzo Beans (1/2 cup)	90	2.0	0.0	0	320
Beans, Garbanzo, Green Giant Garbanzo Beans, 50% Less Salt (1/2 cup)	90	2.0	0.0	0	160
Beans, Garbanzo, IGA Garbanzo Chick Peas (1/2 cup)	90	2.0	(0.2)	(0)	(200)
Beans, Giant Vegetarian Beans (1/2 cup)	130	<1.0	<1.0	0	400
Beans, Great Northern, Eden Great Northern Beans (1/2 cup)	110	<1.0	0.0	0	15
Beans, Great Northern, IGA Great Northern Beans (4 oz)	110	<1.0	(0.0)	0	(450)
Beans, Green or Snap, Bush's Best Cut Green & Shelly Beans (4 oz)	35	0.0	0.0	(0)	290
Beans, Green or Snap, Del Monte Vegetable Classics, Country Green Beans (1/2 cup)	50	2.0	(0.3)	(4)	200
Beans, Green or Snap, no salt added, drained—Most Brands (1/2 cup)	13	0.1	0.0	0	1
Beans, Green or Snap—Most Brands (1/2 cup)	13	0.1	0.0	0	170
Beans, Kidney Beans, all types, canned—Most Brands (1/2 cup)	104	0.4	0.1	0	445
Beans, Kidney, Eden Kidney Beans (1/2 cup)	60	<1.0	(0.0)	0	20

Canned and Shelf-Stable Vegetables (continued)	Calories	Fat g	Saturated Fat g	Choles- terol mg	Sodium mg
Beans, Kidney, Van Camp's New Orleans Style Red Kidney Beans (1 cup)	178	0.6	(0.1)	(0)	940
Beans, Lima, no salt added, undrained—Most Brands (1/2 cup)	93	0.4	0.1	0	5
Beans, Lima, undrained— Most Brands (1/2 cup)	93	0.4	0.1	0	309
Beans, Navy, Bush's Best Navy Beans (4 oz)	60	<1.0	(0.0)	(0)	370
Beans, Navy, Eden Navy Beans (1/2 cup)	70	<1.0	(0.0)	0	15
Beans, Pinto Beans, canned—Most Brands (1/2 cup)	93	0.4	0.1	0	499
Beans, Pinto, Eden Pinto Beans with Kombu (1/2 cup)	70	<1.0	(0.0)	0	15
Beans, Pinto, Eden Pinto Beans with Tamari (1/2 cup)	110	<1.0	(0.0)	0	20
Beans, Progresso Beans, Cannellini (1/2 cup)	80	<1.0	(0.0)	<1	390
Beans, Progresso Beans, Fava (1/2 cup)	90	<1.0	(0.0)	<1	420
Beans, Progresso Beans, Roman (1/2 cup)	110	<1.0	(0.0)	<1	420
Beans, Red, Bush's Best Red Beans (4 oz)	70	<1.0	(0.0)	(0)	350
Beans, Red, IGA Red Beans (4 oz)	80	<1.0	(0.0)	0	(460)
Beans, Red, Van Camp's Red Beans (1 cup)	194	0.6	(0.1)	(0)	928
Beans, Refried (see Refried Beans)					
Beans, Vegetarian, Bush's Deluxe Vegetarian Beans (4 oz)	110	<1.0	(0.3)	(0)	350
Beans, Wax, Giant Wax Beans, Cut (1/2 cup)	20	0.0	0.0	0	20
Beets, Harvard, undrained—Most Brands (1/2 cup)	89	0.1	0.0	0	199
Beets, Pickled, slices, undrained—Most Brands (1/2 cup)	75	0.1	0.0	0	301

Canned and Shelf-Stable Vegetables (continued)	Calories	Fat g	Saturated Fat g	Choles- terol mg	Sodium mg
Beets, slices, drained—Most Brands (1/2 cup)	27	0.1	0.0	0	(324)
Beets, slices, no salt added, drained—Most Brands (1/2 cup)	27	0.1	0.0	0	(57)
Carrots, slices, no salt added—Most Brands (1/2 cup)	17	0.1	0.0	0	31
Carrots, slices—Most Brands (1/2 cup)	17	0.1	0.0	0	176
Chickpeas (see Beans, Garbanzo)					
Chop Suey, La Choy Vegetables (1/2 cup)	10	<1.0	(0.0)	0	320
Corn, Cream Style—Most Brands (1/2 cup)	93	0.5	0.1	0	365
Corn, Cream Style, no salt added—Most Brands (1/2 cup)	93	1.0	0.1	0	4
Corn, Giant White Whole Kernel Corn (1/2 cup)	100	0.0	0.0	0	540
Corn, drained—Most Brands (1/2 cup)	66	0.8	0.1	0	(286)
Corn, no salt added, drained—Most Brands (1/2 cup)	66	0.8	0.1	0	(3)
Garbanzo Beans (see Beans, Garbanzo)					
Green Beans (see Beans, Green or Snap)					
Greens, Collard, Bush's Best Collard Greens, chopped (4 oz)	30	0.0	0.0	(0)	320
Greens, Kale, Bush's Best Kale Greens, chopped (4 oz)	25	0.0	0.0	(0)	230
Greens, Kale, Giant Kale Greens, chopped (1/2 cup)	25	0.0	0.0	0	15
Greens, Mixed, Bush's Best Mixed Greens (turnip and Mustard) (4 oz)	20	0.0	0.0	(0)	300
Greens, Mustard, Bush's Best Mustard Greens, chopped (4 oz)	20	0.0	0.0	(0)	220

Canned and Shelf-Stable Vegetables (continued)	Calories	Fat g	Saturated Fat g	Choles- terol mg	Sodium mg
Greens, Turnip, Bush's Best Turnip Greens with Diced Turnips (4 oz)	25	0.0	0.0	(0)	370
Greens, Turnip, Giant Turnip Greens, chopped (1/2 cup)	20	0.0	0.0	0	15
Greens, Turnip, undrained— Most Brands (1/2 cup)	17	0.4	0.1	0	325
Hominy, Bush's Best Golden Hominy (4 oz)	45	0.0	0.0	(0)	390
Hominy, Giant White Hominy Corn (1/2 cup)	70	0.0	0.0	0	430
Hominy, Town House White Hominy (1 cup)	140	0.0	0.0	0	(710)
Hominy, White, Bush's Best White Hominy (4 oz)	45	0.0	0.0	(0)	450
Hominy, White, IGA White Hominy (4 oz)	70	< 1.0	0.0	0	(430)
Mixed Vegetables, drained— Most Brands (1/2 cup)	39	0.4	0.0	0	122
Mixed Vegetables, Green Giant Garden Medley (1/2 cup)	35	0.0	0.0	0	350
Mixed Vegetables, La Choy Fancy Mixed Chinese Vegetables (1/2 cup)	12	< 1.0	(0.0)	0	30
Mushroom, pieces, drained—Most Brands (1/2 cup)	19	0.6	0.0	0	(330)
Mushrooms, Button, Giant Mushrooms, Button (2 oz)	14	0.0	0.0	0	300
Mushrooms, Giant Mushrooms, Stems and Pieces, No Salt (2 oz)	14	0.0	0.0	0	35
Mushrooms, Giant Mushrooms, sliced (2 oz)	14	0.0	0.0	0	300
Peas, Black-eyed, Bush's Best Blackeye Peas (4 oz)	70	< 1.0	(0.0)	(0)	350
Peas, Black-eyed, Giant Blackeye Peas (1/2 cup)	110	0.0	0.0	0	500
Peas, Black-eyed, Showboat Blackeye Peas (4 oz)	70	< 1.0	(0.0)	(0)	350

Canned and Shelf-Stable Vegetables (continued)	Calories	Fat g	Saturated Fat g	Choles- terol mg	Sodium mg
Peas, Green, no salt added, drained—Most Brands (1/2 cup)	59	0.3	0.1	0	2
Peas, Green—Most Brands (1/2 cup)	59	0.3	0.1	0	186
Peas and Carrots, no salt added, undrained—Most Brands (1/2 cup)	48	0.4	0.1	0	5
Peas and Carrots, undrained—Most Brands (1/2 cup)	48	0.4	0.1	0	332
Peas and Onions, undrained—Most Brands (1/2 cup)	30	0.2	0.0	0	265
Peppers (see Condiments, page 140)					
Peppers, Hot Chili, no salt added, undrained—Most Brands (1 pepper)	18	0.1	0.0	0	(470)
Peppers, Progresso Roasted Peppers (1/2 cup)	20	<1.0	<1.0	0	2
Peppers, Sweet (Bell), halves—Most Brands (1/2 cup)	13	0.2	0.0	0	958
Pork and Beans, Bush's Deluxe Pork & Beans (4 oz)	110	1.0	(0.4)	(9)	350
Pork and Beans, Bush's Showboat Pork & Beans (4 oz)	80	<1.0	(0.0)	(9)	470
Pork and Beans, Bush's Best Baked Beans with Onions (4 oz)	110	1.0	(0.4)	(0)	550
Pork and Beans, Campbell's Canned Beans, Vegetarian Beans (7-3/4 oz)	170	1.0	(0.1)	(0)	780
Pork and Beans, Giant Pork & Beans (1/2 cup)	150	2.0	(0.8)	(9)	445
Pork and Beans, Van Camp's Pork and Beans (1 cup)	216	1.9	1.0	0	1000
Pork and Beans, Van Camp's Vegetarian Style Beans (1 cup)	206	0.6	(0.1)	(0)	950
Potatoes, Whole, Giant Potatoes, Whole, No Salt Added (1/2 cup)	50	0.0	0.0	0	10

Canned and Shelf-Stable Vegetables (continued)	Calories	Fat g	Saturated Fat g	Choles-terol mg	Sodium mg
Potatoes, Whole, drained—Most Brands (1/2 cup)	54	0.2	0.0	0	(452)
Pumpkin—Most Brands (1/2 cup)	41	0.3	0.0	0	6
Refried Beans, IGA Vegetarian Refried Beans (1/2 cup)	130	2.0	(0.8)	(2)	(400)
Refried Beans, Little Pancho Refried Beans and Green Chili (1/2 cup)	80	0.0	0.0	(0)	330
Refried Beans, Old El Paso Mexe-Beans (1/2 cup)	163	1.0	0.0	0	627
Refried Beans, Old El Paso Refried Beans (1/2 cup)	55	< 1.0	0.0	1	200
Refried Beans, Old El Paso Refried Beans with Green Chilies (1/4 cup)	49	< 1.0	(0.0)	(1)	252
Refried Beans, Old El Paso Refried Beans with Jalapenos (1/4 cup)	31	1.0	0.0	1	265
Refried Beans, Old El Paso Spicy Refried Beans (1/4 cup)	35	1.0	0.0	1	280
Refried Beans, Old El Paso Vegetarian Refried Beans (1/4 cup)	70	1.0	< 1.0	0	730
Refried Beans, Rosarita Refried Beans (4 oz)	120	2.0	0.8	2	470
Refried Beans, Rosarita Refried Beans with Green Chilies (4 oz)	120	2.0	0.7	2	430
Refried Beans, Rosarita Refried Beans with Nacho Cheese (4 oz)	140	2.0	0.9	2	490
Refried Beans, Rosarita Refried Beans with Onions (4 oz)	130	2.0	0.8	2	500
Refried Beans, Rosarita Spicy Refried Beans (4 oz)	130	2.0	0.8	2	460
Refried Beans, Rosarita Vegetarian Refried Beans (4 oz)	100	2.0	0.5	0	470
Sauerkraut, Bush's Best Bavarian Kraut (4 oz)	60	0.0	0.0	(0)	400

Canned and Shelf-Stable Vegetables (continued)	Calories	Fat g	Saturated Fat g	Choles-terol mg	Sodium mg
Sauerkraut, undrained—Most Brands (1/2 cup)	22	0.2	0.0	0	780
Spinach, drained—Most Brands (1/2 cup)	25	0.5	0.1	0	(269)
Spinach, no salt added, drained—Most Brands (1/2 cup)	25	0.5	0.1	0	29
Squash, Italian-Style Zucchini, undrained—Most Brands (1/2 cup)	33	0.1	0.0	0	427
Succotash with Corn—Most Brands (1/2 cup)	81	0.6	0.1	0	283
Succotash with Cream-Style Corn—Most Brands (1/2 cup)	102	0.7	0.1	0	325
Sweet Potatoes in syrup, drained—Most Brands (1/2 cup)	106	0.3	0.1	0	38
Sweet Potatoes, mashed—Most Brands (1/2 cup)	129	0.3	0.1	0	96
Three Bean Salad, Green Giant (1/2 cup)	70	<1.0	0.0	0	470
Tomatillos, La Victoria Tomatillo Entero (1 tbsp)	4	<1.0	(0.0)	(0)	102
Tomato Paste, Contadina Italian Paste (1/4 cup)	65	1.0	(0.1)	(0)	520
Tomato Paste, no salt added—Most Brands (1/2 cup)	110	1.2	0.2	0	86
Tomato Paste—Most Brands (1/2 cup)	110	1.2	0.2	0	1035
Tomato Puree, no salt added—Most Brands (1/2 cup)	51	0.1	0.0	0	25
Tomato Puree—Most Brands (1/2 cup)	51	0.1	0.0	0	499
Tomatoes, Contadina Italian Style (Pear) Tomatoes (1/2 cup)	25	<1.0	(0.0)	(0)	220
Tomatoes, Contadina Italian Style Stewed Tomatoes (1/2 cup)	35	<1.0	(0.0)	(0)	250
Tomatoes, Eden Organic Crushed Tomatoes, No Salt Added (4 oz)	35	0.0	0.0	0	0

Canned and Shelf-Stable Vegetables (continued)	Calories	Fat g	Saturated Fat g	Choles-terol mg	Sodium mg
Tomatoes, Old El Paso Tomatoes and Green Chilies (1/4 cup)	14	< 1.0	(0.0)	0	480
Tomatoes, Old El Paso Tomatoes and Jalapenos (1/4 cup)	11	< 1.0	0.0	0	150
Tomatoes, Red with Green Chilies—Most Brands (1/2 cup)	18	0.0	0.0	0	481
Tomatoes, Red, Stewed—Most Brands (1/2 cup)	34	0.2	0.0	0	325
Tomatoes, Red, Whole, no salt added—Most Brands (1/2 cup)	24	0.3	0.0	0	16
Tomatoes, Red, Whole—Most Brands (1/2 cup)	24	0.3	0.0	0	195
Waterchestnuts, sliced, undrained—Most Brands (1/2 cup)	35	0.0	0.0	0	6
Yams, Giant Yams, Cut in Syrup (1/2 cup)	110	0.0	0.0	0	25
Zucchini, Progresso Italian Style Zucchini (1/2 cup)	50	2.0	< 1.0	< 1	540
DEHYDRATED AND FREEZE-DRIED VEGETABLES					
Chives, Freeze-Dried (1 tbsp)	1	0.0	0.0	0	(0)
Corn, Mountain House Freeze Dried Vegetables, Corn (1-1/4 cups)	90	1.0	(0.2)	0	1
Green Beans, Mountain House Freeze Dried Vegetables, Green Beans (1-1/4 cups)	35	1.0	(0.0)	0	1
Parsley, Freeze-Dried (1/4 cup)	4	0.1	0.0	0	5
Peas, Mountain House Freeze Dried Vegetables, Green Peas (1-1/4 cups)	70	1.0	(0.0)	0	90
Potatoes, Arrowhead Mills Potato Flakes (2 oz = 1 cup)	140	0.0	0.0	0	42

Dehydrated and Freeze-Dried Vegetables (continued)	Calories	Fat g	Saturated Fat g	Cholesterol mg	Sodium mg
Potatoes, Giant Instant Mashed Potatoes, prep (w/skim milk, no fat or salt) (1/2 cup)	80	0.0	0.0	0	55
Potatoes, Idahoan Complete Mashed Potatoes, prep (w/water) (1/2 cup)	80	1.0	(0.3)	(0)	175
FRESH VEGETABLES					
Alfalfa Sprouts, raw (1 cup)	10	0.2	0.0	0	2
Artichokes, cooked (1 medium)	53	0.2	0.0	0	79
Artichokes, raw (1 medium)	65	0.3	0.1	0	102
Asparagus, cooked (1/2 cup)	22	0.3	0.1	0	7
Asparagus, raw (4 spears)	14	0.1	0.0	0	1
Basil, fresh, chopped (2 tbsp)	1	0.0	0.0	0	0
Beans, Green or Snap, cooked (1/2 cup)	22	0.2	0.0	0	2
Beets, raw (2)	71	0.1	0.0	0	118
Beets, sliced, cooked (1/2 cup)	26	0.0	0.0	0	42
Broccoli, chopped, cooked (1/2 cup)	23	0.2	0.0	0	8
Broccoli, chopped, raw (1/2 cup)	12	0.2	0.0	0	12
Broccoli, spears, cooked, boiled (1 spear)	53	0.5	0.1	0	19
Brussels Sprouts, cooked (1/2 cup)	30	0.4	0.1	0	17
Brussels Sprouts, raw (1 sprout)	8	0.1	0.0	0	5
Cabbage, shredded, cooked (1/2 cup)	16	0.2	0.0	0	14
Cabbage, shredded, raw (1/2 cup)	8	0.1	0.0	0	6
Cabbage, Chinese, shredded, cooked (1/2 cup)	10	0.1	0.0	0	29
Cabbage, Chinese, shredded, raw (1/2 cup)	5	0.1	0.0	0	23
Cabbage, Red, shredded, cooked (1/2 cup)	16	0.2	0.0	0	6
Cabbage, Red, shredded, raw (1/2 cup)	10	0.1	0.0	0	4

Fresh Vegetables (continued)	Calories	Fat g	Saturated Fat g	Cholesterol mg	Sodium mg
Carrots, Baby, raw, 2-3/4" long (1 medium)	4	0.1	0.0	0	3
Carrots, raw (7-1/2" × 1" diam)	31	0.1	0.0	0	25
Carrots, sliced, cooked (1/2 cup)	35	0.1	0.0	0	52
Cauliflower, 1" pieces, cooked (1/2 cup)	15	0.1	0.0	0	4
Cauliflower, raw, 1" pieces (1/2 cup)	12	0.9	0.0	0	7
Celery, diced, cooked (1/2 cup)	11	0.8	0.0	0	48
Celery, raw (1 stalk = 7-1/2" × 1")	6	0.1	0.0	0	35
Chayote, 1" pieces, cooked (1/2 cup)	19	0.4	0.0	0	1
Chayote, 1" pieces, raw (1/2 cup)	16	0.2	0.0	0	3
Chives, raw, chopped (1 tbsp)	1	0.0	0.0	0	0
Cilantro, fresh (coriander leaf) (1/4 cup)	1	0.1	(0.0)	0	1
Coriander (cilantro), raw (1/4 cup)	1	0.0	0.0	0	1
Corn, Sweet, cooked (1/2 cup)	89	1.1	0.2	0	14
Corn, raw (1/2 cup)	66	0.9	0.1	0	12
Cowpeas, cooked (1/2 cup)	89	0.7	0.2	0	4
Cucumbers, raw (1/2 cup)	7	0.1	0.0	0	1
Dill Weed, fresh (5 sprigs)	0	0.0	0.0	0	1
Eggplant, cubes, cooked (1/2 cup)	13	0.1	0.0	0	2
Eggplant, raw (1 whole = 8-1/2" × 1")	27	0.1	0.0	0	4
Endive, chopped, raw (1/2 cup)	4	0.1	0.0	0	6
Garlic, raw (1 clove)	4	0.0	0.0	0	1
Ginger Root, raw, 1/8" × 1" pieces (5 pieces)	8	0.1	0.0	0	1
Greens, Beet, pieces, cooked (1/2 cup)	20	0.1	0.0	0	173
Greens, Dandelion, chopped, cooked (1/2 cup)	17	0.3	0.0	0	23

Fresh Vegetables (continued)	Calories	Fat g	Saturated Fat g	Choles-terol mg	Sodium mg
Greens, Mustard, chopped, cooked (1/2 cup)	11	0.2	0.0	0	11
Greens, Turnip, chopped, cooked (1/2 cup)	15	0.2	0.0	0	21
Greens, Turnip, chopped, raw (1/2 cup)	7	0.1	0.0	0	11
Jicama (Yam Bean), slices, raw (1 cup)	46	0.1	(0.0)	0	5
Kale, chopped, cooked (1/2 cup)	21	0.3	0.0	0	15
Kale, chopped, raw (1/2 cup)	17	0.2	0.0	0	15
Kohlrabi, slices, cooked (1/2 cup)	24	0.1	0.0	0	17
Kohlrabi, slices, raw (1/2 cup)	19	0.1	0.0	0	14
Leeks, chopped, cooked (1/4 cup)	8	0.1	0.0	0	3
Leeks, chopped, raw (1/4 cup)	16	0.1	0.0	0	5
Lettuce, Iceberg (1/4 head)	18	0.3	0.0	0	12
Mushrooms, pieces, cooked (1/2 cup)	21	0.4	0.1	0	2
Mushrooms, pieces, raw (1/2 cup)	9	0.2	0.0	0	1
Mushrooms, raw (1)	5	0.1	0.0	0	1
Okra, slices, cooked (1/2 cup)	25	0.1	0.0	0	4
Okra, slices, raw (1/2 cup)	19	0.1	0.0	0	4
Onions, chopped, cooked (1/2 cup)	29	0.2	0.0	0	8
Onions, chopped, raw (1/2 cup)	27	0.2	0.0	0	2
Parsley, chopped, fresh (1/2 cup)	11	0.2	0.0	0	17
Parsnips, slices, cooked (1/2 cup)	63	0.2	0.0	0	8
Parsnips, slices, raw (1/2 cup)	50	0.4	0.0	0	7
Peas, Green, cooked (1/2 cup)	67	0.2	0.0	0	2
Peas, Green, raw (1/2 cup)	63	0.3	0.1	0	4
Peppers, Hot Chili, raw (1)	18	0.1	0.0	0	3
Peppers, Sweet (Bell), Green, chopped, raw (1/2 cup)	12	0.2	0.0	0	2
Peppers, Sweet, Red, cooked (1 oz)	5	0.0	0.0	0	1

Fresh Vegetables (continued)	Calories	Fat g	Saturated Fat g	Choles-terol mg	Sodium mg
Peppers, Sweet, Yellow, raw, 5″ long × 3″ diam (1 large)	50	0.4	(0.0)	0	3
Potato with Skin, boiled (1/2 cup)	68	0.1	0.0	0	3
Potato with Skin, baked (1)	220	0.2	0.1	0	16
Pumpkin, Mashed, cooked (1/2 cup)	24	0.9	0.1	0	2
Radicchio, raw, shredded (1/2 cup)	5	0.1	0.0	0	4
Radishes, raw, 1″ diam (10)	7	0.2	0.0	0	11
Rutabagas, cubed, cooked (1/2 cup)	29	0.2	0.0	0	15
Rutabagas, cubed, raw (1/2 cup)	25	0.1	0.0	0	14
Shallots, chopped, raw (1 tbsp)	7	0.0	0.0	0	1
Snow Peas, cooked (1/2 cup)	34	0.2	0.0	0	3
Snow Peas, raw (1/2 cup)	30	0.1	0.0	0	3
Spinach, chopped, raw (1/2 cup)	6	0.1	0.0	0	22
Spinach, cooked (1/2 cup)	21	0.2	0.0	0	63
Squash, Summer, all varieties, slices, cooked (1/2 cup)	18	0.3	0.1	0	1
Squash, Summer, all varieties, slices, raw (1/2 cup)	13	0.1	0.0	0	1
Squash, Winter, all varieties, cubed, cooked (1/2 cup)	39	0.6	<1.0	0	1
Squash, Winter, all varieties, cubed, raw (1/2 cup)	21	0.1	0.0	0	2
Squash, Zucchini, cooked, sliced, boiled (1/2 cup)	14	0.1	0.0	0	2
Succotash, cooked (1/2 cup)	111	0.8	0.1	0	16
Sweet Potatoes, mashed, cooked (1/2 cup)	103	0.1	0.0	0	10
Sweet Potatoes, raw (1/2 cup)	72	0.2	0.0	0	9
Taro, slices, cooked (1/2 cup)	94	0.1	0.0	0	10
Taro, slices, raw (1/2 cup)	56	0.1	0.0	0	6
Tomatillos, raw (1 med = 1-5/8″ diam)	11	0.4	(0.0)	0	0
Tomatoes, Green, raw (1 tomato = 2-3/5″ diam)	30	0.3	0.0	0	16

Fresh Vegetables (continued)	Calories	Fat g	Saturated Fat g	Choles- terol mg	Sodium mg
Tomatoes, Red, cooked (1/2 cup)	30	0.3	0.0	0	13
Tomatoes, Red, fresh (1 tomato = 2-3/5″ diam)	24	0.3	0.0	0	10
Tomatoes, Sun-Dried (1 tbsp)	9	0.1	0.0	0	71
Turnips, cubed, cooked (1/2 cup)	14	0.1	0.0	0	39
Turnips, cubed, raw (1/2 cup)	18	0.1	0.0	0	44
Waterchestnuts, raw (1/2 cup)	66	0.1	0.0	0	9
Watercress, chopped, fresh (1/2 cup)	2	0.0	0.0	0	7
Yam, cubed, cooked (1/2 cup)	79	0.1	0.0	0	6
FROZEN VEGETABLES					
Artichokes—Most Brands (3 oz)	36	0.4	0.1	0	42
Asparagus—Most Brands (4 spears)	17	0.3	0.1	0	2
Beans, Butter, IGA Speckled Butter Beans (3.2 oz)	120	0.0	0.0	0	(30)
Beans, Green or Snap, Birds Eye Combination Vegetables, French Green Beans with Toasted Almonds (3 oz)	50	2.0	(0.4)	0	340
Beans, Green or Snap, Food Club French Cut Green Beans and Almonds with Selected Seasonings (3.3 oz)	45	0.0	0.0	(0)	330
Beans, Green or Snap, Green Giant Cut Green Beans in Butter Sauce (1/2 cup)	30	1.0	<1.0	5	230
Beans, Green or Snap, Green Giant One-Serve Green Beans in Butter Sauce (5.5 oz)	60	2.0	1.0	5	370
Beans, Green or Snap—Most Brands (1/2 cup)	18	0.1	0.0	0	9
Beans, Lima, cooked—Most Brands (1/2 cup)	94	0.3	0.1	0	26
Beans, Lima, Baby—Most Brands (1/2 cup)	94	0.3	0.1	0	26
Beans, Lima, Green Giant Lima Beans in Butter Sauce (1/2 cup)	100	3.0	1.0	5	390

Frozen Vegetables (continued)	Calories	Fat g	Saturated Fat g	Choles- terol mg	Sodium mg
Broccoli, Birds Eye Butter Sauce Combination Vegetables, Broccoli Spears in Butter Sauce (3.3 oz)	45	2.0	(1.2)	5	320
Broccoli, Food Club Broccoli Cuts with Cheese Sauce (3.3 oz)	40	2.0	(0.9)	(4)	230
Broccoli, Green Giant One-Serve Broccoli Cuts in Butter Sauce (4-1/2 oz)	45	2.0	< 1.0	5	420
Broccoli, Green Giant Broccoli Spears in Butter Sauce (1/2 cup)	40	2.0	< 1.0	5	350
Broccoli, Green Giant Broccoli in Cheese Flavored Sauce (1/2 cup)	60	2.0	< 1.0	2	530
Broccoli, Green Giant One-Serve Broccoli Cuts in Cheese Flavored Sauce (5 oz)	70	3.0	< 1.0	5	660
Broccoli, chopped, cooked—Most Brands (1/2 cup)	25	0.1	0.0	0	22
Brussels Sprouts, Giant Brussels Sprouts (3.3 oz)	40	0.0	0.0	0	10
Brussels Sprouts, Green Giant Brussels Sprouts in Butter Sauce (1/2 cup)	40	1.0	< 1.0	5	280
Brussels Sprouts—Most Brands (1/2 cup)	33	0.3	0.1	0	18
Brussels Sprouts, Green Giant Baby Brussels Sprouts in Butter Sauce (1/2 cup)	40	1.0	< 1.0	5	280
Carrots, sliced—Most Brands (1/2 cup)	26	0.1	0.0	0	43
Cauliflower, 1" pieces—Most Brands (1/2 cup)	17	0.2	0.0	0	16
Cauliflower, Green Giant Cauliflower in Cheese Flavored Sauce (1/2 cup)	60	2.0	< 1.0	2	500
Cauliflower, Green Giant One-Serve Cauliflower in Cheese Flavored Sauce (5.5 oz)	80	2.0	< 1.0	5	640
Corn, Green Giant Cream Style Corn (1/2 cup)	110	1.0	0.0	0	370

Frozen Vegetables (continued)	Calories	Fat g	Saturated Fat g	Choles-terol mg	Sodium mg
Corn, Birds Eye Butter Sauce Combination Vegetables, Tender Sweet Corn in Butter Sauce (3.3 oz)	90	2.0	(1.2)	5	250
Corn, Green Giant Niblets Corn in Butter Sauce (1/2 cup)	100	2.0	1.0	5	310
Corn, Green Giant One-Serve Niblets Corn in Butter Sauce (4.5 oz)	120	2.0	< 1.0	5	350
Corn, Green Giant Shoepeg White Corn in Butter Sauce (1/2 cup)	100	2.0	< 1.0	5	280
Corn—Most Brands (1/2 cup)	67	0.1	0.0	0	4
Greens, Mustard—Most Brands (1/2 cup)	14	0.2	0.0	0	19
Greens, Turnip—Most Brands (1/2 cup)	24	0.4	0.1	0	12
Mixed Vegetables, IGA California Blend (1/2 cup)	40	0.0	0.0	0	(220)
Mixed Vegetables, IGA Italian Blend (1/2 cup)	40	0.0	0.0	0	(220)
Mixed Vegetables, IGA Oriental Blend (1/2 cup)	35	0.0	0.0	0	(220)
Mixed Vegetables, IGA San Francisco Blend (1/2 cup)	40	0.0	0.0	0	(220)
Okra—Most Brands (1/2 cup)	34	0.3	0.1	0	3
Pea Pods, Chun King Chinese Pea Pods (1.5 oz)	20	0.0	0.0	(0)	< 10
Pea Pods, Giant Pea Pods (1/2 cup)	25	< 1.0	< 1.0	0	5
Peas, Field, IGA Field Peas with Snaps (3.2 oz)	130	1.0	0.0	0	(70)
Peas, Food Club Green Peas and Pearl Onion with Special Seasoning (3.3 oz)	80	0.0	0.0	(0)	120
Peas, Green Giant One-Serve Le Sueur Baby Early Peas in Butter Sauce (4.5 oz)	90	2.0	< 1.0	5	400
Peas, Green Giant Le Sueur Baby Early Peas in Butter Sauce (1/2 cup)	80	2.0	< 1.0	5	440
Peas, Green Giant Sweet Peas in Butter Sauce (1/2 cup)	80	2.0	< 1.0	5	410

Frozen Vegetables (continued)	Calories	Fat g	Saturated Fat g	Choles- terol mg	Sodium mg
Peas, Green—Most Brands (1/2 cup)	63	0.2	0.0	0	70
Peas, Le Sueur Early Peas in Butter Sauce (1/2 cup)	80	2.0	<1.0	5	400
Peas, Petite, IGA Petite Peas (3.3 oz)	60	0.0	0.0	0	(70)
Peas and Carrots—Most Brands (1/2 cup)	38	0.3	0.1	0	55
Peas and Onions—Most Brands (1/2 cup)	40	0.2	0.0	0	(78)
Potatoes, Ore-Ida Country Style Dinner Fries, baked (3 oz)	110	3.0	<1.0	0	15
Potatoes, Ore-Ida Hash Browns, Cheddar, baked (3 oz)	80	2.0	1.0	5	420
Potatoes, Ore-Ida Hash Browns, Potatoes O'Brien, baked (3 oz)	60	<1.0	0.0	0	25
Potatoes, Ore-Ida Hash Browns, Shredded Hash Browns, baked (3 oz)	70	<1.0	0.0	0	40
Potatoes, Ore-Ida Hash Browns, Southern Style, baked (3 oz)	70	<1.0	0.0	0	30
Potatoes, Ore-Ida Home Style Potato Wedges, baked (3 oz)	110	3.0	<1.0	0	25
Potatoes, Ore-Ida Lites Crinkle Cuts, baked (3 oz)	90	2.0	<1.0	0	35
Snow Peas, La Choy Snow Pea Pods (7/8 cup)	42	0.2	(0.0)	0	4
Snow Peas—Most Brands (1/2 cup)	42	0.3	0.1	0	4
Spinach, Green Giant Creamed Spinach (1/2 cup)	70	3.0	1.0	2	480
Spinach, Green Giant Cut Leaf Spinach in Butter Sauce (1/2 cup)	40	2.0	<1.0	5	380
Spinach—Most Brands (1/2 cup)	27	0.2	0.0	0	82
Squash, Giant Squash, Cooked (4 oz)	45	0.0	0.0	0	0
Stew Vegetables, IGA Stew Vegetables (3.2 oz)	50	0.0	0.0	0	(35)

Frozen Vegetables (continued)	Calories	Fat g	Saturated Fat g	Cholesterol mg	Sodium mg
Succotash—Most Brands (1/2 cup)	79	0.8	0.1	0	38
Sweet Potatoes, Mrs. Paul's Prepared Vegetable, Candied Sweet Potatoes (4 oz)	170	0.0	0.0	0	40
Sweet Potatoes, Mrs. Paul's Prepared Vegetable, Candied Sweets 'N Apples (4 oz)	160	0.0	0.0	0	60
Sweet Potatoes, cubed—Most Brands (1/2 cup)	88	0.1	0.0	0	7
MIXED VEGETABLES					
Bel-Air Vegetables, Chinese Style (3-1/3 oz)	30	0.0	0.0	(0)	280
Bel-Air Vegetables, Hawaiian Style (3-1/3 oz)	50	0.0	0.0	0	250
Bel-Air Vegetables, Japanese Style (3-1/3 oz)	35	0.0	0.0	0	210
Bel-Air Vegetables, Rancho Fiesta Style (3-1/3 oz)	70	0.0	0.0	0	110
Bel-Air Vegetables, Winter Mix (3-1/3 oz)	40	2.0	(1.0)	0	230
Birds Eye Butter Sauce Combination Vegetables, Broccoli, Cauliflower and Carrots in Butter Sauce (3.3 oz)	45	2.0	(1.2)	5	290
Birds Eye Custom Cuisine, Chow Mein Vegetables in Oriental Sauce (4.6 oz)	80	2.0	(0.5)	0	570
Birds Eye Custom Cuisine, Vegetables with Creamy Mushroom Sauce for Beef (4.6 oz)	60	2.0	(0.7)	5	450
Birds Eye Custom Cuisine, Vegetables with Dijon Mustard Sauce for Chicken or Fish (4.6 oz)	70	3.0	(0.3)	5	310
Birds Eye Custom Cuisine, Vegetables with Savory Tomato Basil Sauce for Chicken (4.6 oz)	110	3.0	(0.5)	0	360
Birds Eye Custom Cuisine, Vegetables with Wild Rice in White Wine Sauce for Chicken (4.6 oz)	100	0.0	(0.0)	0	510

Frozen Vegetables (continued)	Calories	Fat g	Saturated Fat g	Choles- terol mg	Sodium mg
Birds Eye Farm Fresh Mixtures, Broccoli, Baby Carrots and Water Chestnuts (4 oz)	45	0.0	0.0	0	35
Birds Eye Farm Fresh Mixtures, Broccoli, Cauliflower and Red Peppers (4 oz)	30	0.0	0.0	0	25
Birds Eye Farm Fresh Mixtures, Broccoli, Corn and Red Peppers (4 oz)	60	1.0	0.0	0	15
Birds Eye Farm Fresh Mixtures, Broccoli, Green Beans, Pearl Onions and Red Peppers (4 oz)	35	0.0	0.0	0	15
Birds Eye Farm Fresh Mixtures, Broccoli, Red Peppers, Bamboo Shoots and Straw Mushrooms (4 oz)	30	0.0	0.0	0	20
Birds Eye Farm Fresh Mixtures, Brussels Sprouts, Cauliflower and Carrots (4 oz)	40	0.0	0.0	0	30
Birds Eye Farm Fresh Mixtures, Cauliflower, Baby Whole Carrots and Snow Pea Pods (4 oz)	40	0.0	0.0	0	35
Birds Eye Farm Fresh Mixtures, Cauliflower, Zucchini, Carrots and Red Peppers (4 oz)	30	0.0	0.0	0	25
Birds Eye Farm Fresh Mixtures, Sugar Snap Peas, Baby Carrots and Water Chestnuts (3.2 oz)	50	0.0	0.0	0	20
Birds Eye Farm Fresh Mixtures, Zucchini, Carrots, Pearl Onions and Mushrooms (4 oz)	30	0.0	0.0	0	15
Birds Eye Stir-Fry Vegetables, Chinese Style (3.3 oz)	35	0.0	0.0	0	540
Birds Eye Stir-Fry Vegetables, Japanese Style (3.3 oz)	30	0.0	0.0	0	510
Food Club California Style Vegetables with Cheese Sauce (3.3 oz)	40	2.0	(0.9)	(4)	230

Frozen Vegetables (continued)	Calories	Fat g	Saturated Fat g	Choles- terol mg	Sodium mg
Food Club Chinese Style Vegetables with Seasoned Sauce (3.3 oz)	30	0.0	0.0	0	280
Food Club Hawaiian Style Vegetables with Seasoned Sauce (3.3 oz)	50	0.0	0.0	0	250
Food Club Japanese Style Vegetables with Seasoned Sauce (3.3 oz)	35	0.0	0.0	0	210
Giant Broccoli Cauliflower Carrots (3.2 oz)	25	0.0	0.0	0	30
Green Giant American Mixtures, California (1/2 cup)	25	0.0	0.0	0	40
Green Giant American Mixtures, Heartland (1/2 cup)	25	0.0	0.0	0	35
Green Giant American Mixtures, Manhattan Style (1/2 cup)	25	0.0	0.0	0	15
Green Giant American Mixtures, New England (1/2 cup)	70	1.0	(0.0)	0	75
Green Giant American Mixtures, San Francisco (1/2 cup)	25	0.0	0.0	0	35
Green Giant American Mixtures, Santa Fe (1/2 cup)	70	1.0	(0.0)	0	0
Green Giant American Mixtures, Seattle (1/2 cup)	25	0.0	0.0	0	35
Green Giant American Mixtures, Western Style (1/2 cup)	60	2.0	0.0	0	25
Green Giant Broccoli, Cauliflower and Carrots in Butter Sauce (1/2 cup)	30	1.0	< 1.0	5	240
Green Giant Broccoli, Cauliflower and Carrots in Cheese Flavored Sauce (1/2 cup)	60	2.0	< 1.0	2	490
Green Giant Mixed Vegetables in Butter Sauce (1/2 cup)	60	2.0	< 1.0	5	300
Green Giant One-Serve Broccoli, Cauliflower and Carrots in Cheese Sauce (5 oz)	80	2.0	< 1.0	5	650

Frozen Vegetables (continued)	Calories	Fat g	Saturated Fat g	Choles-terol mg	Sodium mg
Green Giant One-Serve, Broccoli, Carrots and Rotini in Cheese Sauce (5.5 oz)	100	2.0	< 1.0	5	440
Green Giant Pantry Express, Corn, Green Beans, Carrots, Pasta in Tomato Sauce (solids and liquids) (1/2 cup)	80	2.0	0.0	0	330
Green Giant Pantry Express, Green Beans, Potatoes and Mushrooms in a Lightly Seasoned Sauce (1/2 cup)	60	3.0	< 1.0	0	440
Green Giant Pantry Express, Mixed Vegetables (Green Beans, Potatoes, Carrots, Corn) (1/2 cup)	35	< 1.0	0.0	0	300
Green Giant Valley Combinations, Broccoli Fanfare (1/2 cup)	80	2.0	0.0	0	340
Green Giant Valley Combinations, Broccoli Cauliflower Medley (1/2 cup)	60	2.0	0.0	0	340
Green Giant Valley Combinations, Le Sueur Style (1/2 cup)	70	2.0	0.0	0	400
La Choy Tropical Fruit & Vegetable Medley (5/8 cup)	30	0.2	(0.0)	0	10
La Choy Vegetable Chow Mein (1/3 cup)	45	1.6	(0.4)	0	256
La Choy Vegetables, Oriental Stir-Fry (3/4 cup)	35	0.2	(0.0)	0	20
McCain Vegetables, Florentine (1/2 cup)	30	0.1	0.0	0	30
McCain Vegetables, Normandie (1/2 cup)	23	0.1	0.0	0	27
McCain Vegetables, Parisienne (1/2 cup)	31	0.1	0.0	0	35
McCain Vegetables, Scandia (1/2 cup)	31	0.1	0.0	0	35
Mixed Vegetables—Most Brands (1/2 cup)	54	0.1	0.0	0	32
Ore-Ida Stew Vegetables (3 oz)	60	< 1.0	0.0	0	50

SUBSTITUTIONS TO BE USED IN A CHOLESTEROL-LOWERING DIET

When your recipe calls for . . .	Try substituting . . .
bacon	lean ham, Canadian bacon, artificial bacon bits
baking chocolate (1 square)	3 tablespoons cocoa plus 1 tablespoon tub margarine or 1 teaspoon oil
butter	tub margarine (use same amount)
buttermilk (1 cup)	15 tablespoons (1 cup minus 1 tablespoon) skim, ½%, or 1% low-fat milk plus 1 tablespoon vinegar
cheese	low-fat or nonfat cheese
coconut	coconut extract (texture of product will be different)
cream—whipping or half-and-half	canned evaporated skim milk (can be whipped)
eggs (1 whole)	egg substitute (check label for amount equal to 1 egg) or 2 egg whites
evaporated milk	canned evaporated skim milk
nondairy creamer	skim, ½%, or 1% low-fat milk; nonfat dry milk powder; canned evaporated skim milk
salt pork for seasoning vegetables	lean ham, Canadian bacon, artificial bacon bits
shortening or lard (½ cup)	½ cup tub margarine or ⅓ cup oil
tub margarine (½ cup)	⅓ cup oil
sour cream	low-fat sour cream
white sauce made with milk or cream and butter	white sauce made with skim, ½%, or 1% low-fat milk and tub margarine

OTHER HANDY SUBSTITUTIONS IN THE KITCHEN

1 teaspoon baking powder	=	1 teaspoon baking soda plus ½ teaspoon cream of tartar
1 teaspoon baking powder	=	3 teaspoons low-sodium baking powder
1 teaspoon sugar	=	½ teaspoon fructose
1 tablespoon cornstarch (used for thickening)	=	2 tablespoons flour or 2 teaspoons arrowroot
1 tablespoon flour (used for thickening)	=	1½ teaspoons arrowroot

⅛ teaspoon garlic powder	=	1 small garlic clove
½ teaspoon powdered ginger	=	1 teaspoon fresh ginger
1 teaspoon dried herbs	=	1 tablespoon fresh herbs
2 tablespoons bottled horseradish	=	1 tablespoon fresh horseradish
1 medium onion or ¼ cup finely minced raw onion	=	1 tablespoon instant minced onion plus 2 tablespoons water

SOME INTERESTING FOOD FACTS TO MAKE COOKING EASIER

Baking Ingredients

1 pound of all-purpose flour is 4 cups (sifted)
1 pound of cake flour is about 4½ cups (sifted) to 5 cups (unsifted)
1 pound of whole-wheat flour is about 3½ cups (stirred, not sifted)
1 pound of granulated sugar is 2 cups
1 pound of light brown sugar is 2⅔ cups

Cheese

½ pound of cottage cheese is about 1 cup
1 pound of cheese yields about 4 cups grated
1 ounce of cream cheese is about 2 tablespoons

Eggs

1 egg white equals about 2 tablespoons
1 whole egg equals about ¼ cup

Meat, Poultry, and Fish

1 chicken (broiler) yields about 3½ cups of cooked meat
1 chicken breast (2 halves) yields about 6 to 7 ounces of cooked meat
1 pound of flaked fish is about 2 cups
1 pound ground meat is about 2 cups

Cereals

1½ ounces (about 4⅓ tablespoons) of dry corn grits yields 1 cup plus 4 teaspoons cooked
1½ ounces (scant ¼ cup) of dry farina yields 1⅓ cups cooked
1½ ounces (about 7 tablespoons) of dry oat bran yields about 1⅕ cups cooked
1½ ounces (about ½ cup) of dry oatmeal yields about 1⅛ cups cooked
1½ ounces (3 tablespoons) of dry bulgur yields ½ cup plus 1 tablespoon cooked

Rice

1 pound (2 cups) of uncooked rice yields 6 cups cooked
2 ounces (scant ⅓ cup) of dry long-grain brown rice yields 1 scant cup cooked
2 ounces (scant ⅓ cup) dry medium-grain brown rice yields 1 scant cup (1 cup minus 1 tablespoon) cooked

2 ounces (scant ⅓ cup) dry long-grain regular white rice yields ¾ cup
plus ½ tablespoon cooked

2 ounces (⅗ cup or 9½ tablespoons) dry long-grain precooked or instant
white rice yields 1⅓ cups cooked

2 ounces (scant ⅓ cup) dry medium-grain white rice yields about ¾ cup
cooked

2 ounces (¼ cup plus ½ tablespoon) dry short-grain white rice yields
about ¾ cup cooked

2 ounces (about ⅓ cup) dry wild rice yields 1⅕ cups cooked

Pasta

1 pound (4 cups) dry macaroni yields approximately 8 cups cooked

1 pound (5 cups) dry spaghetti yields approximately 10 cups cooked

2 ounces (about ½ cup) dry macaroni yields about 1 cup plus 1
tablespoon cooked

2 ounces (about ⅔ cup) dry vegetable macaroni yields about 1¼ cups
cooked

2 ounces (about ½ cup) dry whole-wheat macaroni yields about 1⅛ cups
cooked

2 ounces (about 1½ cups) dry egg noodles yields about 1 cup cooked

2 ounces (about 1½ cups) dry spinach and egg noodles yields about 1
cup cooked

2 ounces (about ¼ cup) dry spaghetti yields 1 cup plus 1 tablespoon
cooked

2 ounces (¼ cup) dry spinach spaghetti yields 1 cup plus 2½ tablespoons
cooked

2 ounces (¼ cup) dry whole-wheat spaghetti yields 1 cup plus 2
tablespoons cooked

Dried Beans

1 pound (1½ cups) kidney beans yields 9 cups cooked

1 pound (2⅓ cups) lima beans yields 6 cups cooked

1 pound (2⅓ cups) navy beans yields 6 cups cooked

1 pound (2 cups) soybeans yields 6 cups cooked

Fruits and Vegetables

1 pound of fresh apples is about 3 medium and yields about 3½ cups
peeled and sliced

1 pound of bananas is about 3 medium

1 large lemon contains ¼ cup (2 fluid ounces) of juice and 1 medium
lemon yields about 3 tablespoons of juice and about 1 tablespoon of
grated rind

1 pound of fresh tomatoes is about 3 medium to large

1 pound of fresh potatoes is about 3 medium and yields about 2¼ cups
cooked

CONVERSION TABLES

Tbsp = tablespoon; tsp = teaspoon; fl oz = fluid ounce; pt = pint; qt = quart; gal = gallon; ml = milliliter; l = liter; oz = ounce; lb = pound; g = gram; kg = kilogram; kcal = kilocalorie; kj = kilojoule.

Volume

1 tsp	=	⅓ Tbsp	=	⅙ fl oz	=	5 ml	
1 Tbsp	=	3 tsp	=	½ fl oz	=	15 ml	
4 Tbsp	=	¼ cup	=	2 fl oz	=	60 ml	
16 Tbsp	=	48 tsp	=	1 cup	=	8 fl oz = 240 ml	
1 cup	=	½ pt	=	¼ qt	=	1/16 gal	
2 cups	=	1 pt	=	16 fl oz	=	480 ml	
2 pt	=	1 qt	=	32 fl oz	=	960 ml or 0.95 l	
1 qt	=	4 cups	=	32 fl oz	=	960 ml or 0.95 l	
4 qt	=	1 gal	=	128 fl oz	=	3840 ml or 3.8 l	
10 ml	=	0.34 fl oz					
30 ml	=	1.00 fl oz					
1 l	=	33.3 fl oz	=	1.057 qt	=	0.264 gal	
2 l	=	66.7 fl oz	=	2.11 qt	=	0.53 gal	
3 l	=	100 fl oz	=	3.17 qt	=	0.79 gal	
4 l	=	133.3 fl oz	=	4.23 qt	=	1.06 gal	
5 l	=	166.7 fl oz	=	5.28 qt	=	1.32 gal	
6 l	=	200 fl oz	=	6.34 qt	=	1.59 gal	
7 l	=	233.3 fl oz	=	7.40 qt	=	1.85 gal	
8 l	=	266.7 fl oz	=	8.45 qt	=	2.11 gal	
9 l	=	300 fl oz	=	9.51 qt	=	2.38 gal	
10 l	=	333.3 fl oz	=	10.57 qt	=	2.64 gal	

Weight

1 oz	=	0.06 lb	(1/16 lb)	=	28.35 g
2 oz	=	0.12 lb	(⅛ lb)	=	56.70 g
3 oz	=	0.19 lb	(3/16 lb)	=	85.05 g
4 oz	=	0.25 lb	(¼ lb)	=	113.40 g
5 oz	=	0.31 lb	(5/16 lb)	=	141.75 g
6 oz	=	0.38 lb	(⅜ lb)	=	170.10 g
7 oz	=	0.44 lb	(7/16 lb)	=	198.45 g
8 oz	=	0.50 lb	(½ lb)	=	226.80 g
9 oz	=	0.56 lb	(9/16 lb)	=	255.15 g
10 oz	=	0.62 lb	(⅝ lb)	=	283.50 g
11 oz	=	0.69 lb	(11/16 lb)	=	311.85 g
12 oz	=	0.75 lb	(¾ lb)	=	340.20 g
13 oz	=	0.81 lb	(13/16 lb)	=	368.55 g
14 oz	=	0.88 lb	(⅞ lb)	=	396.90 g
15 oz	=	0.94 lb	(15/16 lb)	=	425.25 g
16 oz	=	1.00 lb		=	453.59 g
1 lb	=	0.45 kg	6 lb	=	2.72 kg
2 lb	=	0.91 kg	7 lb	=	3.18 kg
3 lb	=	1.36 kg	8 lb	=	3.63 kg
4 lb	=	1.81 kg	9 lb	=	4.08 kg
5 lb	=	2.27 kg	10 lb	=	4.54 kg

Weight

1 g	=	0.035 oz	1 kg	=	2.21 lb
2 g	=	0.07 oz	2 kg	=	4.41 lb
3 g	=	0.11 oz	3 kg	=	6.61 lb
4 g	=	0.14 oz	4 kg	=	8.82 lb
5 g	=	0.18 oz	5 kg	=	11.01 lb
6 g	=	0.21 oz	6 kg	=	13.23 lb
7 g	=	0.25 oz	7 kg	=	15.43 lb
8 g	=	0.28 oz	8 kg	=	17.64 lb
9 g	=	0.32 oz	9 kg	=	19.84 lb
10 g	=	0.35 oz	10 kg	=	22.05 lb
1000 g	=	1 kg			

Volume and Weight

2 Tbsp	=	1 oz	=	⅛ cup	=	30 g	
4 Tbsp	=	2 oz	=	¼ cup	=	60 g	
16 Tbsp	=	8 oz	=	1 cup	=	240 g	
2 cups	=	16 oz	=	1 pint	=	480 g (0.45 kg)	

Food Energy

1 kj	=	4.184 kcal
1 kcal	=	0.239 kj

SUPPLEMENTING SINGLE-SERVING ENTRÉES AND DINNERS

Single-serving entrées and dinners may start out low in calories and fat, but the calorie and fat content of the finished meal will depend on the foods being added. Here are some examples of quick-to-prepare foods that can be served with single-serving entrées and dinners that are low in calories and fat to round out a meal. Menus for three sample meals at different calorie levels are also provided.

The calories listed for the following foods are estimates only, and they will vary somewhat with your individual choices.

Suggested Foods to Supplement Single-Serving Entreés and Dinners	Serving Sizes	Approximate Calories
Tossed green salad	2 cups	30
Salad dressing, fat-free	2 tablespoons	10
Vegetable, cooked (ex. spinach, broccoli, green beans, summer squash)	1 cup	60
Bread, regular	1 slice	80
Bread, diet	2 slices	80
Roll, hard type	1 average	80
Fresh fruit	1 average piece	60
Skim milk	1 cup	90
Frozen yogurt, low-fat or nonfat	½ cup	110
Tub margarine, regular	1 teaspoon	35
Tub margarine, diet	2 teaspoons	35

The following sample menus for adults are based on three calorie levels—1,200, 1,500, and 2,200. Each one includes a lunch or dinner meal. The goal for dividing calories among the meals is about 20% for breakfast, 40% for lunch, and 40% for dinner. This division of calories does not include snacks.

1,200-CALORIE EATING PLAN
EXAMPLE OF LUNCH OR DINNER PROVIDING
500 CALORIES

Foods	Serving Sizes	Approximate Calories
Single-serving dinner	1	300
Tossed green salad	2 cups	30
Salad dressing, fat-free	2 tablespoons	10
Broccoli, steamed	1 cup	60
Bread, diet	1 slice	40
Tub margarine, diet	1 teaspoon	18
Fresh fruit	1 average piece	60
Total for the meal		518

1,500-CALORIE EATING PLAN
EXAMPLE OF LUNCH OR DINNER PROVIDING
600 CALORIES

Foods	Serving Sizes	Approximate Calories
Single-serving dinner	1	300
Tossed green salad	2 cups	30
Salad dressing, fat-free	2 tablespoons	10
Summer squash, steamed	½ cup	30
Bread, diet	1 slice	40
Tub margarine, diet	2 teaspoons	35
Skim milk	1 cup	90
Fresh fruit	1 average piece	60
Total for the meal		595

2,200-CALORIE EATING PLAN
EXAMPLE OF LUNCH OR DINNER PROVIDING
900 CALORIES

Foods	Serving Sizes	Approximate Calories
Single-serving dinner	1	300
Tossed green salad	2 cups	30
Salad dressing, fat-free	2 tablespoons	10
Green beans, cooked	1 cup	60
Hard rolls	2 average	160
Tub margarine, regular	3 teaspoons	105
Skim milk	1 cup	90
Fresh fruit	1 average piece	60
Frozen yogurt, low-fat	½ cup	110
Total for the meal		925

QUESTIONS ABOUT FOOD PREPARED OUTSIDE THE HOME

The following sample questions (and preferred answers) will help you determine whether foods purchased from a deli, caterer, or restaurant are low in fat, saturated fat, and cholesterol.

Key questions that you should ask about entrées include:

Q. *Was the fat trimmed off the meat before it was cooked?*
A. Yes, of course.

Q. *What type of fat (if any) was used in cooking the entrée?*
A. We use a small amount of oil, which is either olive or soybean oil.

Q. *Does the entrée include a sauce or gravy?*
A. Yes, but we can serve it on the side.

Q. *Did you use cream, sour cream, or cheese in the casserole?*
A. Yes, but if you give us enough notice, we can prepare it with cheese and sour cream that contain less fat or with yogurt.

In the case of salads and vegetables, ask the following questions:

Q. *Are your cooked vegetables seasoned with butter?*
A. Yes, but we can prepare them without fat or use corn oil margarine.

Q. *What type of cheese do you use to make your sauce?*
A. We normally use regular cheese, but we can make a sauce for you without cheese.

Q. *Does your tossed green salad have the dressing on it?*
A. No, we package it separately.

Q. *Does the dressing on your fruit salad contain whipped cream or mayonnaise?*
A. Normally it does, but we can either prepare a plain mixed fruit salad for you or use a low-fat yogurt dressing.

Q. *What do you use as the dressing in your potato salad?*
A. We normally use mayonnaise, but we have a potato salad that is lower in fat, which uses a mixture of low-calorie mayonnaise and mustard.

Ask the following questions about desserts (those fancy desserts can supply a lot of fat, saturated fat, and cholesterol):

Q. *What type of fat was used to make the cake (or pie or cookies)?*
A. We use all-vegetable shortening, but we can use oil or margarine.

Q. *Was butter or cream cheese used to make the frosting?*
A. No, we make our frosting from powdered sugar and milk.

Q. *Do you put whipped cream on top of your pie?*
A. Yes, but we can make it with a meringue topping if you ask us ahead of time.

REFERENCES

American Heart Association. 1989 Heart Facts. 1988.

American Heart Association and the National Heart, Lung and Blood Institute. The cholesterol facts [AHA Medical/Scientific Statement Special Report]. Circulation 1990; 81:1721–1733.

Anderson J.W., Zettwoch N., Feldman T., Tietyen-Clark J., Oeltgen P., Bishop C.W. Cholesterol-lowering effects of psyllium hydrophilic mucilloid for hypercholesterolemic men. Arch. Intern. Med. 1988; 148:292–296.

Blair S.N., Kohl III H.W., Paffenbarger Jr. R.S., Clark D.G., Cooper K.H., Gibbons L.W. Physical Fitness and All-Cause Mortality—A Prospective Study of Healthy Men and Women. JAMA 1989; 262:2395–2401.

Bonanome A., Grundy S.M. Effect of dietary stearic acid on plasma cholesterol and lipoprotein levels. N. Engl. J. Med. 1988; 318:1244–1248.

Center for Healthcare Communications. Nutrition Update, 1991.

Centers for Disease Control. Prevalence of overweight—behavioral risk factor surveillance system. Morbidity and Mortality Weekly Report 1989; 38:421–423.

Davidson M.H., Dugan L.D., Burns J.H., Bova J., Story K., Drennan K.B. The hypocholesterolemic effects of β-glucan in oatmeal and oat bran. JAMA 1991; 265:1833–1839.

Ekelund L., Haskell W.L., Johnson J.L., Whaley F.S., Criqui M.H., Sheps D.S. Physical fitness as a predictor of cardiovascular mortality in asymptomatic North American men [The lipid research clinics' mortality follow-up study]. N. Engl. J. Med. 1988; 319:1379–1384.

Food Marketing Institute. Trends—Consumer Attitudes & the Supermarket, 1990. Washington, D.C.: Food and Marketing Institute, 1990.

Food Marketing Institute. Trends—Consumer Attitudes & the Supermarket, 1991. Washington, D.C.: Food Marketing Institute, 1991.

Gaziano J.M., Manson J.E., Ridker P.M., Buring J.E., Hennekens C.H. Beta Carotene Therapy for Chronic Stable Angina [Abstracts of the 63rd Scientific Session]. Dallas: American Heart Association, 1990.

IFIC Food Education Foundation. Carrageenan Helps Trim the Fat. Food Insight, March/April 1991:6.

Keys A., ed. Coronary heart disease in seven countries. Circulation 1970; 41(suppl 1):1–211.

Landvik S. The Antioxidant Nutrients. RD 1991; 10:1, 4–8.

Lissner L., Odell P.M., D'Agostino R.B., Stokes J., Kreger B.E., Belander A.J., Brownell K.D. Variability of body weight and health outcomes in the Framingham population. N. Engl. J. Med. 1991; 324:1839–1844.

Mensink R.P., Katan M.B. Effect of dietary trans fatty acids on high-density and low-density lipoprotein cholesterol levels in healthy subjects. N. Engl. J. Med. 1990; 323:439–445.

National Cholesterol Education Program Expert Panel on Detection, Evaluation, and Treatment of High Blood Cholesterol in Adults. Report of the National Cholesterol Education Program Expert Panel on Detection, Evaluation, and Treatment of High Blood Cholesterol in Adults. Arch. Intern. Med. 1988; 148:36–69.

National Cholesterol Education Program. Report of the Expert Panel on Blood Cholesterol Levels in Children and Adolescents. NIH Publication No. 91-2732. September 1991.

National High Blood Pressure Education Program 120/80. The 1988 Report of the Joint National Committee on Detection, Evaluation, and Treatment of High Blood Pressure. Arch. Intern. Med. 1988; 148:1023–1038.

National Research Council (U.S.) Committee on Diet and Health. Alcohol. In: Diet and Health. Washington: National Academy Press, 1989:431–464.

National Research Council (U.S.) Committee on Diet and Health. Diet and Health. Washington: National Academy Press, 1989:76–77.

Parthasarathy S., Khoo J.C., Miller E., Barnett J., Witztum J.L., Steinberg D. Low-density lipoprotein rich in oleic acid is protected against oxidative modification: Implications for dietary prevention of atherosclerosis. Proc. Natl. Acad. Sci. USA 1990; 87:3894–3498.

Quest for fat substitutes taking many routes. Inform 1991; 2:115, 118–119.

Sodium Labeling. In: Federal Register 1984; 101.13:15534.

NEW FOODS

Use this page to list new foods that do not exceed the cutoff points for fat, saturated fat, and cholesterol. The cutoff points are printed on page 69 and at the beginning of each Food Section of *The Living Heart Brand Name Shopper's Guide*. Please use page 413 to share information with the authors.

Food	Serving Size	Cal.	Fat g	Satu-rated Fat g	Choles-terol mg	Sodium mg

If there are foods that you wish to have evaluated for the next revision of *The Living Heart Brand Name Shopper's Guide,* please list them on a xerox copy of the form below and send to:

Diet Modification Clinic
6550 Fannin, SM 1203
Houston, TX 77030

(713) 798-4150
FAX (713) 798-7203

– –

Name ———————————————————— Date ————————————

Address ——————————————————————————————————

———————————————————————————————————————

Home Phone (———) ————————————— Work Phone (———) ————————————

Please evaluate the following foods for your next revision of *The Living Heart Brand Name Shopper's Guide.* (Print the complete name of the food and the manufacturer's name, address, city, and zip code.)

Food ——————————————————————————————————————
    Manufacturer ——————————————————————————————————

——

Food ——————————————————————————————————————
    Manufacturer ——————————————————————————————————

——

Food ——————————————————————————————————————
    Manufacturer ——————————————————————————————————

——

Food ——————————————————————————————————————
    Manufacturer ——————————————————————————————————

——

Food ——————————————————————————————————————
    Manufacturer ——————————————————————————————————

——

Food ——————————————————————————————————————
    Manufacturer ——————————————————————————————————

——

Additional copies of *The Living Heart Brand Name Shopper's Guide* may be ordered by sending a check for $12.50 (please add the following for postage and handling: $3.00 for the first copy, $1.50 for each added copy) to:
Diet Modification Clinic
6550 Fannin, SM 1203
Houston, TX 77030

If you would like to receive information about the next revision of *The Living Heart Brand Name Shopper's Guide,* make a copy of the form below, fill it out, and mail to:

Diet Modification Clinic
6550 Fannin, SM 1203
Houston, TX 77030

(713) 798-4150
FAX (713) 798-7203

— —

YES, I would like to receive information about the next revision of *The Living Heart Brand Name Shopper's Guide.*
(Please print)
Name _____ Date _____
Address _____
        _____

— —

margarine *(cont'd)*
  substitutes for, 211
  trans fatty acids in, 15
marinara sauce, 250–54
marshmallows, 368–70
marshmallow topping, 375–76
matzo, 154–55
  meal, 262
mayonnaise, 321–22
  mayonnaise-type dressing, 321–22
meals
  breakfast, skipped by adolescents, 23
  planning, 29–31
  preparing foods for, 33
  purchasing foods for, 31–32
  saving money in preparation of,
    34–38
  school lunch program, 24–25
  serving and cleaning up after, 33–34
  snacks, 23–24, 25–26
  storing foods for, 32
meats, 273–75
  Agriculture Department—approved
    labels for, 59
  game, 286–87
  hot dogs, 297
  in "Servings of Food" eating plan,
    45–46
  lamb, 287
  monounsaturated fatty acids in, 10
  red, blood cholesterol levels and, 19
  saturated fatty acids in, 10
  sausages, 297
  storing, 32
  substitutes for, 297–98
  terms on food labels referring to, 62
  USDA grading of, 66
  using less of, 37–38
  see also beef; chicken; pork; processed
    and luncheon meats; turkey
melba toast, 150, 151, 158
men, weight gain by, 7
menus, 29
microparticulated protein, 13–14
milk, 175–76
  buttermilk, 175–76
  flavored, 84–85
  ice milk, 224–32
  in "Servings of Food" eating plan,
    46–47
  substitutes for, 175
mixers (beverages), 97–98
modified-fat desserts, 51–52
molasses, 373
money, saving in meal preparation,
    34–38

monoglycerides, 65
monosodium glutamate (MSG), 65
monounsaturated fatty acids, 9, 10
"more," on food labels, 63
mousses, 200–201
muffins, 197–98
  English muffins, 106–9
mustard, 140

National Cancer Institute, 8
National Cholesterol Education Program
    (NCEP), 8
  blood cholesterol levels classified by,
    4–5
  on blood cholesterol levels in children
    and adolescents, 22
National Marine Fisheries Service, 66
National Research Council, 8
"no added sugar," on food labels, 61
nut butters, 215–16
Nutrition Labeling and Education Act
    (NLEA; U.S., 1990), 58–60, 65
nuts, 215–16
  in "Servings of Food" eating plan, 48
  monounsaturated fatty acids in, 10

obesity, 7–8
oils, 10, 11, 210, 214
  cooking sprays, 211
  hydrogenation of, 15
  in "Servings of Food" eating plan,
    47–48
  monounsaturated fatty acids in, 10
  saturated fats in, 72
olestra, 14
olives, 216
  in "Servings of Food" eating plan, 48
Omega-3 fatty acids, 10, 12
optional foods, 51–52
overweight, 7–8

pancakes, 115
  syrups for, 374–75
partial hydrogenation, 65
pasta, 299–306
  in "Servings of Food" eating plan,
    48–49
  sauces for, 250–54
peanut butter, in "Servings of Food"
    eating plan, 48
peas
  canned, 384–85
  in "Servings of Food" eating plan, 49
pepper, hot, 140–41
"percent of calories from fat," on food
    labels, 63–64

"percent fat," on food labels, 64
"percent fat free," on food labels, 62
Physicians' Health Study, 16–17
picante sauce, 141–44
pickles, 144–45
pies
  cream fillings for, 201–8
  frozen, 198
  fruit fillings for, 198
pimientos, 146–47
pita breads, 109–10
pizza sauce, 254–55
planning meals, 29–31, 37
plum sauce, 147
polyunsaturated fatty acids, 9, 10–11
popcorn, 344–46
  in "Servings of Food" eating plan,
    49
pops and bars, frozen, 232–35
pork
  and beans, canned, 385
  fresh and cured, 297–98
  gravy, 248
  processed and luncheon meats,
    291–93
potatoes in "Servings of Food" eating
  plan, 49
poultry, 273–75
  in "Servings of Food" eating plan,
    45–46
  labeling requirements (FSIS) for, 59
  saturated fatty acids in, 10
  terms on food labels referring to, 62
  USDA grading of, 66
  using less of, 37–38
  see also chicken; turkey
PQRST (Probucol Quantitative
  Regression Swedish Trial), 17
preparation, food
  evaluating foods for Living Heart
    Brand Name Shopper's Guide, 73
  saving money in, 34–38
  saving time in, 29–34
preserves, 371–73
pretzels, 346–48
  in "Servings of Food" eating plan, 49
price comparisons, 35–36
processed and luncheon meats
  beef, 288–90
  beef and pork, 290
  chicken, 290–91
  pork, 291–93
  turkey, 294–97
product dates on food labels, 66
protein, 9, 13–14
puddings, 201–8

purchasing foods, 31–32
  lists for, 29–30

"reduced calorie," on food labels, 61
"reduced cholesterol," on food labels, 61
"reduced fat," on food labels, 62
"reduced saturated fat," on food labels,
  62
"reduced sodium," on food labels, 62
Reference Daily Intake (RDI), 60
refried beans, canned, 386
relishes, 145–46
restaurants
  children's meals at, 25
  increase in money spent at, 34
  takeout food from, 32
rice, 306–7
  in "Servings of Food" eating plan, 49
rice cakes, 163–66
risk factors
  for cancer, polyunsaturated fatty acids
    and, 11
  for coronary heart disease, 5
  reduced by diet, 7
rolls, 115–19
  sweet, 198–200

salad bars, 32
salad dressings, 308
  bacon, 309
  blue cheese, 309
  buttermilk, 309
  Caesar, 310
  Catalina, 310
  cucumber, 310
  French, 310–12
  herb, 312
  in "Servings of Food" eating plan, 48,
    53
  Italian, 312–15
  mayonnaise and mayonnaise-type,
    321–22
  other, 320–21
  ranch, 315–17
  red wine vinegar, 317
  Russian, 317
  thousand island, 317–19
  vinaigrette, 319
salsa, 141–44
salt, 7, 62
"salt free," on food labels, 62
sandwich spreads, 321–22
saturated fat, 9–10
  cutoff point for, 72
  decreasing, in diet, 67
  in "Grams of Fat" eating plan, 54–55

steak sauce, 139
stearic acid, 14–15
stir-fry sauce, 255
storing foods, 32
strokes, alcohol and, 20
substitutes
  for butter, 211
  for eggs, 209
  for margarine, 211
  for meats, 297–98
  for milk, 175
  for sugar, 262
sucrose, definition of, 65
sugar, 262
"sugar free," on food labels, 61
Surgeon General, U.S., 8
surimi (imitation shellfish), 286
sweet rolls, 198–200
sweets, 26, 51–52, 367
  candies and marshmallows, 368–71
  jams, jellies, preserves and honey,
    371–73
  syrups, 373–75
  toppings, 375–76
sweet and sour sauce, 255–56
syrups
  chocolate, 373
  corn, 260
  fruit, 373
  for pancakes, 374–75

taco sauce, 141–44
takeout food, 32
tapioca, 262
tea, 83–84
teriyaki sauce, 256
time, saving in meal preparation, 29–34
tomatoes, canned, 387–88
tomato sauce, 256–57
toppings
  butterscotch, 375
  caramel, 375
  chocolate, 375
  fruit, 375
  fudge, 375
  marshmallow, 375–76
  whipped, 177
tortillas, 110
trans fatty acids, 15–16
triglycerides, 6–7
  alcohol and, 6, 20
  fish oil capsules and level of, 12–13
  reduced by exercise, 21
tropical oils, 15

turkey
  canned, 281
  fresh and frozen, 281–82
  gravy, 248
  processed and luncheon meats,
    294–97
  soups, 361

unit pricing, 35–36
universal product codes (UPCs), 66
unsaturated fatty acids, 9
  See also monounsaturated fatty acids
    and polyunsaturated fatty acids
USDA, see Agriculture, U.S. Department
  of

vegetable juice, 271–72
vegetable oils, 10, 11
vegetables, 377–78
  beans, 378–382
  canned, 378–88
  dehydrated, 388–89
  freeze-dried, 388–89
  fresh, 389–93
  frozen, 393–97
  in "Servings of Food" eating plan,
    48–50, 53
  mixed, frozen, 397–400
  saturated fatty acids in, 10
  soups, 361–64
  storing, 32
vegetable shortening, see shortening
vegetarianism, 18–19
vending-machine snacks, 25–26
"very low sodium," on food labels,
  62
vinegar, 263
VLDL-cholesterol, 28

waffles, 115
waist-to-hip ratio (WHR), 8
warehouse food stores, 36
weight
  diet to reduce, 7
  obesity and, 7–8
whipped topping, 177
women, weight gain by, 7
Worcestershire sauce, 53

yeast, 263
yogurt, 77–85
  frozen, 218–24
  in "Servings of Food" eating plan, 47
"yo-yo" dieting, 7–8

Michael E. DeBakey, M.D., is one of the most eminent heart surgeons in the world. He was among the first to complete a successful heart transplant in the United States and has pioneered new methods for the diagnosis and successful treatment of heart disease. Among Dr. DeBakey's numerous noted surgical accomplishments are the first successful resection and graft replacement of an aneurysm of the thoracic aorta and first successful coronary artery bypass. Currently, he is Chancellor of Baylor College of Medicine, Chairman and Distinguished Service Professor of its Department of Surgery, and Director of the DeBakey Heart Center.

Antonio M. Gotto, Jr., M.D., D.Phil., is one of the world's most important specialists in research on fats in the blood and their role in the development of coronary heart disease. He serves as the Principal Investigator of the Baylor College of Medicine Specialized Center of Research in Atherosclerosis of the National Institutes of Health. Currently, he serves as the Chairman of the Department of Medicine at Baylor College of Medicine and Chief of Internal Medicine Service at The Methodist Hospital, both of Houston, Texas.

Lynne W. Scott, M.A., R.D./L.D., is Assistant Professor in the Department of Medicine and Director of the Diet Modification Clinic at Baylor College of Medicine and The Methodist Hospital. She serves as a member of the National Cholesterol Education Program Expert Panel on Blood Cholesterol Levels in Children and Adolescents. She is a registered dietitian and clinical researcher investigating the effect of dietary components on blood cholesterol. She has 40 publications in the area of nutrition and serves on several nutrition committees of the national American Heart Association.

John P. Foreyt, Ph.D., is a clinical psychologist and the Director of the DeBakey Heart Center's Nutrition Research Clinic at Baylor College of Medicine and The Methodist Hospital, Houston, Texas. Currently, he is Professor in the Department of Medicine at Baylor College of Medicine. He has published ten books and more than 120 articles in the areas of behavior modification, cardiovascular risk reduction, obesity, and eating disorders.

The authors of *The Living Heart Brand Name Shopper's Guide* are available for keynotes and seminars. Please contact MasterMedia's Speakers' Bureau for availability and fee arrangements. Call Tony Colao at (908) 350-1612; fax: (908) 359-1647; or write him at:
MasterMedia Limited
17 East 89th Street
New York, NY 10128

THE PREGNANCY AND MOTHERHOOD DIARY: Planning the First Year of Your Second Career, by Susan Schiffer Stautberg, is the first and only updated appointment diary that shows how to manage pregnancy and career. ($12.95 spiralbound)

CITIES OF OPPORTUNITY: Finding the Best Place to Work, Live and Prosper in the 1990's and Beyond, by Dr. John Tepper Marlin, explores the job and living options for the next decade and into the next century. This consumer guide and handbook, written by one of the world's experts on cities, selects and features forty-six American cities and metropolitan areas. ($13.95 paper, $24.95 cloth)

THE DOLLARS AND SENSE OF DIVORCE, The Financial Guide for Women, by Judith Briles, is the first book to combine practical tips on overcoming the legal hurdles with planning before, during and after divorce ($10.95 paper)

OUT THE ORGANIZATION: How Fast Could You Find a New Job?, by Robert and Madeleine Swain, is written for the millions of Americans whose jobs are no longer safe, whose companies are not loyal and who face futures of uncertainty. It gives advice on finding a new job or starting your own business. ($11.95 paper, $17.95 cloth)

AGING PARENTS AND YOU: A Complete Handbook to Help You Help Your Elders Maintain a Healthy, Productive and Independent Life, by Eugenia Anderson-Ellis and Marsha Dryan, is a complete guide to providing care to aging relatives. It gives practical advice and resources to the adults who are helping their elders lead productive and independent lives. ($9.95 paper)

CRITICISM IN YOUR LIFE: How to Give It, How to Take It, How to Make It Work for You, by Dr. Deborah Bright, offers practical advice, in an upbeat, readable and realistic fashion, for turning criticism into control. Charts and diagrams guide the reader into managing criticism from bosses, spouses, children, friends, neighbors and in-laws. ($9.95 paper, $17.95 cloth)

BEYOND SUCCESS: How Volunteer Service Can Help You Begin Making a Life Instead of Just a Living, by John F. Raynolds III and Eleanor Raynolds, C.B.E., is a unique how-to-book targeted to business and professional people considering volunteer work, senior citizens who wish to fill leisure time meaningfully and students trying out various career options. The book is filled with interviews with celebrities, CEOs and average citizens who talk about the benefits of service work. ($9.95 paper, $19.95 cloth)

MANAGING IT ALL: Time-Saving Ideas for Career, Family, Relationships and Self, by Beverly Benz Treuille and Susan Schiffer Stautberg, is written for women who are juggling careers and families. Over two hundred career women (ranging from a TV anchorwoman to an investment banker) were interviewed. The book contains many humorous anecdotes on saving time and improving the quality of life for self and family. ($9.95 paper)

REAL LIFE 101: The Graduate's Guide to Survival, by Susan Kleinman, supplies welcome advice to those facing "real life" for the first time, focusing on work, money, health and how to deal with freedom and responsibility. ($9.95 paper)

YOUR HEALTHY BODY, YOUR HEALTHY LIFE: How to Take Control of Your Medical Destiny, by Donald B. Louria, M.A., provides precise advice and strategies that will help you to live a long and healthy life. Learn also about nutrition, exercise, vitamins and medication, as well as how to control risk factors for major diseases. ($12.95 paper)

THE CONFIDENCE FACTOR: How Self-Esteem Can Change Your Life, by Judith Briles, is based on a nationwide survey of six thousand men and women. Briles explores why women so often feel a lack of self-confidence and have a poor opinion of themselves. She offers step-by-step advice on becoming the person you want to be. ($9.95 paper, $18.95 cloth)

THE SOLUTION TO POLLUTION: 101 Things You Can Do to Clean Up Your Environment, by Laurence Sombke, offers step-by-step techniques on how to conserve more energy, start a recycling center, choose biodegradable products and proceed with individual environmental cleanup projects. ($7.95 paper)

TAKING CONTROL OF YOUR LIFE: The Secrets of Successful Enterprising Women, by Gail Blanke and Kathleen Walas, is based on the authors' professional experience with Avon Products' Women of Enterprise Awards, given each year to outstanding women entrepreneurs. The authors offer a specific plan to help you gain control over your life and include business tips and quizzes as well as beauty and lifestyle information. ($17.95 cloth)

SIDE-BY-SIDE STRATEGIES: How Two-Career Couples Can Thrive in the Nineties, by Jane Hershey Cuozzo and S. Diane Graham, describes how two-career couples can learn the difference between competing with a spouse and becoming a supportive power partner. Published in hardcover as *Power Partners.* ($10.95 paper, $19.95 cloth)

DARE TO CONFRONT! How to Intervene When Someone You Care About Has an Alcohol or Drug Problem, by Bob Wright and Deborah George Wright, shows the reader how to use the step-by-step methods of professional interventionists to motivate drug-dependent people to accept the help they need. ($17.95 cloth)

WORK WITH ME! How To Make the Most of Office Support Staff, by Betsy Lazary, shows how to find, train, and nurture the "perfect" assistant and how best to utilize your support staff professionals. ($9.95 paper)

MANN FOR ALL SEASONS: Wit and Wisdom from The Washington Post's *Judy Mann,* by Judy Mann, shows the columnist at her best as she writes about women, families and the politics of the women's revolution. ($9.95 paper, $19.95 cloth)

THE SOLUTION TO POLLUTION IN THE WORKPLACE, by Laurence Sombke, Terry M. Robertson and Elliot M. Kaplan, supplies employees with everything they need to know about cleaning up their workspace, including recycling, using energy efficiently, conserving water and buying recycled products and nontoxic supplies. ($9.95 paper)

THE ENVIRONMENTAL GARDENER: The Solution to Pollution for Lawns and Gardens, by Laurence Sombke, focuses on what each of us can do to protect our endangered plant life. A practical sourcebook and shopping guide. ($8.95 paper)

THE LOYALTY FACTOR: Building Trust in Today's Workplace, by Carol Kinsey Goman, Ph.D., offers techniques for restoring commitment and loyalty in the workplace. ($9.95 paper)

DARE TO CHANGE YOUR JOB—AND YOUR LIFE, by Carole Kanchier, Ph.D., provides a look at career growth and development throughout the life cycle. ($10.95 paper)

MISS AMERICA: In Pursuit of the Crown, by Ann-Marie Bivans, is an authorized guidebook to the Pageant, containing eyewitness accounts, complete historical data, and a realistic look at the trials and triumphs of potential Miss Americas. ($27.50 cloth)

POSITIVELY OUTRAGEOUS SERVICE: New and Easy Ways to Win Customers for Life, by T. Scott Gross, identifies what the consumers of the nineties really want and how businesses can develop effective marketing strategies to answer those needs. ($14.95 paper)

BREATHING SPACE: *Living and Working at a Comfortable Pace in a Sped-Up Society,* by Jeff Davidson, helps readers to handle information and activity overload and gain greater control over their lives. ($10.95 paper)

TWENTYSOMETHING: *Managing and Motivating Today's New Work Force,* by Lawrence J. Bradford, Ph.D., and Claire Raines, M.A., examines the work orientation of the younger generation, offering managers in businesses of all kinds a practical guide to better understand and supervise their young employees. ($22.95 cloth)

BALANCING ACTS! *Juggling Love, Work, Family and Recreation,* by Susan Schiffer Stautberg and Marcia L. Worthing, provides strategies to achieve a balanced life by reordering priorities and setting realistic goals. ($12.95 paper)

REAL BEAUTY . . . REAL WOMEN: *A Workbook for Making the Best of Your Own Good Looks,* by Kathleen Walas, National Beauty and Fashion Director of Avon Products, offers expert advice on beauty and fashion for women of all ages and ethnic backgrounds. ($19.50 cloth)

MANAGING YOUR CHILD'S DIABETES, by Robert Wood Johnson IV, Sale Johnson, Casey Johnson, and Susan Kleinman, brings help to families trying to understand diabetes and control its effects. ($10.95 paper, $18.95 cloth)

STEP FORWARD: *Sexual Harassment in the Workplace,* by Susan L. Webb, teaches the reader all the basic facts about sexual harassment as well as furnishing procedures to help stop it. ($9.95 paper)

Authors Lynne W. Scott, M.A., R.D./L.D., and John P. Foreyt, Ph.D., are available for keynotes and seminars. Please contact Tony Colao at MasterMedia's Speaker's Bureau at 1-800 4LECTUR, or fax to (908) 359-1647. You can write to Mr. Colao at:
MasterMedia Limited
17 East 89th Street
New York, NY 10128

NOTES

NOTES

NOTES

NOTES

NOTES

NOTES

NOTES

NOTES

NOTES

NOTES

NOTES

NOTES

NOTES

ORDER FORM FOR A FRIEND

Please send me _____ copy(s) of *The Living Heart Brand Name Shopper's Guide* at $12.50 each. Add $3.00 for postage and handling for the first book and $1.50 for each additional book.

Print Name _____

Address   _____

            _____

City   _____ State _____ Zip _____

Payment by check or money order enclosed for $_____
(Make check or money order payable to Diet Modification Clinic.)

Please return to:

Diet Modification Clinic
6550 Fannin, SM1203
Houston, TX 77030

Phone: (713) 798-4150
Fax: (713) 798-7203

See page 414 to have foods evaluated for the next revision.